The Rail Lines of Northern New England

NEW ENGLAND RAIL HERITAGE SERIES

The Rail Lines of Northern New England

A Handbook of Railroad History

ROBERT M. LINDSELL

MAPS BY RONALD DALE KARR

PEPPERELL, MASSACHUSETTS

©2000 by Robert M. Lindsell

ALL RIGHTS RESERVED

This book or any part thereof may not be reproduced in any form without written permission of the publisher.
Printed in the United States of America

Cover design by Diane B. Karr

Frontispiece: Central Vermont RY No. 465 hauls a time freight from White River Jct., VT, to New London, CT, over joint Central Vermont/Boston & Maine track at Claremont Jct., NH, in January 1957. Photo by David K. Johnson, courtesy Walker Transportation Collection, Beverly Historical Society & Museum.

Library of Congress Card Number 96-78654
ISBN: 0-942147-06-5

Branch Line Press
13 Cross Street
Pepperell, Massachusetts 01463-1508

Email: books@branchlinepress.com
www.branchlinepress.com

10 9 8 7 6 5 4 3 2 1

*To Mike Murray
who inspired this,
and to Geoffrey, Amanda, and Stephanie,
who helped*

Contents

Preface 11
Introduction. 13
Maps 20
1. Delaware & Hudson. 35
2. Rutland. 39
3. Bristol 47
4. Hoosac Tunnel & Wilmington 49
5. Connecticut & Passumpsic Rivers. 53
6. Ashuelot 57
7. Cheshire 60
8. Monadnock 64
9. Peterborough & Shirley 67
10. Nashua & Lowell 69
11. Wilton/Peterborough 72
12. Worcester, Nashua & Rochester. 76
13. Portland & Rochester 80
14. Concord & Montreal. 84
15. Boston & Maine (Original Company) 91
16. Eastern 100
17. Brattleboro & Whitehall 104
18. Manchester & Lawrence 109
19. Manchester & Keene 112
20. Peterborough & Hillsborough 115
21. Concord & Claremont 118

22. New Hampshire Central. 123
23. Portsmouth & Concord 127
24. Suncook Valley 130
25. Portsmouth & Dover 133
26. Cochecho 136
27. Lake Shore 140
28. Portsmouth, Great Falls & Conway 145
29. Wolfeborough 150
30. Portland, Saco & Portsmouth 153
31. York Harbor & Beach. 158
32. Kennebunk & Kennebunkport 162
33. Old Orchard Beach Lines 165
34. Central Vermont 168
35. Springfield Terminal 177
36. Portland & Ogdensburg. 179
37. St. Johnsbury & Lake Champlain 185
38. Bridgton & Saco River 191
39. Maine Central (Original System) 195
40. Androscoggin 201
41. Atlantic & St. Lawrence 205
42. Bangor, Old Town & Milford 213
43. European & North American 216
44. Kennebec & Portland 221
45. Knox & Lincoln 227
46. Wiscasset, Waterville & Farmington 231
47. Kennebec Central 236
48. Clarendon & Pittsford 239
49. Woodstock 242
50. White River 245
51. Northern 248
52. Portland & Rumford Falls 254
53. Rumford Falls & Rangeley Lakes 259
54. Sandy River & Rangeley Lakes 263
55. Somerset 272
56. Belfast & Moosehead Lake 277
57. Sebasticook & Moosehead 280
58. Dexter & Newport 283
59. Bangor & Piscataquis 285
60. Monson 290
61. Bangor & Aroostook 294
62. New Brunswick & Canada 303
63. Bucksport & Bangor 305

Contents

64. Maine Shore Line 308
65. Washington County (Maine) 313
66. St. Croix & Penobscot 317
67. Montpelier & Wells River 321
68. Burlington & Lamoille 325
69. Missisquoi 327
70. White Mountains 330
71. Profile & Franconia Notch. 335
72. Upper Coos 338
73. Canadian Pacific 343
74. Orford Mountain 349
75. Lamoille Valley Extension 351
76. Aroostook Valley 353
77. Aroostook River 358
Appendix: Other Lines 361
Bibliography 373
Station Index 383
Main Index 396

Preface

One hundred and seventy years of northern New England railroad history are compressed in the pages of this handbook, which was seven years in the making. It originated in research notes made during review of the proposal to restore passenger service between Portland and Boston over the former Boston & Maine Railroad's main line.

My initial debt is to Mike Murray of the Northern New England Passenger Rail Authority, for he inspired the original effort. His wit during many hours of conversation is deeply appreciated, as is the detail he provided concerning lines owned by the state of Maine. Several rail history experts helped immensely. Jack Armstrong showed extreme patience but was sedulous in answering a stream of requests for information, particularly on the ever-changing rail scene of the 1980s and 1990s. Tom Humphrey provided almost overwhelming detail from his own collection and research, and spent countless hours over several years scrupulously critiquing two drafts of the manuscript. Although I drove and walked several thousand miles during research, John Roy, Jr., saved me considerably more by providing sketch maps and commentary from his own observations. Len Bachelder, whose booklets on railfan excursions were major sources, provided meticulous geographical and timetable data, much of it specially for this book; unfortunately, only a small part of this could be included. From Toronto, the late Sanborn S. Worthen provided extensive criticism from his research on the northernmost lines. At Branch Line Press, Ron Karr reviewed the text for factual inaccuracies, produced all of the maps, and selected the photographs, many of which are his own. Dick Symmes and the volunteers at the Walker Transportation Collection of the Beverly Historical Society deserve special mention for their efforts in locating vintage photographs, as do Nelson Lawry for pointing out good

Unneeded crossbucks lie near the tracks at Colebrook, NH, where trains no longer run. (R. D. Karr)

photographic sites in Maine, and Chop Hardenburgh for verifying current operating information.

Librarians and archivists must not be forgotten. So many were extremely helpful, at state and university libraries—Harvard University, the University of New Hampshire, the University of Maine at Orono, and Northwestern University Transportation Library in Evanston, IL, particularly—at the Canadian government archives in Ottawa, at my then-local Arlington Heights Memorial Library in Illinois, and at the Chicago Public Library, as well as those in the British Library and the Public Records Office in London. My editor, Diane Karr, deserves more praise than can be offered, for with remarkable forbearance she provided encouragement and steered the way through difficulties, amongst which were lapses into my native tongue.

My family were extremely patient through, at times, my almost continuous absence from home either on work or dealing with research. This book is therefore dedicated to them.

Wealth of available detail does not mean that there are no errors or omissions. Painstaking as research has been, sources often disagree on details or on dates of closure and abandonment. Some readers may be disappointed by the absence of their particular interest. Suggestions to the author or publisher for changes in future editions will be readily considered, especially those based on extensive local knowledge.

Hassocks, England
July 2000

Introduction

Perhaps when traveling you've seen an active railroad or been exhilarated by suddenly-encountered ramps in the pavement, or you've spotted crossbucks in disrepair or embankments or cuttings going off on either side of the road, each indicating an abandoned rail line. This handbook will help answer questions about which line it is or was, how it came about, places it linked, when and why closure and abandonment came about, and what use is made of the alignment today. Nearly every known common carrier which actually operated passenger trains has a separate chapter, although geared-cog tourist lines and a selection of other short lines are described only briefly in an appendix; some minor operations are mentioned in principal chapters.

The Northern New England Rail Network

Industrial development in northern New England spread from Massachusetts in the late eighteenth century and was reflected in the promotion of turnpikes and canals from about 1790. New Hampshire promoted a state-supported plan for a network of canals linking the Merrimack and Connecticut Rivers and continuing across Vermont to Lake Champlain. Surveys concluded that more than 300 locks over the Green Mountains would be required. The legislature changed course in 1827, approving passenger conveyance on tramroads. Oddly, the first use of a steam locomotive in the region was in Maine, in 1836, on the humble Bangor & Old Town Railway (later the Bangor, Old Town & Milford). Indeed, the state set up a Board of Internal Improvements whose activities included surveys of a possible rail route to Canada, but nothing came of that.

During the early 1840s Boston became a hub for railroads. The Eastern had completed a line from Boston to Portsmouth, NH, in 1840, where it connected with the Portland, Saco & Portsmouth, opened in

1842. By 1845 a number of railroads were promoting lines between Boston and Canada, which could make Boston an alternative to the St. Lawrence, which perennially froze in winter.

John Alfred Poor, a lawyer living in Portland, ME, promoted that city's harbor and quays as a better alternative, as days would be saved on trans-Atlantic shipments. He won the case for a broad-gauge (5-foot, 6-inch) line from Portland to Montreal against the standard gauge (4-foot, 8½-inch) proposed by others. Construction of the line, which later became part of the Grand Trunk Railroad, started in 1846. Poor also promoted another broad-gauge line from Portland to New Brunswick and Nova Scotia, but by then standard-gauge lines were gaining ground. A few companies in Maine, such as the Androscoggin & Kennebec/Penobscot & Kennebec (the original Maine Central from 1862) and the Androscoggin opted for the broad gauge in order to access Portland, as did the European & North American Railroad, completed in 1871. Poor, in the meantime, had accumulated considerable wealth by opening a foundry in Portland, the largest in Maine, which built over 600 locomotives for U.S. and Canadian railroads, as well as marine engines, boilers, pulp digesters, snow plows, fire appliances, and during the early years of the twentieth century, automobiles.

Poor's vision could not stay the standard gauge, which gradually extended up the Connecticut River valley from Springfield, MA, to Vermont. Two rival railroads, the Vermont Central (later part of the Central Vermont) and the Rutland & Burlington (later part of the Rutland) fought a major battle over who was to fill the gap to Canada across Vermont. Other railroads, such as the Boston, Concord & Montreal and the Northern had built standard-gauge lines north from the Concord Railroad in New Hampshire to the Connecticut River by 1853. Competition on the eastern seaboard was also rife; the Boston & Maine and Eastern Railroads vied for traffic to and from Portland and the Maritime Provinces of Canada. All broad-gauge lines in northern New England were narrowed to standard width by 1880, and several narrow-gauge (3-foot, 6-inch) branches, primarily extending into the U.S. from New Brunswick, were widened. Some new construction, however, resulted in more gauge differences.

After George Mansfield of Hazelwood, MA (near Boston), had seen the 2-foot-gauge Ffestiniog Railway in Wales, he promoted and built a similar line in 1876, the Billerica & Bedford, in Massachusetts. Al-

The difference in gauge is vividly shown here as 2-foot gauge 2-4-4T locomotive no. 5 of the Bridgton & Saco River meets standard-gauge Maine Central 2-8-0 no. 510 at Bridgton Jct., ME, in 1927. (Courtesy Walker Transportation Collection, Beverly Historical Society & Museum)

though it was unsuccessful, he was invited to construct and operate similar lines in Maine, which eventually extended over 100 miles. Two other lines selected 3-foot gauge.

Consolidation of the standard-gauge systems began in 1884 when the Boston & Maine leased the Eastern Railroad. Further major acquisitions and mergers followed. By the end of the century, most of the rail lines of northern New England had been consolidated into five regional systems: the Boston & Maine, the Maine Central, the Central Vermont, the Rutland, and the Grand Trunk. Construction of a sixth began in 1891. The Bangor & Aroostook Railroad was designed primarily to exploit northern Maine traffic in agriculture, particularly potatoes and their by-products, and it expanded vigorously.

Although the northern New England system greatly increased overall mileage as a result, the underlying fact was that profits were in decline. After the First World War, new or rebuilt highways accommodated many former military vehicles as well as a burgeoning number of mass-produced private automobiles. When the Great Depression began in 1929, the demand for textiles from northern New England mills had already declined significantly; resulting economic difficulties and widespread damage caused by severe storms in 1936 and the Great Hurricane of 1938 led to closure of marginal lines.

After America entered World War II, demand on the railroads increased dramatically. Peace did nothing for railroad prosperity, however. After 1945 operators again had to face road competition, stubborn labor unions, and a rapid decline in traditional traffic such as residential coal (as households converted to oil or natural gas), and textiles, shoes, and quarried stone (as manufacturers shifted to cheaper labor markets and cheaper sources of supply). As a means of lowering operating costs, conversion to diesel locomotives became widespread, and permission to abandon several lines was sought.

In a matter of minutes storms can rip out miles of railroad track. This 1927 view shows damage suffered by the White River RR at Quinn Ford's Meadow near Rochester Village, VT. (Courtesy Walker Transportation Collection, Beverly Historical Society & Museum)

Introduction

Timothy Mellon's purchase and ownership of the Boston & Maine and Maine Central (and for a short time the Delaware & Hudson Railroad), which were consolidated under the banner of Guilford Transportation Industries—now Guilford Rail System—marked the beginning of a new era. By the millennium many new companies entered the scene as short-line operators. Vermont Rail System operated much of the former Rutland System, and the Canadian government sold the Central Vermont to RailTex (operating as the New England Central) and the Grand Trunk line to Portland to the Atlantic & St. Lawrence Railroad. Meanwhile, ownership of the Bangor & Aroostook and Canadian Pacific lines through Maine was acquired by the Iron Road Railroad System.

Passenger service was gone by the early 1960s except for commuter trains to Boston and the Canadian Pacific Montreal–Maritime trains that crossed Maine. The last scheduled passenger trains north of the Massachusetts line ended in 1967, although New Hampshire experimented with a restored Nashua–Boston commuter service in 1980 and 1981. Amtrak restored the *Montrealer* from New York through Vermont to Montreal in 1972. Vermont subsidized restoration of long-distance passenger trains from 1995. Service is returning to Maine with the reintroduction of intercity trains between Portland and Boston, which should begin operation in 2001.

The states of northern New England may not have wealthy economies, but they are rich in railroad history.

How To Use This Book

Maps: Locator maps appear at the beginning of this handbook. Numbers shown refer to the chapters where detail is provided. Abandoned lines are represented by dashes. For those interested in tracing alignments, the atlases published in Freeport, ME, by DeLorme and Hartnett House are invaluable. The U.S. Geological Survey (1-888-275-8747 or on the Internet at www.usgs.gov) can provide the most detailed maps, which are also available free of charge from several sites on the World Wide Web.

Stations: All known passenger stations, freight depots, and junctions are listed, in most cases using the most recent name, with earlier names in parentheses. Supplemental designations, such as "Eastern," appear in brackets. Apostrophes are omitted, as are variations of names derived from Indian dialects used until standardized by Act of the New Hampshire legislature in 1929.

Distance: Numbers shown represent mileage from the point of origin indicated. Intermediate distances outside northern New England are omitted, except for the depots either side of the state line. Distances of less than 100 miles are given to the nearest half mile, except where two depots existed within a one-mile length. Distances in excess of 100 miles are rounded to the nearest whole mile.

Built: Dates given are those of construction. Dates of incorporation or approval to proceed may be different, in which case details are given in the narrative.

Operators: Names given are of the actual operating companies, which may not be the same as the builder or title owner. Guilford is used generically to describe the lines owned by Guilford Rail System (formerly Guilford Transportation Industries) and leased by its subsidiaries, the Maine Central, Boston & Maine, Portland Terminal, and Springfield Terminal companies, and for a short time, the Delaware & Hudson Railroad.

Daily Passenger Trains: The number of passenger trips gives some indication of the importance of a line. Unless otherwise stated, the first figure indicates the number of trips operated over the entire line (from end point to end point in each direction), followed in parentheses by shorter runs and, where appropriate, branch line trips.

Abandonment: Before 1920, approval to abandon a line was required from state authorities, normally the state railroad commission. The 1920 federal Transportation Act transferred authority to the Interstate Commerce Commission (ICC) for lines that could be considered as contributing to interstate trade, which essentially meant all lines. In 1958, the ICC was given power to review proposals for the end of passenger service, to obviate conflicts between intrastate decisions on interstate trains. The ICC was succeeded in 1995 by the Surface Transportation Board. Dates given are for formal approval to abandon and do not necessarily reflect dates when service actually ended. A railroad may seek authority to abandon two ways, (a) Application for Abandonment, when all operations have ceased and other conditions do not apply; or (b) Notice of Exemption, when no traffic has originated or terminated intermediately in the prior two years and any traffic traversing the entire line can be rerouted. A railroad does not lose its right to continue operation after abandonment is approved.

Introduction

Narrative: A brief history describes the formative years of the company, special features of the alignment (including some information about the villages, towns, and cities that provided business), and some interesting events. Names of railroads are fully spelled out on first mention in each chapter; in subsequent references they are abbreviated unless confusion would result. Railroad is abbreviated as RR and Railway as RY throughout.

Sources: Principal sources of background material are cited in abbreviated form in footnotes. Full citations are contained in the bibliography. Annual reports of the state railroad commissions and *Poor's Railroad Guide* provide more detail. Information on current northern New England railroad affairs can be obtained from magazines such as *Railfan & Railroad, Railpace, Trains,* and others. Those with access to the Internet may begin with the railroad links on the publisher's web site at www.branchlinepress.com.

Caution

Railroads, whether active or apparently abandoned, are owned by someone. Going onto a railroad alignment is trespass unless it is a declared public way. Where track is in place there is extreme danger, as a train may run at any time from either direction. Trespassers can be arrested by railroad, state, or local police. Before walking on or near any alignment, check with the assessors at the local town hall to find out who owns the property and whether permission is required for access.

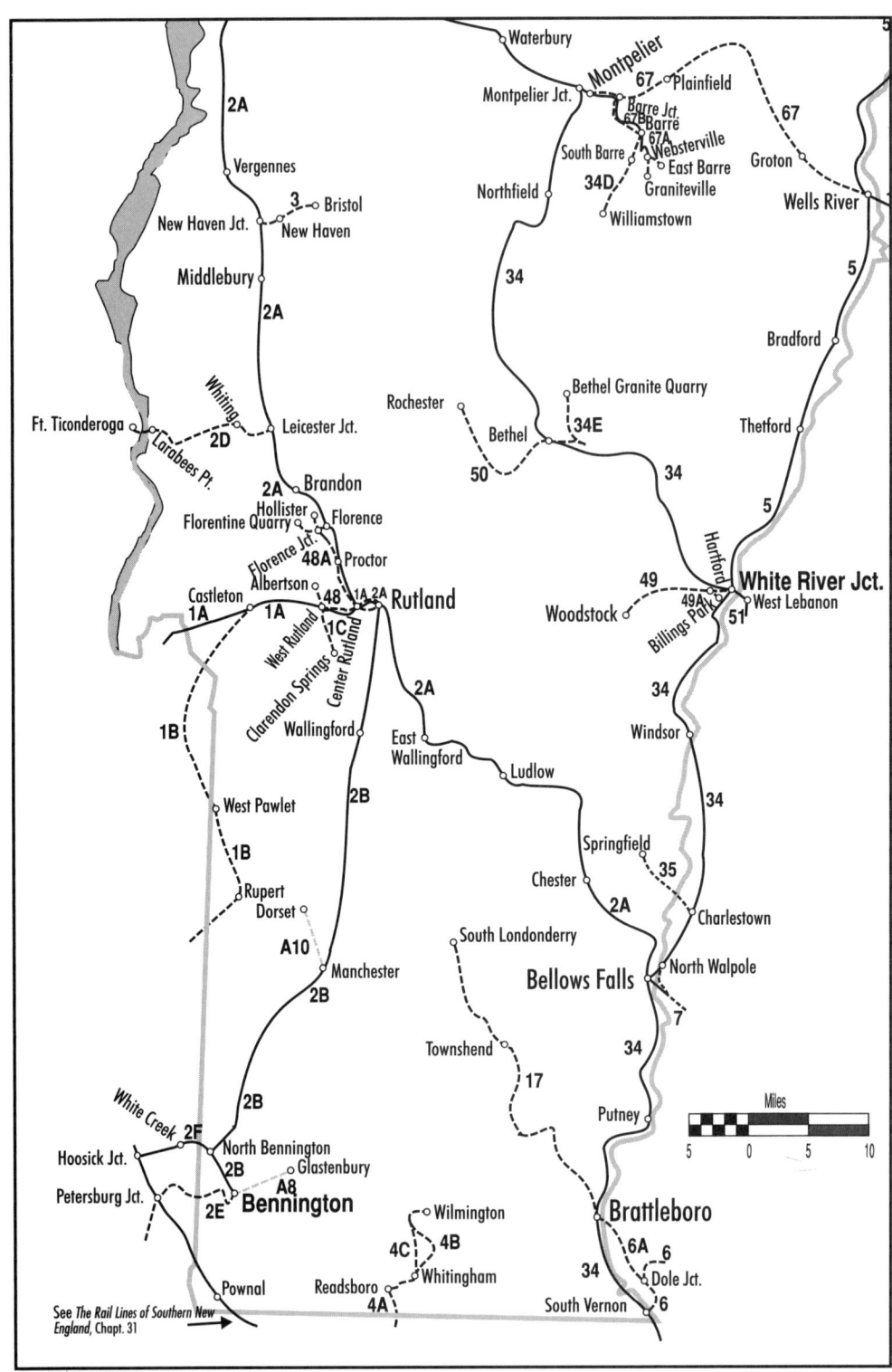

Southern Vermont

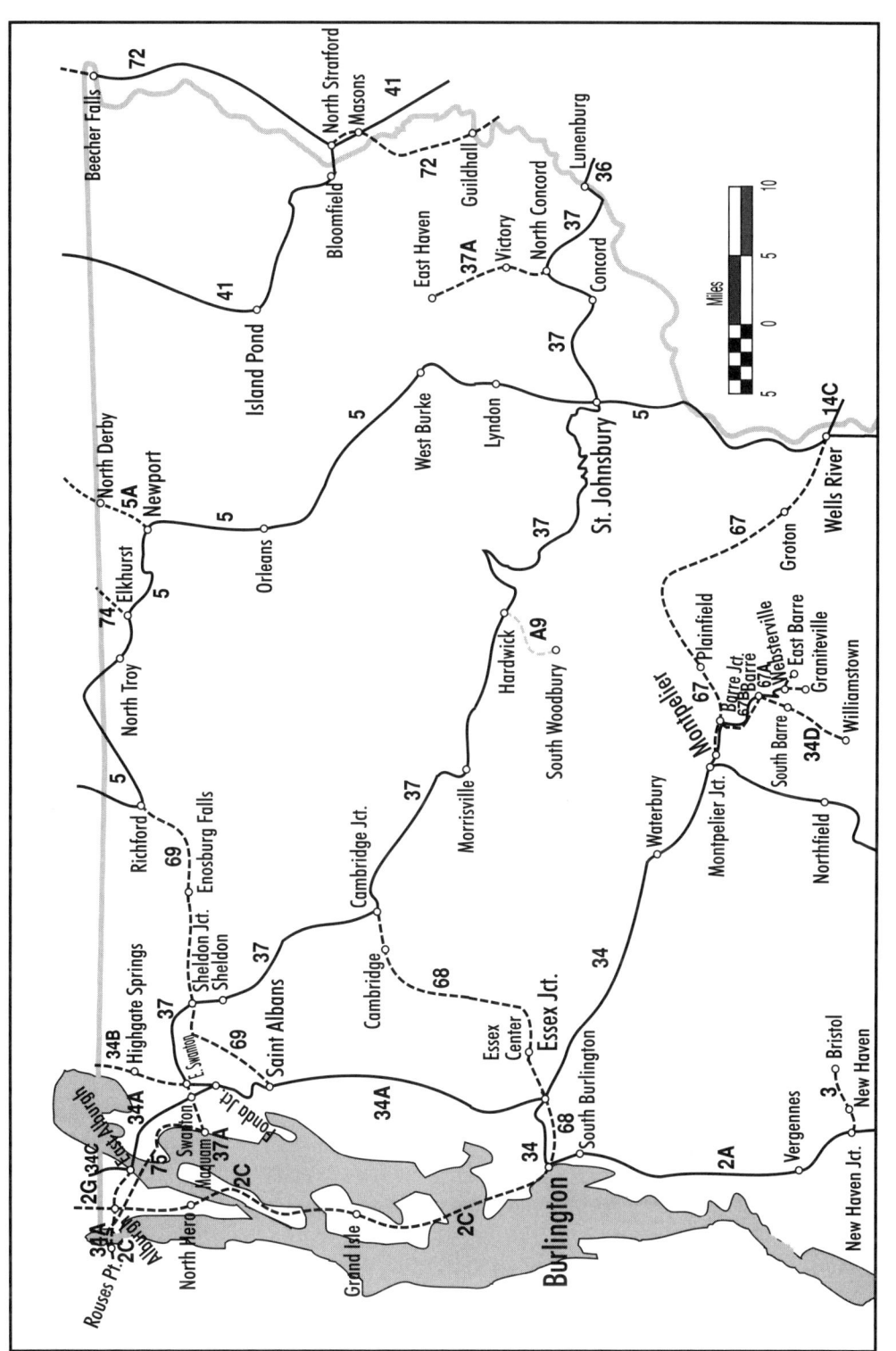

Northern Vermont

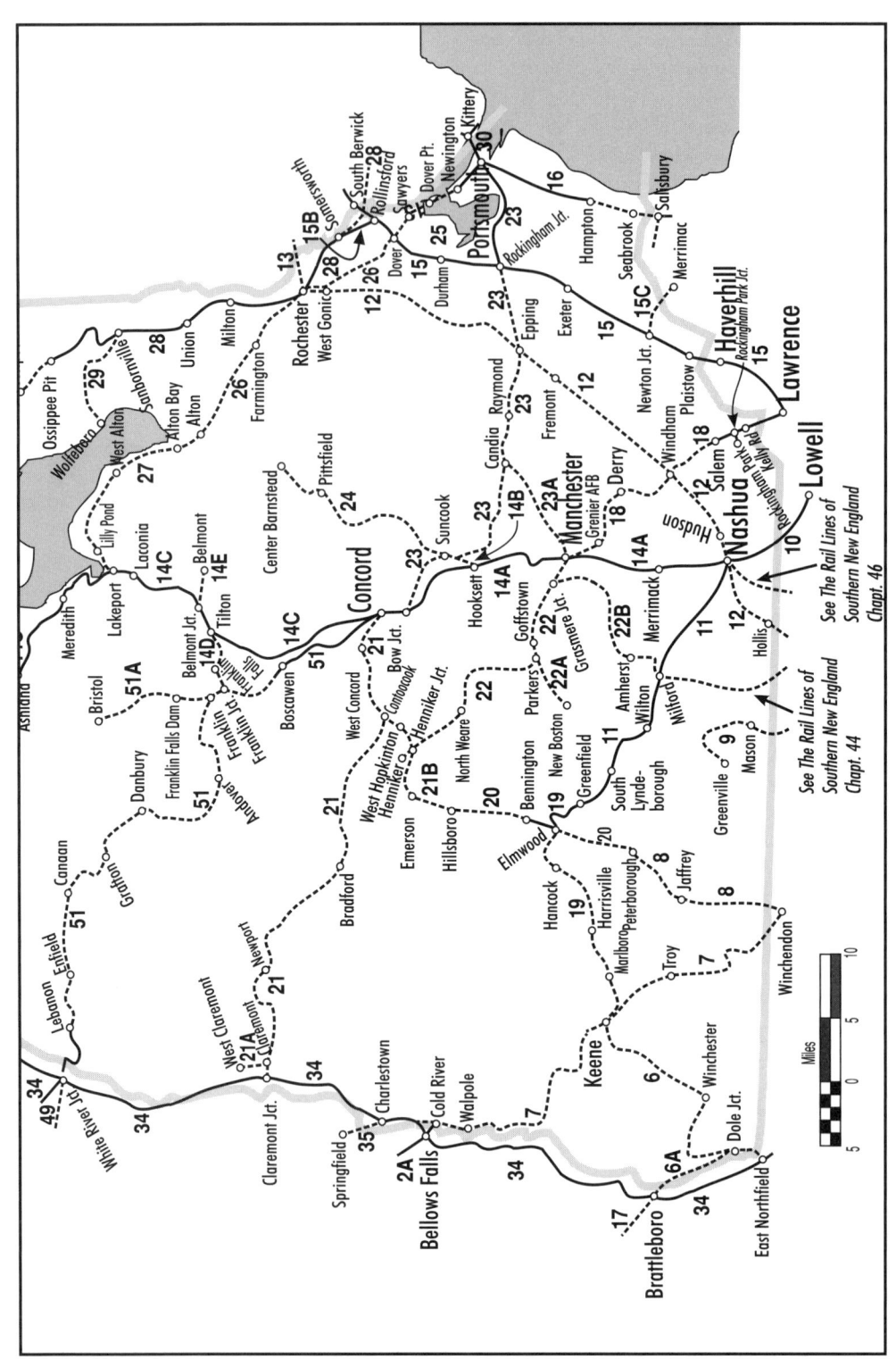

Southern New Hampshire

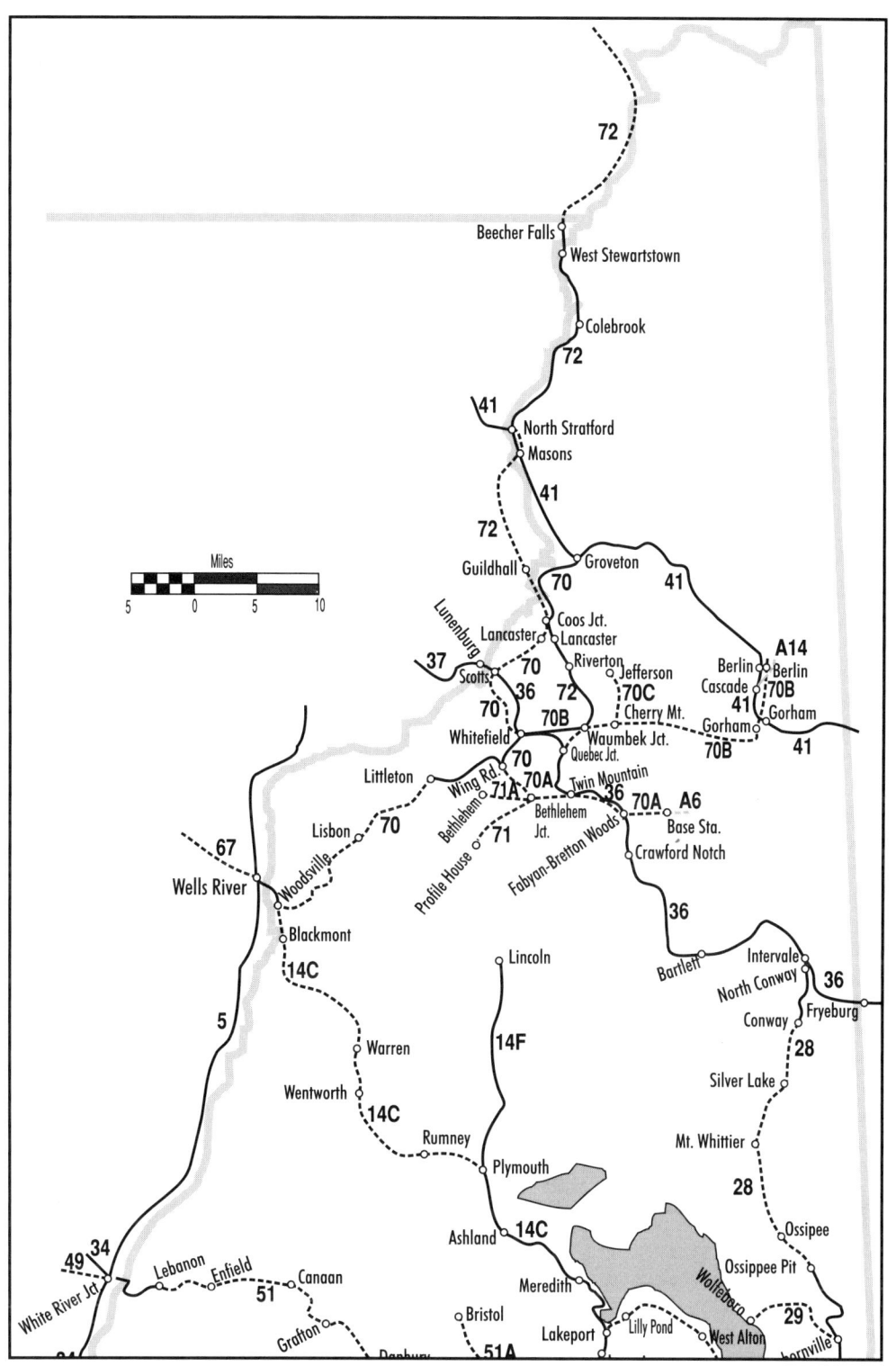

Northern New Hampshire

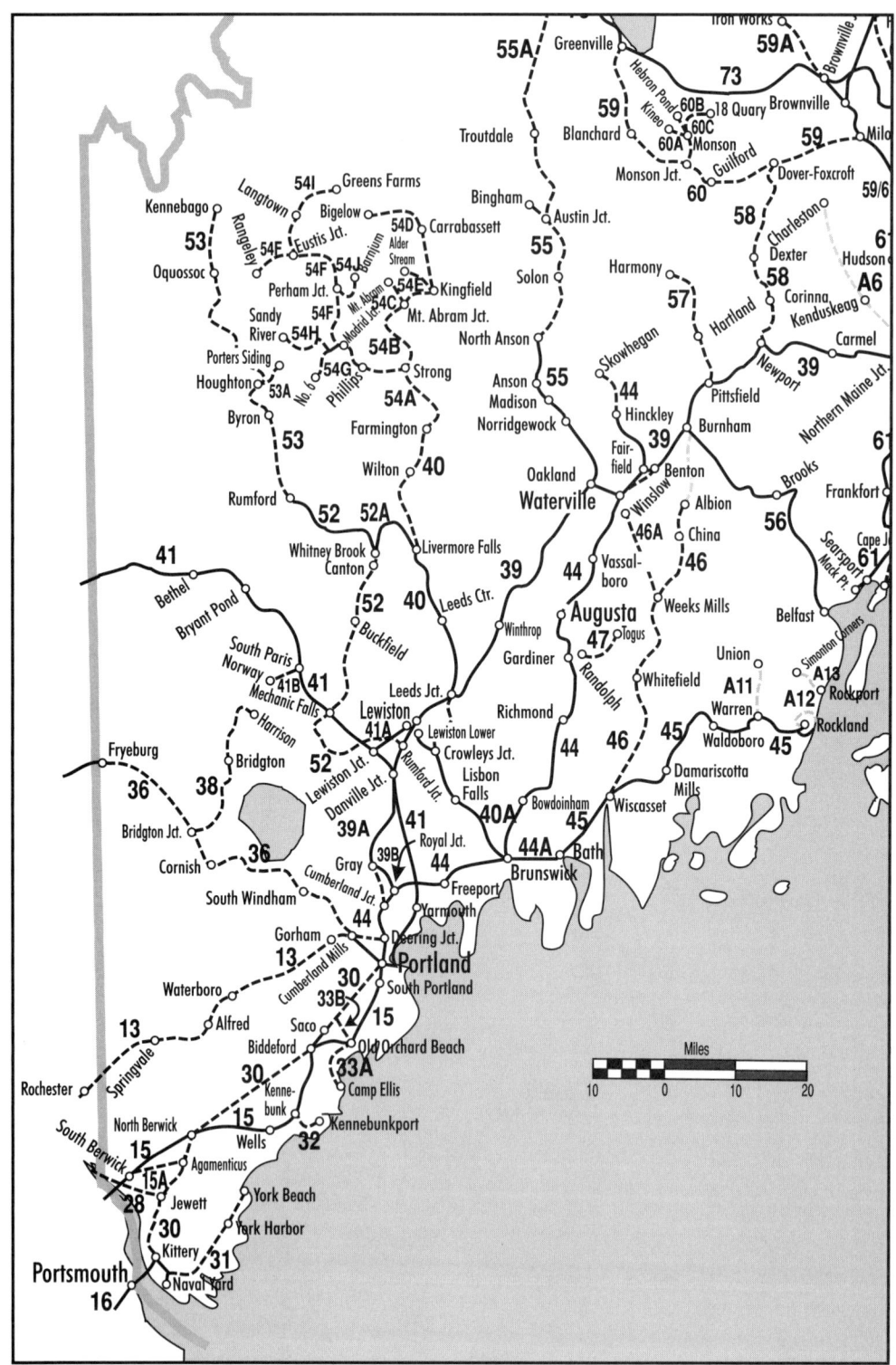

Southern Maine

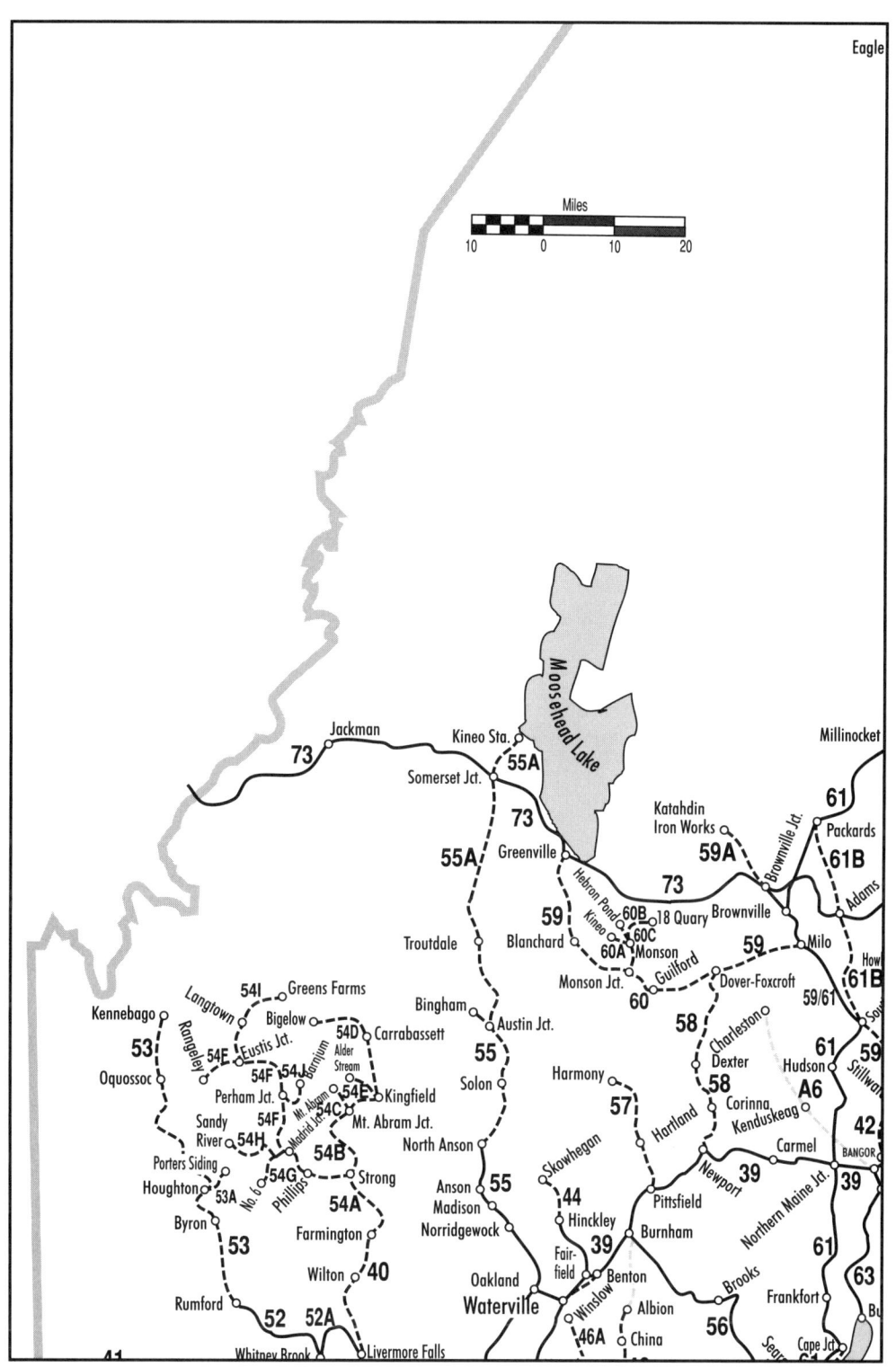

Western Maine

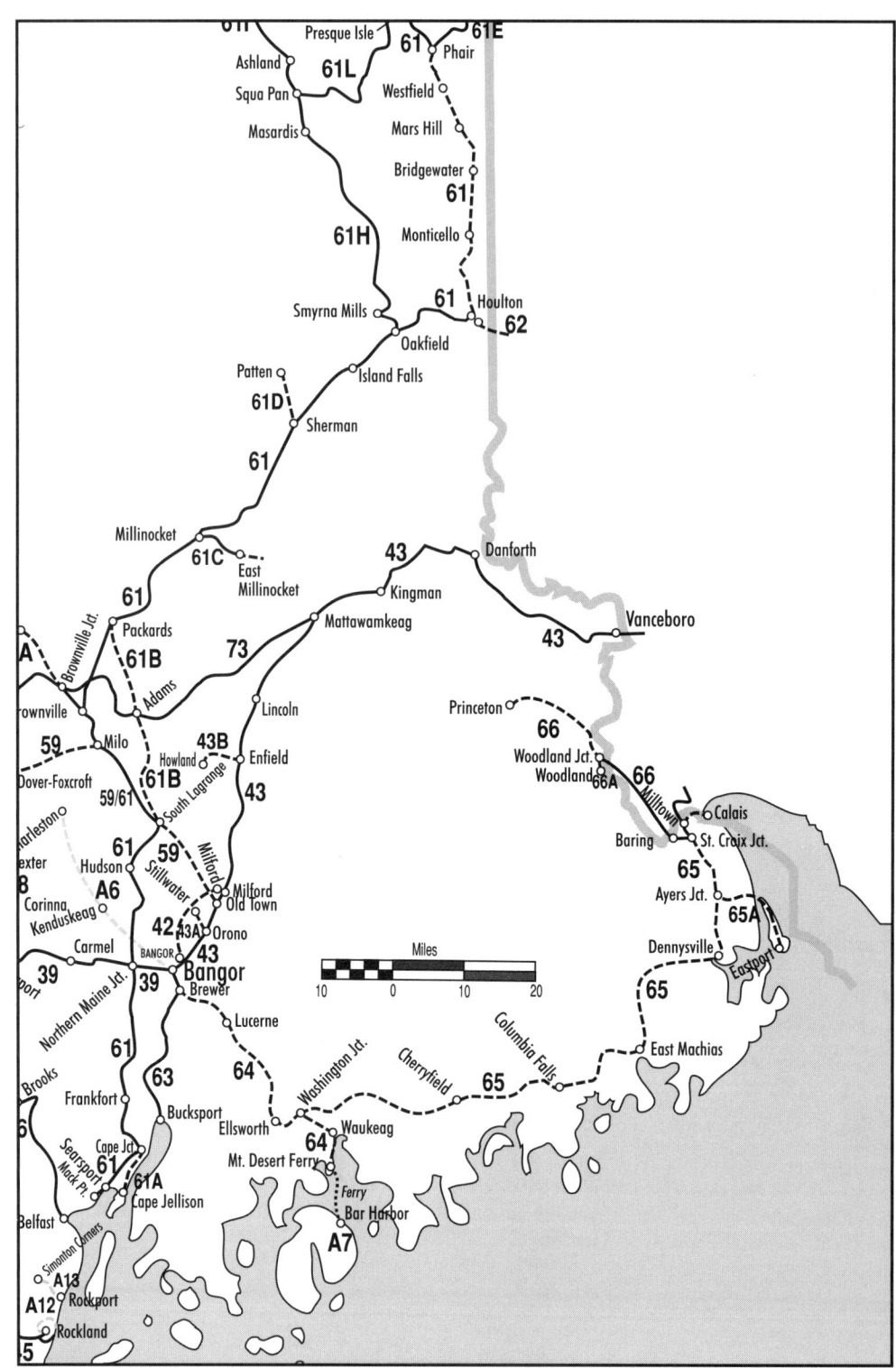

Eastern Maine

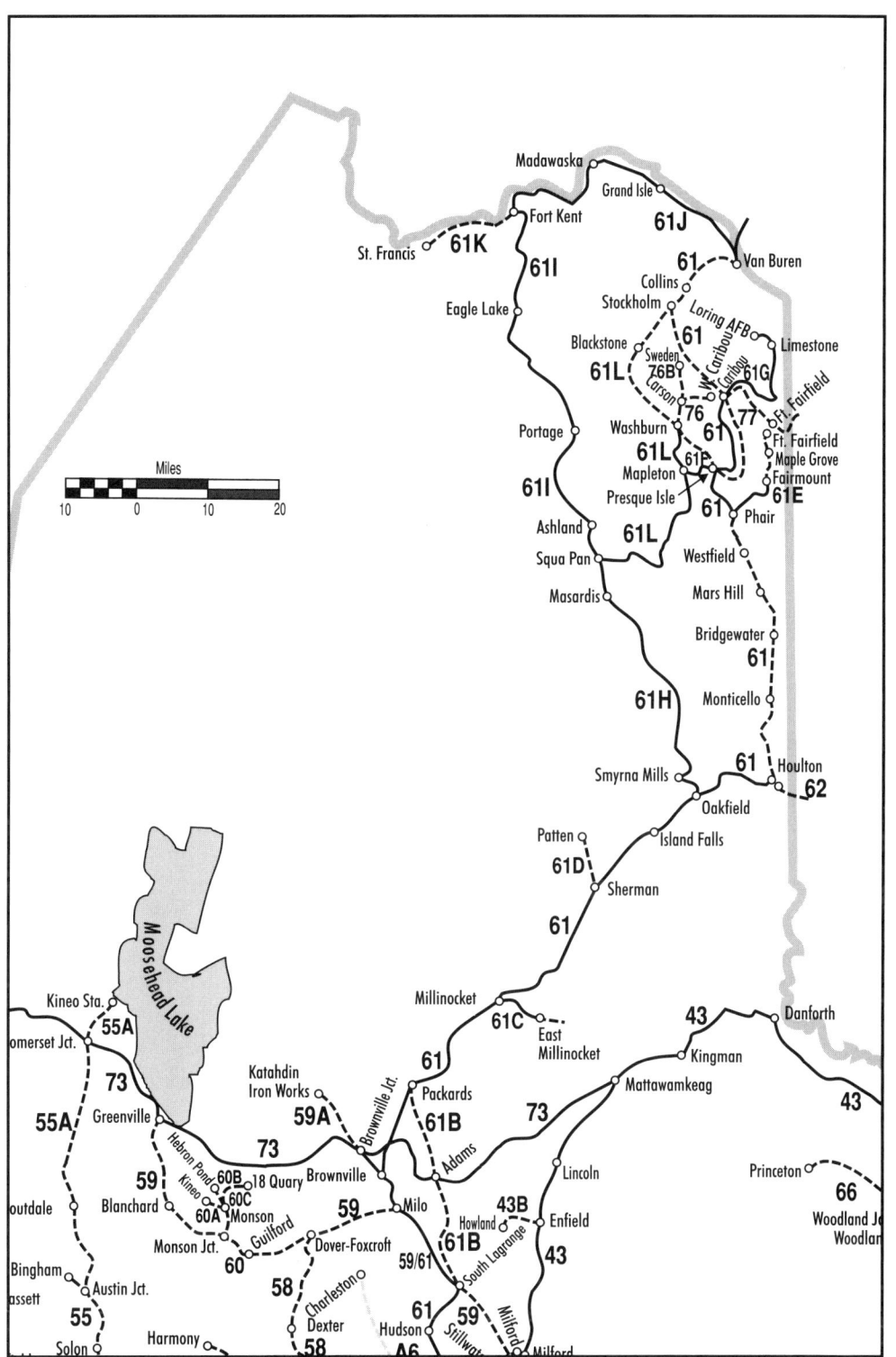

Northern Maine

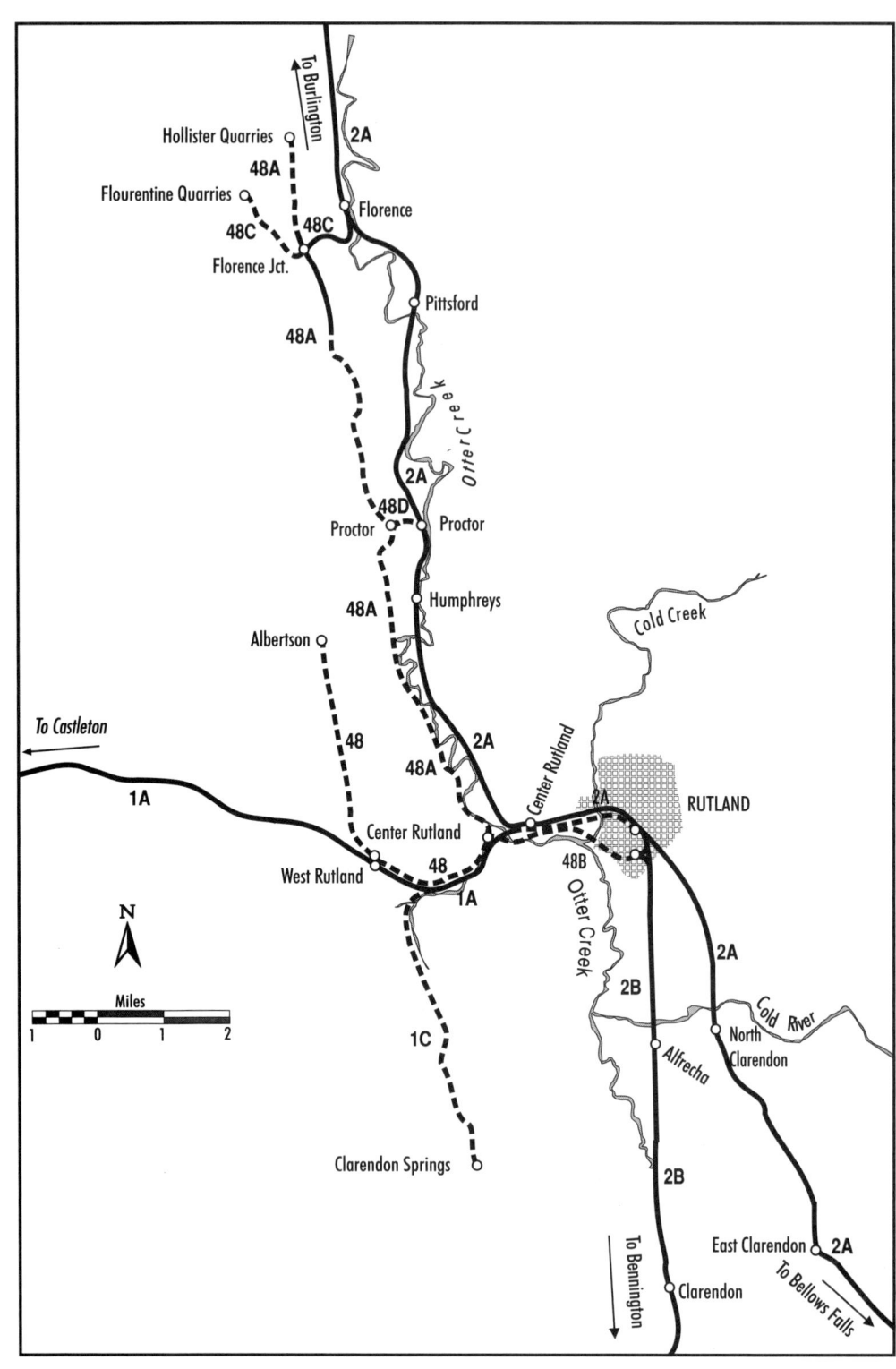

Rutland, VT, and Vicinity

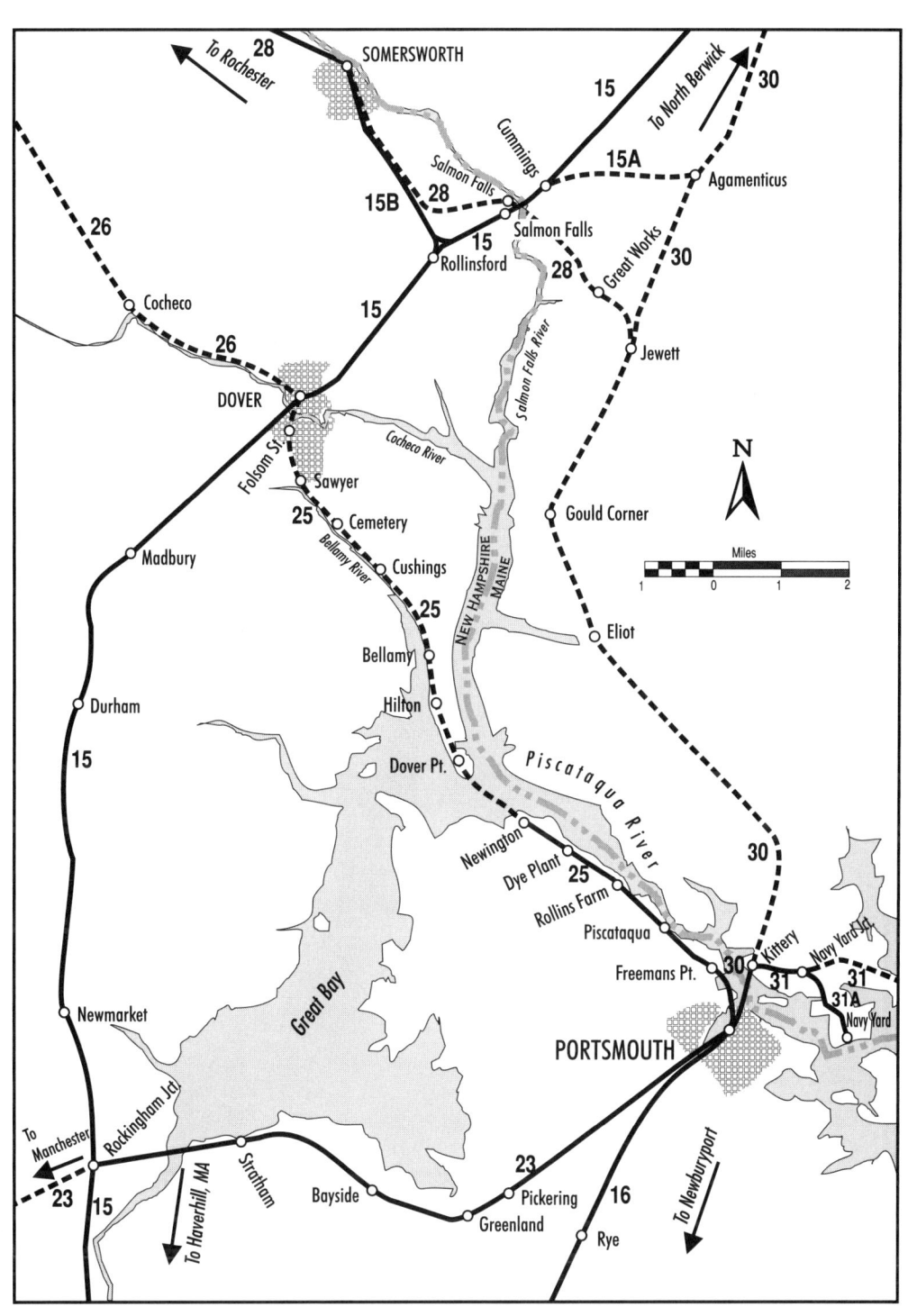

Portsmouth, NH, and Vicinity

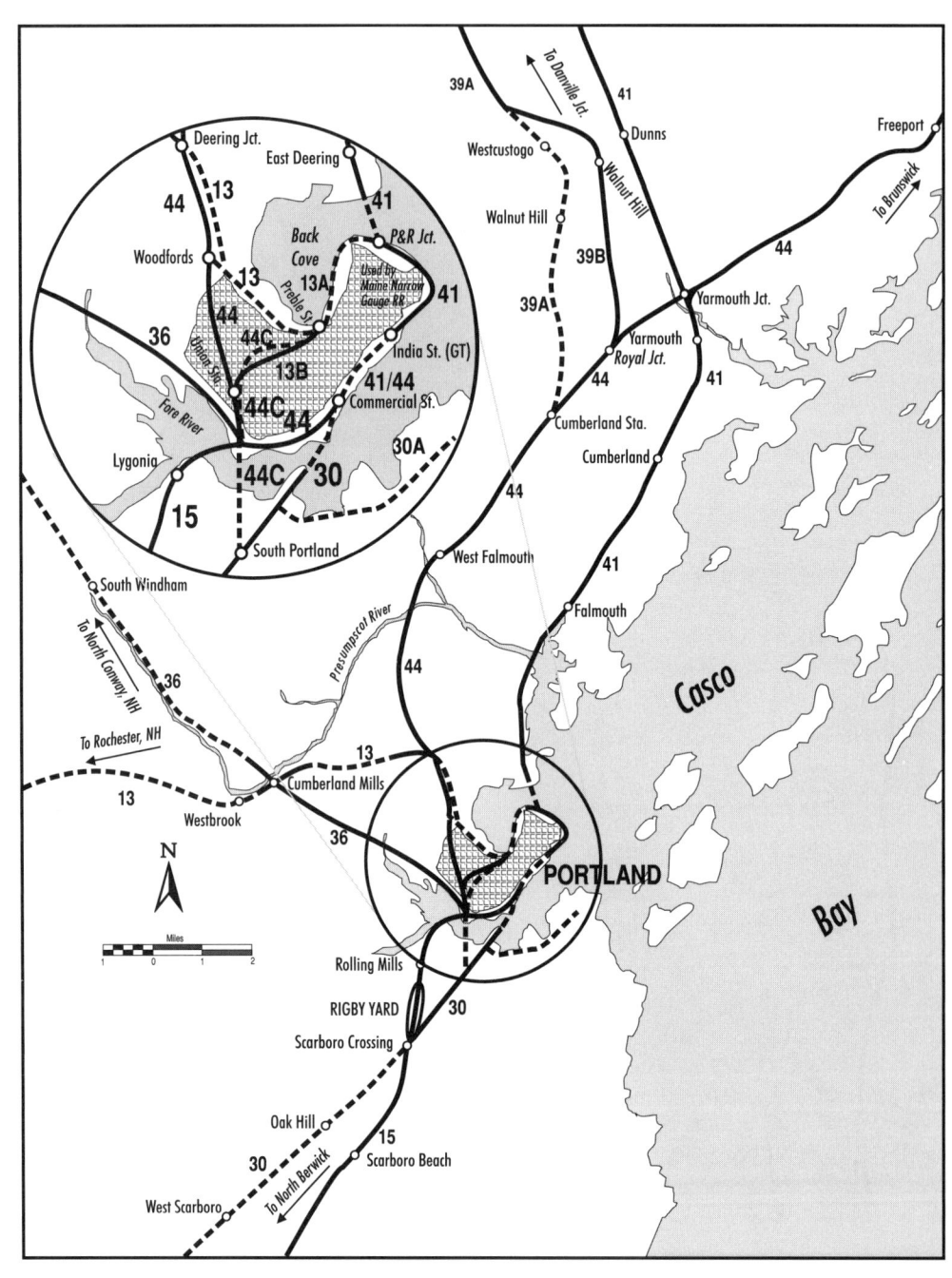

Portland, ME, and Vicinity

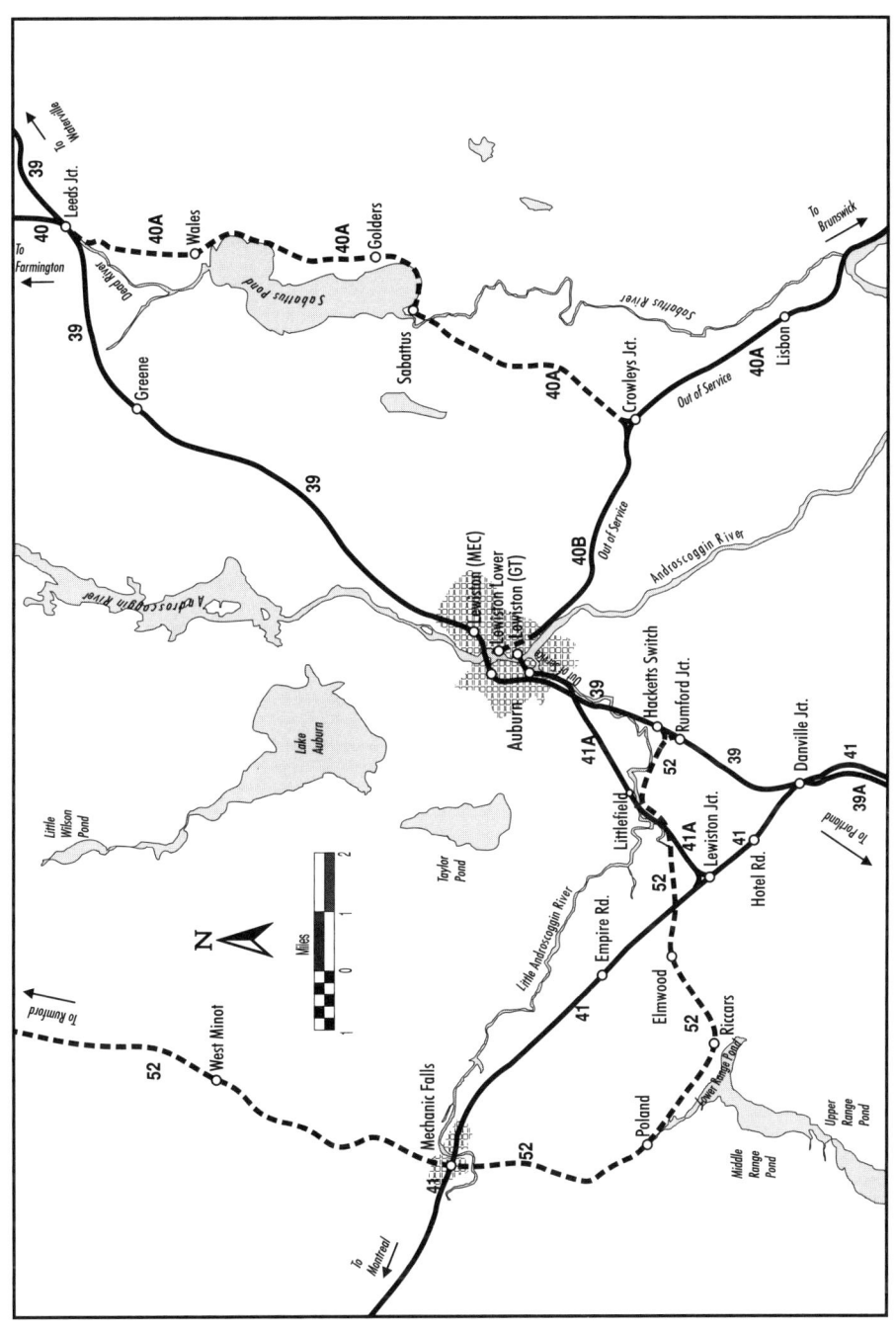

Lewiston-Auburn, ME, and Vicinity

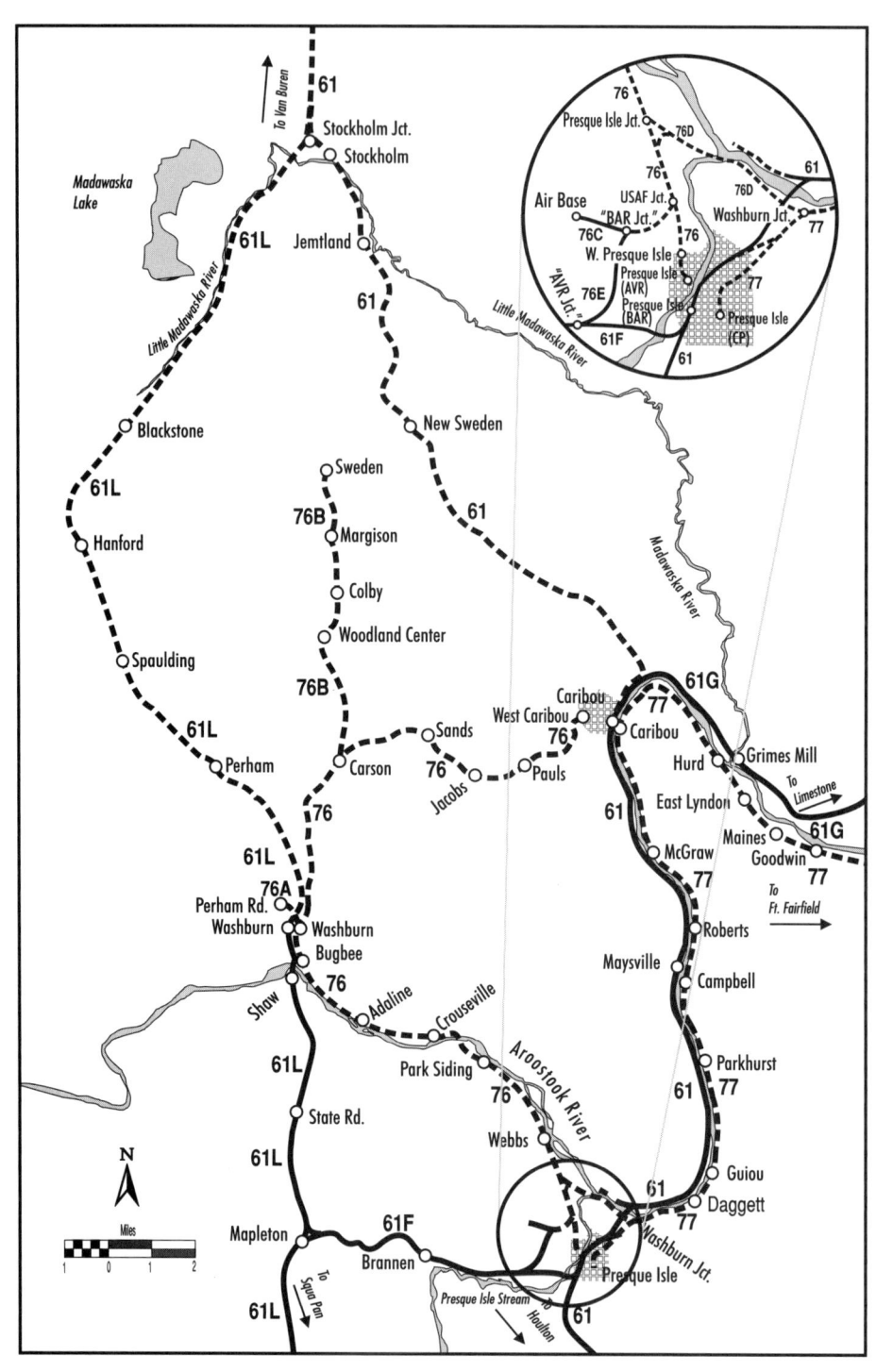

Caribou-Presque Isle, ME, and Vicinity

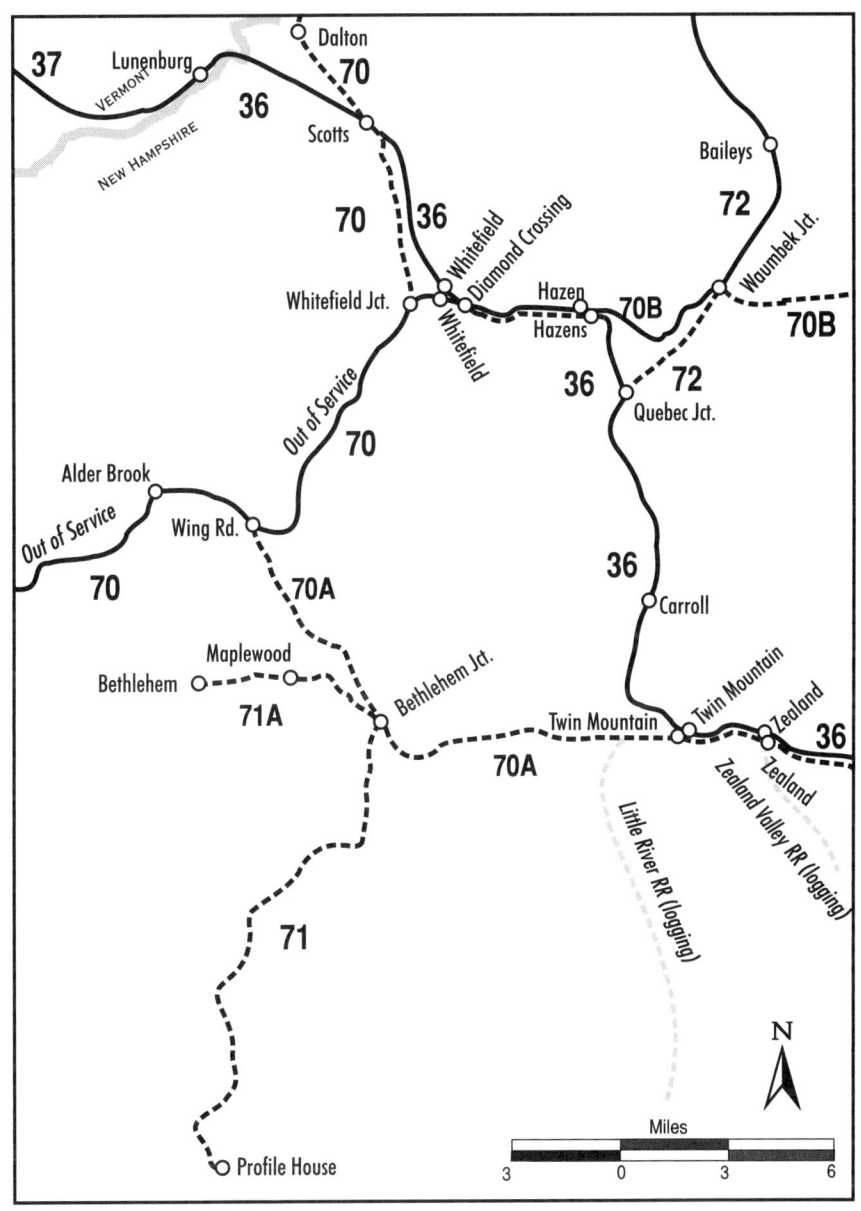

Whitefield, NH, and Vicinity

Amtrak 299, the Ethan Allen Express, *roars through West Rutland on its way to Rutland in late September 1999. (R.D. Karr)*

1. Delaware & Hudson

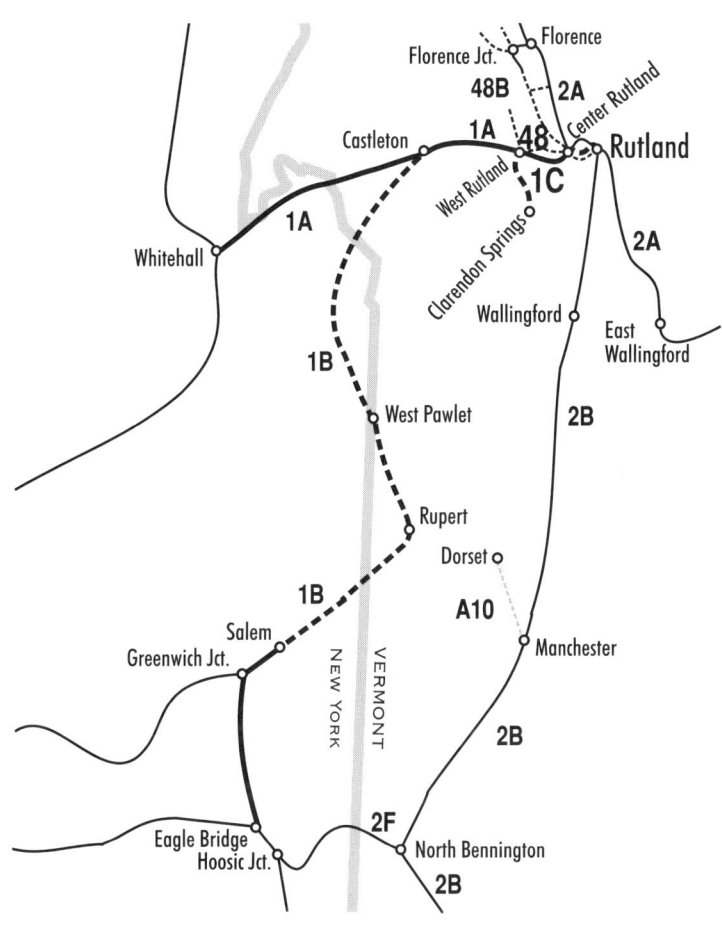

1A. Whitehall Branch	1B. Washington Branch	29 West Rupert, VT
0 Rutland, VT	0 Castleton, VT	35 Salem, NY
2 Center Rutland	1.5 Parker Hill	50 Eagle Bridge, NY
4 West Rutland	2 Blissville	
10 Castleton,	8 Poultney, VT	1C. Clarendon Springs Branch
13 Hydeville	15 Middle Granville, NY	
15 Fairhaven, VT	19 Granville, NY	0 West Rutland, VT
23 Whitehall, NY	20 West Pawlet (Pawlet), VT	3 Clarendon Springs, VT
	27 Rupert	

Built: 1848–52; Clarendon Springs Branch ca. 1920.

Operators: See text.

Daily Passenger Trains: *1869:* Rutland–Eagle Bridge, 4; Rutland-Whitehall, 4; *1893:* Rutland–Eagle Bridge 6; Rutland-Whitehall, 11; *1908:* Rutland-Whitehall, 2; Rutland-Eagle Bridge, 1; *1916:* Rutland–West Rutland, 2; Rutland-Whitehall, 3; *1919:* Rutland–Eagle Bridge, 4; Rutland-Whitehall, 6. Passenger service ended 1933 (resumed by Amtrak, 1996).

Abandonments: Clarendon Springs Branch, 1944; Rutland–Center Rutland, ca. 1947; Castleton–Salem, 1982.

During the late 1840s companies in both Vermont and New York attempted to develop a rail connection between Rutland and the Albany-Troy area. Before 1848 the monopoly on freight traffic that New York had granted to the state-owned Champlain Canal, which had opened in the 1820s from Whitehall to the Erie Canal in Waterford, with regular boats to Troy, discouraged rail competition. The monopoly was eased somewhat in March 1848 when parallel railroads were permitted to haul freight if they paid the equivalent of canal tolls to the state.

Even before New York relaxed its restrictions on railroads, a group of Rutland businessmen obtained a charter for the Rutland & Washington RR on November 13, 1847, with authority to construct a line from Rutland to the New York state line. There it would connect with the Saratoga & Washington RR, a New York line chartered in 1836 but only now constructing its line from Saratoga Springs to Whitehall, NY. The Saratoga & Washington opened the line to Whitehall on December 10, 1848, and obtained permission to extend to the Vermont boundary to connect with the Rutland & Washington.

By this time the Rutland & Washington was under construction from Rutland toward Castleton. The Rutland & Washington abruptly changed its plans, however, when quality slate deposits were found near Poultney and Granville, and obtained permission in 1849 to divert south from Castleton to the state line at Rupert instead. The Troy & Rutland RR was chartered in New York state to extend the line southward to Eagle Bridge, NY, where it would use other railroads to reach Troy and Albany.

This shift in plans left the Saratoga & Washington without a connection to Rutland, so the railroad obtained a Vermont charter for the

1. Delaware & Hudson

Rutland & Whitehall RR from the state line to Castleton, completing the gap between the Saratoga & Washington and the Rutland & Washington on November 1, 1850, a few weeks after the latter railroad had opened the first section of its line between Castleton and Rutland. The Rutland & Washington meanwhile continued to build its own line south from Castleton. On March 9, 1852, the combined route of the Rutland & Washington and Troy & Rutland was opened from Rutland to Eagle Bridge, providing a second route between the Albany-Troy area and Rutland.

Over the next few decades the two rail systems went through a complicated series of bankruptcies, reorganizations, leases, and sales. By 1865 both lines were part of the Rensselaer & Saratoga RR, which in turn was taken over by the Delaware & Hudson RR on May 1, 1871. The D&H designated the line from Castleton to Eagle Bridge as its Washington Branch, and the line between Rutland and Whitehall became the Whitehall Branch. These two Vermont lines formed the eastern-most part of the New York and Pennsylvania-based D&H, one of the nation's oldest railroads.

Under the D&H, passenger and freight service increased, especially after April 1908 following agreement with the Boston & Maine for trackage rights between Eagle Bridge and the major yards at Mechanicville. Switching and exchange of trains to and from the Washington Branch were thereby considerably simplified. Maintenance facilities were built by the D&H at Salem, primarily to service the growing and increasingly higher-powered fleet of Consolidation (2-8-0) locomotives, used for hauling freight.

During the Great Depression passenger service over the Washington Branch ended, with last trips operating on Tuesday, February 28, 1933. By then, the Whitehall line had become the principal D&H route to Rutland, although it too lost passenger service shortly thereafter. In 1947 flood waters at East Creek in Rutland Center took out sections of both the D&H and the closely parallel Rutland RR. The two railroads agreed to rebuild only the Rutland line over which the D&H acquired trackage rights, abandoning its own line between Rutland Center and Rutland. Freight over the Washington Branch justified operation of a six-times-weekly train until the 1960s, generally hauled by an Alco RS-3 road switcher.

The path of a three-mile branch to Clarendon Springs is shown on recent Geological Survey maps, but no published information about it has been found, and it does not appear on D&H system maps. One authority believes it was abandoned in 1944.

With traffic falling, operating costs rising, and the company generally returning annual deficits, the D&H listed the Washington Branch for potential abandonment in June 1980. Service ended on November 15, 1981, when the line was embargoed owing to poor track conditions. The length from Eagle Bridge to Salem was purchased by a new short-line operator, the Batten Kill RR, and operation resumed on October 22, 1982. The remainder to Castleton was abandoned and torn up, the right of way in Vermont later becoming the Delaware & Hudson Recreational Trail. A year later, with purchase of the D&H by Guilford imminent (the deal was completed on January 4, 1984), the Vermont RY made an offer to purchase the Whitehall Branch. Negotiations culminated in sale during August 1983, and operation was taken over by the Clarendon & Pittsford RR.

Nowadays, the Whitehall line sees mainly bridge traffic between the Vermont and Green Mountain RRs (the latter now a part of the Vermont RY system) at Rutland to the D&H. Until 1991 there was some inbound traffic in grain to the Beacon Feed mill at Castleton. Outbound limestone from quarries around Florence continues. A $3.5 million track improvement program, sponsored by state and federal funding, enabled Amtrak to introduce the daily *Ethan Allen* express from New York beginning December 2, 1996; a second train from Albany was added in February 1998.

Sources: Armstrong, *Railfan's Guide*, 30, 36; Bachelder, *Green Mountain Flyer*, 13–17; Drury *Historical Guide*, 378–81; Jones *Railroads of Vermont*, 1: 250; Karr, *Lost Railroads*, 140; Lewis, *American Shortline Railway Guide*, 32; Shaughnessy, *Delaware & Hudson*; Zimmerman, *Decade of the D&H*.

2. Rutland

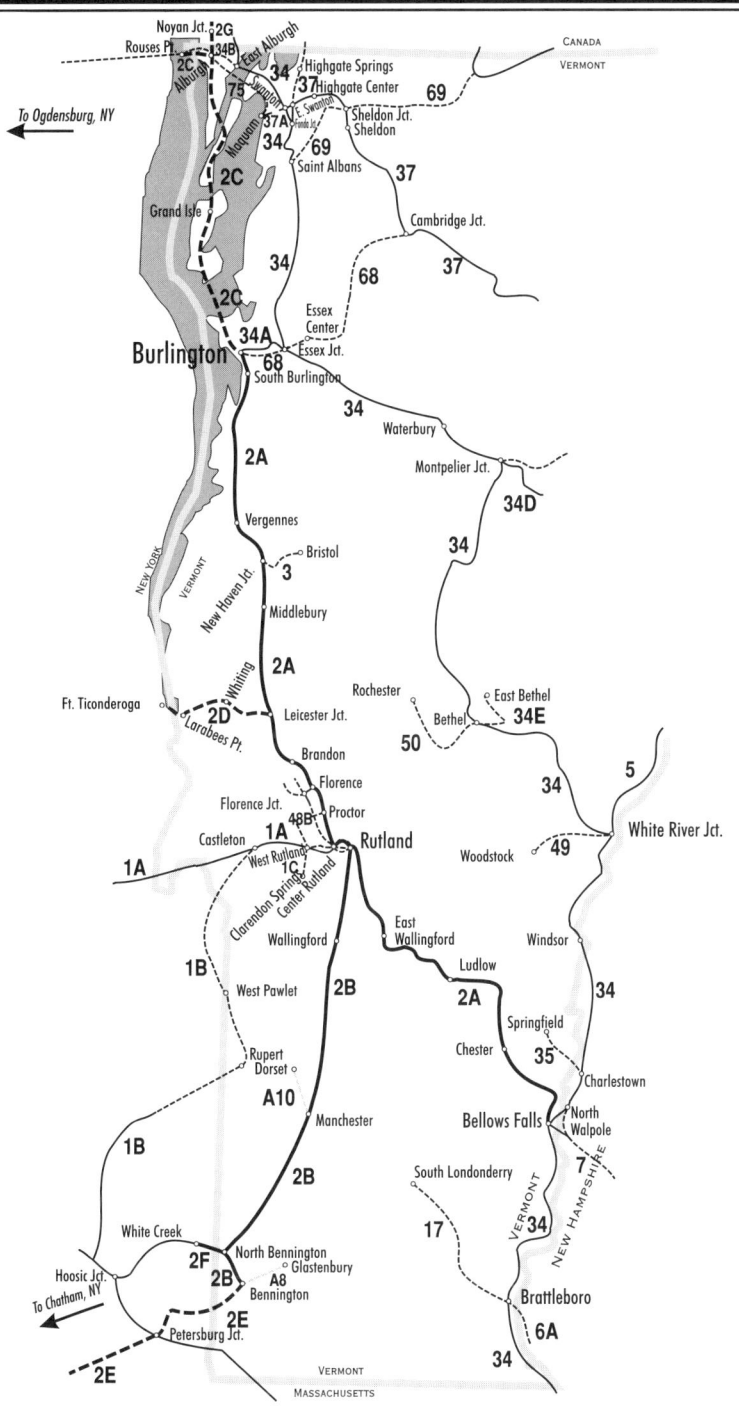

2A. Rutland & Burlington

0 Burlington, VT
0.5 Burlington Yard
5.5 Queen City Park
7 Shelburne
12 Charlotte
15 Thompsons Point
16.5 North Ferrisburg
19.5 Ferrisburg
21.5 Vergennes
26.5 New Haven (New Haven Jct.)
30 Brooksville
32 Beldens
34 Middlebury
41 Salisbury
45.5 Leicester Jct. (Leicester) (Whiting)
51.5 Brandon
57 Florence (Fowler) (Pittsford Quarry)
58 Pittsford
61.5 Proctor (Sutherland Falls)
62.5 Humphreys
66 Center Rutland
67.5 Rutland
70.5 North Clarendon
73.5 East Clarendon (Clarendon)
77 Cuttingsville
80.5 East Wallingford
83 Mount Holly
85.5 Summit
87 Healdville
92.5 Ludlow
96 Proctorsville
97.5 Cavendish
101.5 Gassetts
106.5 Chester
110.5 Bartonsville
112.5 Brockways Mills
114.5 Rockingham
115 Midway
117.5 Riverside
119.5 Bellows Falls, VT

2B. Bennington & Rutland

0 Rutland, VT
3 Alfrecha (Cold River)
5 Clarendon
9.5 Wallingford
13.5 South Wallingford
15 Stafford
18.5 Danby (Danby & Mt. Tabor)
22.5 North Dorset
26 East Dorset
30 Barnumville
31.5 Manchester
37.5 Sunderland
41 Arlington
45.5 Shaftsbury
50.5 South Shaftsbury
52.5 North Bennington
57 Bennington, VT

2C. Rutland & Canadian

0 Burlington, VT
3.5 Star Farm Beach
6.5 Colchester (Colchester Point)
13.5 South Hero
17.5 Grand Isle
19 Knight Point (Abnaki)
25 North Hero
31 Isle La Motte
33 South Alburgh
37 Alburgh, VT
39 Rouses Point, NY

2D. Addison Branch

0 Leicester Jct., VT
3 Whiting
6 Shoreham
8 Orwell
11 Houghs Crossing
13.5 Larrabees Point, VT
14.5 Fort Ticonderoga (Ticonderoga), NY

2E. Chatham Branch

0 Bennington, VT
4.5 Anthony
6.5 Bee Hive Crossing, VT
11.5 Petersburg Jct., NY
57.5 Chatham, NY

2F. White Creek Branch

0 North Bennington, VT
5 White Creek, NY

2G. Rutland & Noylan

0 Alburgh, VT
6 Noyan Jct., PQ

Built: Rutland & Burlington, 1843-49; Bennington & Rutland, White Creek Branch, 1852-53; Chatham Branch, 1869; Addison Branch, 1871; Rutland & Canadian, Rutland & Noylan 1899-1901.
Operators: See text.

2. Rutland

Daily Passenger Trains: *1849:* Bellows Falls-Burlington, 2; Burlington-Rutland, 2; *1851:* Bellows Falls-Burlington, 4; Burlington-Rutland, 2; Bellows Falls-Rutland, 2; *1869:* Rutland-N. Bennington, 4; Bellows Falls-Burlington, 4; *1893:* Rutland-N. Bennington, 8; Bellows Falls-Burlington, 8; Addison Branch, 2; Burlington-Rouses Point, 6; Chatham Branch, 6; *1919:* Rutland-N. Bennington, 8; Bellows Falls-Burlington, 10; Burlington-Rouses Point, 6; Addison Branch, 4; Chatham Branch, 6; *1935:* Rutland-N. Bennington, 6; Bellows Falls-Burlington, 6; Burlington-Rouses Point, 8; Addison Branch, 2; Chatham Branch, 2; *1950:* Rutland-N. Bennington, 2; Bellows Falls- Burlington, 6; Burlington-Rouses Point, 2; Addison Branch, 2 mixed, Tuesdays only. Passenger service ended 1953.

Abandonments: Larrabees Point.-Ft. Ticonderoga, 1923; International Border-Noyan Jct., 1934; Alburgh to International Border, ca.1941; Whiting-Larrabees Point, 1951; Bennington-Chatham, NY, 1953; Leicester Jct.-Whiting, 1961; Burlington-Rouses Point, 1963.

On November 1, 1843, a charter was granted to the Champlain & Connecticut River RR for a line from Burlington to the west bank of the Connecticut River. During construction, the company entered receivership, to emerge on November 6, 1847, as the Rutland & Burlington RR. Work was completed to Burlington on December 18, 1849, with regular service beginning Christmas Eve. An extension to St. Albans was approved, but blocked by the Vermont Central, which made interchange at Burlington difficult. In November 1853 receivers again took over. John B. Page, a trustee since 1863, arranged the reorganization of the R&B as the Rutland RR on July 9, 1867. Oddly enough, on January 16, Page and the chairman of the Vermont Central had personally leased the Bennington & Rutland RR, which ran from Rutland through North Bennington. The B&R had been chartered as the Western Vermont RR in 1845 to build a line from Rutland through North Bennington to connect with the Troy & Boston RR at White Creek, NY. Completed in 1853, it had become the B&R in 1865.

Animosity between the Rutland and Vermont Central continued as both vied for control of Vermont's rail traffic. To the west, the Rutland leased the Whitehall & Plattsburgh RR, from Ft. Ticonderoga to Port Henry, NY, in 1870, and acquired a controlling interest in the Lake Champlain steamers between Burlington and Plattsburgh. This was

A Rutland double-headed freight pulls through East Wallingford in September 1946. (Albert G. Hale, courtesy Walker Transportation Collection, Beverly Historical Society & Museum)

followed by purchase of the Addison RR, a short line opened on December 1, 1871, from Leicester Jct. to Ft. Ticonderoga. These acquisitions featured a 1500-foot trestle and a bridge of barges across Lake Champlain. While the line provided a much-sought international route, it was of minor importance.

The Vermont Central countered by leasing the Rutland as of December 31, 1870. The VC defaulted in 1873, but its successor, the Central Vermont, continued to operate the system in an attempt to keep out the Delaware & Hudson. The CV took a short-term lease of the Rutland in 1890, along with the Bennington & Rutland, which had been independent since 1877. A new lease was negotiated in 1893, only to be abrogated on May 7, 1896, in favor of operation by the D&H.

2. Rutland

The Rutland RR resumed independent operation on October 22, 1898. It obtained a charter in November 1898 for the Rutland & Canadian RR to build from Burlington to Rouses Point, giving it access to Canada independent of the CV for the first time. The new line required a three-mile causeway across Lake Champlain to South Hero, several long trestles between islands, and another causeway to Alburgh, completed in 1901. Between East Alburgh and Rouses Point the new line closely paralleled the CV and shared the CV's bridge across the Richelieu using an unusual gauntlet track that allowed both railroads to use the bridge without the need for switches. A branch from Alburgh, built by the Rutland & Noyan RR, connected to the north with the Grand Trunk RY. Southward, the Chatham & Lebanon Valley was leased in 1899 and merged by 1901. Built as the Lebanon Springs RR, it had opened a line between Bennington and Chatham, NY, in 1869, operating under various names until its acquisition by the Rutland. In 1901 the Rutland absorbed the Ogdensburg & Lake Champlain RR, built by the Northern RR of New York to Rouses Point in 1850.

On May 1, 1902, Dr. William Seward Webb, son-in-law of William H. Vanderbilt of New York Central fame, became the Rutland's president; but by about 1911, through various stock exchanges, the New York, New Haven & Hartford RR had gained control. At Burlington, a Union station designed by Fellheimer & Long of New York City, was opened on January 23, 1916. Though now much altered internally, it retains the original Georgian-style sash windows, with a pediment above a stylized Norman arch entrance.

The Addison Branch barge-bridge system was embargoed in 1917 and formally abandoned in 1923. Significant flood damage in October 1927 throughout the Rutland system cost the company about $1 million. By the mid-1930s the railroad was struggling, and on May 5, 1938, it entered receivership. Administrative economies were made, but proposals for less restrictive work rules were rejected by the operating unions. Management chose a course through the courts, which ordered a further reduction in management costs and a 15 percent reduction in wages, to be recompensed after the restoration of substantial profitability. Although that occurred in 1941, management took no action to restore previous wage levels, and the unions threatened strikes. Animosity lingered for twenty years.

On November 1, 1950, the assets and liabilities of the Rutland were acquired by the Rutland RY. Major cost-cutting measures were taken.

The Addison Branch was truncated at Whiting in 1951, with the final trip to Larrabees Point on May 21. The last trains over the Chatham Branch ran on May 19, 1953, after permission to abandon had been obtained the previous December. Two named passenger trains, however, the *Mount Royal* and the *Green Mountain*, continued to operate daily between New York and Montreal, with a connection to Boston via Bellows Falls. A strike by administrative and managerial staff began on June 26, 1953, and all operations ceased. Passenger service never resumed.

By 1954, diesel had ousted steam, and cost savings enabled a modest wage increase. Further deterioration in the Rutland's finances led to more budget cuts and refusal to accept the 1960 National Rail Wage Agreement. This resulted in a 41-day strike from September 15, which ended after a federal court injunction followed arbitration. When the injunction expired, all service ended on Monday, September 25, 1961.

During the late summer and early fall 1999 the Vermont Railway operated the Ethan Allen Connector *between Rutland and Burlington. With GP-38-2 no. 202 pushing in the rear, the train is passing northbound through Center Rutland in September 1999. (R. D. Karr)*

Rutland no. 28, a 2-8-0 Consolidation, crosses a farm road at Anthony, VT, a few years before diesels replaced steam. (Courtesy Walker Transportation Collection, Beverly Historical Society & Museum)

A petition to abandon the entire system was submitted on December 4, 1961, and approval was given on September 18, 1962. The rail unions and the state lobbied for reconsideration, which postponed abandonment until May 20, 1963. Just over 332 miles in Vermont and New York were given up, but the system was not to die.

On October 25, 1963, the Vermont RY was incorporated and commenced service on January 6, 1964, over the route between Burlington and Bennington. A few months later, on April 3, 1964, the Green Mountain RR was incorporated to operate the line between Bellows Falls and Rutland, resuming April 2, 1965. The two companies carried mainly minerals (particularly talc), lumber, paper, oil, fly ash, and salt. The Vermont RY took control of the Green Mountain RR on May 23, 1997, and now operates much of the old Rutland as a single system. For some years until 1983, when Steamtown moved to Pennsylvania, seasonal steam-hauled passenger excursions were operated out of Bellows Falls.

Between Center Rutland and Rutland, Amtrak uses former Rutland track for its year-round trains from New York. Seasonal passenger trains, such as the *Green Mountain Flyer,* continue. During the summer of 1999 the state of Vermont operated scheduled passenger service between Burlington and Rutland.

Sources: Armstrong, *Railfan's Guide,* 31, 36; Bachelder, *Green Mountain Flyer,* 3-12; Jones, *Central Vermont;* Jones, *Railroads of Vermont,* 2: 152-94; Lewis, *American Shortline Railway Guide,* 115, 271; Nimke, *Green Mountain;* Potter, *Great American Railroad Stations,* 113-18; *Railpace* 16 (Aug. 1997): 37; Shaughnessy, *Rutland.*

3. Bristol

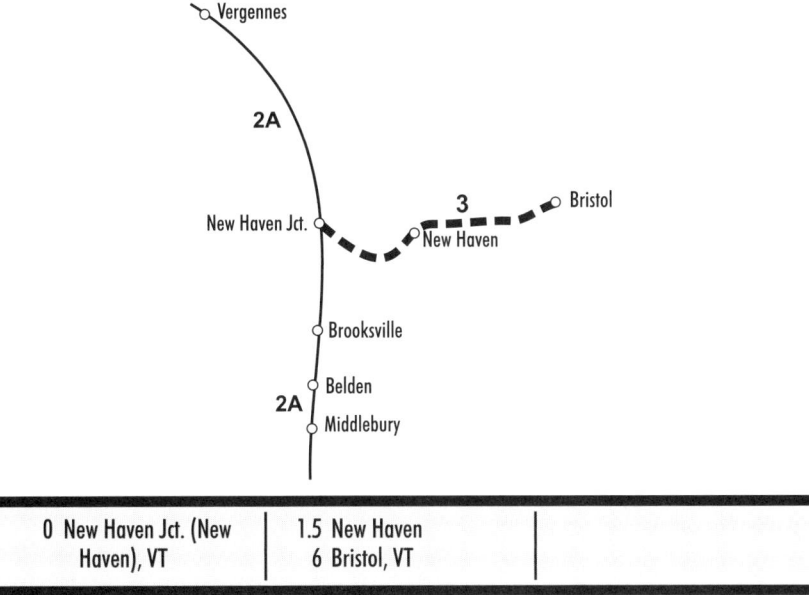

0 New Haven Jct. (New Haven), VT	1.5 New Haven 6 Bristol, VT	

Built: 1890–92.
Operator: *Bristol*, 1892–1930.
Daily Passenger Trains: *1893:* 4; *1919:* 6.
Abandonment: 1930.

Bristol, at the headwaters of the New Haven River, was a most unpromising place for a railroad. Its sole claim to fame—or notoriety—were diggings around the turn of the nineteenth century for supposedly buried treasure, led by a preacher named Nathaniel Wood, who some say had much to do with the origin of Mormonism. The Rutland RR bypassed the town, serving the local communities with a station in New Haven.

Local interests obtained a charter for the Bristol RR in 1890 in hopes of promoting quarry and agricultural traffic, and to serve the one textile mill in the town. Surveys produced a virtually level alignment, which generally followed various upstream branches of Otter Creek south and northeast of New Haven town center. Service began on November 25, 1891, with official opening on January 5, 1892. An 0-4-4 side-tank locomotive coupled to a combine car was the normal consist for handling

Bristol RR 0-4-4T no. 1 at New Haven Jct. in 1916. (Courtesy Walker Transportation Collection, Beverly Historical Society & Museum)

freight and passenger service, with connections generally made with Rutland RR trains. The Rutland showed no interest in lease or acquisition, and the Bristol RR never had a traffic pooling agreement; separate fares and charges were levied. Strict economy allowed the purchase, around 1911, of a gas-mechanical railcar, which remained in use until the early 1920s, when steam haulage resumed.

Always a marginal operation, the company failed during the Great Depression and obtained permission to abandon in 1930. A short distance east of New Haven Jct. was subsequently taken over by State Route 17, but the remainder of the alignment can still be hiked. The station building in Bristol is now a private dwelling. The junction depot, built of variegated brick, is in use by a construction and landscaping company.

Sources: Bachelder, *Green Mountain Flyer*, 32–33; Jones, *Railroads of Vermont*, 1:105–15; Karr, *Lost Railroads*, 85.

4. Hoosac Tunnel & Wilmington

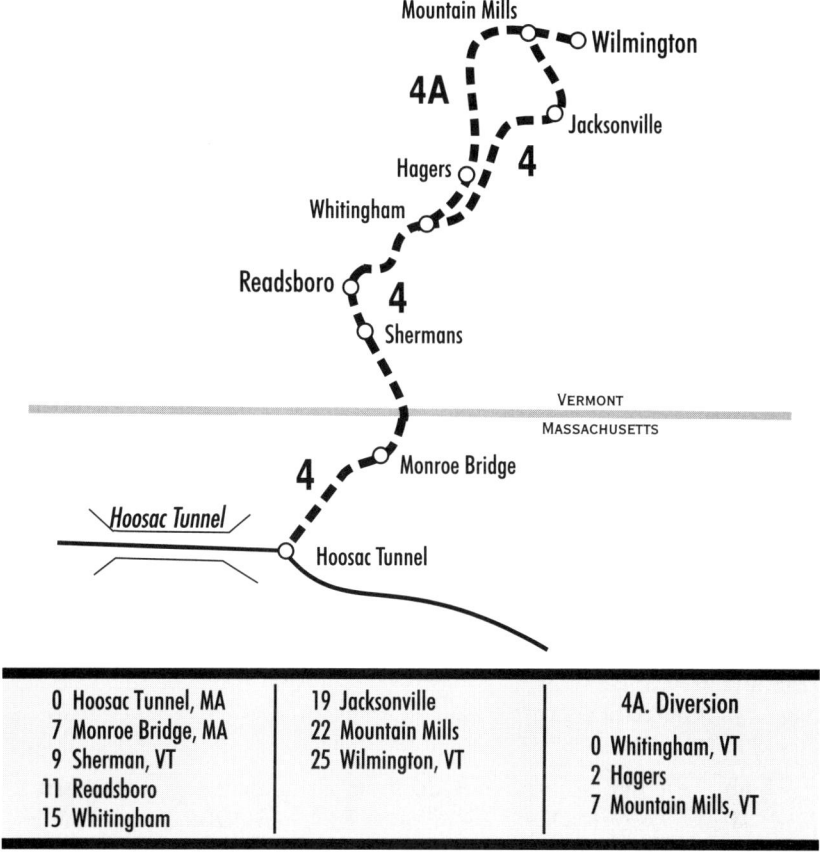

		4A. Diversion
0 Hoosac Tunnel, MA	19 Jacksonville	
7 Monroe Bridge, MA	22 Mountain Mills	0 Whitingham, VT
9 Sherman, VT	25 Wilmington, VT	2 Hagers
11 Readsboro		7 Mountain Mills, VT
15 Whitingham		

Built: Hoosac Tunnel–Readsboro, 1884-85; Readsboro–Wilmington, 1891; Diversion, 1922.

Operators: Deerfield River, 1885-86; Hoosac Tunnel & Wilmington, 1886-1971.

Daily Passenger Trains: *1891:* 2; *1893:* 3; *1895:* 4; *1916:* 4; *1925:* 4. Passenger service ended 1927.

Abandonments: Whitingham–Mountain Mills, 1922 (original line); Readsboro–Wilmington, 1938; Hoosac Tunnel–Readsboro, 1971.

4. Hoosac Tunnel & Wilmington

The Deerfield River RR was chartered and incorporated in Vermont in 1884 by the Deerfield River Co. to build south from Readsboro to the Fitchburg RR at the eastern portal of Hoosac Tunnel. The 3-foot-gauge common carrier line cost roundly $100,000 and opened on July 4, 1885. The owners, the Newton family of Holyoke, MA, incorporated the Hoosac Tunnel & Wilmington RR in Massachusetts during 1886 to acquire the section of line within the state and to lease the remainder. Extension to Wilmington by the nominally independent Deerfield Valley RR opened on November 4, 1891. All three undertakings were consolidated in the HT&W company on January 1, 1892, the registered office being transferred from the pulpwood mill at Readsboro to Wilmington three days later. Several logging-only branches were built.

Initially, the fleet comprised two engines, increasing to five in 1892 and six in 1898, of which four were frequently identified as passenger engines. During the 3-foot-gauge era, ten locomotives were purchased, some as replacements for sold or scrapped stock. The Vermont Railroad Commissioners reported in 1902 that "traffic over the railroad is not very great," but the situation changed when the Newton family expanded its interests into woodwork mills and other industrial ventures during the next several years. Prosperity brought both takeover bids and local consternation when the railroad, deeds to various manufacturing facilities, and rights to felling lumber on 123,000 acres were sold in 1904 to J. P. Kellas of Malone, NY, and his associates for $1.5 million.

Under the new regime over 30 miles of branches were constructed into lumber stands above Readsboro between 1908 and 1914, then dismantled when these resources were depleted. A decision was made to convert the main line to standard gauge, announced in July 1912, to obviate inconvenience and cost of interchange at the tunnel. Preparations were made in spring, and work was completed on August 2, 1913. Two of the original locomotives and some other rolling stock were retained to work the remaining lumber branches, with the rest eventually sold to a Cuban sugar plantation.

Plans were announced in 1920 by the New England Power Company to dam the Deerfield River near Whitingham to create a reservoir with flood relief in Sadawga Pond south of Whitingham, incidentally flooding the line in Wilmington where it entered from Whitingam Township. Kellas and the local communities rejected a suggestion for

4. Hoosac Tunnel & Wilmington

substitute ferry service, compelling the power company to purchase the line in January 1922, which it needed for material delivery, and to construct a diversion to higher ground westward, involving two switchbacks and the closure of Jacksonville station. Jacksonville lay several miles east of the original line, so loss of the depot was not serious. Henry I. Harriman succeeded Kellas as president of the railroad; when complete, the earthwork dam was the largest of its kind in the world and it, together with the reservoir, were named in Harriman's honor.

No longer interested in owning a railroad that had served its purpose and was not producing returns, the NEPC sold the line to local interests in 1926. Parts of the line were extensively flooded on November 3, 1927, with extensive damage to the timber trestle near Wilmington. Freight traffic resumed in 1929 after repairs, but passenger service was suspended and replaced by busses. The line hosted the first American railfan excursion on Sunday, August 26, 1934, sponsored by the National Association of Railroad Enthusiasts (later to become the Massachusetts Bay Railroad Enthusiasts, Inc.).

Lumber traffic had virtually ceased when, on March 18, 1936, the spring thaw accompanied by heavy rainfall washed out the trestle west of Wilmington and caused considerable damage elsewhere. Unable to finance reconstruction, the company was put up for sale. It was purchased by the H. E. Salzberg Company which sold it to Salzberg's son-in-law, Samuel M. Pinsly, as his first railroad in 1937. Pinsly reopened the line south of Readsboro in 1938 but had obtained ICC permission to abandon northward on December 3, 1937.

The "Great Hurricane" of September 1938 caused severe damage but the line was again restored. Three years later accounts showed a profit—the first in 15 years—and modest returns continued to be recorded for many years, aided by conversion to diesel traction in 1949, until the mid-1950s. Award of a contract to convey material for construction of the Yankee Atomic Power Station near Monroe Bridge, MA, revived company fortunes somewhat, but plans for a pumped-storage hydroelectric plant at Bear Swamp brought about the line's demise. Compensation for costs of another realignment were regarded as inadequate, and the railroad agreed to seek permission to abandon. Permission was given by the ICC in September 1971, and operation ended on Wednesday, October 13, 1971.

The Yankee facility shut down in 1984 but was not dismantled until more than a decade had passed. Ironically, the railroad that had brought in the plant's equipment could have facilitated shipment of many large components to Barnwell in South Carolina for reprocessing, instead of costly and dangerous transfer along winding narrow roads to Guilford trackage at Hoosac Tunnel. What better epitaph could there be for a small branch line that nobody needed?

Sources: Bachelder, *Half-Century Ltd.*, 4-9, 50-51; Carman, *Hoot, Toot & Whistle*; Cornwall and Smith, *Names First*, 35, 50-51; Hilton, *American Narrow Gauge*, 538-39; Karr, *Rail Lines*, 170-72; Karr, *Lost Railroads*, 129-30; Nelligan, *Bluebirds*; 224 ICC 255.

5. Connecticut & Passumpsic Rivers

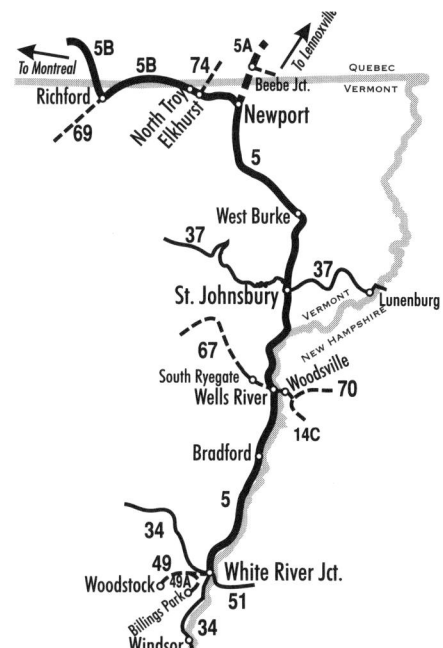

0 White River Jct. (White River Falls), VT	54 Inwood (East Barnet) (McLarans) (Norrisville)	2 Derby
2 Wilder (Olcott)	58 Passumpsic	5 North Derby, VT
4 Norwich (Norwich-Hanover)	61 St. Johnsbury	6 Beebe Jct. (Stanstead Jct.), PQ
9 Kendall (Pompanoosuc)	64 Centervale (St. Johnsbury Centre)	37 Lennoxville, PQ
14 Thetford	69 Lyndon	
17 Northboro (North Thetford)	70 Lyndonville	**5B. South Eastern RY**
19 Ely	77 West Burke	0 Newport, VT
22 Fairlee (Fairlee & Orford)	80 Summit	4 Lake Park
27 Bradford	83 Sutton	8 Newport Center
31 Conicut (South Newbury)	89 Willoughby (South Barton) (Kimball)	14 Elkhurst (Troy Jct.)
34 Newbury	94 Barton	15 North Troy, VT
41 Wells River	98 Orleans (Barton Landing)	18 Highwater, PQ
45 East Ryegate (Rye Gate)	102 Coventry	21 Glenton, PQ
49 McIndoes (McIndoes Falls) (McIndoe)	104 Newport, VT	24 Missisquoi, VT
50 Barnet		27 Stevens Mills
	5A. Massawippi Valley RY	29 Richford, VT
	0 Newport, VT	34 Abercorn, PQ
		108 Windsor Sta., Montreal, PQ

5. Connecticut & Passumpsic Rivers

Built: 1846-67; Massawippi Valley, 1868-70; South Eastern, 1869-73.

Operators: *Connecticut & Passumpsic Rivers,* 1848-87; *South Eastern,* 1873-75, 1879-83; *Boston, Concord & Montreal,* 1875-77; *Boston & Lowell,* 1887; *Canadian Pacific,* 1883-1996; *Boston & Maine,* 1887-1983; *Guilford,* 1983-98; *Northern Vermont,* 1996-; *Vermont,* 2000.

Daily Passenger Trains: *1869:* 2; *1893:* 9; *1919:* 6; *1935:* 6; *1950:* 4; *1960:* 2. Passenger service ended 1965.

Abandonments: Massawippi Valley (Lenoxville-Beebe Jct., ca. 1990; Bebe Jct.-Newport [1 mile north], 1996).

A railroad from the Massachusetts-Vermont border to Canada along the valleys of the Connecticut, Passumpsic, and Barton Rivers was granted a charter in Vermont on November 10, 1835, and renewed in 1843. Nothing was done, however, for lack of capital. On November 5, 1845, a charter amendment split the proposed line between the Connecticut & Passumpsic Rivers RR, which was to build from "a place at or near the mouth of the White River" to the Canadian border, and a Connecticut River RR to build south to its namesake at the Massachusetts state line. Nothing more was heard of the latter.

Work began on the C&PR in 1846, with the first rails laid at Norwich in July 1848. The line was completed from the Northern and Vermont Central RRs at White River Jct. to Wells River on November 6. The line was opened to McIndoes in October 1850 and to St. Johnsbury on November 28. Three years later the Boston, Concord & Montreal RR connected at Wells River. With refusal of the Canadian government to allow the BC&M access to Montreal, the C&PR pushed forward slowly. Barton was reached in fall 1857, Barton Landing two years later, Newport on October 14, 1863, and the international border at North Derby on May 1, 1867. It was assumed that other railroads would complete the route to Montreal.

In Canada, Royal Assent had been given in 1853 to the Stanstead, Shefford & Chambly RY, in 1862 to the Massawippi Valley RY, and in 1866 to the South Eastern Counties Jct. RY. The C&PR agreed on July 31, 1867, to lease and operate the MV on completion of the line from Lennoxville to Stanstead Jct., on the U.S. border. Regular service began on July 1, 1870, for which the broad-gauge Grand Trunk laid a

5. Connecticut & Passumpsic Rivers

third rail on the three-mile length from Lennoxville to Sherbrooke, PQ. The MV also built a short line from Beebe east to Stanstead, PQ, with a branch from Rock Island to the border abutting Derby Line, VT, a truly international town, these days with a public library straddling the border, and a theater where the stage is in Canada and the audience in the U.S.

The interchange at Sherbrooke was inconvenient and costly. The South Eastern Counties Jct. RY, whose enabling act of August 15, 1866, specifically empowered construction "from West Farnham or some other convenient point on the [Stanstead, Shefford & Chambly] to a point on the international border...as may best suit for connecting with the [C&PR]," began construction in 1869. On November 11 that year, the Missisquoi & Clyde Rivers RR obtained a charter in Vermont to build either side of Richford and from the border near North Troy to Newport. The SECJ, which had agreed to lease the Missisquoi & Clyde Rivers on completion, faltered and was reorganized as the South Eastern RY in 1872. Although special trains operated over the two lines in the winter of 1872–73, scheduled service did not begin until July 9, 1873.

Competition and low traffic resulted in a joint lease of the South Eastern by the C&PR and BC&M from March 1, 1875, to ensure its survival. However, the BC&M withdrew in 1877, whereupon the SE claimed that maintenance had not been to the standards required by the lease. The SE blocked the line with a stationary locomotive and removed several rails, although through service resumed on September 10, 1879. In 1883 the SE was acquired by the Canadian Pacific RY, and on January 1, 1887, the Boston & Lowell RR leased the C&PR. When the Boston & Maine leased the Boston & Lowell later that year, the line eventually formed the B&M's Passumpsic Division with headquarters in the former C&PR offices at Lyndonville. For many years the line was an important link for traffic between Montreal and Boston, although it was never a money spinner.

On January 6, 1926, the B&M leased the C&PR north of Wells River to the Canadian Pacific. The CP in turn sublet the line north of Newport to its subsidiary, the Quebec Central RY. Passengers were then invited to use newly named trains—the daytime *Alouette* and the overnight *Red Wing*—which took up to 11 hours to journey between Boston and Montreal, although from 1931 the *Alouette* was diverted

In August 1977 a dozen years had passed since the last passenger boarded a train at the CP's St. Johnsbury station. (R. D. Karr)

over the Central Vermont line (it was later restored to the C&PR). For many years the CP pooled rolling stock with the B&M. Passenger trains from Boston to Montreal continued via the C&PR until the fall of 1965.

In 1995 Guilford discontinued freight service on its section of the C&PR north of Wilder after the bridge between Wells River and Woodsville was condemned. Two years later Guilford placed the White River Jct.-Wells River segment for sale. In December 1998 a bridge at Wilder was damaged by a truck. Rather than repair it, Guilford embargoed the line. Only one customer, a lumber dealer who received an occasional shipment at Wilder, was left. The state of Vermont bought the line in December 1999, and the Vermont RY began operating occasional freights to Wells River starting in February under state contract.

The CP sold their portion of the C&PR to the Iron Road system in September 1996. Iron Road now operates the line between Wells River and Canada as the Northern Vermont RR, and in May 2000 the state of Vermont chose the NV to operate the C&PR south of Wells River as well. Most of the former Massawippi Valley between Newport and Beebe is an international bike trail, which opened in June 1999.

Sources: Bachelder, *Alouette*, 6-10; Bachelder, *Half-Century Ltd.*, 46-48; Baker, *Formation*, 146, 172, 229; Drury, *Historical Guide*, 368; Kistler, *Rise of Railroads*, 41, 57-65, 202-04; *Railpace* 17 (Feb. 1998): 37.

6. Ashuelot

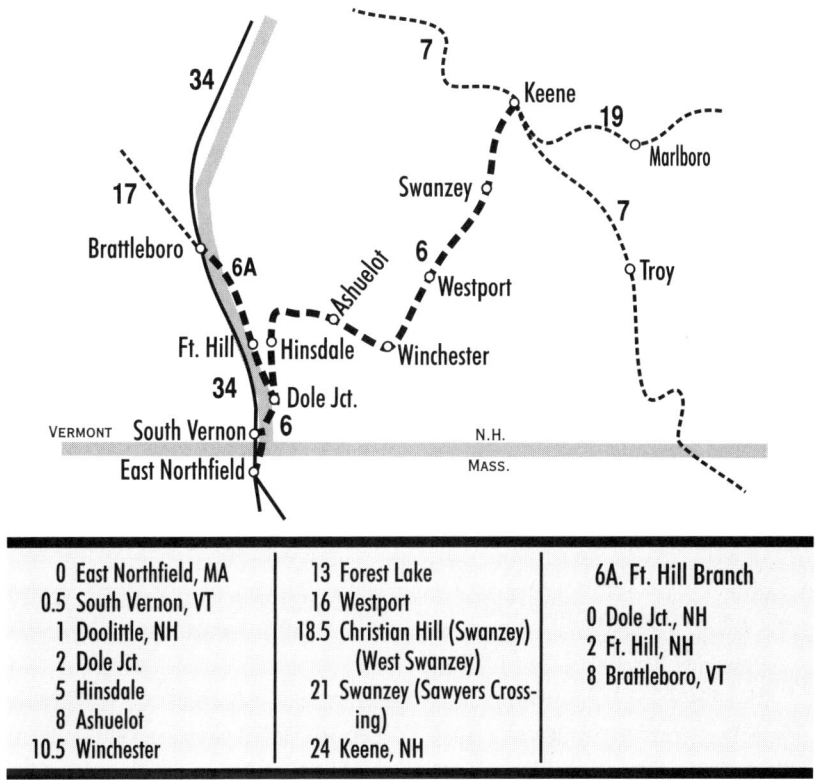

0 East Northfield, MA	13 Forest Lake	**6A. Ft. Hill Branch**
0.5 South Vernon, VT	16 Westport	0 Dole Jct., NH
1 Doolittle, NH	18.5 Christian Hill (Swanzey)	2 Ft. Hill, NH
2 Dole Jct.	(West Swanzey)	8 Brattleboro, VT
5 Hinsdale	21 Swanzey (Sawyers Crossing)	
8 Ashuelot		
10.5 Winchester	24 Keene, NH	

Built: 1849–51; Fort Hill Branch, 1913.
Operators: *Connecticut River*, 1851-60; *Cheshire*, 1860-77; *Connecticut River*, 1877-93; *Boston & Maine*, 1893-1981; *Green Mountain*, 1981-83.
Daily Passenger Trains: *1869:* 4; *1893:* 6; *1919:* 8; *1935:* 4; *1950:* 4. Regular passenger service ended 1958; unscheduled mixed service until ca. 1964.
Abandonment: 1983.

The Cheshire RR reached Keene, in the heartland of New Hampshire, in 1848. The following year Keene was chosen as the terminal of the Ashuelot RR, which planned to connect at its southern end in South Vernon, VT, with the Vermont & Massachusetts RR.

The Ashuelot negotiated with the V&M, then controlled by the Fitchburg RR, to obtain trackage rights southward to reach the Connecticut River RR at East Northfield, MA. When these negotiations failed, the Ashuelot built a parallel line, about a half mile long, to East Northfield.

Surveys indicated that the easiest alignment was along the Ashuelot River, because a more direct route would have required extensive tunnels between South Vernon and Ashuelot. As constructed, the line entailed a bridge over the Connecticut River and four crossings of the Ashuelot River, although each of them were made where the river narrowed. The Connecticut River RR leased the Ashuelot from its opening in January 1851. Until completion of the Vermont Valley RR between Bellows Falls and Brattleboro at the end of the year, the line briefly formed part of the through route between Vermont, Springfield, MA, and points south.

Traffic receipts were small. The CR decided not to renew its lease, and the line was placed in receivership. The Cheshire RR, which had no potential for growth of its own system, leased the line in 1860. Years later Ashuelot shareholders brought suit over unsatisfactory performance, which resulted in termination of the lease on April 20, 1877. The Ashuelot was again leased by the CR, which lasted until the Boston & Maine RR took over in 1893.

In 1912, the B&M built a new line to avoid dependence on Central Vermont trackage between South Vernon and Brattleboro. An alignment was surveyed from north of the Connecticut River bridge through Hinsdale to Brattleboro. Construction from a remote location known as Dole Jct. followed the river and required a causeway and trestle between islands in a bay northwest of Hinsdale. It opened on June 23, 1913, as the Fort Hill Branch, forming part of the Connecticut River line, which was jointly operated by the B&M and the CV. The usual practice was for northbound trains between South Vernon and Brattleboro to use the Fort Hill Branch while southbounds took the CV. Failure of the Connecticut River bridge at South Vernon in 1970 ended this through route. The Ashuelot could thereafter be accessed only from Brattleboro.

Traffic to and from Keene declined significantly from the late 1920s. The connection with the Manchester & Keene branch went in 1935 with the closure of that line. Still the Ashuelot eked out a reasonable return that justified its retention by the B&M until the 1970s. The

6. Ashuelot

Cheshire route eventually closed and was abandoned in 1972, although 3.1 miles of yard trackage in Keene and the length from Keene to Swanzey were retained. Track on the latter was dismantled in 1975 (although not formally abandoned until 1981), and closure of the remainder was threatened at the same time. At this point the Green Mountain RR stepped in with a proposal to take over switching in Keene, together with trackage rights over the Ashuelot. The GM took over switching at Keene on January 23, 1978, and took over the entire Ashuelot on January 1, 1982. After cost-cutting had reduced the line to a long siding the GM gave up and abandoned the yard at Keene on January 3, 1983. The remainder of the Ashuelot was abandoned in November of that year.

Sources: Jones, *Central Vermont*; Karr, *Lost Railroads*, 130, 131, 144–45; Karr, *Rail Lines*, 188–89; Nimke, *Green Mountain*.

7. Cheshire

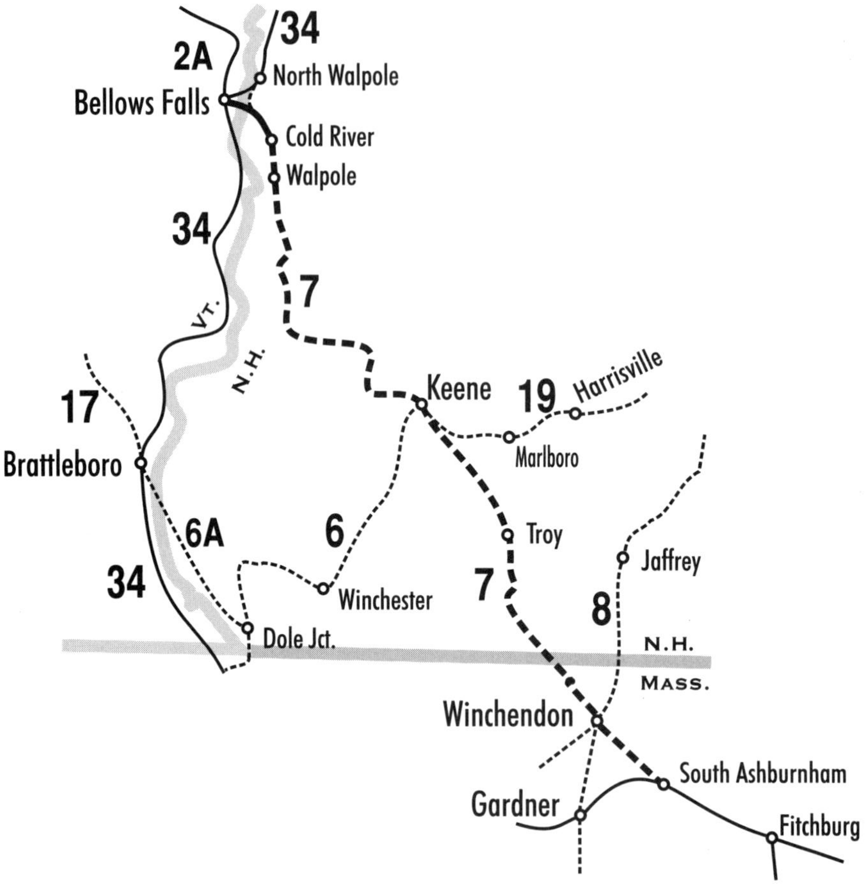

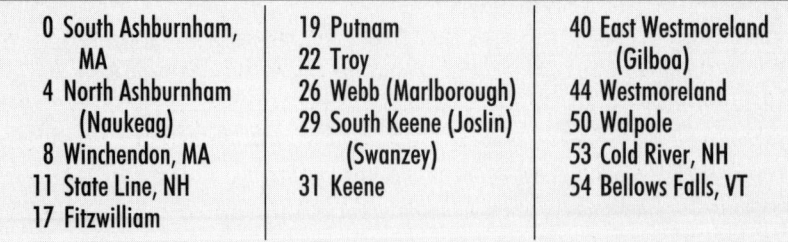

0 South Ashburnham, MA	19 Putnam	40 East Westmoreland (Gilboa)
4 North Ashburnham (Naukeag)	22 Troy	44 Westmoreland
8 Winchendon, MA	26 Webb (Marlborough)	50 Walpole
11 State Line, NH	29 South Keene (Joslin) (Swanzey)	53 Cold River, NH
17 Fitzwilliam	31 Keene	54 Bellows Falls, VT

7. Cheshire

Built: 1845-49.
Operators: *Cheshire*, 1847-90; *Fitchburg*, 1890-1900; *Boston & Maine*, 1900-83; *Guilford*, 1983-91; *Green Mountain*, 1977-.
Daily Passenger Trains: *1868:* 6; *1893:* 10; *1906:* 10; *1924:* 8; *1941:* 9; *1952:* 7; *1954:* 5. Passenger service ended June 1958.
Abandonments: Keene-Cold River, Winchendon-South Keene, 1972; South Keene-Keene, 1975 (see text); South Ashburnham-Winchendon, 1984; at South Ashburnham, 1993.

Businessmen in Keene received a New Hampshire charter in 1844 for the Cheshire RR, with authority to build a line from the Massachusetts border to Bellows Falls, and the following year also chartered the Winchendon RR in Massachusetts to extend to the unbuilt Vermont & Massachusetts RR. The V&M planned to extend the newly completed Fitchburg RR west from Fitchburg to Brattleboro, VT. As chartered, this line was to pass through Gardner, MA, but management decided that a course through Winchendon made more sense. When work commenced in October 1845, the charter had not been changed to allow the new route. When the alignment was nearly complete, attempts to alter the charter proved unsuccessful. Massachusetts insisted on the more direct route to the west through Gardner for traffic to and from New York state. The V&M sold the incomplete line between South Ashburnham and Winchendon to the Keene proprietors, who completed it in the fall of 1847.

The Cheshire reached Troy, NH, in December and Keene in May 1848, ironically ahead of the V&M line to Brattleboro. By then the proprietors had reincorporated all three constituents as the Cheshire RR, which completed the line from Keene to Bellows Falls in June 1849. Traffic proved to be profitable, and in 1851 the V&M readily agreed to grant the Cheshire trackage rights over the ten miles from South Ashburnham to Fitchburg to minimize operating costs. In 1860 the Cheshire leased the Ashuelot RR, with which it connected in Keene, but relinquished it in 1877 because of financial difficulties. Recovery by 1880 allowed the Cheshire to lease the Monadnock RR.

By 1874 Winchendon had become a junction with two other railroads, the Ware River and the Boston, Barre & Gardner. The Fitchburg RR bought control of the Cheshire in 1890 to keep competitors out. With the Fitchburg and the Rutland RR, the Cheshire formed part

7. Cheshire

The Cheshire comes to an abrupt end in Cold River. Most of the short surviving section is used by the Green Mountain RR for car storage, as shown here May 1999. (R. D. Karr)

of a through route between Boston and Montreal, which continued after the Boston & Maine leased the Fitchburg in 1900. Major expresses were the *Mount Royal* and *Green Mountain Flyer*, which remained until 1953 when the Rutland RR discontinued passenger service. Local passenger trains were continued by the B&M until 1958.

Local freight trains operated until the early 1970s when proposals were submitted for abandonment of the line. A temporary stay of execution was secured through proceedings by New Hampshire in the state courts on the basis that short-line haulers might be willing to take over operation. Permission to abandon was merely postponed by six months in 1972, whereupon all service ceased between Winchendon and Cold River. The B&M offered terms for purchase to the state of New Hampshire, but they were not accepted, owing to continuing court proceedings and unavailability of funding. Anxious to recover the value of the Cheshire's assets, the B&M tore up tracks between Winchendon and Cold River, except for a short section in Keene that survived for another three years and yard trackage that lasted until 1983. Court proceedings ended in 1979 when the state of New Hampshire agreed to purchase the section between Bellows Falls and Cold River. This short length was leased to the Green Mountain RR as an extension of its Vermont (former Rutland RR) operations. Parts of the line in Massachusetts remained in service as late as 1991, and the final 0.7 miles at South Ashburnham were abandoned in 1993.

Sources: Bachelder, *Half-Century Ltd.*, 40; Baker, *Formation*, 196; Karr, *Lost Railroads*, 130-33, 145, 147, 155; Karr, *Rail Lines*, 188-89; Poor, *History*, 52; Valentine "Brief History."

8. Monadnock

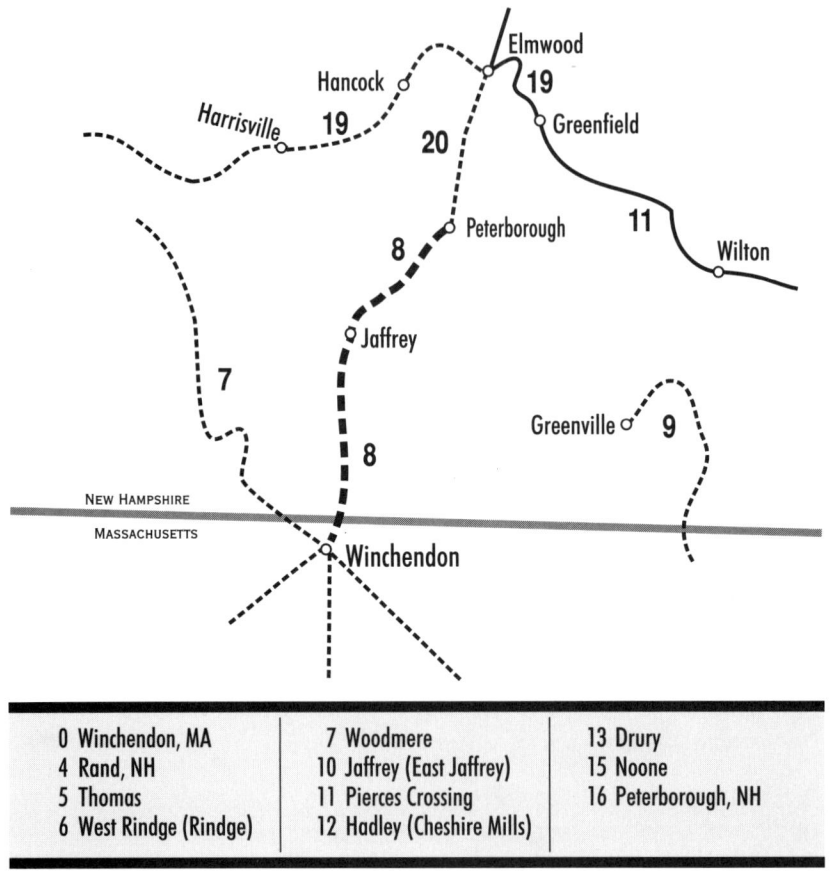

0 Winchendon, MA	7 Woodmere	13 Drury
4 Rand, NH	10 Jaffrey (East Jaffrey)	15 Noone
5 Thomas	11 Pierces Crossing	16 Peterborough, NH
6 West Rindge (Rindge)	12 Hadley (Cheshire Mills)	

Built: 1870-71.

Operators: *Monadnock*, 1871-74; *Boston, Barre & Gardner*, 1874-80; *Cheshire*, 1880-90; *Fitchburg*, 1890-1900; *Boston & Maine*, 1900-83; *Guilford*, 1983-84.

Daily Passenger Trains: *1893:* 6; *1906:* 10; *1919:* 8; *1935:* 6; *1950:* 2. Passenger service ended 1953.

Abandonments: Jaffrey-Peterborough, 1972; Winchendon-Jaffrey, 1984.

8. Monadnock

Lakes and ponds in Rindge and Jaffrey, in the New Hampshire foothills of the Appalachians, are the sources of the Contoocook River north to Concord and streams flowing south to Millers River in Massachusetts. By the 1840s, the western slopes of Pack and North Pack Manadnock had become a resort for those seeking to escape Boston summers. After the Cheshire RR reached Winchendon, MA, on its route from Bellows Falls, VT, to South Ashburnham, MA, in December 1847, a branch line was chartered to Peterborough in 1848 as the Monadnock RR. Raising capital proved difficult, since potential investors were more interested in operations with year-round traffic. The project stagnated until the post-bellum economic boom.

Jaffrey received regular service from December 1870 and operation was extended to Peterborough in June 1871. In November 1873 the Ware River RR reached Winchendon, followed in January 1874 by the Boston, Barre & Gardner RR from Gardner, MA, which leased the Monadnock line almost immediately. In 1878 the route was extended northward when the Peterborough & Hillsborough RR, under lease to the Northern RR, opened its line from Peterborough to Hillsboro, where it connected with the Contoocook Valley RR to Concord. The BB&G had hoped to use this line to reach Concord, but it could not afford rent and surrendered the Monadnock lease in 1880. The Cheshire RR stepped in with a new lease of the Monadnock to guard against expansion of the Boston & Albany, which had leased the Ware River line from mid-1873. The Cheshire and Monadnock were taken over in 1890 by the Fitchburg RR, which had acquired the BB&G in 1885. Less than ten years later the Monadnock became part of the Boston & Maine RR, forming the Worcester & Hillsboro or Worcester & Contoocook Branch. The goal of a through route to Concord finally was realized.

To reduce costs, the B&M introduced a parallel bus service from June 20, 1927, beginning a pattern of decline in rail passenger service. Flooding in Hancock ended passenger service north of Peterborough in 1936. Through freight traffic ceased by 1941, and the link with Elmwood, NH, was formally abandoned in 1942. Thereafter, the line was a modest but picturesque affair. Trains pulled by ancient Moguls displaced from the main lines traveled at a leisurely pace on deteriorating track over minimal grades. Passenger trains went in 1953, but freight traffic sustained the line well into the diesel age.

B&M gas-electric 151 pauses at Peterborough on June 17, 1929. (Courtesy Walker Transportation Collection, Beverly Historical Society & Museum)

Service beyond Jaffrey to Peterborough ceased entirely in 1972, although just over a mile of track was left in place for switching purposes. What remained became a casualty of Guilford's first economy program following purchase of the B&M in 1983. Dismantling took place two years later.

In 1999 the state of New Hampshire finally agreed to purchase the right of way for $500,000.

Sources: Baker, *Formation*, 17, 178, 192, 196; Cornwall & Smith, *Names First*, 71; Karr *Lost Railroads*, 130, 147; Karr, *Rail Lines*, 190-91; Valentine, "Brief History."

9. Peterborough & Shirley

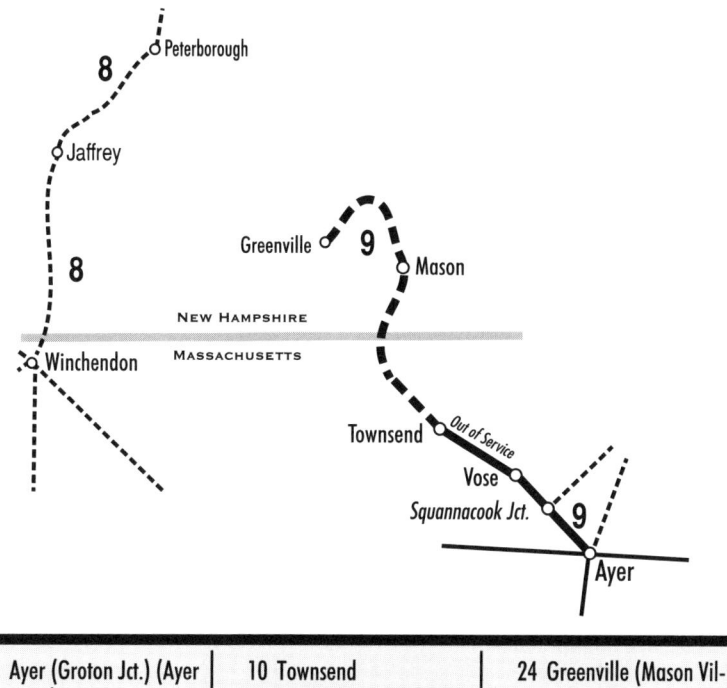

0 Ayer (Groton Jct.) (Ayer Jct.), MA	10 Townsend	24 Greenville (Mason Village), NH
3 *Squannacook Jct.*	12 West Townsend, MA	
4 West Groton	16 Mason (Mason Centre), NH	
8 Townsend Harbor	19 Pratt (Pratts) (Wilton)	

Built: 1847-50.

Operators: *Fitchburg*, 1848-1900; *Boston & Maine*, 1900-83; *Guilford*, 1983- .

Daily Passenger Trains: *1869:* 4; *1893:* 7; *1916:* 6; *1932:* 4; *1933:* 2. Passenger service ended 1933.

Abandonment: Townsend-Greenville, 1979.

After the Fitchburg RR opened in 1845, several branch lines were promoted, one of which envisaged a 36-mile route from Groton Jct. (Ayer), MA, to Peterborough, NH. Construction of the Peterborough & Shirley RR to the New Hampshire line got underway in Massachusetts in 1847. A separate company was incorporated in

New Hampshire under the same name to carry the line onward through Mason and Wilton to Peterborough. The line from Ayer to West Townsend opened in January 1848, and construction reached Mason in November 1850. Concern by the Fitchburg RR that the line might attract the Nashua & Lowell resulted in their leasing the P&S before opening.

The line never reached Peterborough or Wilton. Instead, under a revision of the New Hampshire charter, the alignment turned south, four miles from the N&L, to end in Mason Village (now Greenville). A mile from the terminal, a wrought iron trestle with ashlar abutments was built across the Souhegan River gorge. Purchase of both companies by the Fitchburg was completed in 1860. The line remained a modest operation throughout its life, even though some improvements were made under Boston & Maine ownership in 1911, primarily strengthening of the Souhegan trestle by the addition of intermediate stone piers to support higher axle loads.

In New Hampshire, the line served a quarry in Mason but was almost entirely dependent on Greenville's textile mills, so mill closures there seriously affected it in the 1930s. Passenger trains ceased on July 8, 1933, and were replaced by B&M Transportation Co. bus service from Ayer to West Townsend until June 22, 1936. Freight continued beyond West Townsend to Greenville until May 1972, when the B&M took advantage of several relatively minor washouts in New Hampshire to close the line beyond West Townsend. The B&M sold the section of the P&S in Massachusetts to the Massachusetts Bay Transportation Authority in 1976. The length beyond Townsend Center remained open a few more years to serve the Bates Corrugated Box factory and to switch sidings there, but the B&M cut back service to the Hollingsworth-Vose paper mill in West Groton in November 1981. Most of the track between there and Townsend Center remains in place, though long disused. Permission to abandon the line west of Townsend Center was obtained in 1979. Guilford continued to serve the West Groton paper mill for many years. Nine miles of the P&S right of way in Mason and Greenville now form the Mason Railroad Trail.

Sources: Bachelder, *Half-Century Ltd.*, 35; Baker, *Formation*, 178, 181; Della Penna, *Great Rail Trails*, 126-31; Karr, *Rail Lines*, 206-08.

10. Nashua & Lowell

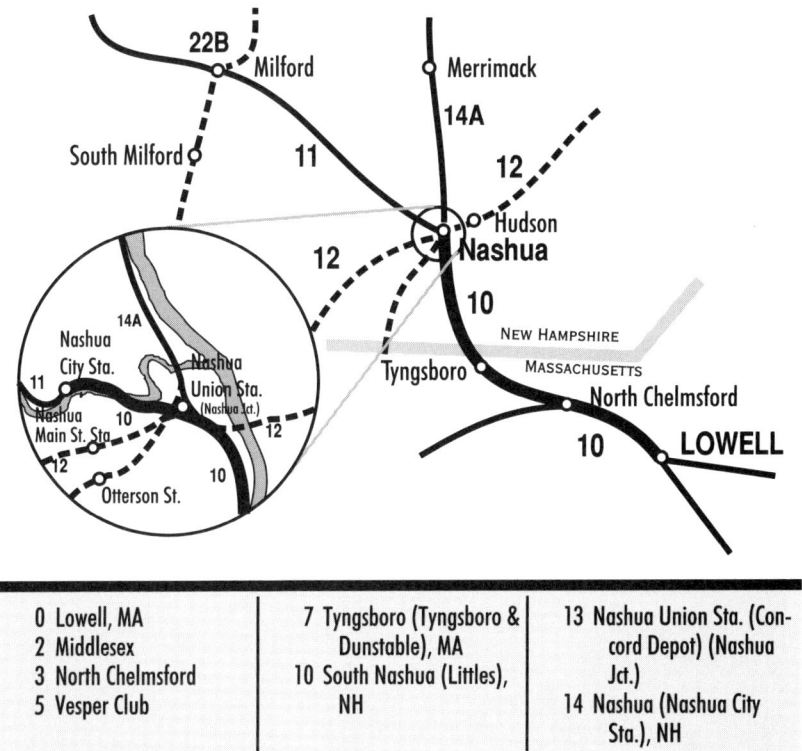

0 Lowell, MA	7 Tyngsboro (Tyngsboro & Dunstable), MA	13 Nashua Union Sta. (Concord Depot) (Nashua Jct.)
2 Middlesex		
3 North Chelmsford	10 South Nashua (Littles), NH	14 Nashua (Nashua City Sta.), NH
5 Vesper Club		

Built: 1837–38.

Operators: *Nashua & Lowell*, 1838–57; *Nashua & Lowell/Boston & Lowell* (jointly), 1857–78; *Nashua & Lowell*, 1878–80; Boston & Lowell, 1880–87; *Boston & Maine*, 1887–1983; *Guilford*, 1983–.

Daily Passenger Trains: *1869:* 11; *1893:* 19; *1919:* 26; *1935:* 35; *1950:* 18; *1960:* 14. Passenger service ended 1967 (restored on trial basis 1980–81).

Abandonments: None.

Lowell, MA, was reached by the Boston & Lowell RR in 1835. With Nashua just 15 miles away, extension was promoted by the Nashua & Lowell RR, which obtained a charter in New Hampshire that year and in Massachusetts the year after. A route along the

Merrimack River was surveyed and construction started in 1837. A single track reached South Nashua in 1838, with service commencing on October 8, and the line was completed by December. It was the first railroad in New Hampshire.

Traffic developed rapidly, after the Concord RR extended north from Nashua through Manchester to Concord four years later. A second track was laid progressively over the next several years and completed throughout in 1848.

The N&L and Boston & Lowell entered into an agreement to operate as a single company in 1857, an arrangement that lasted for over twenty years until the B&L leased the N&L in 1880. The B&L and N&L were in turn leased by the Boston & Maine in 1887, and formed part of the B&M's Southern Division. Under a B&M reorganization program implemented on October 14, 1930, the line formed a part of the New Hampshire Division.

Local Guilford freight NA-2, returning from Lowell, passes through Tyngsboro along the Merrimack River just south of the New Hampshire line in October 1999. (R. D. Karr)

10. Nashua & Lowell

After World War II the N&L went into decline, although surviving the most drastic B&M economy measures. It was reduced to a single track with passing sidings and centralized traffic control. Long-distance passenger service using the line ended on January 4, 1965, except for a single weekday round trip between Boston and Concord that the B&M was ordered to continue running; it operated until June 30, 1967. New Hampshire politicians instigated an experimental commuter service from Concord to Boston, which commenced on January 28, 1980. Both of the two daily round trips were far longer than either the former railroad running time or an automobile trip. An intermediate stop at Merrimack was introduced on April 27; savings measures, which included import of a prototype railbus from Britain, failed to produce satisfactory results. When federal and state funds ran out, the experiment ended on February 28, 1981.

The N&L now forms part of Guilford's Northern Main Line. Nashua-area officials are hopeful of restoring passenger service, particularly as Route 3 between Nashua and Boston grows increasingly congested.

Sources: Baker, *Formation*, 105-07; Bradlee, *Boston & Lowell*; Harlow, *Steelways*, 285-87; Karr, *Rail Lines*, 220-22; Kirkland, *Men, Cities, and Transportation*, 1: 162-63.

11. Wilton/Peterborough

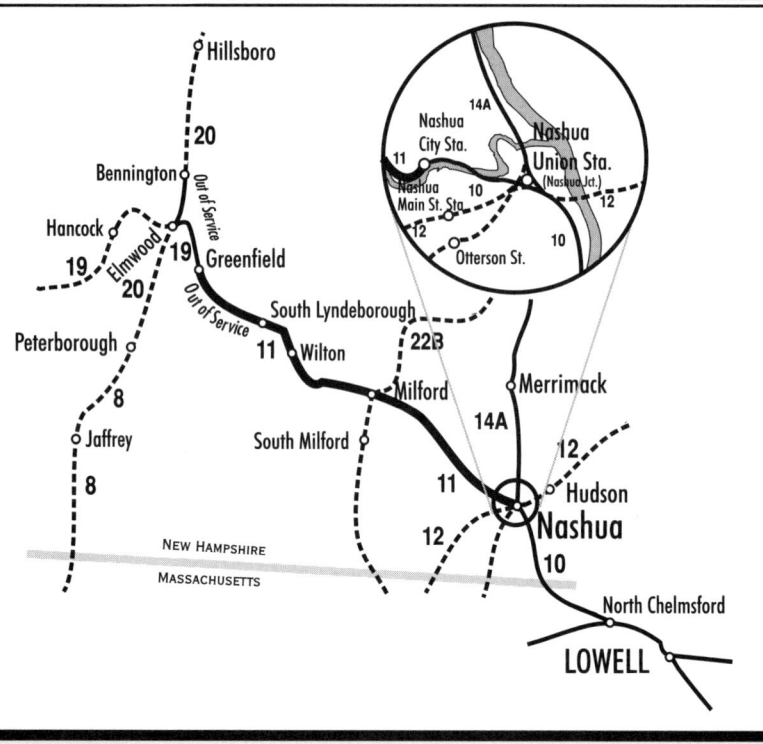

0 Nashua (Nashua City Sta.), NH	8 Amherst (Danforths Corners) (Ponemah)	15 Pine Valley
4 Blood	10 East Milford	16 Wilton
6 South Merrimack	11 Milford	19 South Lyndeborough
	13 Richardson	23 Russell
		25 Greenfield, NH

Built: 1847-74.

Operators: *Nashua & Lowell*, 1838-57; *Nashua & Lowell/Boston & Lowell* (jointly), 1857-78; *Nashua & Lowell*, 1878-80; *Boston & Lowell*, 1880-87; *Boston & Maine*, 1887-1983; *Guilford*, 1983-; *Milford-Bennington*, 1992-.

Daily Passenger Trains: *1893:* 6; *1906:* 7; *1916:* 7; *1926:* 4; *1933:* 4. Passenger service ended 1935; mixed train service Nashua-Wilton, 1936-49.

Abandonments: None.

11. Wilton/Peterborough

The Wilton RR received a charter in 1844 to build west from the Nashua & Lowell at Nashua through Wilton or Peterborough to Marlow on the Ashuelot River. Construction began in 1847, and the first length to Danforths Corners was completed by the end of 1848. Thereafter the company faltered but was rescued by the N&L, enabling completion to Milford in 1850 and to Wilton in 1851. The N&L operated the line from the outset, and formally leased it by 1854. With no major sources of traffic between Wilton and Marlow, and in fear that rail lines in western New Hampshire would divert traffic to the Connecticut River RR, the N&L allowed the charter for the remainder of the line to lapse. In 1857 the N&L and Boston & Lowell entered into agreement to operate all of their lines, including the Wilton, as a single company, an arrangement that lasted for over twenty years.

In 1864 a charter was obtained for the Manchester & Keene RR to build eastward from the Cheshire RR at Keene. Its fears of a Connecticut River takeover renewed, the N&L reacted by backing the Peterborough RR, a nominally independent venture, in building northwest from Wilton through Greenfield, then southwest to Peterborough. Both schemes languished but were revived when it became apparent that the Monadnock RR would be built to Peterborough from the south in 1870 and might extend north along the Contoocook Valley. The threat of a through route from the Cheshire RR at Winchendon, MA, to Concord, NH, forced the N&L's hand. The Peterborough and M&K companies agreed to extend each of their lines to a meeting point in Greenfield, abandoning the proposed routes to Peterborough and Manchester. The Peterborough reached Greenfield from Wilton in 1874, but funding difficulties postponed the M&K's completion from Keene until 1878. The Boston & Lowell eventually leased the N&L in 1880. When the Boston & Maine in turn leased the B&L in 1887, the Wilton/Peterborough became part of the B&M's Southern Division's Keene Branch.

In 1926, bus services began to replace some trains. Following a landslide at Hancock on the M&K in 1934, passenger service from Nashua was cut back to Elmwood before ceasing on September 30, 1935, to be replaced by busses. A daily (except Sunday) mixed train ran between Nashua and Wilton, however, from November 5, 1936, until about 1949. Bus service continued to be provided by the Boston & Maine Transportation Co. until the spring of 1956 when the last routes were sold to Hancock-based Community Bus Lines.

Milford-Bennington no. 901, an ex-Canadian National SW900, waits at the Granite State Concrete plant in Milford in September 1999. (R. D. Karr)

After connecting tracks west and south of Elmwood were abandoned in 1939 and 1942, the Wilton/Peterborough provided the only connection to Hillsboro. The line between Nashua and Hillsboro became designated the Hillsboro Branch. The B&M served a number of customers in Nashua and Milford. Beyond Milford, quarries in South Lyndeborough, a grain mill at Greenfield, and the Monadnock Paper Mill in Bennington provided steady traffic for several years. The grain mill was destroyed by fire in 1963. Operation continued until after Guilford's takeover of the B&M in 1983. A few years later Guilford closed the line beyond the quarries. When a petition for abandonment was submitted, the state of New Hampshire purchased the route from Wilton to Greenfield to Elmwood, then north to Bennington. The Milford-Bennington RR leased this line from the state in 1992.

The Milford-Bennington hauls gravel from a pit near South Lyndeborough to the Granite State concrete plant in Milford, using trackage rights over Guilford from Wilton. A reciprocal agreement allows Guilford to operate to the quarry as needed for rebuilding Guilford's

11. Wilton/Peterborough

Boston–Portland line for Amtrak service. West of South Lyndeborough the line remains out of service. Guilford continues to operate local freights from Nashua to Milford and Wilton.

Sources: Baker, *Formation,* 105-07; Bradlee, *Boston & Lowell;* DiFalco, "Milford-Bennington Railroad"; Harlow, *Steelways,* 285-87; Karr, *Rail Lines,* 220-22; Kirkland, *Men, Cities, and Transportation,* 1: 162-63.

12. Worcester, Nashua & Rochester

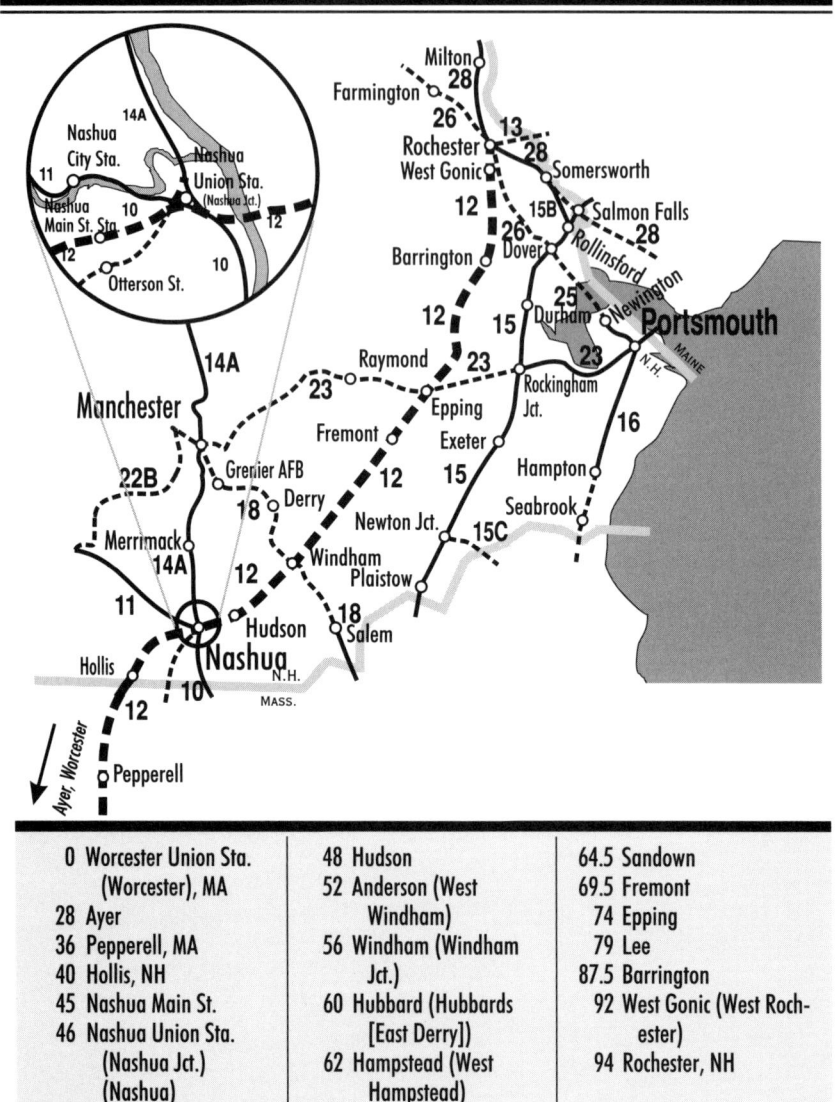

0 Worcester Union Sta. (Worcester), MA	48 Hudson	64.5 Sandown
28 Ayer	52 Anderson (West Windham)	69.5 Fremont
36 Pepperell, MA	56 Windham (Windham Jct.)	74 Epping
40 Hollis, NH		79 Lee
45 Nashua Main St.	60 Hubbard (Hubbards [East Derry])	87.5 Barrington
46 Nashua Union Sta. (Nashua Jct.) (Nashua)	62 Hampstead (West Hampstead)	92 West Gonic (West Rochester)
		94 Rochester, NH

Built: 1846–74.

Operators: *Worcester & Nashua,* 1848–83; *Worcester, Nashua & Rochester,* 1883–86; *Boston & Maine,* 1886–1983; *Guilford,* 1983–93.

12. Worcester, Nashua & Rochester

Daily Passenger Trains: *1851:* 6 (Worcester-Nashua); *1869:* 6 (Worcester-Nashua); *1893:* 4 (plus Worcester-Nashua, 8; Nashua-Rochester, 3); *1919:* Worcester-Nashua, 8; Nashua-Rochester, 4; *1930:* Worcester-Nashua, 8; Nashua-Rochester, 2. Passenger service ended 1934.

Abandonments: Epping-West Gonic, 1935; Hudson-Fremont, 1935; Nashua-Hudson, 1942; Hollis-Nashua, 1942; West Gonic-Rochester, ca. 1981; Fremont-Epping, 1982; at Nashua, 1993.

Nashua, NH, was a developing textile manufacturing center when the Worcester & Nashua RR completed the line between its titular cities in December 1848. The line prospered from considerable freight and passenger traffic. Trains to and from Nashua carried not only mill products, but also agricultural traffic and the gamut of goods and materials that support a local economy. Rochester, far to the north, developed rapidly about the same time, and by 1849 was served by both the Great Falls & Conway and Cochecho RRs.

After the Civil War the York & Cumberland RR, originally promoted to connect Portland and Berwick, reorganized as the Portland & Rochester RR, and finally completed its line to Rochester in 1871. It had obtained financial support from the city of Portland on the promise that the W&N would be extended to Rochester. For that purpose, the W&N obtained a charter for the Nashua & Rochester RR in 1871, and work started without delay. The timing for this expansion proved inauspicious. The B&M, locked in rivalry with the Eastern RR over the Portland, Saco & Portsmouth line, built another line to Portland while construction of the N&R was in progress. The formerly prosperous N&R, which barely rode out the crash of 1873, opened its line in November 1874, but struggled to survive.

The merger of the W&N and N&R as the Worcester, Nashua & Rochester RR was agreed to in 1883. The B&M acquired a lease of the WN&R from January 1, 1886, creating the Worcester, Nashua & Portland Division, although the P&R was not absorbed until 1900. From June 1887 crack trains, such as the *Bar Harbor* and *State of Maine Express*, were diverted to or introduced over the line to avoid congestion on the seaboard routes. The main line remained unsignalled until the 1911-12 capital improvements program, when a second track was completed between Worcester and Nashua. By then, however,

The old depot in Sandown, NH, has been beautifully restored as a town museum. (R. D. Karr)

most through passenger and freight runs to and from Portland had been diverted through Lowell and Haverhill, MA, to Dover, NH, and in 1925 the WN&P Division was abolished. North of Nashua, the line became part of the Portland Division; the remainder was operated by the Southern Division.

Agents were removed from several stations during the 1920s, and after 1928 passenger trains did not connect at Rochester, presumably because the inconvenience would help the B&M to be rid of them (a ploy apparently adopted to support the massive railway closure program in Great Britain during the 1960s). Just one passenger round trip operated north of Nashua after 1930, using gas-electric "doodlebugs."

In 1932 the B&M sought permission to abandon north of Nashua, except for the lengths to Hudson and between Fremont and Epping. When the New Hampshire Attorney General raised objections, permission to abandon within the state was made conditional on the tracks remaining in place. In January 1934 the ICC approved abandonment of

12. Worcester, Nashua & Rochester

service only, effective that spring. Passenger service ended north of Nashua on March 3, 1934, followed on April 14 between Ayer and Nashua. The discontinued sections were barricaded in March 1934, with the rails remaining in place. In September 1935 the B&M received permission to physically abandon the two segments when the state changed its mind and decided it wanted some of the right of way to build a highway. Even so, recovery of materials did not take place until 1942, by which time the war effort had created demand for used steel. During that same year the B&M abandoned the line from Nashua across the Merrimack to Hudson and west to Hollis, retaining two miles within Nashua to serve local customers.

Hollis continued to receive cars from Ayer until traffic ended about 1981, as did the spur in Rochester to West Gonic, and the Epping–Fremont line which served the New England Brick company. Parts of the former main line in Nashua survived to enter Guilford ownership but were abandoned by 1993.

Much of the WN&R in New Hampshire is now buried under highways, particularly State Route 111 from Hudson to Windham. From there, the alignment forms the Rockingham Recreational Trail as far as Fremont, where the timber-framed station building, north of Route 107, is now a private residence. Northward, Route 125 occupies the alignment as far as Route 9 in Barrington. Sandown station survives as a museum.

Sources: Bachelder, *Half-Century Ltd,*. 36; Baker, *Formation*, 146; 166-67; Crouch and Frye, "Worcester, Nashua & Portland"; Karr, *Lost Railroads*, 49-53; 89; 106; 141; Karr, *Rail Lines*, 195-99.

13. Portland & Rochester

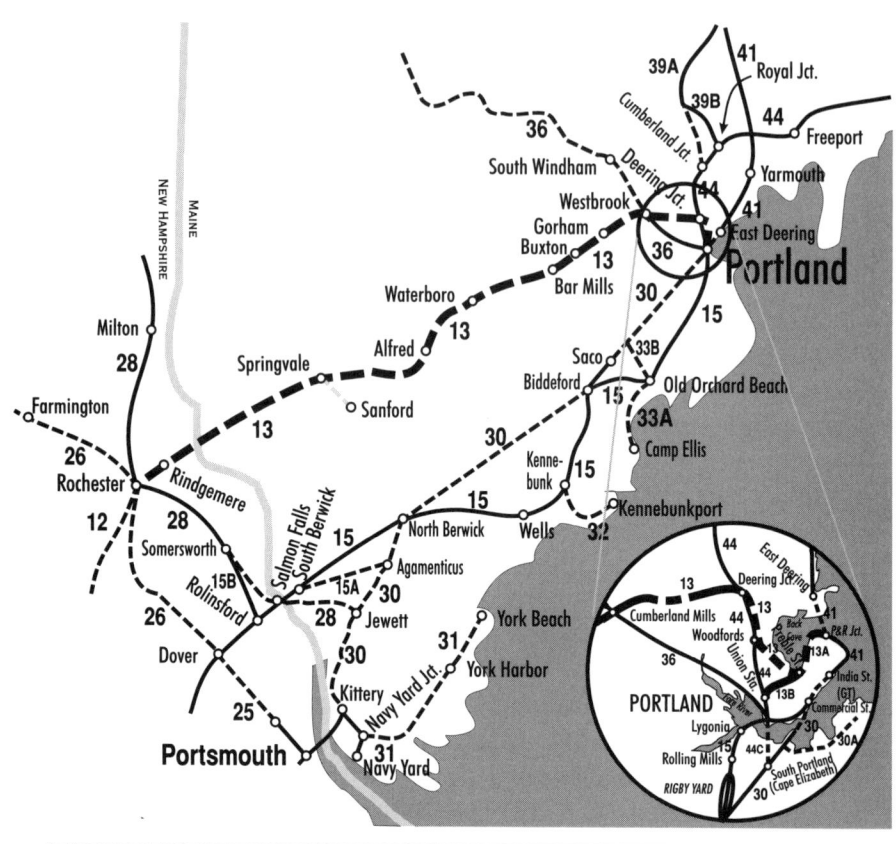

0 Portland, Preble St. Sta., ME	25 Wescott (East Waterboro) (Centre Waterboro)	**13A. GT Extension**
1.5 Woodfords	28 Waterboro (South Waterboro)	0 Portland, Preble St. Sta., ME
2.5 Deering Jct. (Westbrook Jct.) (Morrills)	32.5 Alfred	1.5 GT Jct. (Portland & Rochester Jct.), ME
5 Main St.	36.5 Sanford & Springvale (Springvale)	
5.5 Cumberland Mills (Cumberland Mills Jct.)	43 Eastwood (East Lebanon), ME	**13B. Union Station Branch**
6.5 Westbrook (Saccarappa)	50 Rindgemere (East Rochester), NH	0 Portland, Preble St. Sta., ME
10.5 Gorham	52.5 Rochester, NH	1 Portland Union Sta., ME
15.5 Buxton (Buxton Centre)		
18 Bar Mills (Saco River)		
20 Bradbury (Hollis Centre)		

13. Portland & Rochester

Built: 1850-71; GT Extension, 1874; Union Station Branch, 1891.

Operators: *York & Cumberland*, 1853-65; *Portland & Rochester*, 1865-1900; *Boston & Maine*, 1900-49; *Portland Terminal*, 1911-83; *Sanford & Eastern*, 1949-61; *Guilford*, 1983-.

Daily Passenger Trains: *1853:* 6 (Portland-Saco River); *1869:* 6 (Portland-Saco River); *1898:* 6 (plus Portland-Gorham, 6); *1919:* 6; *1929:* 4. Passenger service ended 1932.

Abandonments: Woodfords-Preble St. Sta., 1911; GT Extension, ca. 1950; Springvale-Rochester, 1952; Deering Jct. [west]-Cumberland Mills [east], ca. 1954; Westbrook-Springvale, 1961.

To break the Portland, Saco & Portsmouth RR monopoly south of Portland, the York & Cumberland RR obtained a charter in 1846 to build from Portland to the Boston & Maine RR at South Berwick. The B&M, then cooperating with the Eastern RR through joint lease of the PS&P, showed no interest in the new line. Despite unpromising circumstances, the company pressed on from 1850, taking three years to reach the Saco River at Bar Mills, 18 miles from its depot on Preble St. in Portland.

Near the end of the Civil War the company was reorganized, on March 25, 1865, as the Portland & Rochester RR. The new owners took possession in November, with grand visions of a line through Rochester and beyond to Nashua, or to the Hoosac Tunnel, and even a line to Boston. The City of Portland, keen on obtaining a new route to compete with the PS&P, invested $700,000. This enabled work on the extension to begin, but it was not until further loans were made by the city that the impoverished company reached Rochester in 1871. Financing for further southward extension could not be obtained. Rochester was already served by the Dover & Winnipiseogee RR (former Cocheco) and the Portsmouth, Great Falls & Conway RR, which connected with the Boston & Maine and Eastern; the P&R therefore was barely able to eke out an existence based primarily upon agricultural and mill traffic.

In 1874 the Worcester & Nashua RR reached Rochester from the south through a subsidiary, the Nashua & Rochester RR. That same year the P&R built a direct connection in Portland with the Grand Trunk RY. By then, however, the B&M had completed its own route to Portland, breaking the monopoly enjoyed by the PS&P. Portland

Passengers at Eastwood Station circa 1908 are about to board a B&M passenger train. (Courtesy Walker Transportation Collection, Beverly Historical Society & Museum)

authorized the sale of its stake in the P&R for a fraction of the original value in 1877, and two years later shares in the P&R were purchased by the Eastern RR. The B&M acquired 20 percent of the P&R in 1882, and its share reached 80 percent by 1890. A short branch built in 1891 enabled the P&R to move its Portland terminal to Union Station and abandon its Preble St. facility. The P&R continued to operate independently until 1900, however, when it was taken over by the B&M and made part of its Worcester, Nashua & Portland Division. In 1911 the original section of the P&R between Woodfords and the old Preble St. station was abandoned.

Budget-cutting measures, including on-train ticketing, brought about closure of station agencies by 1932. Passenger trains ceased to connect at Rochester in 1928, and only two round trips by a gas-electric unit operated from 1929 until January 4, 1932, when one was discontinued. The remaining trip between Portland and Rochester ended on June 25, 1932. From then on the freight-only line was almost totally dependent on cloth mills.

When the B&M petitioned to abandon the P&R south of Westbrook in 1949, Samuel M. Pinsly stepped in with an acceptable offer to

13. Portland & Rochester

purchase the line under the aegis of the Sanford & Eastern RR. Two miles of the former electric Atlantic Shore Line in Sanford and Springvale were also acquired from York Utilities on April 1; the Goodall-Sanford mills produced most of the traffic. The section of the line from Springvale to Rochester was officially abandoned in 1952, although operation continued sporadically to Rindgemere until about 1954. When the Goodall-Sanford mills closed in 1961 the line west from Westbrook was closed and abandoned almost immediately in April that year, along with the former Atlantic Shore trackage.

Around 1954 the B&M abandoned part of the P&R between Deering Jct. and Cumberland Mills when the turnpike was constructed, with customers on the section between Cumberland Mills and Westbook thereafter served by Portland Terminal local freights using the Maine Central's Mountain Division. This operation passed to Guilford in the 1980s. Part of the short Union Station branch in Portland continues in operation as a freight spur.

The tracks remain in use a short distance westward from Deering Jct. to a Georgia-Pacific plant. At Cumberland Mills, Guilford still serves the Southern Container and S. D. Warren (now SAPPI) plants. Between Westbrook and Rochester only parts of the right of way remain intact, serving as informal snowmobile trails. These include sections through Gorham to Buxton and between Waterboro and Sanford. Here the alignment runs alongside Route 202 and some lengths can be glimpsed from the road. From East Lebanon nearly to the New Hampshire line Route 202 has been built on the old rail bed.

Sources: Baker, *Formation*, 146, 166-67; Crouch and Frye, "Worcester, Nashua & Portland"; Karr, *Lost Railroads*, 49-53, 89, 106, 141; Karr, *Rail Lines*, 195-99.

14. Concord & Montreal

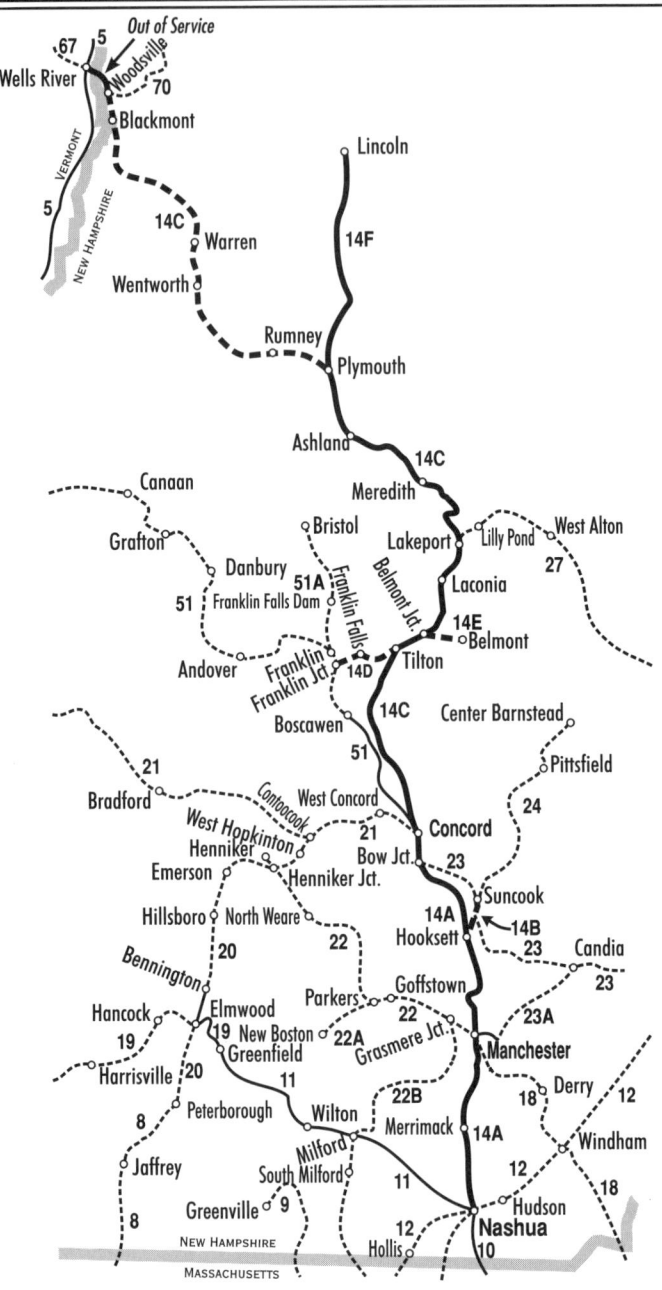

14. Concord & Montreal

14A. Concord

- 0 Nashua Union Sta. (Nashua Jct.) (Nashua [Concord Depot]), NH
- 6 Thorntons Ferry (Thorntons)
- 7.5 Merrimack
- 9 Reeds (Reeds Ferry)
- 13 Moores Cossing
- 13.5 Goffs (Goffs Falls)
- 15 South Manchester
- 16.5 Manchester
- 20 Amoskeag
- 22.5 Martin (Martins) (Martins Ferry)
- 25 Hooksett
- 29.5 Robinsons Ferry
- 32.5 Bow (Bow Jct.) (Bow Mills)
- 34 Concord, NH

14B. Suncook Branch

- 0 Hooksett, NH
- 1.5 Suncook, NH

14C. Boston, Concord & Montreal

- 0 Concord, NH
- 2 East Concord (Eastside)
- 5 Sewalls Falls (Sewalls)
- 7 North Concord (Boyce)
- 10 Canterbury
- 13 Northfield
- 18 Tilton (Sanbornton Bridge)
- 21 Belmont Jct.
- 22 Lochmere (East Tilton) (Union Bridge)
- 25 Winnisquam
- 27 Laconia (Meredith Bridge)
- 29 Lakeport (Lake Village)
- 34 Weirs Beach (Weirs)
- 37 Meredith (Meredith Village)
- 40 New Hampton (Foggs Rd.)
- 46 Ashland (Holderness)
- 51 Plymouth
- 54 West Plymouth
- 57 Quincy
- 59 Rumney
- 62 West Rumney (Swainboro)
- 67 Wentworth
- 70 Warren
- 75 Glencliff (Warren Summit)
- 80 East Haverhill (Oliverion)
- 82 Pike
- 85 Haverhill (Haverhill & Newbury)
- 88 Blackmount (North Haverhill)
- 91 Horse Meadow
- 92 Woodsville, NH
- 94 Wells River, VT

14D. Franklin & Tilton Branch

- 0 Tilton, NH
- 3 Franklin Falls
- 4 Franklin Jct., NH

14E. Tilton & Belmont Branch

- 0 Belmont Jct., NH
- 1 Gardners Grove
- 2 Tioga
- 4 Belmont, NH

14F. Pemigewasset Valley Branch

- 0 Plymouth, NH
- 2 Livermore Falls
- 4 Blair
- 5.5 Beebe River
- 8 Campton (Campton Village)
- 9 Lyfords Siding
- 11 Thornton
- 14 West Thornton
- 17 Woodstock
- 18 Mountain Park
- 19 Fairview
- 20 North Woodstock
- 21 Lincoln, NH

Built: 1836–95.

Operators: *Concord*, 1838–89; *Boston, Concord & Montreal*, 1847–84; *Boston & Lowell*, 1884–87; *Boston & Maine*, 1887–89, 1895–1983; *Concord & Montreal*, 1889–95; Suncook Valley, 1943–53; *Guilford*, 1983–; *Wolfeboro*, 1975–76; *Goodwin*, 1976–81; *New England Southern*, 1982–; *Winnipesaukee*, 1984–90; *Hobo*,

1987–; *Winnipesaukee & Pemigewasset Valley*, 1991-94; *Winnipesaukee Scenic*, 1995–.

Daily Passenger Trains: *1869:* Nashua-Concord, 10; Concord-Wells River, 2; *1893:* Nashua-Concord, 19; Concord-Wells River, 10; *1919:* Nashua-Concord, 26; Concord-Wells River, 8; *1935:* Nashua-Concord, 16; Concord-Wells River, 8; *1950:* Nashua-Concord, 17; Concord-Wells River, 6; *1960:* Nashua-Concord, 14; Concord-Laconia, 2. Passenger service ended Tilton & Belmont Branch, 1929; Woodsville Plymouth, 1954; Plymouth-Laconia, 1959; Wells River-Woodsville, 1961; Laconia-Concord, 1965; Nashua-Concord, 1967 (temporarily restored 1980-81).

Abandonments: Tilton & Belmont Branch, 1934; Franklin & Tilton Branch (Franklin Jct.-Franklin Falls., 1942; Franklin Falls-Tilton, 1975); Franklin-Hooksett-Suncook [0.5 miles south], 1943; Suncook-[0.5 miles south], 1953; Plymouth-Blackmount, 1954; Blackmount-Woodsville, 1981.

From the mid-1830s, the New Hampshire towns of Nashua, Merrimack, Manchester, and Concord began to develop with the textile industry's rapid spread northward along the Merrimack River from Lowell, MA. Both the Nashua & Lowell and Concord RRs were chartered on June 27, 1835. The N&L was completed on December 1, 1838, but the Concord's single line opened progressively and was not finished to Concord until 1842. Built to high standards, the Concord was double tracked throughout by 1848. It soon became one of the most profitable railroads in New England.

The Boston, Concord & Montreal RR was chartered in New Hampshire on December 27, 1844, but failed to secure approval in Canada. With another line progressing along the Connecticut River, attention was concentrated on the section between Concord and Wells River. Simultaneously, the Northern RR was under construction from Concord to White River Jct. The massive boom in railroad construction, when money was available for almost any project, was almost over, and the BC&M found it difficult to obtain share subscriptions. Service to Plymouth started in early 1850, extended to Warren during 1851, and Wells River depot finally became a junction in May 1853. A two-deck timber trestle was built across the Connecticut River to replace a turnpike bridge, and under the rights of the Coos Turnpike Corporation,

Lincoln, at the end of the Pemigewasset Valley Branch, as it appeared in August 1974, just before the B&M sold the line to the state. (R. D. Karr)

given in 1805, the railroad imposed tolls for non-rail crossings. Shortly before, the BC&M had leased the White Mountains RR, then under construction. Seasonal vacation travel and limited freight was not enough for prosperity.

Leases and mergers became the order of the day. The BC&M, Concord, Manchester & Lawrence, New Hampshire Central, and Concord & Portsmouth companies agreed to a pooling arrangement, though it began to unravel in 1869 through a bizarre sequence of events. That year, the Great Northern RR was promoted to merge the three smaller lines with the Northern company, but the merger was rejected by the New Hampshire legislature. To the south, the Boston & Lowell sought a merger with the Fitchburg RR in the face of strenuous opposition by the Boston & Maine, which resulted in lease by the B&L of the BC&M. The Concord RR sparked a row in the New Hampshire legislature and courts, arguing that the B&L was "not legally operating in the State of New Hampshire." The costs of litigation were substantial, and they were one reason that the B&L was taken over by the Boston & Maine RR in June 1887. The New Hampshire Supreme Court determined, in spring 1889, that by leasing itself to the B&M, the B&L had in effect sub-leased the BC&M, and so was not legally operating it.

Merger of the BC&M and Concord took place under a charter for the Concord & Montreal RR, issued on September 19, 1889. The new company embarked on an ambitious expansion program. It subscribed to Lake Shore and Tilton & Belmont RR stock and laid out money for

Trains no longer crossed this fragile-appearing trestle across the Winnipesaukee River into Franklin Falls, at the end of the Franklin & Tilton Branch, when this picture was taken in August 1974. (R. D. Karr)

14. Concord & Montreal

the Pemigewasset Valley RR and for a second connection with the Suncook Valley RR. Chartered in 1874, the PV had been completed from Plymouth to Woodstock in 1883. With BC&M backing it eventually reached Lincoln but never made a proposed connection with the Profile & Franconia Notch RR. At Lincoln, traffic was provided by the East Branch & Lincoln RR. The T&B, only four miles long, opened shortly before the merger. Both the PV and the T&B had been leased on opening by the BC&M. The EB&L, a logging line built by J. E. Henry starting in 1892, survived until 1948 and continued to switch cars at Lincoln until 1972. Henry should be remembered for description in local newspapers as Heartless Lumber King, Mutilator of Nature, King Contractor of the Mountains, and Grand Duke of Lincoln. A quote from him says it all: "I never see the tree yit that didn't mean a damned sight more to me goin' under the saw than it did standin' on a mountain" (Heffernan and Stecker, *New Hampshire*, 157).

The Franklin & Tilton Branch, built in 1892, was leased on completion. By 1895, however, the C&M was bearing heavy debts and the original Concord line, once so prosperous, was in disrepair. The B&M took over, guaranteeing stockholders a 7 percent return. Apart from completion of work already in hand, capital expenditure ceased. In the years following World War I there was some expansion of service over the main line, although branches suffered severe losses during the 1920s. Passenger service over the Franklin & Tilton ceased in September 1926. In April 1929, passenger trains over the Tilton & Belmont ended. The final freight ran in August 1930. Flood damage in 1936 closed the F&T west of Franklin Falls, and the line was abandoned in 1942. The connection between Hooksett and the yard at Suncook was closed in 1935 when the bridge at Hooksett was taken out of service. Any chance that the B&M might repair it ended when the severe floods of March 1936 destroyed it. The B&M then leased the remainder of the Suncook Loop to the Suncook Valley RR.

After World War II the main line enjoyed a brief revival, but only until October 31, 1954, when the last through passenger trains ran from Boston to Wells River following permission to abandon from Plymouth to Blackmount. The B&M ended remaining passenger service on the BC&M in 1967. What was left of the F&T closed in November 1972 and was abandoned in 1975. In 1973 the B&M embargoed the C&M north of Meredith, prompting the state of New Hampshire to buy the entire line beyond a point 1.5 miles north of Concord in 1975.

How far from the days when the clerestory Pullman cars, *Passaconway* and *Lafayette,* plied the route!

Leases by the Wolfeboro and then the Goodwin RRs were unsuccessful. The New England Southern RR took over from September 1982. The only current freight customer north of Concord is the Quinn-T Corp. in East Tilton (whose spur is located on the first half-mile of the old T&B), who occasionally receives a carload of clay slurry. Trackage rights over Guilford from Concord to Manchester were obtained in 1985. New England Southern traffic is mainly lumber, feed, and rock salt, with occasional general freight.

Guilford, which still owns the old Concord RR from Nashua to Concord, regularly uses the line north of Manchester only for unit coal trains to the Bow electric plant. Customers between Nashua and Manchester are served by a local freight out of Nashua.

Excursion passenger trains have been operated over portions of the C&M by various operators since the 1970s. The Winnipesaukee Scenic RR operates scheduled trains between Meredith and Lakeport summers, and from time to time runs special excursions as far south as Tilton. The Hobo RR, under the same management, operates trains over the Pemigewasset Valley Branch and sometimes south to Meredith.

Sources: Armstrong, *Railfan's Guide,* 32–33; Baker, *Formation,* 123–24, 141–44; Kirkland, *Men, Cities, and Transportation,* 1: 161–63, 435; Mead, *Up-Country Line;* Wood, *Turnpikes,* 211.

15. Boston & Maine (Original Company)

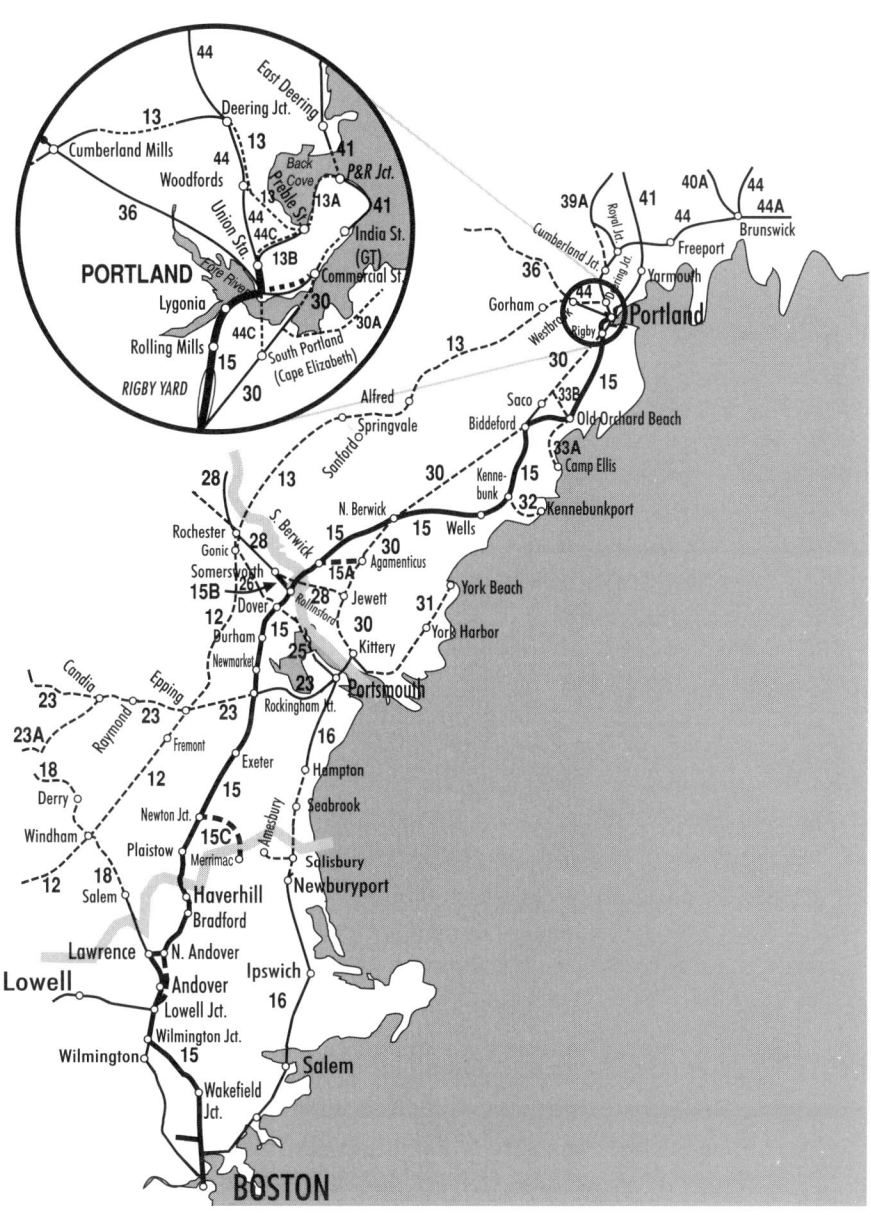

15. Boston & Maine

0 Boston, MA	71.5 Cummings (South Berwick) (Berwick Jct.), ME	115 Portland Union Sta. (Congress St.), ME
33 Haverhill, MA		
36.5 Atkinson, NH		
37.5 Westville	77.5 North Berwick	**15A. PS&P Connection**
38.5 Plaistow	82 Merriland	
41 Newton Jct. (Newton)	85 Wells (Wells Beach)	0 Cummings (South Berwick) (Berwick Jct.), ME
42 Russ Crossing	85.5 Elms (The Elms)	
44.5 Powwow River	90 Kennebunk	2 Agamenticus (South Berwick Jct.), ME
45.5 East Kingston	92 Arundel	
50.5 Exeter	96 West Biddeford	
54.5 Newfields (South New Market)	99 Biddeford	
	99.5 Saco	**15B. Somersworth Branch**
55.5 Rockingham Jct. (Rockingham) (Newmarket Jct.) (South Newmarket Jct.)	102.5 Temple Ave.	0 Rollinsford, NH
	103 Camp Ground	1 Crocketts Crossing
	104 Old Orchard Beach	2 Foundry
	105 Surfside	3 Somersworth (Great Falls), NH
57 Newmarket	105.5 Grand Beach	
59 Bennett Rd.	107 Pine Point (Blue Point) (Pine Point Beach)	
61.5 Durham		**15C. West Amesbury Branch**
64 Madbury	109 Scarboro Beach (Scarboro)	
67 Dover		0 Newton Jct., NH
70 Rollinsford	111 Scarboro Crossing (Rigby) (Pleasant Hill)	1.5 Newton, NH
71 Salmon Falls, NH		4.5 Merrimac (West Amesbury), MA
	113 Rolling Mills	
	114 Ligonia	

Built: 1840-74; Somersworth Branch, 1843; West Amesbury Branch, 1872-73.

Operators: *Boston & Maine,* 1842-1983; *Portland Terminal,* 1911-83; *Guilford,* 1983-; *New Hampshire Northcoast,* 1986-.

Daily Passenger Trains: *1842:* 6 (Boston-Dover); *1869:* 10 (Boston-Agamenticus); *1893:* 10; *1919:* 14; *1935:* 15; *1950:* 17; *1960:* 10; *1965:* 2. Passenger service ended PS&P connection, 1873; West Amesbury Branch, 1927; Somersworth Branch, 1961; Dover-Portland, 1965; Haverhill-Dover, 1967.

Abandonments: PS&P connection, 1879; West Amesbury Branch, 1972.

In 1833 Massachusetts issued a charter to the Andover & Wilmington RR for an eight-mile branch from Wilmington on the as yet unbuilt Boston & Lowell line, to Andover. Two years later extension

A Guilford work train waits at the Oak Street yard in Dover, NH, in June 1999. (R. D. Karr)

Guilford freight NESE heads south through Madbury, NH, on a fine spring day in 1999. (R. D. Karr)

was authorized to Haverhill. The A&W opened in 1836. North of the state line two railroads were chartered to extend toward Portland. A charter for a Boston & Maine RR was granted on June 27, 1835, in New Hampshire, followed by the Maine, New Hampshire & Massachusetts RR in Maine on March 30, 1836. A financial crisis prompted the state of Massachusetts to step in with a vote of funds to enable completion to Bradford, south of the Merrimack River, in October 1837. The A&W was renamed the Andover & Haverhill RR, with consent for extension to the Hew Hampshire state line. It became the Boston & Portland RR in 1839. The B&M line was completed from Plaistow to East Kingston on January 1, 1840, to Exeter on June 26, to Newmarket on July 28, 1841, and to a temporary depot in Coffins Cut, south of Dover, on September 24. Extension over the Cocheco River into Dover was completed before year end. A charter amendment in April 1841 permitted connection with other lines, and as a result a link was made with the Portland, Saco & Portsmouth RR at Agamenticus, ME, on February 2, 1843, completing the through route to Portland. A branch from Rollinsford to Somersworth opened on July 24. The B&P,

15. Boston & Maine

B&M, and MNH&M companies were consolidated using the New Hampshire company title, and in July 1845, an extension south from Wilmington into Boston was built.

When the joint lease of the PS&P by the B&M and Eastern between 1847 and 1870 ended, the B&M was deprived of its Portland connection. The B&M obtained a charter for a new line from South Berwick to be built east of the PS&P alignment. Authorization was given in 1871, and the 41-mile line—largely single-track—was completed in 1873. The new line ran through the Ligonia section of Cape Elizabeth (now South Portland), where a station was provided at the steel rolling mills. North of the Fore River, the line paralleled Portland & Kennebec (later Maine Central) tracks to reach its terminal north of the renamed Commercial Street. Grade crossings of the PS&P were required at two locations. At North Berwick, where the B&M and Eastern (PS&P) converged, station and depot facilities were shared, although there was no physical connection. There, William C. Briggs promoted his "restorator"—forerunner of the station buffet—to sell his wife's Berwick sponge cake during what became for many years a mandatory ten-

This is the view south from a rare, soon-to-be-removed, box pony truss wooden bridge at Berwick, ME, in July 1999. (R. D. Karr)

minute stop. The fastest trains took three and a half hours to run the intercity trip, and the slowest five and a half. Immediately north of the Fore River bridge, an interchange station, known as B&M Jct. or Transfer Station, was provided for passenger interchange with the MEC. After the B&M took over the Eastern, and with it, the PS&P, the various passenger terminals in Portland were replaced in 1888 by a facility south of Congress Street, owned by the Portland Union Railway Station Company. Rigby Yard was constructed around 1913 in South Portland as the principal freight interchange point, and the Somersworth branch was connected to the Portsmouth, Great Falls & Conway line.

Three branches were built by independent companies. The West Amesbury Branch RR from Newton station to the Merrimack River in Massachusetts opened in 1873. To obtain the 2.2 percent ruling gradient mandated in New Hampshire, wetlands east of Newton were filled with ash and clinker, and track comprised worn 85-pound rail, all obtained from the B&M, which leased the line from opening in 1873. Tender engines were used, so turntables were required at both ends; the one at Newton Jct. was located south of the station and west of the main line. The Old Orchard Beach RR and Kennebunk & Kennebunkport RR were completed in 1880 and 1883, respectively, and leased from completion.

Following capital improvements made in 1911, the main line carried several crack express passenger trains, such as the *State of Maine*, the *Pine Tree Limited*, and the *East Wind*. Freight traffic was enormous, comprising agricultural products, textiles and other mill output, lumber, grist, a wide range of industrial goods, and for many years, ice from East Kingston. Continuous improvement was required. By 1879, 16.5 miles of steel rail had been laid in New Hampshire. Telegraphic control was introduced in the 1870s to replace the timetable order system, along with the Miller platform, electric signal, power brake, and safety switch. Double track was gradually introduced beginning in 1888, although the second track to Dover was not completed until 1912. The widened bridge across the Salmon Falls River between Rollinsford, NH, and South Berwick, ME, is a magnificent spectacle and a monument to the over-engineering of the time. An additional station, originally named The Elms, was built north of Wells to serve the farm of George Lord, president of the company. Between August 1893 and May 1894, the B&M opened a new North Union Station in Boston to

With CSX locomotives in the lead, Guilford symbol freight SENE crosses the splendid 1888 Warren steel undertruss bridge from Salmon Falls, NH, into South Berwick, ME, in July 1999. (R. D. Karr)

combine its railhead and those of the Eastern, the Fitchburg, and the Boston & Lowell. Additional sidings north of Newton Jct. were installed in 1896 and a new turntable was installed in 1907.

Expansion of the University of New Hampshire campus in Durham (formerly the New Hampshire College of Agriculture and the Mechanic Arts, which had moved from Hanover in 1891) had enveloped the line when, in 1910, an arch over the Oyster River about 0.5 miles south of the town caved in, owing to use of heavier locomotives. The line through Durham was shifted westward the following year, and today the old alignment is part street and part dirt trail. A granite quoin and yellow brick station building from East Lynn, MA, was rebuilt north of Main Street. With most West Amesbury Branch trains running to and from Dover, an additional lead was provided in 1911 at Newton Jct. to form a wye, and the turntable was removed. By 1920 the entire route was double tracked, except between North Berwick and Kennebunk.

15. Boston & Maine

In May 1999 Kennebunk station looked much the same as it did a century ago. (R. D. Karr)

The B&M brought a new 40-stall round house into service on December 25, 1923, in Dover. In 1928, the railroad moved the track north of Newmarket slightly to the west and built a new causeway and 60-foot timber trestle across the Lamprey River. Considerably longer trestles were built over the Nonesuch and Scarborough Rivers. Double tracking was completed from North Berwick through to Portland in 1944, when the former PS&P was abandoned. By 1946 freight was hauled by diesels, although steam locomotives continued on passenger trains until about 1952.

The fortunes of the route declined rapidly after the completion of the parallel I-95 in 1958. Stations at Dover and Old Orchard Beach were demolished. Budd rail diesel cars (RDCs) were purchased to replace locomotive-hauled passenger rolling stock. Local freight had all but disappeared by the mid-1960s when passenger service north of Dover ended. Much of the line had been reduced to a single track. The B&M filed for bankruptcy in 1970. Since 1983 the original B&M has become Guilford's Freight Main Line, with four or five freight trains daily. The branch from Rollinsford has been operated by the New Hampshire Northcoast RR since 1986.

Maine's Senator George Mitchell, then Senate Majority Leader, secured authorization for more than $40 million for the restoration of rail passenger service between Boston and Portland in the Intermodal Surface Transportation Act of 1991. The Northern New England Passenger Rail Authority was created in 1995 to implement the project, which includes upgrading of track and provision by local communities of new or rehabilitated stations in Portland, Old Orchard Beach, Biddeford/Saco, Wells, Dover, Durham, and Exeter. Work did not commence until 1999, following a decision by the Surface Transportation Board that settled an acrimonious debate between Guilford and the NNEPRA.

The station at Old Orchard Beach is in use by the local Chamber of Commerce. In Biddeford, the original depot is a restaurant. Kennebunk station is almost unaltered; a mother and children seen on the platform during a summer trip a few years ago made it seem that a train might appear in minutes to take them to Portland. Wells station has been much modified as a private residence. The timber-clad passenger building at Madbury has been moved, and is now a flower shop known for Killarney roses. Rockingham depot survives almost intact, although derelict. Durham station is now the extremely popular university dairy bar, used to educate students in the basic arts of catering; the university advocates the restoration of passenger service. At Exeter, a pizza parlor occupies the old station, its emanations as powerful as a blast of steam from a coal-fired locomotive. East Kingston depot is a private residence, restored by a former B&M employee, with several railroad artifacts transferred from elsewhere. Plaistow station is occupied by a building contractor. Stations also survive at Dover, The Elms, and North Berwick.

Sources: Armitage, *Railroads of America*; Baker, *Formation*, 145-48; Barnum, *Atkinson*; Bradlee, *Boston & Maine*; Cobb and Shaw, "Dover," 11, 12; Drury, *Historical Guide*, 365-70; Drury, *Train-Watcher's Guide*, 122-25; Hurd, *Rockingham and Strafford*, 406; Jager and Jager, *New Hampshire*, 61; Karr, *Rail Lines*, 236-42; Karr, *Lost Railroads*, 71, 72, 84; Waite, "Recycling."

16. Eastern

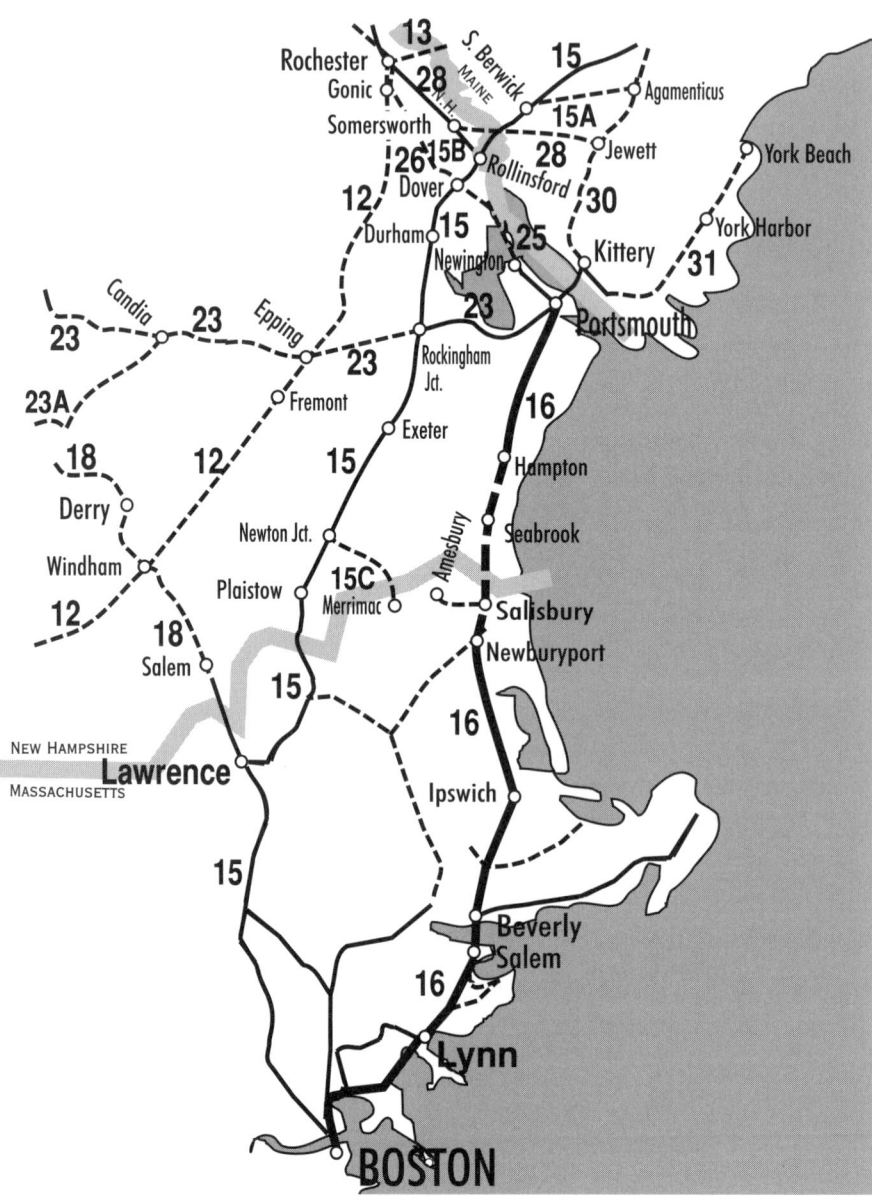

16. Eastern

0 Boston, MA	43 Seabrook	51 Breakfast Hill (Greenland)
37 Newburyport	44 Hampton Falls	57 Portsmouth, NH
39 Salisbury, MA	47 Hampton	
41 Atlantic (Smithtown) (State Line), NH	49 North Hampton	

Built: 1839–40.

Operators: *Eastern*, 1840–84; *Boston & Maine*, 1885–1983; *Guilford*, 1983–.

Daily Passenger Trains: *1869:* 10; *1893:* 14; *1919:* 21; *1935:* 16; *1950:* 22; *1960:* 12. Passenger service ended 1965 (Newburyport–Portsmouth).

Abandonments: Salisbury–Seabrook, 1982; Seabrook–Hampton, 1997.

The Eastern RR of Massachusetts, which had begun building north from East Boston in 1836, had reached the state border near Smithtown in November 1840. There it connected with the Eastern RR of New Hampshire, which had built south from the southern outskirts of Portsmouth to meet it end-on. Work continued through Portsmouth to a terminus at Vaughan Street the following month, enabling the opening of the entire line on December 31. With completion of the Portland, Saco & Portsmouth RR in November 1842, a through route to Portland became available, but the Eastern monopoly of traffic to and from Maine ended when the B&M also extended to the PS&P in February 1843. In 1847 the Eastern and the B&M took a joint lease of the PS&P. Until 1854 the Eastern was disadvantaged by a terminal in East Boston with a connection to the city by ferry, and competition from coastal steamers.

After three decades of intense competition with the B&M, the Eastern was bankrupt. By 1870 about 80 percent of Maine traffic was passing over the B&M. Lawsuits stemming from a major collision at Revere, MA, on the night of August 26, 1871, and the construction by the B&M of its own route to Portland after the Eastern had paid a high cost to acquire the PS&P, brought the Eastern to its knees in 1875. After a decade of negotiations and political maneuvering, the B&M leased the entire Eastern in December 1884, effective at the beginning of 1885.

16. Eastern

North of Massachusetts, revenue on the Eastern principally came from freight to and from Portsmouth and local passenger trains serving the intermediate beach resorts. Most passenger service between Boston and Portland used the B&M route, and all through trains to Portland over the PS&P ended in 1944; remaining trains north of Portsmouth stopped running in 1952. Passenger service from Boston was cut back to Newburyport, MA, as of January 4, 1965. The segment of former main line between Salisbury, MA, and the nuclear power plant just south of Seabrook went in 1982. To the north the remaining trackage is served by local freights operating out of Portsmouth as far south as the Foss Manufacturing plant in Hampton. From there to Seabrook the tracks remain in place unused, although the line was formally abandoned in 1997. In 1995 the Seacoast Scenic RR was formed to operate tourist trains to Hampton, but selectmen blocked this effort, alleging potential ecological damage. The Rockingham Planning Commission recently studied the possibility of extending commuter service from Newburyport to Portsmouth.

Sources: Baker, *Formation*, 147-48; Bradlee, *Eastern*; Karr, *Rail Lines*, 257-59; Karr, *Lost Railroads*, 143; Kirkland, *Men, Cities and Transportation*, 1:195-99,2: 2-12; Poor, *History*, 115-16.

Officially abandoned since 1997, the overgrown tracks of the Eastern stretch south from Hampton toward the Seabrook Nuclear Power Plant, visible here on the horizon in this October 1999 view. (R. D. Karr)

17. Brattleboro & Whitehall

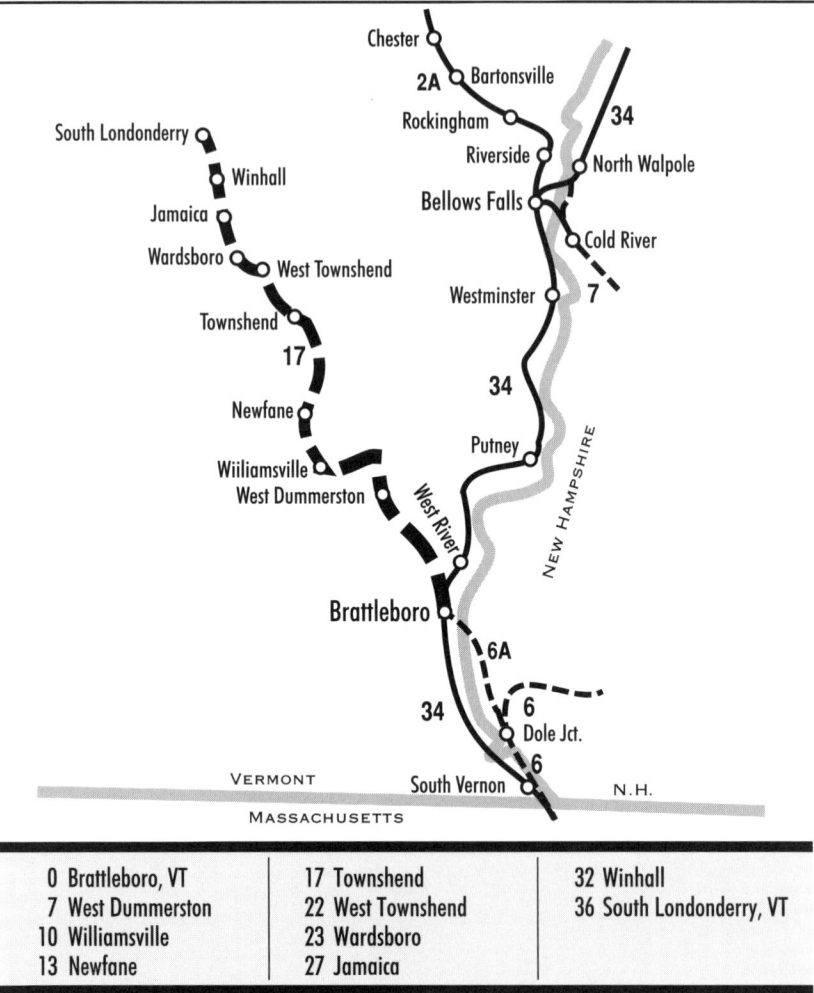

0 Brattleboro, VT	17 Townshend	32 Winhall
7 West Dummerston	22 West Townshend	36 South Londonderry, VT
10 Williamsville	23 Wardsboro	
13 Newfane	27 Jamaica	

Built: 1878–80.

Operators: *Central Vermont*, 1880-1927; *West River*, 1931-36; *Vermont White Granite*, 1936-38.

Daily Passenger Trains: *1880:* 4; *1905:* 4; *1925:* 2. Passenger service ended 1927. Restored 1931, 1933-34.

Abandonments: West Dummerston–South Londonderry, 1936; Brattleboro–West Dummerston, 1938.

17. Brattleboro & Whitehall

A railroad through the Green Mountains from the Connecticut River had been considered in the late 1840s to compete with the Vermont Central, but nothing happened until 1867 when the Rutland seemed about to dominate the scene. That year, a group of entrepreneurs organized the West River RR and obtained a charter in Vermont for a standard-gauge line from Brattleboro to Jamaica. An alignment was surveyed, but no other work was done.

In 1876 the project was revived, with a charter by the Brattleboro & Whitehall company, which envisaged a 3-foot-gauge line extending from Brattleboro to the Delaware & Hudson RR at Whitehall, NY. The directors were persuaded to adopt 2-foot gauge, following inspection of the new Billerica & Bedford RR in Massachusetts, but they reversed the decision before construction began. Ceremonial groundbreaking took place at Newfane on November 11, 1878. Money ran out when grading was completed as far as South Londonderry in the summer of 1879.

Faced with an enormous debt compared with expected revenue, the company negotiated a lease by the Central Vermont through its New London Northern RR subsidiary. Track work was completed on Octo-

A passenger train pulls into Newfane station, probably around the begining of the twentieth century. (Courtesy Walker Transportation Collection, Beverly Historical Society & Museum)

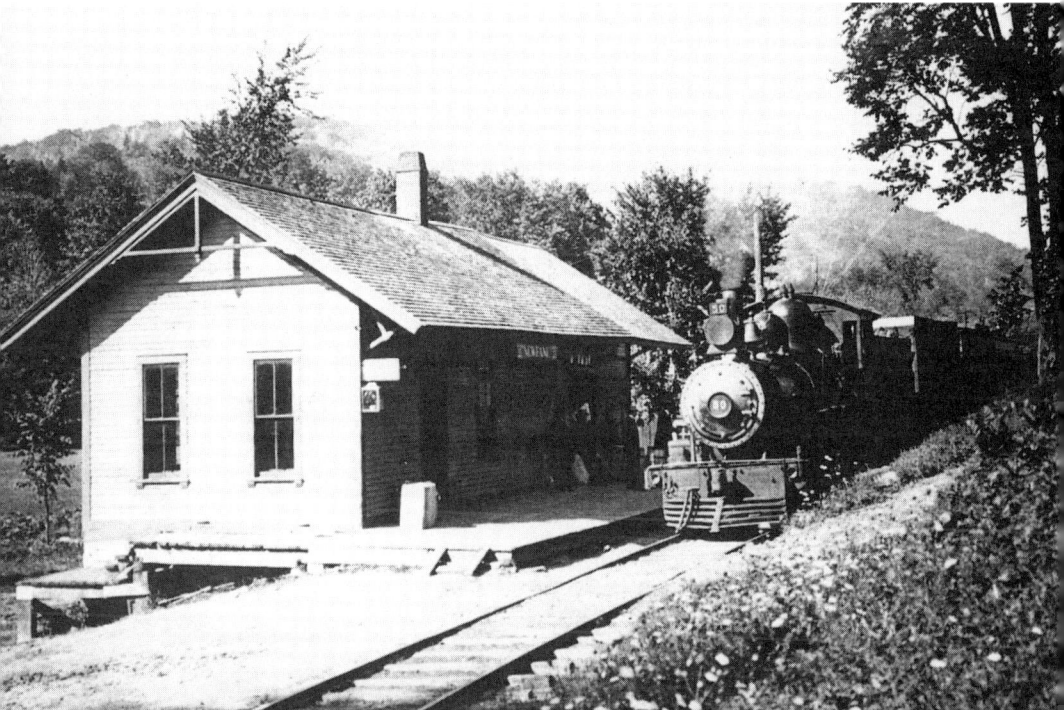

The collapse of this trestle across the West River in Brattleboro in 1886 cost two lives. It was replaced by an iron bridge. (Courtesy Walker Transportation Collection, Beverly Historical Society & Museum)

ber 20, 1880, and service commenced on November 18. One mixed train in each direction conveyed stone from a quarry in West Dummerston owned by Lyons Granite Co. A second train, required by the lease, was passenger only. One coal- and three wood-burning locomotives provided motive power.

At first revenues covered the cost of the lease but produced no return on the stockholders' investment, although modest dividends were paid in several later years. Extension of the line was never again considered. The line was susceptible to spring flooding and washouts, culminating in collapse of the timber trestle across the mouth of the West River at Brattleboro under a mixed train in 1886, with the loss of two lives. The trestle was replaced by an iron bridge, and a program followed to rebuild several other bridges before 1898. These were done, however, at the expense of track maintenance, which declined to the basic minimum after 1895, particularly north of the quarry. Derailments were frequent. B&W shareholders and the granite company pressured the CV to improve safety and to convert the line to standard gauge in order to eliminate the gauge change at Brattleboro. The addi-

17. Brattleboro & Whitehall

tion of a third running rail enabled standard-gauge trains to operate as far as West Dummerston by 1901.

Inadequate maintenance continued, and derailments remained such a problem that in 1903 the B&W petitioned for receivership and cancellation of the lease. After two years in the courts, a compromise was reached under which the B&W agreed to foreclosure in exchange for some compensation, and the CV agreed to improve maintenance and complete gauge-widening throughout.

Thus on April 20, 1905, the B&W was reorganized as the West River RR. Conversion to standard gauge started on Sunday, July 30, with the final mile commissioned the next day. Maintenance remained minimal, however. Repairs after severe damage to major portions of the line in 1927 were beyond the means of the company. Aid from the state of Vermont enabled mixed train service to resume on February 6, 1931, as an independent short line. There were still no promising sources of traffic north of the West Dummerston quarry, and competition from motor vehicles was taking a toll. Mixed train service ended in September.

In 1933, James G. Ashley of Greenfield, MA, largely took over operation of the line. He introduced a gasoline-motor passenger car on September 3, 1933, which ran until the car was destroyed by fire on June 1, 1934. Operation of the railroad was suspended during the winter of 1934, but resumed on an as-required basis in the spring of 1935. A petition to abandon was submitted, and approval was obtained during 1936. The length to the quarry was taken over by the Vermont White Granite Co. (successors to Lyons), but damage from the Great Hurricane of 1938 brought about the end.

Sources: Hilton, *American Narrow Gauge*, 137–38; Karr, *Lost Railroads*, 92; Morse, *36 Miles*.

18. Manchester & Lawrence

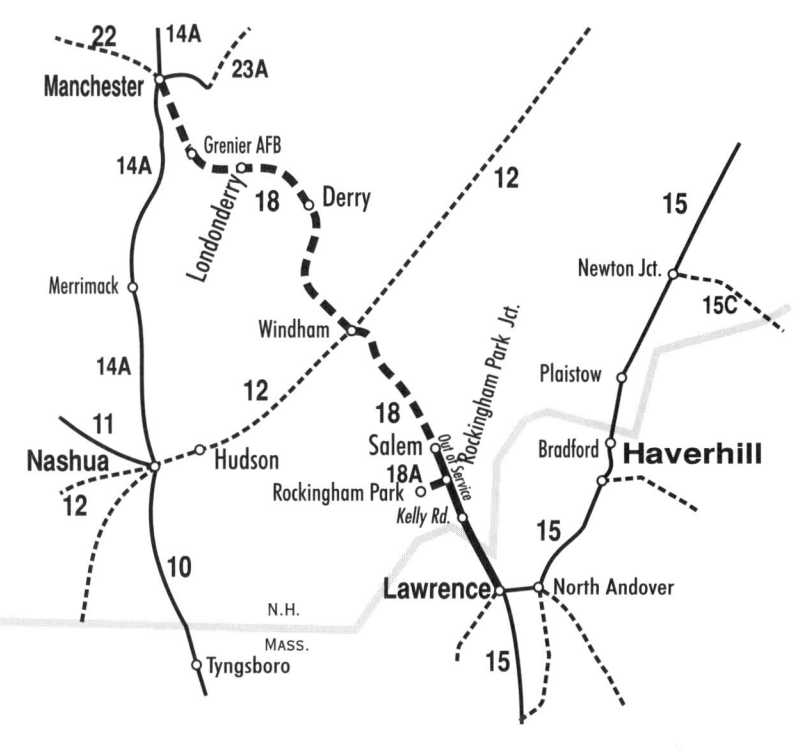

0 Lawrence, MA	9 Canobie Lake	27 Manchester, NH
1 North Lawrence (Lawrence Essex St.)	13 Windham (Windham Jct.)	**18A. Rockingham Park Branch**
2 Methuen, MA	16 Derry	
3 Hampshire Rd. (Messers), NH	18 Wilson (Wilsons)	0 Rockingham Park Jct., NH
4 Kelly Rd.	21 Londonderry	0.5 Rockingham Park, NH
6 Rockingham Park Jct.	24 Manchester Airport (Grenier AFB) (Willey)	
7 Salem	25 Nutts Pond	

Built: 1848–49.

By June 1999, around the time of its official abandonment, the northern segment of the M&L near Manchester Airport had long deteriorated beyond use. (R. D Karr)

This informal barricade marked the end of the line at Kelly Rd. in Salem in June 1999. The tracks just north of this point have been lifted. (R. D. Karr)

Operators: *Manchester & Lawrence*, 1849-50, 1853-56; *Concord*, 1850-53, 1856-87, *Boston & Maine*, 1887-1983; *Guilford*, 1983-.

Daily Passenger Trains: *1869:* 6; *1893:* 8; *1919:* 10; *1935:* 6; *1950:* 2. Regular passenger service ended 1953.

Abandonments: Salem-Derry, 1983; Derry-Londonderry, 1986; Rockingham Park Branch, ca. 1999; Londonderry-Manchester, 2000.

By the mid-1840s, both Manchester and Lawrence were rapidly growing mill towns, as were several intermediate communities. To link them, and to provide a new route to Boston, entrepreneurs in Manchester promoted the Manchester & Lawrence RR in 1847. It was to connect at the state line with the projected Methuen branch of the Boston & Maine, which had been approved by charter amendment in 1846. The M&L opened in November 1849, leased the Methuen Branch, and the next year was leased by the Concord RR, which sent the B&M traffic that would otherwise have gone to the

18. Manchester & Lawrence

Boston & Lowell. Aside from 3 years of independent operation in the 1850s, the M&L was operated by the Concord for the next 37 years.

The line never became an important through route. In 1887 the M&L was leased to the B&M. Service improvements followed. Rockingham Park racetrack was served by a short branch from 1935. A single round trip passenger train, a gas-electric car, operated until July 1953, although special trains continued to run to the race track until 1960.

For many years the line survived on a few local freight trips. They ended in the early 1980s, prior to abandonment of the nine-mile section between Salem and Derry that severed the line into two branches. The section between Derry and a point in Londonderry just south of Manchester International Airport (formerly Grenier AFB) was abandoned in 1986. In November 1998 the northern section lost its last shipper. Without regulatory approval, the city of Manchester removed track for extension of the main runway at the airport. In 1999 Guilford petitioned to abandon the entire remaining northern part of the M&L, and this was granted in May 2000.

At the south end, a plastics pellets company at Kelly Road in Salem provides some traffic. The track north of this point to Salem station is out of service, and some of it was recently removed without waiting for formal abandonment. The town of Derry plans to purchase the old depot there to house its chamber of commerce and perhaps a museum.

Sources: Baker, *Formation*, 105–06, 123–27; Harlow, *Steelways*, 148; Karr, *Rail Lines*, 243–44; Kirkland, *Men, Cities, and Transportation*, 1: 183-84; Poor, *History*, 57; *Railpace* 18 (Aug. 1999), 37.

19. Manchester & Keene

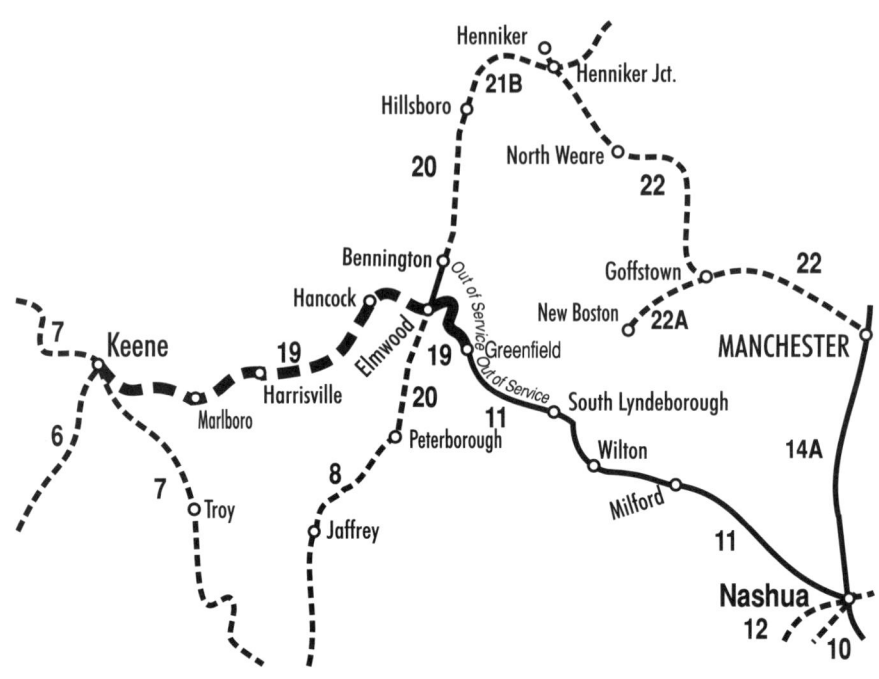

0 Greenfield, NH	7 Hancock	23 Marlboro (Marlboro Village)
4 South Bennington	13 Dublin (East Harrisville)	
5 Elmwood Jct. (Hancock Jct.) (Elmwood)	(Eastview)	29 South Keene
6 Coolidge Crossing	16 Harrisville	30 Keene, NH
	19 Chesham	

Built: 1875-78.

Operators: *Manchester & Keene*, 1878-79; *Connecticut River*, 1879-80; *Boston & Lowell*, 1880-87; *Boston & Maine*, 1887-1983; *Guilford*, 1983-86.

Daily Passenger Trains: *1880:* 4; *1893:* 6; *1915:* 6; *1920:* 6; *1924:* 4; *1926:* 4; *1935:* 4 (Greenfield-Elmwood). Passenger service ended Keene-Elmwood, 1934; Elmwood-Greenfield, 1935.

19. Manchester & Keene

Abandonments: Keene–Coolidge Crossing, 1938; Coolidge Crossing–Elmwood, 1939.

Keene, a wool mill town, was an intermediate stop on the Cheshire RR main line from 1849 and became the terminal of the Ashuelot RR two years later. Local interests promoted a link with the Concord RR at Manchester and obtained a charter for the Manchester & Keene RR in 1864. Nothing happened until the post-bellum economic boom in 1872, when the scheme was revised. The Nashua & Lowell RR sought to extend its Nashua–Wilton line westward. The N&L and the M&K agreed to meet at Greenfield, to which the N&L was to extend from Wilton, and the M&K dropped its plans of extending to Manchester. While the N&L extension was completed in 1874, the impecunious M&K did not connect with it until August 13, 1878, a month after opening of the Peterborough & Hillsborough RR, which it crossed at Elmwood. The entire route from Greenfield to Keene was completed on November 29.

The M&K was in trouble from the outset. The only real sources of traffic were the wool mill at Keene, two other wool mills in Harrisville, two cotton mills in Marlboro, and one in Nelson, north of Harrisville; but they were all relatively small operations. Agricultural traffic was minimal. The line shut down in March or April 1879 as a result of operating losses. The N&L resumed service from Greenfield to Harrisville on September 6, 1879, but withdrew on January 1, 1880. After failed attempts by the N&L and the Connecticut River RR to restore operations, the Boston & Lowell and the Concord each bought 50 percent of the M&K bonds—the two companies were planning joint management of their systems—and reopened the line. It was operated by the B&L, with revenue and cost divided equally. The arrangement lasted until July 1, 1884, when the Concord leased its interest to the B&L. After 1887 Elmwood became a minor nexus in the Boston & Maine system. The M&K was retained partly because it could be used occasionally as an alternative through route for freight.

On January 9, 1934, torrential rains following a thaw caused Moose Brook, northeast of Hancock, to overflow, and Rice's Trestle, which bridged the brook a few hundred yards beyond Coolidge Crossing (Longview Road) in Hancock, collapsed. The entire line west of that point to Keene was taken out of service. The B&M decided that the line's low revenue could not justify reinstatement. Both daily round-trip passenger trains to Keene from Nashua were diverted to Peterborough, with bus connections provided from Elmwood for Hancock and from Peterborough for Keene; the Hancock runs ended sometime around the turn of the year. Trains to Peterborough were replaced by busses in September 1935.

Local freight service continued between Elmwood and Coolidge Crossing. When the great hurricane in September 1938 caused still more damage the cost of replacement could not be justified. Freight service west of Elmwood ended. The section between Keene and Hancock was formally abandoned that year, and the length from Elmwood to Coolidge Crossing in 1939. A stub west of Elmwood was retained, which together with a spur to the former Peterborough & Hillsboro line formed a wye for switching trains to and from Hillsboro. The remaining section between Greenfield and Elmwood became part of the B&M's Hillsboro Branch.

About 1948 the stub and diamond at Elmwood were eliminated by installation of a new spur, but reversal of trains to and from Hillsboro was still required. In 1952, the B&M secured title to additional land near the station (which had closed in 1938) to build a direct connection. Shortly after commissioning in September that year, all redundant track was taken up and the station building razed.

In the 1950s, a daily round-trip freight train used the line between Greenfield and Elmwood on its way to Hillsboro, mainly for stone and aggregate traffic, but it had become a "run-as-required" operation by the 1980s, when Guilford decided to include the line in its 1984 five-year plan for potential abandonment.

During abandonment proceedings, the state of New Hampshire stepped in with an offer to purchase the right of way and track west of Greenfield to Elmwood, along with the former Peterborough & Hillsboro length north to Bennington and the former Greenfield RR between Wilton and Greenfield. A price was negotiated and title duly passed, but the state did not find a short line operator until 1992, when a lease was taken by the Milford-Bennington RR, which has yet to operate revenue trains beyond Greenfield. The last remnant of the M&K west of Greenfield remains in place, gradually rotting.

Sources: Baker, *Formation*, 17, 178, 192, 196; Cornwall and Smith, *Names First*, 64; DiFalco, "Milford-Bennington Railroad"; Karr, *Lost Railroads*, 100, 106, 137; Hancock History Committee, *Second Hundred Years*, 259-72; Morison and Elton, *New Hampshire*, 134-78.

20. Peterborough & Hillsborough

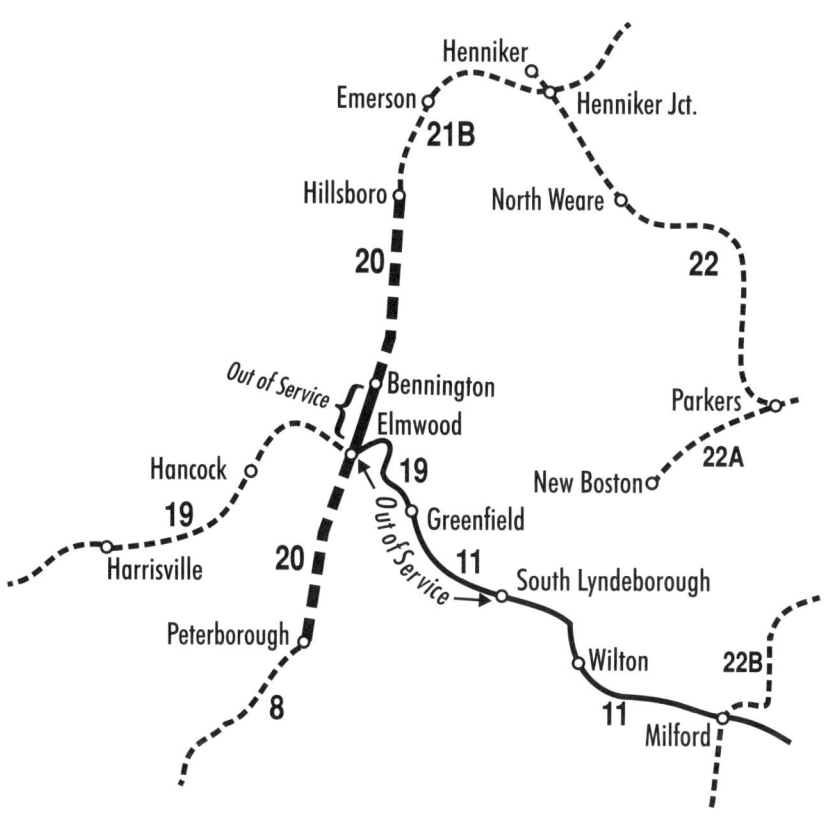

0 Peterborough, NH	6.5 Elmwood Jct. (Hancock Jct.) (Elmwood)	13 Deering (West Deering)
2 Tarbell		14 Holton
3 Nahor	8.5 Bennington	17 Hillsboro, NH
4 Cavender	10.5 Antrim	

Built: 1877-78.

Operators: *Northern,* 1878-84, 1887; *Boston & Lowell,* 1884-87; *Boston & Maine,* 1888-1983; *Guilford,* 1983-84.

Daily Passenger Trains: *1887:* 4; *1908:* 6 (plus Peterborough-Elmwood, 4; Elmwood-Hillsboro, 2); *1919:* 6 (plus Peterborough-Elmwood, 2; Elmwood–Hillsboro, 2); *1935:* 2. Passenger service ended 1936.

Abandonments: Peterborough–Elmwood, 1942; Bennington–Hillsboro, 1979.

Peterborough was the northern terminal of the Monadnock RR from 1871. The Boston, Barre & Gardner RR leased the Monadnock in anticipation that locally subscribed capital would enable building of a link with the Contoocook Valley RR at Hillsboro, to establish a through route to Concord. Previous promises of support for the link by the BB&G were not fulfilled owing to debt from construction of its Massachusetts main line. Work on the link, the Peterborough & Hillsborough RR, finally began in 1877, on the understanding that the Northern RR would lease it upon completion.

The Contoocook River valley though which the P&H passed formed a natural division between the manufacturing region of New

Elmwood, where the P&H crossed the Manchester & Keene, was a busy junction, as can be seen in this view from around 1910. A Nashua-bound M&K train (right) has the road after connecting with a northbound train to Hillsboro. Note the ball signal protecting the crossing. (Courtesy Walker Transportation Collection, Beverly Historical Society & Museum)

20. Peterborough & Hillsborough

Hampshire and the predominantly farm-based economy to the west. Antrim depot was actually located in Bennington, immediately east of the river. Hillsboro (the railroad adopted the abbreviated form here and elsewhere) was entered on a skew bridge over the river and the tracks crossed what is now State Route 149 to the existing terminal. The line was opened in July 1878, and was operated by the Northern RR and the Boston & Lowell until January 1, 1888, when the Boston & Maine took over and included it as part of its Southern Division. From 1913 the line formed part of the Worcester & Hillsboro Branch of the Worcester, Nashua & Portland Division. Timetables for passenger trains were stable until the late 1920s.

On March 13, 1936, a storm took out parts of the line south of Elmwood. Passenger service over the entire P&H ended, and freight service between Peterborough and Elmwood never resumed. With heavy increases in train movements over the main lines to the west and east, and the need to divert finance and maintenance resources to them, the B&M abandoned the Peterborough–Elmwood section along with the Contoocook Valley south of Emerson to Hillsboro in 1942. Hillsboro from then on was served from Nashua only.

By the 1950s, a daily round-trip freight train used the line, mainly for stone and aggregates from quarries and for the Monadnock Paper Co. mill in Bennington, but operation declined to "as required" by the early 1980s. The segment between Bennington and Hillsboro was abandoned in 1979.

Guilford, which had included the remainder of the line in its 1984 five-year plan for potential abandonments, embargoed the route, depriving the paper mill of service. The state of New Hampshire purchased the line, along with the Elmwood–Wilton segment of the former Manchester & Keene and Peterborough Railroads, and eventually reached agreement with the Milford-Bennington RR to be the designated operator. A state grant to reconstruct the line to Bennington to serve the paper mill resulted in some work, but the Milford-Bennington has yet to restore service to any part of the P&H, and at last report the mill no longer wanted rail service.

Sources: Baker, *Formation*, 101, 142–46; DiFalco, "Milford-Bennington Railroad"; Hancock History Committee, *Second Hundred Years*, 259–72; Karr, *Lost Railroads*, 106, 137; Karr, *Rail Lines*, 184–91.

21. Concord & Claremont

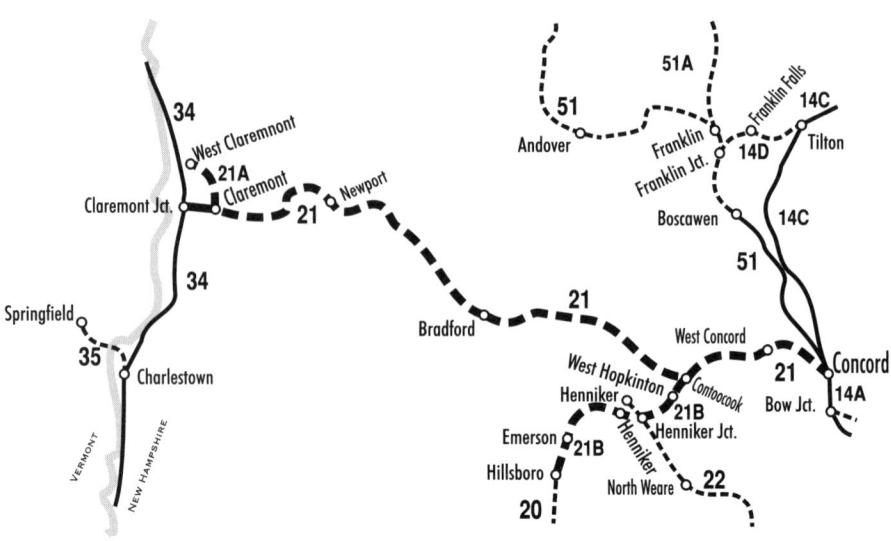

0 Concord, NH	34 Lake Sunapee	**21A. Claremont RY**
4 Garrison (West Concord)	35 Mt. Sunapee (Edgemont)	
6 Riverhill	40 Sunapee	0 Claremont [Mulberry St.]
8 Mast Yard	42 Guild	3.5 West Claremont, NH
10 Tyler	44 Newport	
12 Contoocook	47 Northville (North New-	**21B. Contoocook Valley RR**
15 Dimond Corner	port)	
(Dimonds)	49 Kellyville	0 Contoocook, NH
17 Bagley	50 Chandler	3 West Hopkinton
18 Lower Warner	55 East Claremont (Wash-	7 Henniker Jct.
19 Warner	ington St.)	8 Henniker
21 Waterloo	56 Claremont Center	9.5 Emerson (West
23 Roby (Robys Corner)	(Pleasant St.)	Henniker)
25 Melvin (Melvin Mills)	*56.5 Claremont [Mulberry St.]*	14.5 Hillsboro (Hillsboro
28 Bradford	58.5 Claremont Jct., NH	Bridge), NH
33 Newbury		

Built: 1848-73; Contoocook Valley RR, 1848-49; Claremont RY, 1903.

Operators: *Concord & Claremont*, 1848-53; *Contoocook Valley*, 1849-53; *Northern*, 1853-84; *Boston & Lowell*, 1884-87; *Boston &*

21. Concord & Claremont

Maine, 1887-1954; *Claremont RY*, 1903-54; *Claremont & Concord*, 1954-88; *Claremont Concord* 1988-.

Daily Passenger Trains: *1869:* 2 (Concord-Bradford); *1893:* 6; *1919:* 6; *1935:* 4; *1950:* 4. Passenger service ended Contoocook-Hillsboro, 1936; Concord-Claremont Jct., 1955.

Abandonments: Emerson-Hillsboro, 1942; West Concord-Contoocook and West Hopkinton-Emerson, 1960; West Hopkinton-Contoocook-Bradford, 1961; Bradford-Newport, 1964; Newport-East Claremont, 1977; Concord-West Concord, 1984; East Claremont-Claremont Center, 1988; Claremont RY (Claremont [Mulberry St.] [0.5 miles north]-West Claremont, 1988; Claremont [Mulberry St.]-[0.5 miles north], 1994).

During the mid-1840s, various schemes emerged for what were essentially rural branch lines west of Concord, NH, to the Connecticut River. The most ambitious was the Concord & Claremont RR, which planned a through route to the Connecticut River and connection with the Sullivan RR. The first twenty miles of the surveyed alignment were somewhat circuitous along the Contoocook River valley to West Hopkinton; the remainder struck out northwest through Warner and Newport to Claremont. Each of these towns had wool mills and were agricultural centers. A charter was obtained for a line from Concord to Claremont on June 24, 1848, at the same time as the New Hampshire Central and Contoocook Valley lines.

Construction of the C&C started from just north of the joint Concord/Boston, Concord & Montreal station in Concord. The line was opened to Mast Yard in the Penacook section of Concord that year. It was extended to Contoocook in 1849, where connection was made with the Contoocook Valley RR which had opened its fifteen-mile long line to Hillsboro the same year. The Contoocook sought to extend south from Hillsboro to meet the proposed Monadnock RR running north from the Cheshire main line at Winchendon, MA. The C&C was extended another 16 miles west to Bradford in 1850. Meanwhile, the New Hampshire Central opened between Manchester and the Contoocook Valley in Henniker. In 1853 the C&C and NHC merged to form the Merrimac & Connecticut Rivers RR, which then leased the Contoocook Valley.

B&M gas-electric car and trailer skirt the shores of Sunapee Lake in Newbury, NH, sometime before the Claremont & Concord resumed independent operation in 1954. (Dwight A. Smith, Jr., Courtesy Walker Transportation Collection, Beverly Historical Society & Museum)

The Northern RR operated the M&CR from 1853, initially under contract, but soon it acquired a controlling financial interest. Capital for extension of the C&C beyond Bradford could not be raised. With mounting annual losses, the Contoocook Valley failed, to be reorganized in 1857 as the Contoocook River RR. In 1858, the M&CR merger came apart but the components were still operated by the Northern. C&C results improved, but were insufficient to justify extension beyond Bradford.

The economic boom of the early 1870s enabled the C&C to complete its line to Claremont. Along the proposed route major sheep farming communities had been established. There were wool mills in Hopkinton and Warner and four in Newport. Claremont had two wool and two cotton mills. A separate company, the Sugar River RR, was incorporated to revive the original charter; it completed the line to Newport in 1871 and to Claremont in September 1872. In 1873 the C&C

21. Concord & Claremont

absorbed the Sugar River and acquired the Contoocook River line, although the Northern continued to operate the entire C&C system until 1884 when the Boston & Lowell leased the Northern. Three years later the Boston & Maine in turn took over the Boston & Lowell.

From August 1903 increased service between Claremont Center and Claremont Jct. was provided by the Claremont RY and Lighting Company's electric street railway line, built after merger in 1901 of the Claremont Street RY and the Claremont Electric Light Co. At its zenith, the company operated cars over almost 8.5 miles of track, including a second track between Claremont Center and West Claremont. Passenger service was provided until 1930.

After World War II the Concord & Claremont was in trouble. In 1954 the B&M proposed that the line beyond West Concord be abandoned. Samuel M. Pinsly, who owned other New England short lines, proposed to purchase the line, including the original Contoocook Valley line to Emerson. A new Claremont & Concord RY, was incorporated on July 12, 1954, to complete the acquisition, although

Among the three surviving Claremont & Concord covered bridges is this one across the Sugar River near Kellyville, shown in August 1999. (R. D. Karr)

operation did not commence until much later that year. The Pinsly company also acquired the Claremont RY from the four freight customers that jointly owned it and converted it to diesel traction.

Passenger service between Concord and Claremont ended in 1955. All service ceased east of Contoocook in 1958 owing to serious flood damage to a trestle over the Contoocook River. An extensive Army Corps of Engineers flood control project for the river valley would have required realignment, the cost of which could not be justified. Abandonment of the West Concord–Contoocook length was approved in 1960, along with the portion of the Contoocook Valley from Emerson to West Hopkinton. Mill closures brought about a gradual death: the C&C east of Bradford to Contoocook and on to West Hopkinton was abandoned in 1961; further cutbacks, to Newport in 1964, and to East Claremont on September 1, 1977, were approved. The B&M ceased to operate the West Concord line in 1981, but it was left to Guilford to formally abandon during 1984.

At the western end, the Pinsly group maintained operations until 1988. Their application to abandon throughout was approved; but LaValley Building Supply formed the Claremont Concord RR Corporation, supported by three other freight customers, to purchase it instead on October 19, 1988. Most of the old Claremont RY was abandoned, however, and another mile and a half of track in Claremont was given up.

Operation over the rest of the Claremont RY continued until 1994 when service to the CPM paper mill on the Sugar River ceased. The track was removed during the summer of 1997. Three customers survived: LaValley itself, an Akzo salt unloading facility (now gone), and a scrap dealer. Only the final two miles between Claremont and Claremont Jct. remain of the old Concord & Claremont. The C&C's workshops in Claremont now rehabilitate locomotives and other rolling stock for other railroads as well.

Sources: Baker, *Formation*, 101, 123; Karr, *Lost Railroads*, 117, 118, 120, 136, 150; Lewis, *American Shortline Railway Guide*, 64; Mead, *Through Covered Bridges*; *Railpace* 16 (Nov. 1997): 37; 17 (May 1998): 37.

22. New Hampshire Central

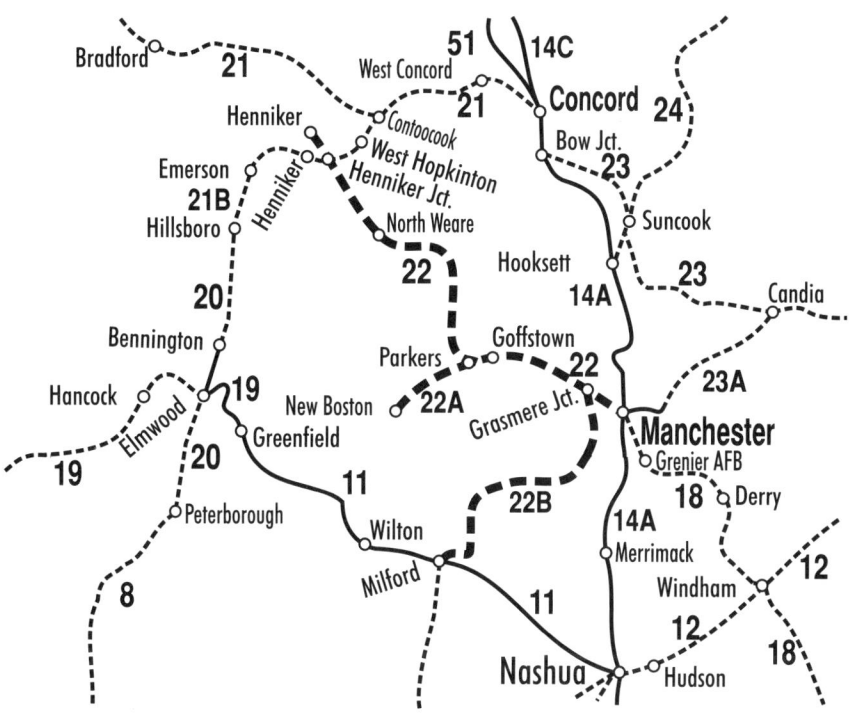

0 Manchester, NH	12.5 Sargent	2.5 Lang
1 West Manchester (Bedford)	15 South Weare (Everett)	6 New Boston, NH
4 Pinardville	16 East Weare	
5 Grasmere (Grasmere Jct.)	19 North Weare	**22B. Manchester & Milford Branch**
7 Shirley Hill (Shirley)	22 Colby	
8 Goffstown (Goffstown Center)	24 Henniker Jct.	0 Grasmere Jct., NH
	24.5 Henniker (Crescent St.), NH	2 Tirell Hill
10 Parkers (Parker)		6 Bedford
10.5 Riverdale (Oil Mills)	**22A. New Boston RR**	16 Amherst
	0 Parkers, NH	18.5 East Milford, NH

22. New Hampshire Central

Built: 1849-50; New Boston RR, 1893; Manchester & Milford, 1899-1900.

Operators: *New Hampshire Central*, 1850-53; *Merrimac & Connecticut Rivers*, 1853-58; *Concord*, 1858-89; *Concord & Montreal*, 1889-95; *Boston & Maine*, 1895-1980.

Daily Passenger Trains: *1869:* 2; *1893:* 4; *1915:* 4; *1929:* 4 (Parkers-New Boston, 4); *1932:* 2. Passenger service ended Grasmere Jct.-Milford, 1924; Parkers-New Boston, 1931; Manchester-Henniker, 1936.

Abandonments: North Weare-Henniker, 1858 (restored North Weare-Henniker Jct., 1891; finally abandoned 1937); Grasmere Jct.-Milford, 1926; Parkers-New Boston, 1935; west of Goffstown-North Weare, 1937; in Goffstown, 1976; Manchester-Goffstown, 1981.

Manchester business interests promoted the New Hampshire Central RR, which obtained a charter on June 24, 1848, for a line from Manchester to Claremont. The Contoocook Valley and Concord & Claremont Valley RRs received charters the same day. This was railway mania, for such development could hardly be justified by traffic potential. The C&C and NHC merged as the Merrimac & Connecticut Rivers RR in 1853, and leased the Contoocook Valley. A connection was installed at Henniker between the NHC and CV from north to west. The primary focus of the M&CR was completion of the C&C west from Bradford, but this had not been accomplished when the M&CR entered receivership five years later. The Concord RR leased the former NHC on condition that the tracks between North Weare and Henniker be removed to prevent their use to bypass the Concord's Manchester-Concord main line. It was the first railroad abandonment in northern New England. Renamed the Manchester & North Weare RR, the company was sold to the Concord in 1868.

For twenty years the line eked out an existence exporting agricultural produce and importing fertilizer and other material necessary to sustain a rural economy. The Concord & Montreal RR took over in 1889 and reconstructed the North Weare-Henniker Jct. link in 1891, although reopening was delayed until 1893. The final portion of the original line from the junction across the river into Henniker Center was not rebuilt.

22. New Hampshire Central

While all this was going on, the C&M supported a project by the New Boston RR for a branch railroad along the Piscataquog River south branch to a connection with the Nashua & Lowell RR at Milford. A charter was obtained in February 1891, and opening to New Boston was in June 1893 under lease by the C&M. The New York-based architect Bradford Lee Gilbert had been appointed to design a lavish through station at New Boston. A fire destroyed all but the stone and stucco in 1895, and Gilbert was again appointed to undertake rebuilding, producing an even more grandiose structure, featuring a rotunda and spire-capped roof and an exposed fieldstone chimney piercing a mock half-timbered gable.

When the B&M took over in 1895, thoughts of extending beyond New Boston ended. The Fitchburg RR had reached Milford via the Brookline & Milford RR that year. To deter the Fitchburg from extending this line into Manchester, the B&M built the Manchester & Milford Branch, with junctions at each end deliberately laid in the "wrong" direction, in order to discourage Fitchburg RR traffic. By the time the line was completed in 1900, it was an anachronism, for that year the B&M took over the Fitchburg. The B&M now had a virtually useless line, owing to inappropriate junction layouts and almost no local traffic. The line was abandoned in 1926, but the track was not removed until 1930. Some of the alignment in Bedford and Goffstown is now occupied by State Highways 114 and 101.

Passengers at the East Weare depot near the end of the nineteenth century are about to board a train. (Courtesy Walker Transportation Collection, Beverly Historical Society & Museum)

By 1930 maintenance of the rest of the NHC was minimal. The track to New Boston was embargoed in 1931, and all service ceased on June 15; abandonment was approved on December 28, 1934. New Boston Station remains today; it was sold and eventually became a police station, with shared use by the local Chamber of Commerce and a kindergarten; it is now a private residence. A small stone waiting shelter at Lang also survives.

Flooding in March 1936 caused by heavy rainfall and early thaw of snow and ice took out parts of the line between Goffstown and Henniker Jct. Permission to abandon was obtained almost immediately, and track was removed in 1937. Goffstown continued to be served as a branch from Manchester, with the station and yard layout retained, together with about 4000 feet of the main line to the west for switching purposes. Fire destroyed a covered bridge over the Piscataquog River in Goffstown in 1976, and freight service was cut back to a passing siding on the east bank. Four years later even that ceased; permission to abandon was obtained in 1981. It is possible to walk the line from Manchester to Goffstown, although bridges over the Piscataquog River at West Manchester and west of Goffstown are derelict.

Sources: Baker, *Formation*, 130-31; Karr, *Rail Lines*, 209-11; Karr, *Lost Railroads*, 72, 82, 91, 93, 141; Potter, *Great American Railroad Stations*, 103-4.

23. Portsmouth & Concord

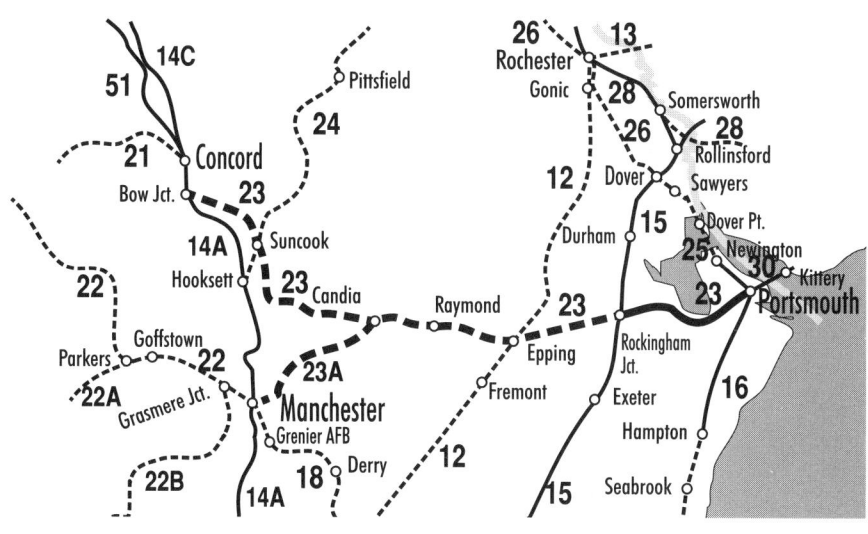

		23A. Manchester Line
0 Portsmouth, NH	17 Epping	
3 Pickering	20.5 West Epping	0 Candia, NH
3.5 Greenland	22 Raymond	4 Auburn
5 Bayside	25 Onway Lake	5 Severance
7 Stratham	27 East Candia	7 Massabesic
9 Rockingham Jct.	29 Candia	9 East Manchester
(Newmarket Jct.)	32 Rowes Corner	(Hallsville)
(Rockingham)	36 Suncook	12.5 Manchester, NH
12.5 Littlefield	38 Pembroke	
15 Hedding (East Epping)	39 Bow Jct., NH	

Built: 1847–62.

Operators: *Portsmouth & Concord*, 1852–57; *Concord & Portsmouth*, 1857–58; *Concord*, 1858–89; *Concord & Montreal*, 1889–95; *Boston & Maine*, 1895–1983; *Guilford*, 1983–.

Daily Passenger Trains (Portsmouth–Manchester): *1869:* 4; *1893:* 6; *1915:* 7; *1920:* 5; *1935:* 4; *1950:* 4. Regular passenger service ended 1954; mixed train service ca. 1963.

Abandonments: Candia–Suncook, 1862 (see text); Bow Jct.–Suncook, 1953; Rockingham Jct.–East Manchester, 1982.

23. Portsmouth & Concord

On July 1, 1845, the state of New Hampshire approved charters for two railroads: the Portsmouth, New Market & Concord to build a line from Portsmouth or the Boston & Maine line to some location between Concord and Manchester; and the Portsmouth, New Market & Exeter. Both were intended to promote Portsmouth as a seaboard outlet for manufactured goods, primarily textiles. They merged on December 23, 1845, as the Portsmouth & Concord RR, and the new line's charter was amended in 1848 to include a branch from Candia or Hooksett to Manchester. Portsmouth was already served by the Eastern and the Portland, Saco & Portsmouth RRs by 1842. Completion of the P&C was long drawn out; the terminals of the Eastern RR in Portsmouth and the Concord RR in Concord were finally linked in 1852.

The P&C failed in 1855 but was reorganized in 1857 as the Concord & Portsmouth RR. Still struggling, the company was forced to accept an egregious five-year lease by the Concord RR effective from September 11, 1858. The Concord demanded that the previously pro-

On the only active section of the P&C, a Guilford switcher pauses at Rockingham Jct. in April 1999. (R. D. Karr)

23. Portsmouth & Concord

posed branch to Manchester be built from Candia and that the existing line between Candia and Concord be abandoned, thus blocking a potentially competitive route between Manchester and Concord. Upon opening of the branch in 1862, the Candia–Suncook length was torn up, and the Concord itself bought the segment of the P&C between Suncook and Bow Jct. This later became part of the Suncook Valley RR and was finally abandoned along with that line in 1953.

By the 1870s Manchester had become the manufacturing center of New Hampshire with five cotton and two wool mills (Concord had just two of each), and the line had adequate traffic to sustain existence for over one hundred years. The station at Epping was rebuilt in 1874 as a joint facility with the Nashua & Rochester RR, with which rail connections were provided from the east. The Concord continued to operate the line until 1889 when the lease passed to the Concord's successor, the Concord & Montreal RR. Six years later the B&M gained control when it took over the C&M. The B&M gained a majority of stock in 1940, and purchased the line outright in 1944.

Scheduled passenger service lasted until 1954, provided by gas-electric units. Mixed trains, carrying passengers in the caboose, continued to operate until the early 1960s. Regular freight service was eventually discontinued by the B&M between Raymond and East Manchester (near Lake Massabesic) during 1981. A short length in Manchester remained to serve an industrial park north of Massabesic Street, but this is no longer in use. The track east of Raymond to Rockingham was used sporadically for another year, but permission to abandon was eventually obtained. East of Rockingham, the line is now part of Guilford's Portsmouth Running Track, with up to two switching operations daily, providing Portsmouth's only rail access. This is the only part of the Portsmouth & Concord still in use.

The alignment west of Rockingham to Massabesic Street in Manchester can be walked. It is an extremely pleasant contrast with the parallel US Route 101. The original passenger depot in Raymond lives on and is occupied by the local historical society.

Sources: Baker, *Formation*, 125–130; Boston & Maine Railroad, *Corporate History*; Niles, "Change Trains at Rockingham Junction"; Karr, *Lost Railroads*, 72, 89, 140, 141.

24. Suncook Valley

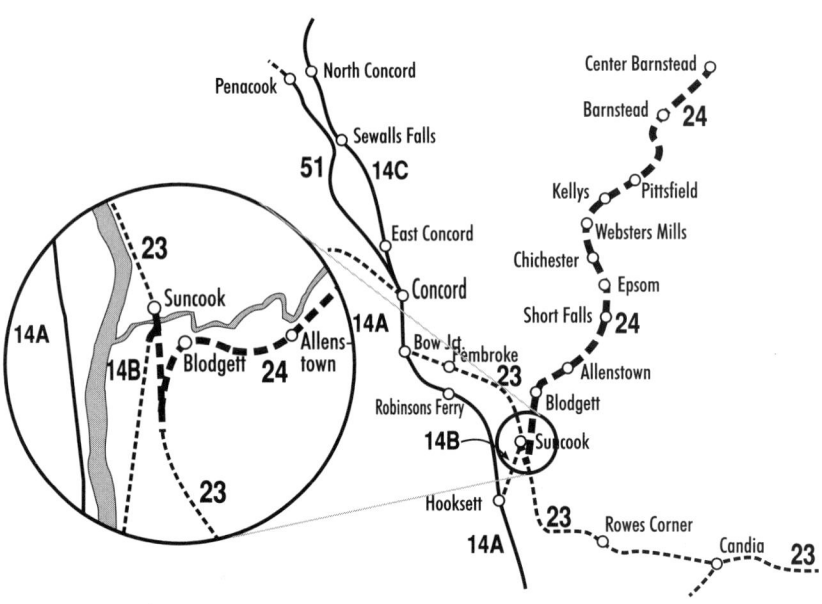

0 Suncook, NH	9 Chichester (North	15.5 Barnstead
1 Blodgett	Chichester)	18.5 Center Barnstead (Centre
2 Allenstown	11 Websters Mills	Barnstead), NH
5 Short Falls	12 Kellys	
7.5 Epsom	13.5 Pittsfield	

Built: 1869-89.

Operators: *Concord*, 1869-89; *Concord & Montreal*, 1889-95; *Boston & Maine*, 1895-1924; *Suncook Valley*, 1924-53.

Daily Passenger Trains: *1869:* 2; *1889:* 4; *1910:* 4; *1925:* 4; 1951 (Suncook Valley Jct.-Center Barnstead) : 4. Passenger service ended Pittsfield-Center Barnstead, 1943; Bow Jct.-Pittsfield, 1952.

Abandonments: Pittsfield-Center Barnstead, 1947; Suncook Valley Jct.-Pittsfield, 1953.

24. Suncook Valley

To serve the area in east central New Hampshire east of Concord the Suncook Valley RR was chartered on January 4, 1849, to build northeastward along the Suncook River valley to Pittsfield. Another charter was obtained in the name of the Suncook Valley Extension RR on July 6, 1849, to extend the line to Alton on Lake Winnipesaukee, partly in an attempt to block extension of the Boston & Maine over the Cochecho RR. The B&M, however, took no interest in the Cochecho until 1864. Until then, the SV schemes languished, but were revived in the mid-1860s with backing by the Concord RR. From Suncook, two miles southeast of Concord, the line was completed to Pittsfield in December 1869. The Concord RR used the western end of the former Portsmouth & Concord line, which it had acquired in 1862, to provide a connection with Bow Jct., and also built a 1.7-mile link south to Hooksett to complete the Hooksett Loop. The SV also took over a short section of the abandoned P&C south from Suncook with which it connected by way of switchback.

Traffic was never substantial. During the mid-1880s, however, during the Boston, Concord & Montreal RR's debacle with the Boston &

A Suncook Valley mixed train pulls into Chichester station in April 1949. (Courtesy Walker Transportation Collection, Beverly Historical Society & Museum)

Maine over the Lake Shore RR, the Suncook Valley Extension charter was revived. Grading toward Alton was begun, but work stopped when negotiations for merger of the Concord and BC&M commenced and construction of the Lake Shore RR was no longer a potential threat. The extension opened as far as the small wool mill town of Center Barnstead in the fall of 1889, but never went any further. The SV became another B&M branch line in 1895.

The entire line was a rural backwater conveying primarily agricultural traffic. As part of the first major B&M economy program, the SV was returned to local management on September 28, 1924. Company offices were located in Pittsfield. From then until 1933 SV passenger trains connected with B&M trains operating between Concord and Portsmouth over the Hooksett Loop, although the Suncook–Hooksett line was out of service owing to flood damage to bridges between March and August 1927.

When passenger service over the loop ended around the end of 1934, passengers made a bus connection at Blodgett for either Manchester or Concord. Floods in March 1936 again took out the link with Hooksett and also a bridge across the Merrimack River south of Bow Jct. Thus isolated, the SV negotiated lease of the Hooksett loop from the Hooksett bridge to Bow Jct. and obtained trackage rights into Concord. Trains began running on May 12, 1936. All service was suspended in spring 1943 following a derailment, but was not resumed between Pittsfield and Center Barnstead after repair. The ICC was petitioned for abandonment of the SV north of Pittsfield on December 8, 1944, and approval was granted effective March 31, 1947.

By 1950 just one locomotive hobbled over deteriorated track hauling a twice-daily (except Sundays) mixed train. The shortest end-to-end journey time for a trip to or from Concord was 1 hour 40 minutes. The SV company bought the Bow Jct.–Suncook section from the B&M in December 1950. When creditors threatened to take possession of the SV's sole locomotive, closure was inevitable; the final train ran on December 15, 1952. Freight cars were removed to Concord on December 20. Permission to abandon was obtained in 1953. Almost all of the alignment between Suncook and Allenstown has been obliterated by roads, but most of the rest of the right of way can still be traced.

Sources: Hutchins, *Blueberry Express,* 49, 54, 55–57; Karr, *Lost Railroads,* 72, 107, 108, 112.

25. Portsmouth & Dover

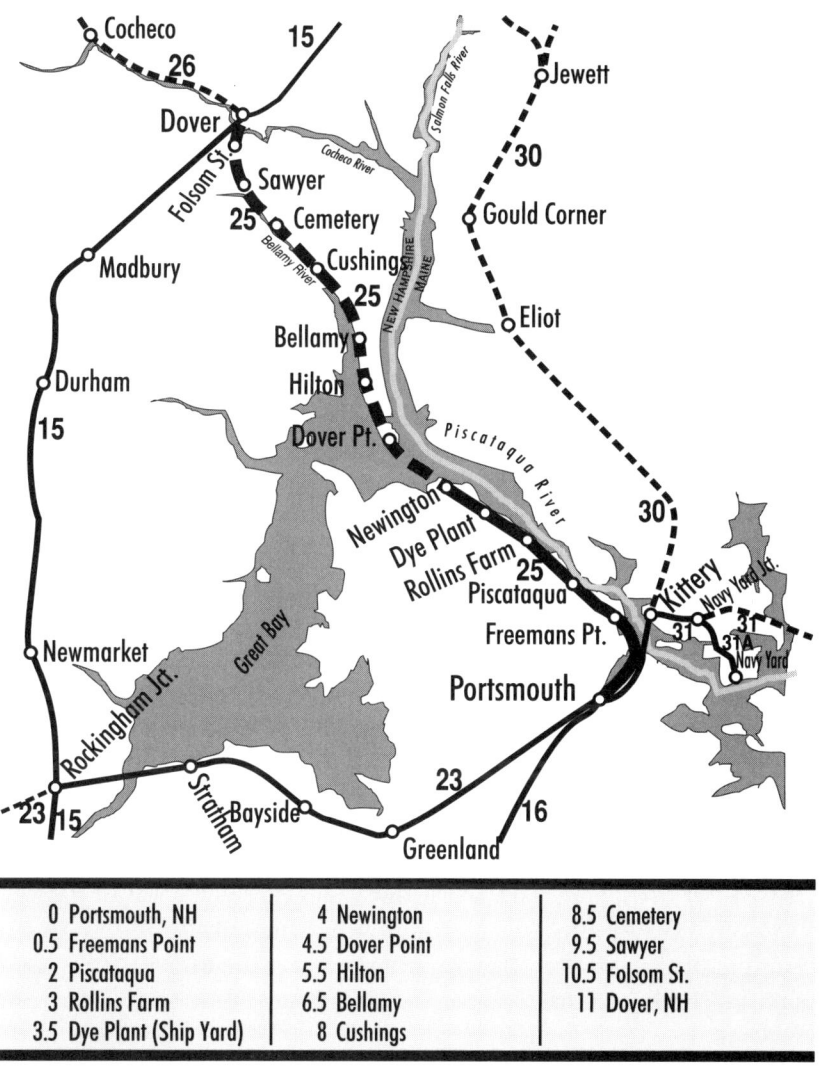

0 Portsmouth, NH	4 Newington	8.5 Cemetery
0.5 Freemans Point	4.5 Dover Point	9.5 Sawyer
2 Piscataqua	5.5 Hilton	10.5 Folsom St.
3 Rollins Farm	6.5 Bellamy	11 Dover, NH
3.5 Dye Plant (Ship Yard)	8 Cushings	

Built: 1873–74.

Operators: *Eastern*, 1874–84; *Boston & Maine*, 1884–1983; *Guilford*, 1983–.

Daily Passenger Trains: *1893:* 11; *1915:* 4; *1920:* 4; *1924:* 2; *1926:* 6; *1933:* 6. Passenger service ended 1933.

Abandonments: Newington–Dover Point, 1934; Dover Point–Sawyers, 1941; Sawyers–Dover, 1986.

Backed by the Eastern RR, the Portsmouth & Dover RR was chartered on July 7, 1866. The new line would serve the expanded wharves, quays, and industrial facilities in Portsmouth on the west bank of the Piscataqua River, and provide a shorter route to the coast for Dover mill traffic. Construction did not get underway until 1873.

Most of the line was single track. The first few miles, from a junction with the Portland, Saco & Portsmouth RR at the south end of its Piscataqua River bridge, required some grading over low-lying land. Bridging of the Great Bay involved a 1700-foot through truss bridge to provide headroom for seagoing vessels. Approaches to the bridge required considerable earthwork to meet the maximum permitted ruling gradient of 2.2 percent. In Dover, the line turned generally northward to cross the Cocheco River and enter Dover center. During the eighteenth century the river had been diverted by a cut across the narrow neck of an ox-bow, creating an island; the P&D filled the southern gap with a causeway and built a wrought-iron undertruss bridge at the northern end to maintain navigation. Dover had been an inland port since dredging of the river in the early nineteenth century. A sizable passenger terminal was provided on Chestnut Street entirely separate from the B&M facility. A spur led to a junction just east of the B&M/Cochecho RR connection, where a freight house was built.

Upon opening on February 1, 1874, the line was leased to the Eastern RR. It prospered with the growth and diversification of industry between Portsmouth and Newington and manufacturing in Dover. During the decade after the line became part of the B&M Eastern Division in 1884, various changes were made to facilitate operating arrangements. The junction freight facility at Dover was closed in the mid-1890s following construction of extensive yard facilities near Oak Street. The original P&D depot in Dover closed in 1897 when the B&M station was remodeled.

Competition from southern textile mills toward the end of the century and a flood in 1896 eroded Dover's economic base. Many mills were closed in the first decades of the new century. Passenger and

25. Portsmouth & Dover

freight service was reduced dramatically. During the 1920s, the state raised the possibility of shared use of the Great Bay bridge by road traffic, and terms were readily accepted. The deck was reconstructed and traffic signals installed for control of vehicular movements when a train was crossing. The bridge became, in effect, an extremely long grade crossing.

Passenger trains were withdrawn in 1933, with the last trip on August 12, after the state had completed an independent crossing of Great Bay by what is now Route 16. Through freight service ceased at the same time. Permission to abandon the bridge was obtained in 1934. Contraction of service took place rapidly thereafter. Service south of Dover was cut back to a mill located about 0.6 miles south of Sawyer in 1936 and reduced further in March 1938.

Industry on the length between Portsmouth and Newington provided—and still provides—considerable traffic. Chemical and oil companies were the main customers in Newington. When Pease Air Force Base was built during the mid-1950s, a spur was built from just east of Newington.

When Guilford bought the B&M, returns on the Sawyer spur were, at best, marginal, but the Portsmouth–Newington branch produced significant return. Guilford closed the line from just north of the Cocheco River bridge in Dover, but retained about 600 feet south from the Third Street station site, as a layover and for switching long trains from Oak Street Yard. Use of this spur caused considerable inconvenience to road traffic, particularly at the complex Chestnut Street/Third Street intersection, and Guilford finally agreed to sell the land to the city of Dover for use as a parking lot. The Cocheco River bridge is fenced and gradually rotting. Southward the line has been reclaimed by nature and by the Spaulding Turnpike from just north of where it left the Bellamy River valley at Sawyer.

The track from Portsmouth to Newington remains in daily use, serving Sprague Energy terminals and a wire and cable factory two or three times daily. The former Pease AFB, now an airport and industrial park, has not seen trains for many years.

Sources: Baker, *Formation*, 146, 158; Cobb and Shaw, "Dover"; Karr, *Lost Railroads*, 89, 104, 148; Maine Dept. of Transportation, *Historical and Archeological Resources*.

26. Cochecho

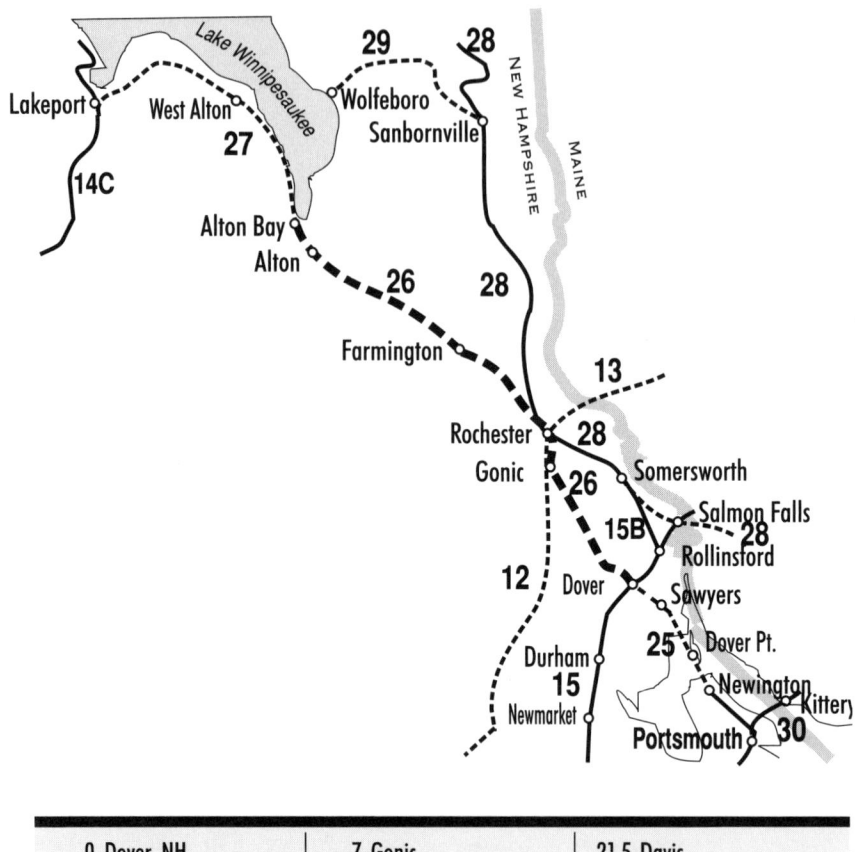

0 Dover, NH	7 Gonic	21.5 Davis
4 Cocheco (Cocheko)	8.5 Rochester	24 New Durham
(Cochecho)	14 Place	27 Alton
6 Pickering	16.5 Farmington	29 Alton Bay, NH

Built: 1847-51.

Operators: *Cochecho*, 1849-62; *Dover & Winnipiseogee*, 1862-64; *Boston & Maine*, 1864-1983; *Guilford*, 1983-93; *New Hampshire Northcoast*, 1993-95.

Daily Passenger Trains: *1869:* 4; *1893:* 6; *1910:* 6; *1919:* 6; *1926:* 4; *1931:* 1. Passenger service ended 1935.

26. Cochecho

Abandonments: Dover [0.5 miles north]-Gonic, 1943; Farmington-Alton Bay, 1942; Gonic-Rochester, 1983; at Dover, 1984; Rochester-Farmington, 1995.

Dover was originally known as Cochecho, a variant spelling of the river to the east of which the original settlement lay. In 1847 a railroad adopting that name was chartered to build from the Boston & Maine RR in Dover to Rochester and onward along the south shore of Lake Winnipesaukee to a connection with the Boston, Concord & Montreal RR at some undetermined location. Like similar lines, the venture was planned with the goal of leasing the line to the B&M. The alignment commenced in Dover from a junction facing southbound at the site of the later passenger station and curved sharply northward to parallel the river.

Completion in stages took place over the next few years, but money ran out when Alton Bay was reached in 1851. While the line conveyed some freight traffic, the B&M refused to lease it because it was incomplete. The Cochecho struggled for several years before declaring bankruptcy in 1861. Operations continued, however, and the company was reorganized as the Dover & Winnipiseogee RR on July 1, 1862. Tourist traffic to Alton Bay, where connections were made with lake steamers, was a mainstay during summers. There matters rested until 1864, when the B&M yielded to local public opinion and reluctantly agreed to a lease. Apathy soon disappeared; the B&M *Annual Report* for 1866 said that

> Since we came into possession of the Dover & Winnipisoegee [sic] Railroad, Dover has become more of a centre [sic] than formerly. Consequently, arrangements have been made to have the rails repaired and other mechanical work done at that Junction, which was formerly done at the Rollinsford Junction and other places.

The line throughout was progressively upgraded to B&M standards, although most effort was devoted to the length between Dover and Rochester, over which a proportion of traffic could be diverted from the Eastern-controlled Portsmouth, Great Falls & Conway RR. Nothing was done to extend beyond Alton Bay despite continued public pressure on the New Hampshire legislature. Connection with the BC&M was eventually established by the Lake Shore RR at Alton Bay in 1889. Passenger train service then grew, but both freight and passen-

26. Cochecho

ger traffic declined significantly after 1930. The B&M closed the Lake Shore RR in 1935 and withdrew all passenger service on the former Cochecho after July 8. The line west of Farmington to Alton Bay was closed in 1941 and abandoned the following year, along with the length from just north of Dover to Gonic.

The remaining tracks were retained for many years as freight spurs serving Davidson Rubber in Farmington and Eastern Propane in Gonic. The Rochester–Gonic branch was officially abandoned in 1983, but continued in use as an industrial spur until the single customer moved its facility to the New Hampshire Northcoast RR line at North Rochester in 1990.

On October 10, 1993, Guilford sold the Farmington line to the NHN, which had some years earlier taken over operation of the Conway Branch from Rollinsford. There was little traffic, and operation ceased in June 1995. The line was dismantled, rails and ties were salvaged for reuse, and the right of way was sold to the state for $200,000; in the absence of rail traffic, it is now a recreational trail.

Sources: Karr, *Lost Railroads*, 105, 143; Lenk, "Birth of the Boston & Maine"; Maine Dept. of Transportation, *Historical and Archeological Resources*, Appendix C, 14; Philbrook, "Lake Shore Railroad"; *Railpace* 16 (Nov. 1997): 37.

A Boston & Maine train rounds a curve on the Cochecho near Alton in the first decade of the twentieth century. (Courtesy Walker Transportation Collection, Beverly Historical Society & Museum)

27. Lake Shore

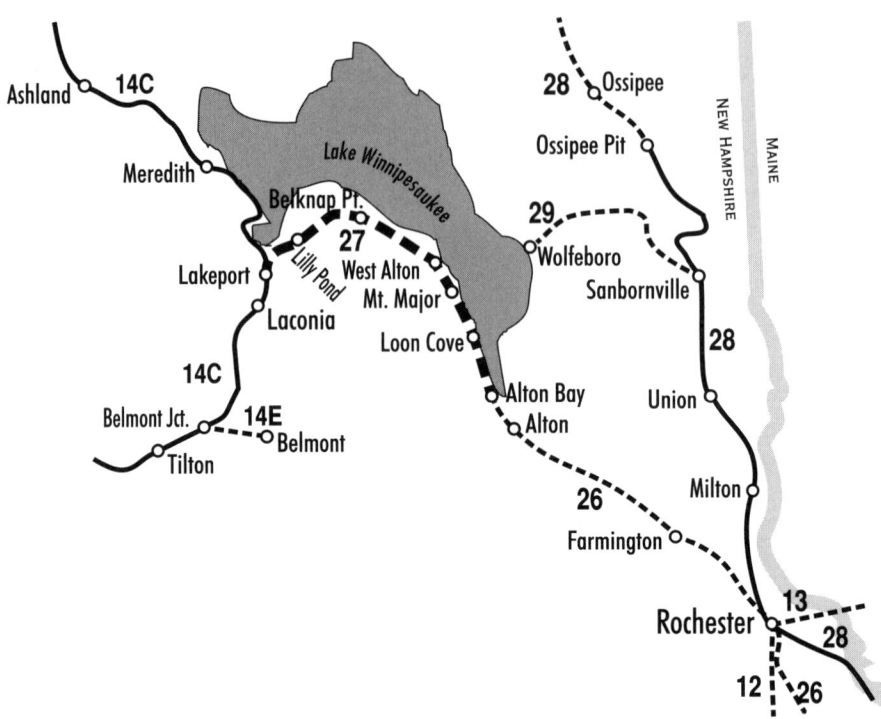

0 Lakeport, NH	7 Lake Shore Park	13.5 Mt. Major
2.5 Lily Pond	(Ellacoya)	14.5 Brookhurst
3.5 Meadowbrook	7.5 Terrace Hill	15 Buckley
4 Gilford (Sanders)	8.5 Ames	15.5 Loon Cove
(Saunders)	9 Spring Haven	16 Keewaydin
4.5 Glendale	10 Smiths Point	17 Alton Bay, NH
5.5 Belknap Point	10.5 West Alton	
6.5 Greystone	12 Woodlands	

Built: 1888-90.

Operators: *Concord & Montreal,* 1890-95; *Boston & Maine,* 1895-ca. 1980.

Daily Passenger Trains: *1893:* 6; *1907:* 8; *1915:* 4; *1930:* 4. Passenger service ended 1935.

27. Lake Shore

Abandonments: Lily Pond–Alton Bay, 1935; Lakeport [1 mile north]–Lily Pond, 1942; at Lakeport, ca. 1980.

In 1847 the Cochecho RR obtained a charter to build a line from the Boston & Maine RR in Dover to some point on the Boston, Concord & Montreal line in Belknap County. The Cochecho opened its line from Dover to Alton Bay in 1851. The Lake Shore RR, intended to complete the missing link between Alton Bay and Lakeport, took almost forty years to come to fruition.

Public pressure on the New Hampshire legislature to force one or the other main lines to complete the link was unsuccessful, in part because of opposition from the BC&M. Charles A. Busiel, a locally-based trustee of the BC&M and later state governor, approached the B&M but was rebuffed. A slight softening of opposition occurred in 1884 when the B&M and the BC&M agreed that if the line were to be built, the latter should have the right to subscribe to and lease it if substantial completion took place by January 1, 1889; otherwise, the B&M would have an option on the rights.

Busiel organized the Lake Shore Railroad in July 1884, proposing an alignment to pass through his property at Lake Village in Lakeport. A dispute over acquisition of the BC&M by the Boston & Lowell RR, protracted by the B&M's lease of the B&L in 1887, delayed action again. The BC&M was reluctant to aid the LS, but at the annual shareholders meeting on May 28, 1888, a motion in favor of construction was passed, and the directors voted to take $300,000 of stock. With less than five months left in the construction season, completion was scheduled for December 10, 1888.

The schedule was ambitious to say the least. The prime contractor awarded three subcontracts to enable around-the-clock activity. Some months later, a large group of BC&M stockholders sought an injunction barring subscription to LS stock on the grounds that overall company indebtedness was affecting their rights to a fair and reasonable return on investment. A temporary stay on the company resulted in an almost general strike September 21 when one crew was not paid wages. The case was referred to the State Supreme Court, which ruled against the contractor on September 27.

Just two and a half months remained until the deadline for completion. The BC&M made it happen with an injection of capital. To complete the line, worn rail recovered from the main line between Concord

A Concord & Montreal passenger train, hauled by a vintage 4-4-0 American locomotive, approaches Belknap Point station on a wintry day in the 1890s, not long after the Lake Shore finally opened. (Courtesy Brent S. Michiels, Walker Transportation Collection, Beverly Historical Society & Museum)

and Tilton was laid on new oak and hemlock ties. A July 1889 opening was proposed by the BC&M's successor, the Concord & Montreal, which would operate the line. Late rail deliveries caused postponement to fall. Although inauguration ceremonies were held on October 25, more work was required during the winter. The first revenue train of pulpwood ran from West Alton to Lakeport in the third week of January 1890, followed by shipment of 500,000 tons of ice valued at almost $2 million over the ensuing months. At the formal opening on June 17 trains carried guests to a ceremony at Alton Bay, followed by a sumptuous repast at the Hotel Wonolancet in Laconia.

Passenger business was foremost. Advertisements promoted lots along the line. Lake Shore Point was developed as a resort, a hotel there opening on June 26, 1891. Two steamboats of the C&M's Winnipesaukee Steamboat Company subsidiary plied the lake. Passenger train timetables were designed around connections with main line services through Lakeport and Dover. Freight traffic was minimal.

27. Lake Shore

When the B&M took over in 1895 significant changes were made. Promotion of passenger traffic continued. The first consolidated schedule published in October that year included a through passenger train between Lakeport and Dover. Three additional stations introduced in the early 1900s brought the average spacing close to that of a rapid transit system. To reduce journey time and operating cost, all stations except Glendale and West Alton (and Lake Shore Park in the summer season) were designated as flag stops. Freight was handled by one daily train on weekdays and Saturdays. In 1911, the line and its connection with Dover, the former Cochecho RR, had become the Lakeport Branch.

The summers-only *Maine Coast Special*, operated in 1930, 1931, and 1932, was a last-ditch effort to keep the line viable. Through sleeping cars were run over the Lake Shore as part of a through route between Montreal and Portland. Connections at Lakeport became increasingly inconvenient, and between 1930 and 1934 passenger traffic was almost halved; freight traffic declined 97 percent as goods were transferred to highways. Abandonment was inevitable; the last trains ran on July 9, 1935. Passenger service over the line to Dover ceased simultaneously.

At Alton Bay, a short length was retained for freight switching until 1942. From Lakeport to Lily Pond just over a mile of track remained in use as an industrial spur to serve Grossman's lumber yard, but this was closed about 1980. Some of the right of way has been taken for road improvements, but most of it can be hiked. Several station buildings remain, although some have been much altered. Belknap Point depot has been moved a short distance away from the alignment.

Sources: Blaisdell, *Three Centuries;* Karr, *Lost Railroads*, 91, 106; Philbrook, "Lake Shore Railroad."

Boston & Maine no. 3800, an EMD E-7 locomotive, hauls train 2918 through Sanbornville in September 1954. (Donald Robinson, courtesy Walker Transportation Collection, Beverly Historical Society & Museum)

28. Portsmouth, Great Falls & Conway

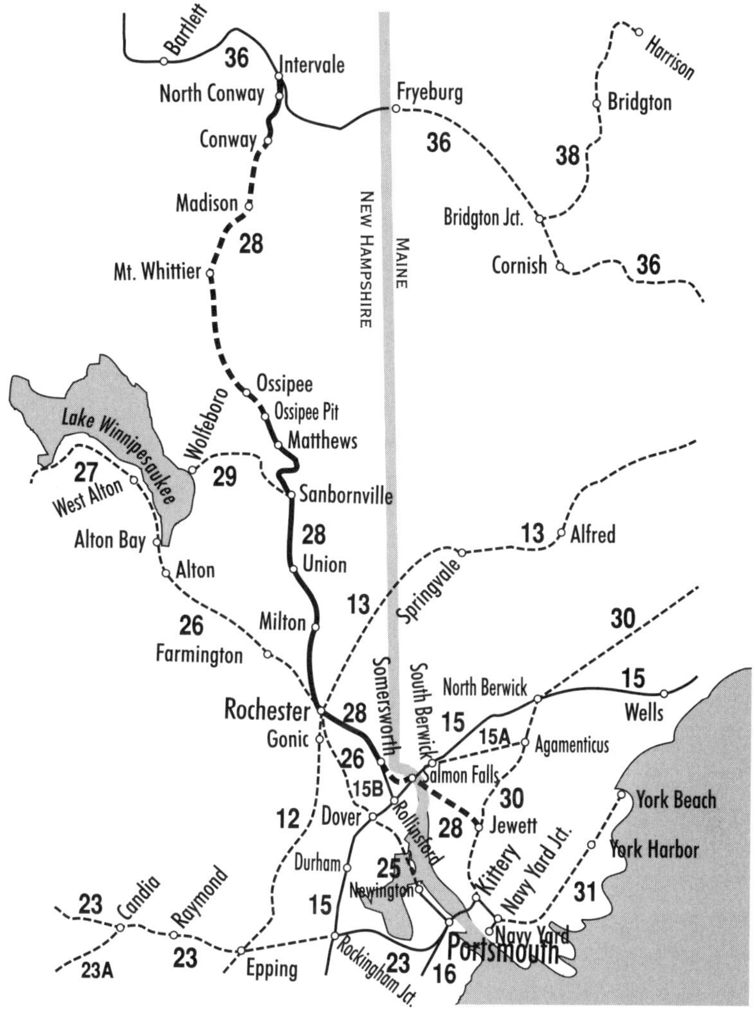

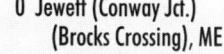

0 Jewett (Conway Jct.) (Brocks Crossing), ME	5 Somersworth (Great Falls)	30 Sanbornville Union Sta. (Sanbornville) (Wolfeboro Jct.)
1 Great Works, ME	12 Rochester	32 Wakefield
3 Salmon Falls (Cotton Mill), NH	17 Hayes (Hayes Crossing)	36 Burleyville (Hillsdale) (East Mathews) (East Wakefield)
4 Foundry	18 South Milton	
	20 Milton	
	26 Union	

28. Portsmouth, Great Falls & Conway

39 Mathews (North Wakefield)	51 Lakewood (Ossipee Valley)	71 North Conway
42 Ossipee Pit	55 Mt. Whittier (West Ossipee)	73 Intervale, NH
44 Ossipee	59 Madisn (Silver Lake)	
49 Mountainview (Centre Ossipee)	60 Conway	

Built: 1848-72.

Operators: *Great Falls & Conway*, 1849-55; *Great Falls & South Berwick*, 1855-58, 1861-65; *Portsmouth, Great Falls & Conway*, 1865-70; *Eastern*, 1870-84; *Boston & Maine*, 1885-1983; *New Hampshire Northcoast*, 1986-; *Conway Scenic*, 1974-.

Daily Passenger Trains: *1869:* 4 (Jewett-Union); *1893:* 4; *1915:* 6; *1920:* 6; *1923:* 8; *1935:* 4; *1957:* 4 (Somersworth-Intervale); *1958:* 2 (Somersworth-Intervale). Passenger service ended Jewett-Somersworth, 1941; North Conway-Intervale, 1958; Somersworth-North Conway, 1961. Excursion trains operated North Conway-Conway, 1974-; North Conway-Intervale, 1995-.

Abandonments: Jewett-Somersworth, 1941; Mt. Whittier-Conway, 1972; Ossipee-Mt. Whittier, 1998.

The Portsmouth, Great Falls & Conway RR originated as the Great Falls & South Berwick RR, which was chartered on March 31, 1841, to run from the Portland, Saco & Portsmouth line to several mills at Somersworth. The scheme failed when a Boston & Maine branch from Rollinsford to Somersworth was approved and built in 1843. The Great Falls & Conway RR, with B&M backing, began operation from Somersworth to Rochester on March 6, 1849, in direct competition with the Cochecho RR from Dover. A year later the line was extended to South Milton, and five years later, in 1855, to Union.

By then, the GF&C was first pawn in a game of chess between the Eastern and the B&M. The Eastern guaranteed a mortgage bond issue that enabled the extension to Union; to the south, the Eastern revived the Great Falls & South Berwick, which opened on February 5, 1855. Both the GF&C and the GF&SB were bankrupt and reorganized during 1857. The GF&SB went bankrupt again within a year and closed until 1861, when trustees resumed operation. The Eastern foreclosed in 1865 in order to have both companies taken over by a new venture,

The PGF&C featured distinctive passenger depots, with steeples and gingerbread trim, such as this one at Wakefield, NH. (Courtesy Walker Transportation Collection, Beverly Historical Society & Museum)

the Portsmouth, Great Falls & Conway RR, chartered that year. Debts were paid through stock issued by the new company. In 1870 the Eastern leased the PGF&C and subscribed almost $500,000 of its stock. Construction resumed, and the line was completed north to West Ossipee in October 1871, and to North Conway in the spring of 1872. Through passenger service from Boston via Portsmouth commenced on June 3, 1872. An extension to Intervale, on the Portland & Ogdensburg line, was completed in 1875.

Nathaniel J. Bradlee designed a grand new North Conway station, described by Potter as a "Victorian interpretation of Russian provincial architecture." The B&M took over the lease of the PGF&C along with the rest of the Eastern system in 1885. Legal existence of the PGF&C ended on May 9, 1890, when it merged with the B&M.

A major customer, Salmon Falls Manufacturing Co., was dissolved in 1915 (although weaving continued until 1927), and lumber traffic was reduced in 1920 with closure of the Conway Lumber Co. mill, once the largest in New England. Thereafter the line was maintained primarily to convey through freight, sand from quarries north of Mathews, and Yield House furniture products from West Ossipee. All passenger trains south of Somersworth were diverted via Dover and Rollinsford from April 25, 1936. By 1941 the line between Jewett and Somersworth served just one freight customer, and abandonment followed in November.

When MEC passenger trains over the Portland & Ogdensburg line ceased in 1958, the B&M promptly cut back service to North Conway, subsequently removing all passenger trains on December 3, 1961. A gravel pit north of Mathews became the end of the line in October 1972. The B&M had petitioned to abandon the line from Mt. Whittier to Intervale in 1969; the ICC approved in 1972, provided that sale of the line should be to any party willing to continue rail operation. The North Conway Depot Co., which had owned the North Conway facilities since 1968, purchased the remaining property in Conway in 1974.

The site of the old PGF&C turntable at Jewett, ME, has been preserved as a monument to the railway era. (R. D. Karr)

28. Portsmouth, Great Falls & Conway

The company was the progenitor of the Conway Scenic RR, which began operation that year.

Guilford, which had taken over the B&M in 1983, sought permission to abandon north of Rochester in August 1985. The state of New Hampshire stepped in with an offer to purchase this section so that Ossipee Aggregates, Inc., the owner of the quarry at Ossipee Pit, could operate the railroad as the New Hampshire Northcoast Corporation. The new line started running on May 27, 1986, under a trackage rights agreement. Completion of the sale to the state in 1995 was followed by a track improvement program. The Surface Transportation Board authorized abandonment of 10.8 miles north of the quarry, unused for more than 25 years, effective January 2, 1998, apart from 3500 feet, which, ironically, Guilford retains. The tracks remain in place.

Between Jewett and South Berwick part of the alignment is used by State Route 236, and the rest is overgrown, although parts can be walked. Only the concrete abutments and stone piers of the bridge across Salmon Falls River, which also carried the station platforms, survive. The wooden depot building at Salmon Falls survived until 1995, gradually rotting, and with floors collapsed into the brick basement; someone with a sense of humor daubed "For Sale" on the exterior. The building's fate was to be deliberately burned down by the local fire department. Volunteers are converting the site into an attractive park. Northward to Somersworth the line is a broad trail owned by the state.

Sources: Bachelder, *Mountaineer*, 2-3, 12, 14-15; Baker, *Formation*, 146, 158-59; Bradlee, *Eastern*, 6, 8, 10; Cobb and Shaw, *Dover*, 11; Karr, *Lost Railroads*, 103,130-31; Lenk, "Birth of the Boston & Maine"; Lewis, *American Shortline Railway Guide*, 181; Potter, *Great American Railroad Stations*, 103-4; Waite, "Recycling," 32.

29. Wolfeborough

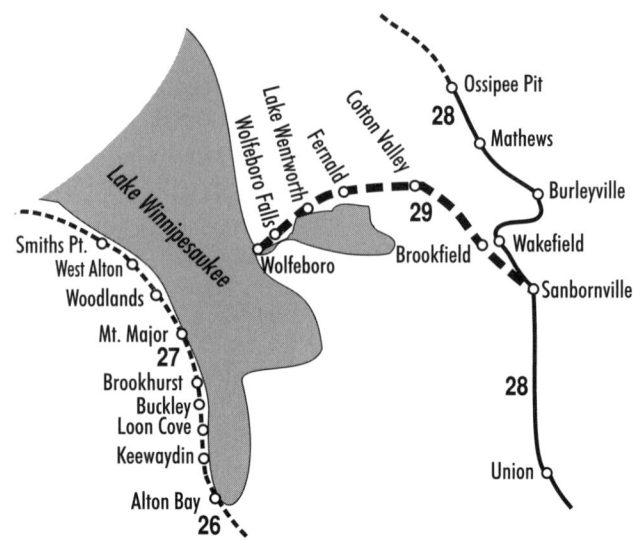

0 Sanbornville Union Sta. (Sanbornville) (Wolfeboro Jct.), NH	6 Cotton Valley (Cottonboro)	11.5 Wolfeboro Falls (Mill Village)
2 Brookfield	9.5 Fernald	12 Wolfeboro
	10 Lake Wentworth	12.1 "Wolfeboro Lake", NH

Built: 1869–70; 1900.

Operators: *Eastern*, 1872–84; *Boston & Maine*, 1884–1972; *Wolfeboro*, 1972–84.

Daily Passenger Trains: *1893:* 4; *1919:* 8; *1935:* 6. Passenger service ended 1938 (mixed trains until ca. 1950); re-opened as a tourist operation, 1972–1984.

Abandonments: Wolfeboro–"Wolfeboro Lake," 1935; Sanbornville–Wolfeboro, 1986.

Wolfeborough residents promoted this branch line in anticipation of connecting with the then incomplete Portsmouth, Great Falls & Conway RR at Sanbornville. After grant of a charter in 1868, the line was built through Brookfield and immediately north of Lake Wentworth (with its curiously named Stamp Act Island).

29. Wolfeborough

A long trestle across the western part of the lake was required to reach Wolfeborough, where a lavish two-story station was built, with ten dormer windows, extensive gingerbread valances at two levels, and a twenty-foot steeple surmounted by a locomotive-shaped weathervane.

Completed in 1870, the line did not realize its full potential until October 1871, when the PGF&C opened. Passenger trains were introduced in August 1872, operated under lease by the Eastern RR. The Eastern promoted the lakes as a summer resort to make the line competitive with the B&M-leased Cochecho and Lake Shore lines.

In 1900 the B&M extended the Wolfeborough about a tenth of a mile to the shore of Lake Winnipesaukee, where another station was built on the docks used by the steamships. This station, informally called Wolfeboro Lake, was open summers-only for many years, though, oddly enough, was apparently never shown in timetables. Freight traffic was conveyed by a single train each day, but passenger trains were relatively frequent, particularly during the summer season.

Resort traffic declined rapidly in the 1930s. There were no more passenger trains after 1938, although a mixed freight operated until around 1950, and most of the station buildings were sold or fell into ruin. By the 1960s freight was carried on an "as required" basis. Inevitably, a petition to abandon was filed in 1972.

With assistance from the town, a group of rail enthusiasts led by Donald Hallock, then with the Strasburg RR in Pennsylvania, incorporated a new Wolfeboro RR company. Steam-hauled passenger trains were operated, and the stations at Wolfeboro and Wolfeboro Lake were painstakingly rehabilitated. At Wolfeboro the platform canopy, steeple, and dormers were rebuilt by a high school industrial arts class.

By the early 1980s the line experienced financial difficulties, in part owing to competition from the Conway Scenic RR and later the Winnipesaukee RR. After the 1985 season the line closed, and it was not reopened the next year. Permission to abandon was given on April 6, 1986, just six weeks before the New Hampshire Northcoast commenced operation over the former PGF&C.

Wolfeboro station was struck by lightning in 1987. Fire damage repair was paid for by the town. The waiting room was converted to offices for the local Chamber of Commerce, with other parts of the building used for a kindergarten. The nearby freight house is privately owned and used for storage. Wolfeboro Lake station became an ice cream parlor. Although the line is abandoned, the Cotton Valley

A B&M passenger train meets the Lake Winnipesaukee steamer Mt. Washington at the so-called Wolfeboro Lake station in 1907. (Courtesy Walker Transportation Collection, Beverly Historical Society & Museum)

group, based at Fernald, maintains the track from Sanbornville to Wolfeboro Falls for testing track speeders.

Sources: Della Penna, *Great Rail Trails*, 144–50; Karr, *Lost Railroads*, 149; Potter, *Great American Railroad Stations*, 107–8.

30. Portland, Saco & Portsmouth

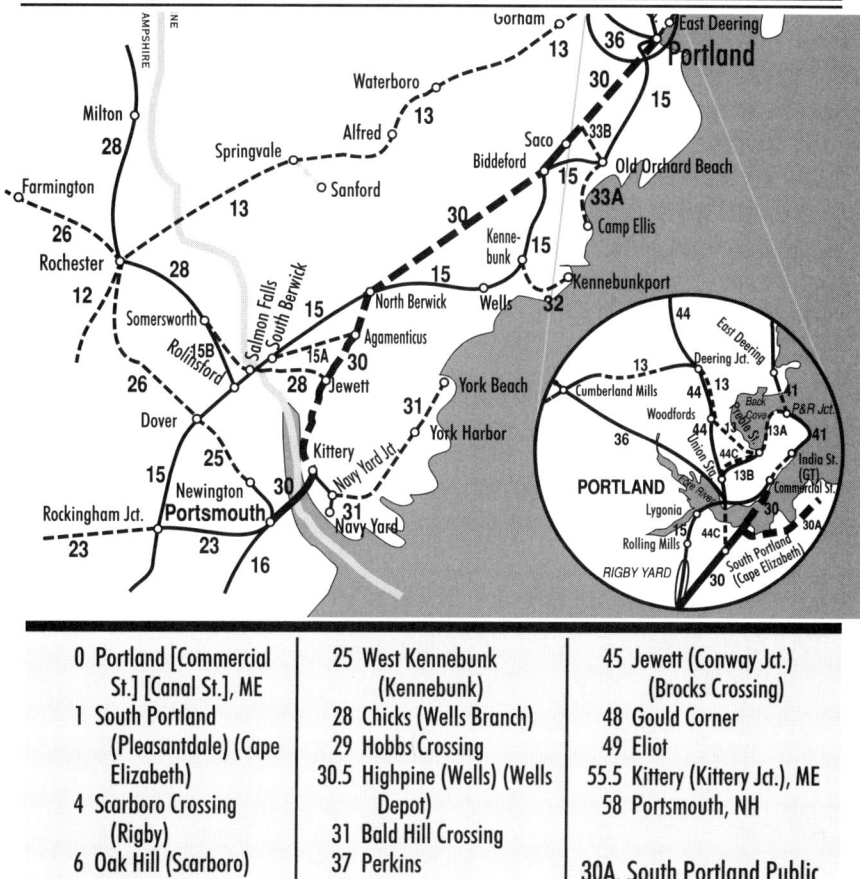

0 Portland [Commercial St.] [Canal St.], ME	25 West Kennebunk (Kennebunk)	45 Jewett (Conway Jct.) (Brocks Crossing)
1 South Portland (Pleasantdale) (Cape Elizabeth)	28 Chicks (Wells Branch)	48 Gould Corner
	29 Hobbs Crossing	49 Eliot
	30.5 Highpine (Wells) (Wells Depot)	55.5 Kittery (Kittery Jct.), ME
4 Scarboro Crossing (Rigby)	31 Bald Hill Crossing	58 Portsmouth, NH
6 Oak Hill (Scarboro)	37 Perkins	
8.5 West Scarborough (Dunstan)	39 North Berwick	30A. South Portland Public Development Branch
14 Saco [East] (Saco)	43.5 South Berwick Jct. (Agamenticus)	0 South Portland, ME
16 Biddeford		2 Shipyards, ME

Built: 1840–42; South Portland Public Development Branch, ca. 1943.

Operators: *Eastern*, 1842–47; *Portland, Saco & Portsmouth* (see text), 1847–73; *Eastern*, 1873–84; *Boston & Maine*, 1885–1983; *Guilford*, 1983–; *Turner Island*, 1998–.

Daily Passenger Trains: *1869:* 8; *1893:* 12; *1915:* 5 (plus Portsmouth–North Berwick and Western route, 3; via Jewett to Conway

Branch, 6; via Kittery Jct. to York Beach, 6); *1920:* 6 (plus Portsmouth–North Berwick and Western route, 3; via Jewett to Conway Branch, 6; via Kittery Jct. to York Beach, 4); *1926:* 5 (plus Portsmouth–North Berwick and Western route, 4; via Jewett to Conway Branch, 6); *1927:* 5 (Portsmouth–North Berwick, plus Portsmouth–Jewett to Rochester, 2); *1939:* 5 (Portsmouth–North Berwick) *1944:* 7 (Portsmouth–North Berwick); *1952:* 3 (Portsmouth–North Berwick). Scheduled passenger service ended North Berwick–Portland, 1927 (see text); Portsmouth–North Berwick, 1952.

Abandonments: Portland–South Portland, ca. 1916; Rigby–Saco [1.5 miles north], Biddeford–North Berwick [0.8 miles north], 1944; North Berwick–Kittery, 1952; at North Berwick, 1983; South Portland Development Branch, ca. 1990.

A charter for the Portland, Saco & Portsmouth RR was obtained from the Maine legislature in 1837, a year after the Eastern RR was chartered from East Boston to Portsmouth. The financial crisis of 1837 stalled progress, but construction started in 1840 and was completed in 1842. The PS&P opened on November 21, under a five-year lease by the Eastern. The northern terminus in Portland was located near wharves in Canal (now Commercial) Street at State Street and was reached through Turners Island and a drawbridge over the Fore River. Saco, the most important intermediate town, was home from 1829 to one of the largest textile mills in America. Other towns on the route included North Berwick, known for manufacture of plows, and Kittery, a major fishing center. To reach the Eastern RR terminal at Vaughan Street in Portsmouth, a second major bridge was required to cross the Piscataqua River. The Boston & Maine RR, which had extended to Berwick in 1842, completed a connection with the PS&P at South Berwick Jct. (Agamenticus) the following year.

When the Eastern's lease expired in 1847, the PS&P was jointly leased by the competitive main lines, although the line operated independently and had its own small fleet of locomotives and rolling stock. Eastern and B&M trains generally met at Agamenticus, where they were coupled and hauled by a single locomotive to Portland to complete their five-hour journey from Boston. These arrangements continued for 23 years, until the PS&P became a central player in the escalating war that developed between the Eastern and B&M.

A westbound passenger train passes Saco East station on the PS&P during the time when the B&M still maintained two routes between Boston and Portland. (Courtesy Walker Transportation Collection, Beverly Historical Society & Museum)

In 1870, the PS&P abrogated the joint lease and sought better terms. The Eastern, B&M, and MEC all submitted bids; the Eastern won, but paid a high price. In retaliation, the B&M obtained a charter in 1871 for its own seaboard route from Berwick to Portland, serving Biddeford, Saco, and the growing communities toward the Atlantic coast. The B&M's partly single-track line opened in 1873, and its link between South Berwick and Agamenticus closed at the same time. From about 1875 MEC passenger trains used the PS&P terminal in Portland. In later years, after absorption of the Eastern by the B&M, trains not required to make local stops could be directed over either main line south of Rigby. Passenger service to the PS&P Portland terminal ended by 1894, and the track between Scarboro Crossing and South Portland became a freight-only branch line. The bridge across the Fore River into Portland, shown on maps as late as 1916, was abandoned, probably shortly thereafter.

With two lines to Portland maintained to passenger standards, the B&M ended passenger service between North Berwick and South

Portland over the PS&P in 1926, and maintenance of the length was reduced accordingly. Express passenger trains continued to use the PS&P between North Berwick and Rigby to bypass congestion on the B&M line as the need arose.

The bridge over the Piscataqua River to Portsmouth was originally a side-by-side rail and road corridor, with tolls levied on vehicular traffic until 1924. In 1939–40, a new double-deck bridge was constructed, now named for Sarah Mildred Long, featuring a lifting span over the main channel of the Piscataqua River and a retractable span for small craft at the Kittery end. On the night of September 10, 1939, construction material broke loose and damaged the old bridge. Under the weight of B&M Class P2b Pacific no. 3666, hauling a westbound local, the bridge collapsed, taking with it the tender and an empty wooden coach. The engine crew perished, but the locomotive remains on the river bottom as their memorial, although dragged some distance from its original grave to avoid hazard to ocean-going craft. For almost a year, most trains were diverted over the Western route to North Berwick. The new bridge opened on November 11, 1940.

This overgrown culvert near Agamenticus, ME, once carried the rails of the PS&P. (R. D. Karr)

30. Portland, Saco & Portsmouth

The Portsmouth, Great Falls & Conway connection at Jewett was removed in 1941, and through freight to and from Portland was routed over the B&M (Western) route in November 1944, which enabled the abandonment of the PS&P between North Berwick and Rigby. In Biddeford/Saco, a spur known as the Saco Industrial Branch was retained from Alfred Road (now US Route 111) through the former Eastern station to serve several freight customers in Biddeford. Additional spurs were built to serve new industries, among them the Maremont Corporation (now Saco Defense, Inc.), established in 1952, manufacturers of the M-16 rifle. During World War II a branch was constructed to reach the South Portland shipyards. Known locally as "the Burma Road," it was later taken over by a state agency, the Greater Portland Public Development Commission, and operated by the Portland Terminal Co. It is now abandoned.

Closure of the remainder of the PS&P main line between Portsmouth and North Berwick came in September 1952, and tracks were gone by the end of the year, although two lengths were retained as spurs. One in North Berwick served Swensons Granite quarry; the other was the Piscataqua River crossing for trains to and from Kittery Navy Yard. The Swenson quarry spur was closed in 1983.

After ownership of the remaining PS&P passed to Guilford in 1983 there were no major changes. Traffic over the Rigby-Pleasantdale spur declined, and by 1993, the terminal yard—no. 3 in Portland Terminal nomenclature—was no longer in regular use. The spur's use as a siding for storage of freight cars ended in 1998 when the line was reopened by the Fore River Dock and Dredge Company, operating as the Turner Island RR. Quarried granite from Stonington on Deer Isle provides seasonal traffic, generally destined for Providence, RI.

The track bed from just north of Kittery to Jewett is now interred beneath Maine Route 236. Between Jewett and North Berwick it is a path over a natural gas pipeline. Most of the alignment toward Biddeford is traceable, and the Eastern Trail Alliance is promoting its conversion into a rail trail.

Sources: Bradlee, *Eastern*, 50, 51; Drury, *Historical Guide*, 365; Eugley, "Eastern Route"; Karr, *Lost Railroads*, 107-10; Kirkland, *Men, Cities & Transportation*, 2: 4-7; Kyper, "Saco Branch."

31. York Harbor & Beach

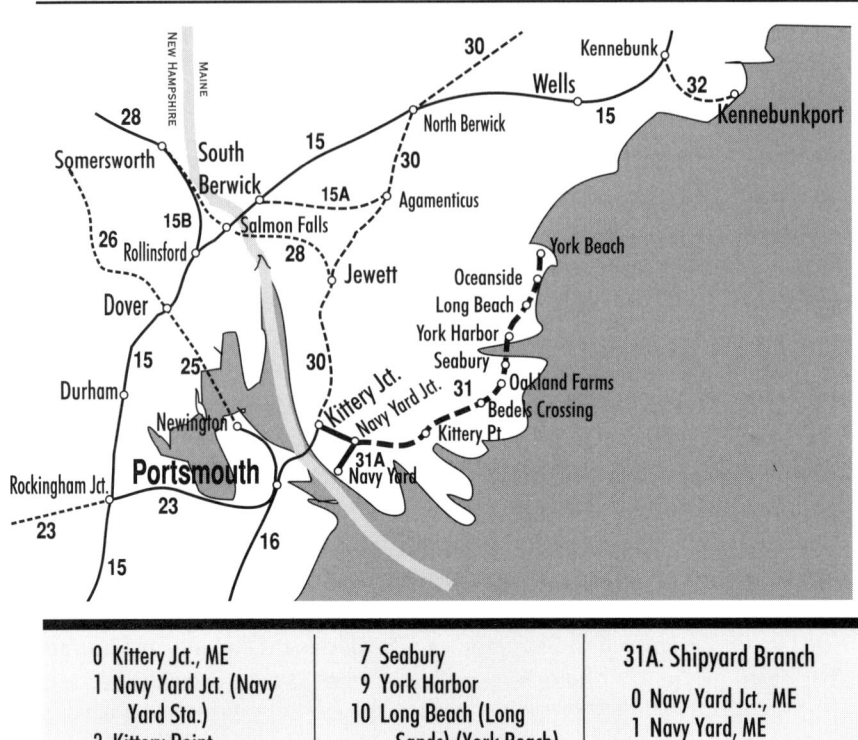

0 Kittery Jct., ME	7 Seabury	**31A. Shipyard Branch**
1 Navy Yard Jct. (Navy Yard Sta.)	9 York Harbor	0 Navy Yard Jct., ME
3 Kittery Point	10 Long Beach (Long Sands) (York Beach)	1 Navy Yard, ME
4.5 Bedels Crossing (Bedells) (Bedell)	11 Oceanside (Pavilion)	
5.5 Oakland Farms	12 York Beach (Union Bluffs), ME	

Built: 1887-88; Shipyard Branch, 1901.
Operators: *Boston & Maine*, 1888-1983; *Guilford*, 1983-.
Daily Passenger Trains: *1887:* 10; *1893:* 12; *1919:* 6; *1922:* 8. Passenger service ended Navy Yard Jct.-York Beach, 1925; Portsmouth-Navy Yard, ca. 1931.
Abandonments: Navy Yard Jct.-York Beach, 1927.

York promoted itself as a resort from 1868, when a hotel was opened, followed in 1871 by the more splendid facilities of the Marshall House. Growth was limited, however, by erratic boat and stage service. A coastal rail line from Portsmouth to Saco through

31. York Harbor & Beach

Wells Beach and Kennebunkport, which would also serve the Navy Yard in Kittery, was suggested as early as 1872.

A decade passed before a committee of local people approached the Eastern RR, then in control of the Portland, Saco & Portsmouth RR, to build a line from Kittery to York Beach. With the Eastern embroiled in heated competition with the Boston & Maine, the proposal was rejected. Instead, in 1883 a charter was obtained for an independent line. Among others, Frank Jones, a brewer in Portsmouth and a B&M board member, bought stock. When a narrow-gauge line was proposed, Jones negotiated an agreement with the B&M to construct a standard-gauge line; the local company agreed to raise sufficient capital for land acquisition, just over $51,000, and the B&M would take up the remaining stock, about $250,000, for construction. The B&M would operate the line on opening.

Work proceeded rapidly. Track installation by the B&M began on June 4, 1887, from a junction in Oak Terrace immediately north of the Piscataqua River bridge in Kittery. The line was completed to Kittery Point on June 28, and to Brave Boat Harbor on the York River in mid-July, and to a short distance beyond Long Sands by the planned date of opening on Monday, August 8, 1887. The inaugural train consisted of two B&M passenger cars with Baldwin 4-4-0s at both ends, since the turntable was inaccessible. From 1893, when Jones was elected chairman, several other directors served on both boards, and officers were shared. By then the B&M held 90 percent of the stock, and soon after, Jones became president of the B&M.

Although freight was conveyed to and from York Village and York Harbor year round—mainly consumable goods which included considerable quantities of fish—passenger traffic was always most important. Connections were provided in Portsmouth with trains to and from Boston during daylight. Through parlor cars that were subsequently introduced gave well-heeled Bostonians a comfortable journey to their summer homes. Dividends were paid until 1914, despite competition from the almost parallel Kittery & York Electric RR. Incorporated in 1893 and built in 1897, the trolley line was of no use to main line passengers, but it creamed off local traffic and also obtained the local contract for conveyance of mail. This was not the only problem the line experienced: on April 30, 1900, a mixed train from Portsmouth was climbing the grade to York Harbor depot when five of its cars broke loose and ran back downhill toward an open drawbridge. The combine

York Beach Station, at the end of the YH&B, as it appeared around 1917. (Courtesy Walker Transportation Collection, Beverly Historical Society & Museum)

at the rear overturned in the river, but the following freight car impacted a concrete bridge foundation, causing the cars to telescope. Fortunately there were no fatalities among the nine people in the combine, all of whom had jumped clear, although the company's supply agent had a leg amputated as a result.

A narrow-gauge system known as the Shipyard RR had been built by the navy within the dockyard on Dennett Island in 1901 and was expanded considerably in 1905. A spur from a junction west of Navy Yard Station was built by the YH&B in 1901, and the Shipyard RR was converted to standard gauge in 1910. In 1922 merger with the B&M was approved by the stockholders of both companies. The competing trolley lines, now part of the Atlantic Shore Line, ceased operation early in 1923, and YH&B losses declined during the next couple of years. However, the B&M applied for consent to a replacement bus route from Portsmouth to Saco in April 1925. Permission was given on June 27, and busses were introduced on July 8, after which just one round freight trip ran to York Beach three times each week. Passenger trains to the Navy Yard, however, continued for nearly six more years.

After a hearing in Portsmouth in November 1926, the ICC on February 19, 1927, gave approval for the B&M to completely abandon the

31. York Harbor & Beach

line east of Navy Yard Jct. A contractor started dismantling the line west from York Beach in May, although the track at Navy Yard Jct. was retained for switching and for the occasional freight car to Kittery.

Together with the branch to the naval docks, this spur saw regular use into the 1990s. The navy is still said to send nuclear waste over the line about twice a year, and rarely bulky or heavy items, such as timber, waste oil, and propellers, are conveyed by rail. Aside from these rare and unpredictable navy moves, the line is never used. Several former station buildings are now private residences, although some have been moved. Otherwise, the alignment can be traced, albeit requiring a machete in difficult areas.

Sources: Bradlee, *Eastern*; Cummings, *Atlantic Shore Line*; Hilton and Due, *Electric Interurban Railways*, 323; Karr, *Lost Railroads*, 84; Lawry, "It's Government Work"; Tobey, "York Harbor & Beach Railroad."

32. Kennebunk & Kennebunkport

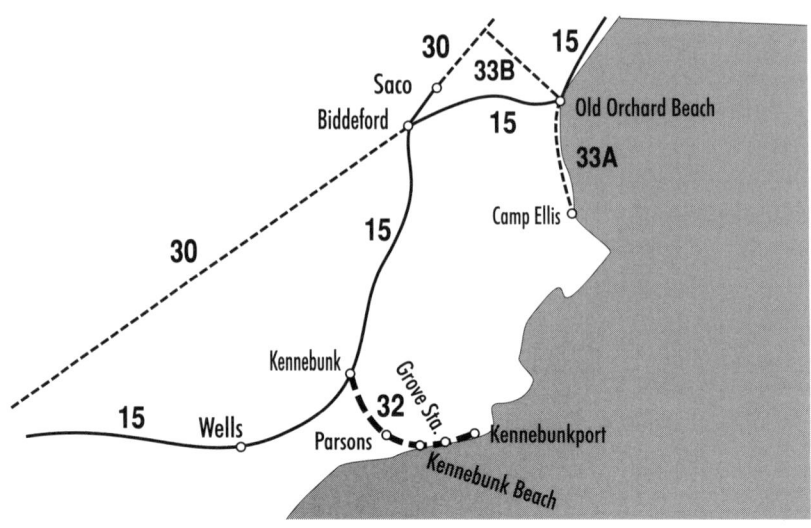

| 0 Kennebunk, ME | 3 Kennebunk Beach | 4.5 Kennebunkport, ME |
| 2.5 Parsons | 3.5 Grove Sta. | |

Built: 1883.
Operators: Boston & Maine, 1883–1926.
Daily Passenger Trains: *1886:* 12; *1893:* 16; *1903:* 12; *1908:* 26; *1919:* 10 (one mixed); *1925:* 4 (one mixed). Passenger service ended 1926.
Abandonment: 1926.

From the 1870s, coastal towns in southern Maine promoted themselves as beach resorts to attract Boston residents. One successful local enterprise was the Kennebunk & Kennebunkport RR, organized on August 16, 1882, to build a line from the Boston & Maine RR station in Kennebunk, south of Summer Street and east of the old town center, to Kennebunkport. The line turned south into the Mousam River valley, which it then followed to Four Corners, two miles west of central Kennebunkport, and then turned east to a terminal a short distance south of Coopers Corner (now the intersection of State Routes 9

32. Kennebunk & Kennebunkport

and 9A/35). Sidings beyond, to the west bank of the river, served the local fishing industry. The line was leased by the B&M upon opening on June 6, 1883, and year-round service was operated.

Until the line's demise in 1926, the number of trips during winters averaged about six. At its zenith between 1908 and 1916, as many as 26 trips were made daily during summers, generally considered to be late June to late September. No trains ran on Sundays. Kennebunk Beach station was open only in summers after 1907. From about 1914 one summer train included a through parlor car from Montreal, and sleeper, combination cars, and coaches were included in through trains to and from Portland.

Decline set in around 1917, perhaps owing to restrictions imposed during World War I. Summer service comprised no more than ten trips. Mixed consists for some trains had been introduced in October

Boston & Maine 4-4-0 American locomotive number 987 pulls a typical New England mixed train up to Kennebunk Beach in the 1920s. (Courtesy Walker Transportation Collection, Beverly Historical Society & Museum)

1916. Absorption by the B&M was approved in 1919. Some trains continued to run to and from Portland to facilitate locomotive maintenance. On September 8, 1926, all rail service was discontinued. Objections were lodged by local residents, but none came from the proprietors of resort hotels. Today, almost all of the line is a dirt track used for hiking and biking. Kennebunk station remains, a rust-colored clapboard structure in typical B&M style, now a private residence. A hump in the road north of Wharf Lane and Wallace Street represents a former grade crossing.

Sources: Bradlee, *Boston & Maine*; Karr, *Lost Railroads*, 83; Maine Dept. of Transportation, *Historical & Archeological Resources,* Appendix C, 16; 111 ICC 500 (1926).

33. Old Orchard Beach Lines

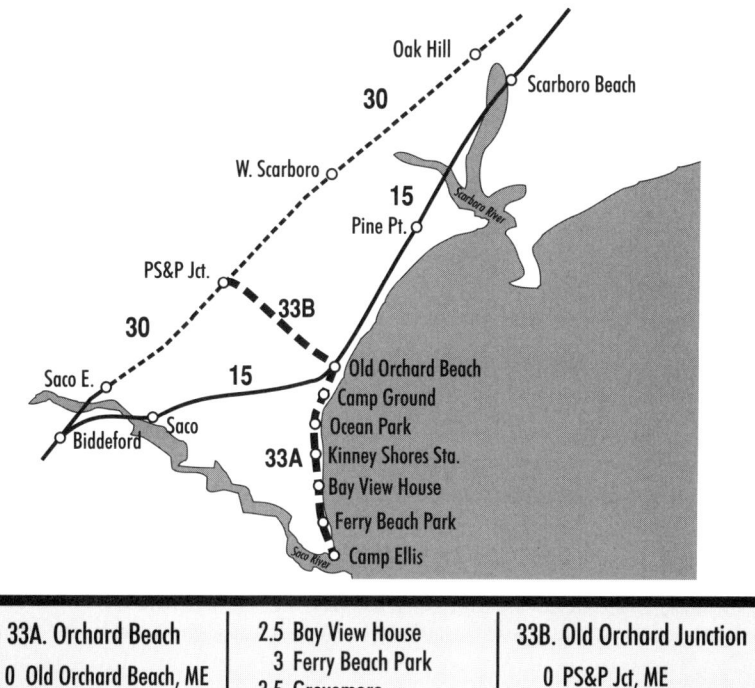

33A. Orchard Beach		33B. Old Orchard Junction
0 Old Orchard Beach, ME	2.5 Bay View House	0 PS&P Jct, ME
0.5 Camp Ground	3 Ferry Beach Park	2.5 Old Orchard Beach, ME
1 Ocean Park	3.5 Grovemore	
1.5 Kinney Shores Sta.	4 Camp Ellis, ME	

Built: Orchard Beach, 1880; Old Orchard Junction, 1881.

Operators: *Orchard Beach*, 1880-83; *Old Orchard Junction*, 1881-82; *Boston & Maine*, 1883-1923.

Daily Passenger Trains: (Orchard Beach) *1901:* 26; *1910:* 46; *1915:* 46; *1918:* 36. Passenger service ended Old Orchard Junction, 1882; Orchard Beach, 1923.

Abandonments: Old Orchard Junction, ca. 1885; Orchard Beach, 1923.

By the late 1870s, after construction of the Boston & Maine line to Portland, Old Orchard Beach and the coast to the south had become popular as a seaside vacation area and summer home for businessmen. Local interests obtained a charter for the Orchard Beach

A young passenger waits at Kinney Shores Station for one of the frequent trains on the Orchard Beach line around 1910. (Courtesy Walker Transportation Collection, Beverly Historical Society & Museum)

RR on February 27, 1876, but opening along the shore line to Camp Ellis at the mouth of the Saco River was delayed until June 26, 1880. The four-mile line was operated summers for more than 40 years. The tracks ran along the beach, directly in front of seaside cottages. Diminutive 0-4-0 steam engines, in streetcar parlance known as dummies, were used with open-sided cars with transverse bench seating for passengers and luggage. Operation was "push-pull" as no turntable or wye was provided at either terminal.

Local residents called the train "the Dummy" until its discontinuation, even though the fleet was replaced by standard equipment some time after the Boston & Maine took over operation of the line in 1883. A passing siding between Kinney Shores and Bay View was required during years of intensive service, but in later years service was provided by a single consist, apparently with reversing time at Camp Ellis of just one minute. By the 1920s, improved roads and automobile competition brought about the line's demise; operation ended at the end of the season on September 5, 1923. In 1924, after obtaining permission to abandon the line, the B&M sold it to the Old Orchard Transportation

33. Old Orchard Beach Lines

Company, which apparently operated it briefly before dismantling the line.

Chartered and constructed in 1881, the Old Orchard Junction RR ran from the Eastern's Portland, Saco & Portsmouth line about four miles east of Biddeford to about half a mile north of what are now Union Avenue and T for Turn Road in Old Orchard Beach. Rolling stock was rented from the Eastern as required. The intention appears to have been to give Old Orchard Beach another rail outlet to compete with the B&M, but neither the Eastern or the B&M showed interest in lease or acquisition. After operation in the summers of 1881 and 1882, the line closed; it was dismantled about three years later.

Sources: Cornwall and Smith, *Names First*, 93-94; Karr, *Lost Railroads*, 74, 81; Maine State Archives; Peverly and McLin, *Dummy*, 90 ICC 474 (1924).

34. Central Vermont

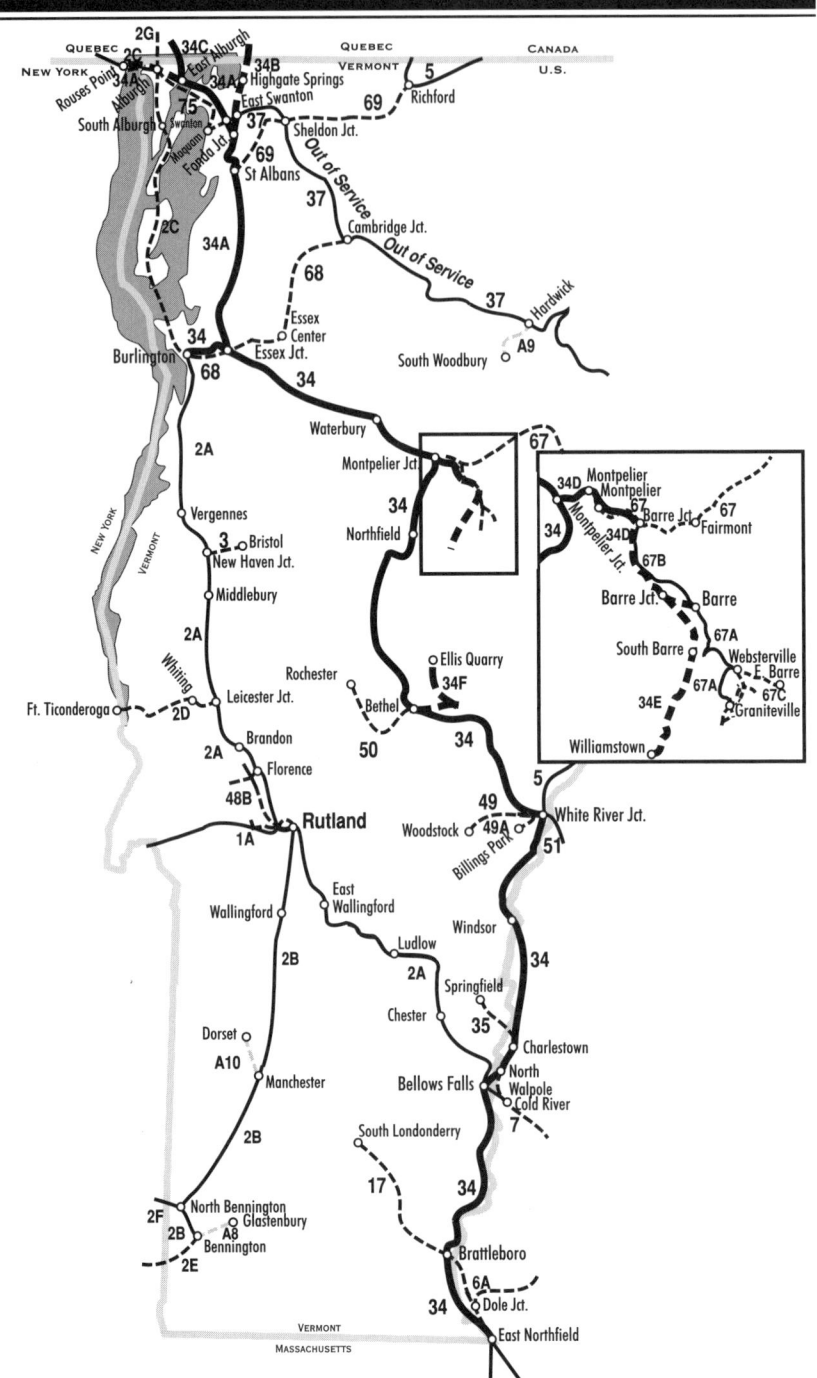

34. Central Vermont

0 East Northfield (West Northfield), MA	127 Northfield Falls	**34B. St. Armand Subdivision**
3 Central Park, VT	131 Riverton (West Berlin)	0 Swanton Jct. (Fonda Jct.), VT
5 Vernon	134 Montpelier Jct.	9 East Swanton, VT
10 Brattleboro	139 Middlesex	13 Highgate Springs, VT
12 West River	140 North Moretown	*18 St. Armand, PQ*
15 Dummerston	143 Duxbury	*43 St. Johns (St-Jean), PQ*
19 Putney	144 Waterbury	
22 East Putney	148 North Duxbury (Ridleys)	
30 Westminster	151 Bolton	**34C. Canada Atlantic Extension**
34 Bellows Falls, VT	154 Jonesville (Jones's)	
35 North Walpole, NH	157 Richmond	0 East Alburgh, VT
41 Charlestown	162 Williston	*2 Rogers, PQ*
47 North Charlestown	166 Essex Jct.	*9 Cantic, PQ*
51 Claremont Jct. (Claremont), NH	168 Ft. Ethan Allen	
59 Windsor, VT	171 Winooski	**34D. Montpelier & White River RR**
64 Hartland	174 Burlington, VT	
68 Evarts (North Hartland)		0 Montpelier Jct., VT
73 White River Jct. (White River Falls)	**34A. Vermont & Canada**	2 Montpelier
74 White River Village (Hartford)	0 Essex Jct	7 CV Barre Jct.
76 Woodstock	4 Colchester	8 Barre, VT
80 West Hartford	7 Milton	
85 Sharon	10 Georgia	**34E. Williamstown Branch**
90 South Royalton	15 Oakland (East Georgia) (North Georgia)	0 CV Barre Jct.
91 Royalton	20 St. Albans	3 South Barre
97 Bethel	22 North Jct.	7 Williamstown, VT
100 Beanville	26 Fonda	
104 Randolph	27 Fonda Jct. (Swanton Jct.)	**34F. Bethel Granite RY**
110 Braintree	29 Swanton	
113 East Granville	35 Lakewood (West Swanton)	0 Bethel, VT
117 Roxbury Flat	36 East Alburgh (Alburgh Springs) (Missisco)	5.5 Ellis Quarry [East Bethel], VT
119 Roxbury	39 Alburgh	
124 South Northfield	42 West Alburgh, VT	
126 Northfield	*44 Rouses Point, NY*	

Built: 1845–51; Vermont & Canada, 1847–51; St. Armand Subdivision, 1864; Barre Branch, 1875; Williamstown Branch, 1888; Canada Atlantic Extension, 1897; Bethel Granite, 1905.

Operators: *Vermont Central*, 1848–73; *Central Vermont RR*, 1873–99; *Connecticut River*, 1877–93; *Central Vermont RY*, 1899–

1995; *New England Central,* 1995–; *Boston & Maine,* 1893– 1983; *Amtrak,* 1972–87, 1989–; *Guilford,* 1983–.

Daily Passenger Trains (White River Jct.–St. Albans) *1869:* 4; *1893:* 8; *1915:* 8; *1935:* 8 (plus 2, Essex Jct.–White River Jct.; 2, Essex Jct.–Burlington; 10, White River Jct.–Windsor); *1950:* 6 ; *1960:* 6. Passenger service ended East Alburgh–Rouses Point, 1929; Burlington–Essex Jct. and Barre Branch, 1938; St. Armand Subdivision, 1946; East Swanton–Phillipsburg, 1946; St. Albans–White River Jct., 1966. Restored by Amtrak, 1972–87, 1989–.

Abandonments: Bethel Granite RY, 1937; Williamstown Branch (Williamstown–South Barre, 1939; South Barre–CV Barre Jct., 1950); St. Armand Subdivision (Canadian portion, 1952; East Swanton–Canadian border, 1956); Montpelier & White River (CV Barre Jct.–Montpelier [2 miles east], 1958); Rouses Point–East Alburgh, 1962.

Led by Charles Paine of Northfield, a former governor of Vermont, the Vermont Central RR incorporated on November 1, 1843, to build a line from "some point on the eastern shore of Lake Champlain" to the Connecticut River. As the owner of a wool mill in Northfield, Paine saw to it that the line passed through his home town. Despite its local origin, the VC from the beginning was conceived as a through route, and it raised three quarters of its initial capital in Boston. The VC opened its line between Windsor and Northfield in February 1849, and completed the route to Burlington by the end of the year.

To the south the Sullivan RR had opened its first section in January 1849 between the Cheshire RR at Bellows Falls and Charlestown, NH. The inaugural train was described in the *Bellows Falls Gazette* of January 4, 1849:

> [On Monday, January 1] the engine came up in grand style and when opposite our village, the monster gave one of its most savage yells, frightening men, women, and children considerably, and bringing forth the most deafening howls from all the dogs in the neighborhood. This day, Thursday, the Sullivan road is to be opened, with the usual ceremonies, to Charlestown, and then the arrival of cars will be a common, everyday business affair.

The next month the Sullivan completed its line to Windsor, where it connected with the Vermont Central, thus opening a direct rail route

Central Vermont's massive 2-10-4 number 706 heads a long freight somewhere north of Essex Jct. (Courtesy Walker Transportation Collection, Beverly Historical Society & Museum)

from Burlington to Springfield, MA, albeit by way of a circuitous route through Keene, NH. In 1850 the Vermont & Massachusetts RR completed an extension from East Northfield, MA, to Brattleboro, VT. The final gap between Brattleboro and Bellows Falls was closed when the Vermont Valley RR connected these points in 1851.

At the same time that the VC had been established, the Champlain & Connecticut River RR was also chartered, with authority to build another line between Burlington and the Connecticut River. Soon reorganized as the Rutland & Burlington RR, it engaged the VC in a bitter rivalry over the next two decades. The first round in this competition involved the Vermont & Canada RR, for which a St. Albans banker, John Smith, had obtained a charter in October 1845. As chartered, the V&C was supposed to connect with both the VC and the R&B and extend the rails northward to Canada. But while the line was still under construction in 1849 the VC leased it, built its own connection at Essex

Jct., and never extended the V&C to Burlington, as required by its charter. The VC made sure that the transfer of freight and passengers to the R&B in Burlington was difficult, and Essex Jct. became infamous for long waits and inconvenient connections.

To connect with the Northern RR of New York, then under construction from Ogdensburg to Rouses Point, the V&C built a causeway across the northern end of Lake Champlain. Plans for a mile-long bridge between Alburgh and Rouses Point had been delayed by New York authorities, who insisted on an unobstructed navigable width far in excess of contemporary bridge design and construction technology. To get the line in operation, a rail-equipped barge was used from opening on January 10, 1851. Not until 1868 did the VC replace the barges with a bridge. Meanwhile, in 1864, the VC had opened an alternative to the route through Rouses Point when it built northward from Swanton Jct. to the Canadian border, and then under a Canadian charter for the Montreal & Vermont Junction RY to St. Johns, PQ, where it connected with a subsidiary of the Grand Trunk RY to reach Mon-

Amtrak 56, the Vermonter, *heads north along the banks of the Connecticut River in Vernon, VT, on May 1, 1999. (R. D. Karr)*

34. Central Vermont 173

treal. For the next 80 years this more direct route, the St. Armand Subdivision, was used by VC (and subsequently Central Vermont) passenger trains to and from Montreal.

At the southern end of its route, the VC leased the Sullivan RR in 1861, which brought it to Bellows Falls, a town already served by the R&B. In 1865 the R&B (soon to be the Rutland RR) retaliated by leasing the Vermont Valley RR between Bellows Falls and Brattleboro, and five years later the Vermont & Massachusetts line from Brattleboro to Millers Falls, MA. On December 31, 1870, the VC put an end to the rivalry by leasing the Rutland RR system. A year later the VC also leased the New London Northern RR of Massachusetts and Connecticut and the Missisquoi RR as it was completed during 1871–72.

The high costs of these acquisitions led to the failure of the VC in 1873. It emerged from bankruptcy as the Central Vermont RR, at first retaining all leases of other lines. But financial troubles soon cost it two important lines, the Sullivan County (formerly the Sullivan RR) and the Vermont Valley (which had been leased to the Rutland). By 1880 both lines were leased to the Connecticut River RR, which connected with the Vermont Valley at Brattleboro (via trackage rights over the CV), and in 1893 the B&M assumed these leases when it acquired the Connecticut River RR. The CV now had to depend on trackage rights between Windsor and Brattleboro to connect the northern and southern parts of its system between New London, CT, and Canada. Meanwhile, the ambitiously titled Montpelier & White River RR, had completed a branch as far as Barre in 1875 and was immediately taken over by the CV.

On the morning of February 5, 1887, a six-car train with about eighty passengers aboard was traveling northbound to Montreal. As the train crossed the 650-foot bridge over the White River about midway between White River Jct. and West Hartford, the rear four cars derailed and plunged into the river. Thirty-two people died, some on impact, and others in the fire that ensued or in the icy stream beneath the bridge. The accident was attributed to a broken rail about 200 feet south of the bridge.

Extension of the Montpelier & Wells River branch to Williamstown took place in 1888, but it was never to proceed beyond to the White River. In 1897 the Canada Atlantic RY from Ottawa, using a subsidiary, the Vermont & Province Line RY, built a line from Cantic, PQ, to East Alburgh, and ran its own trains as far as Swanton. In 1905 this

Central Vermont 4-4-0 no. 53 at Montpelier circa 1895. (Courtesy Walker Transportation Collection, Beverly Historical Society & Museum)

three-mile line became part of the Grand Trunk RY, and was used extensively by CV trains.

The financial panic in 1893 and the ensuing trade depression forced the CV into bankruptcy in March 1896. Its lease of the Rutland was canceled on May 7. Aid from the Grand Trunk RR enabled its reincarnation as the Central Vermont RY on January 1, 1899, and the CV became a GT (Canadian National after 1923) subsidiary. Effective October 1, 1900, the CV and the B&M agreed to jointly operate their tracks from South Vernon (later from East Northfield) to White River Jct. For the next 80 years all trains between these points were dispatched by the B&M. The short Bethel Granite RY, built in 1905, was operated by the CV as a common carrier, although no scheduled passenger trains ran.

Heavy floods in 1927 washed out most of the line between Essex Jct. and White River Jct. Although the CN funded reconstruction, the disaster forced the CV into receivership; it was reorganized in Vermont on January 30, 1930. The last trains ran on the Bethel Granite line in November 1933, with abandonment in 1937. The Williamstown branch was trimmed back to South Barre in 1939.

34. Central Vermont

After World War II, the CV discontinued its use of the St. Armand Subdivision and rerouted its trains over the Canada Atlantic, now another CN subsidiary. The Montpelier & White River branch was sold to the Montpelier & Barre RR in 1957, which abandoned the part of it south of Montpelier. Further savings were made by replacing steam power with diesel traction. Remaining passenger service between East Northfield and Montreal ended in September 1966.

After Guilford acquired the B&M in 1983 and the Delaware & Hudson RR in 1984, most of its Canadian traffic was routed over the D&H, and maintenance on the B&M's Connecticut River section between Brattleboro and Windsor (used by CV trains) declined. Amtrak, whose *Montrealer* from New York to Montreal had been operating over the CV from September 29, 1972, until April 1987, brought action against the B&M. In 1988 the ICC ordered the B&M to sell the line to Amtrak, which immediately resold it to the CV. Subsequent track improvements enabled reintroduction of the *Montrealer* in 1989

Amtrak 56, the Vermonter, *pulls north out of Bellows Falls station in May 1999. (R. D. Karr)*

A Canadian National locomotive hauls a CV train over a bridge in Milton, VT. (David K. Johnson, courtesy Walker Transportation Collection, Beverly Historical Society & Museum)

entirely over CV lines from New London, CT, to East Alburgh, although budget cuts eliminated the train again on April 1, 1995. The next day the state-subsidized *Vermonter* began operation from New York over Amtrak and Conrail lines through Springfield and Palmer, MA, thence over the CV to St. Albans.

A year earlier CN had placed the CV for sale. RailTex (recently bought by Rail America) was the successful bidder, and after taking control in January 1995, commenced operation as the New England Central RR. Traffic is primarily paper, lumber, grain, cement, and LP gas, much of which crosses the international border.

Sources: Armstrong, *Railfan's Guide*, 13-15; Baker, *Formation*, 229; Jones, *Central Vermont*; Jones, *Railroads of Vermont*, 1: 140-43; Karr, *Rail Lines*, 100-104; Karr, *Lost Railroads*, 84; 101, 109, 115; Kirkland, *Men, Cities & Transportation*, 1: 166-75.

35. Springfield Terminal

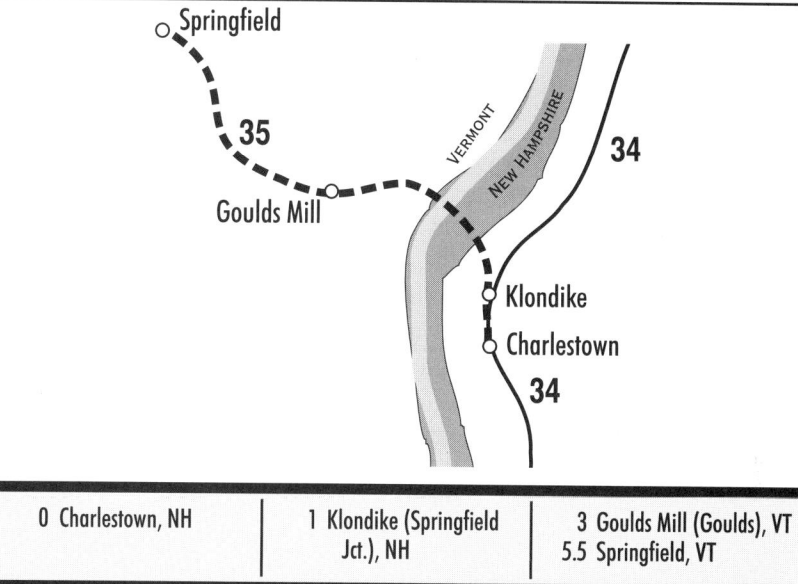

0 Charlestown, NH	1 Klondike (Springfield Jct.), NH	3 Goulds Mill (Goulds), VT 5.5 Springfield, VT

Built: 1894–97.
Operators: *Springfield Electric,* 1897–1923; *Springfield Terminal,* 1923–83; *Guilford,* 1983–84.
Daily Passenger Trains: *1916:* 22. Passenger service ended 1947.
Abandonment: 1991.

Springfield Terminal RY holds an extraordinary place in New England railroad history, not because of its construction and operation but for what it has become under the ægis of Guilford Transportation Industries. Chartered and incorporated in 1894 as the Springfield Electric RY, the line was built up the Black River Valley to Springfield, VT, from a junction with the Boston & Maine's Connecticut River line at Charlestown, NH. An existing bridge, the Cheshire Bridge of 1804, carried the line across the Connecticut River using rails set in the deck roadway; highway bridge tolls provided the trolley with a major source of revenue. Opened on August 4, 1897, the alignment featured 4 percent grades and tight curves. "Steeple cab" electric locomotives were used for freight service and passengers were conveyed in streetcars. Power was supplied from a hydroelectric plant at Goulds.

Sidings were built at Charlestown to handle car load interchange traffic, which proved relatively heavy, since Springfield lacked any other rail service. Passenger connections were provided with each train on the Connecticut River line.

The company declared bankruptcy in 1918 but continued to operate until 1923 when it was reorganized as the Springfield Terminal RY. The B&M eventually bought the company in 1930 but continued its operation as a separate entity. Passenger service continued until January 1947, when the ST retired its 1925-vintage steel Wason combines. By then it was the last rural electric line in New England to have maintained passenger service. Diesel locomotives replaced electric traction for freight service on October 31, 1956, amid high ceremony presided over by the Governor of Vermont. By about 1962 the last mile into Springfield had closed. A decade later traffic was in severe decline, and around 1980 rail traffic over the Connecticut River bridge ceased. The line remained nominally in service to retain the toll revenue from the bridge company.

A year after Guilford acquired the line as part of the B&M package, average daily hauled traffic consisted of one car. Upon closure on June 14, 1984, the former interchange sidings at Charlestown were retained together with a lumber yard spur at the junction, although in later years they saw little use. Again the line was not abandoned.

During 1985 Guilford, struggling with debts and high labor costs, leased the former MEC Woodland Branch to the ST to take advantage of the latter's lower wage rates. By 1987 all Guilford subsidiaries (except the Delaware & Hudson) were similarly leased to the ST, provoking considerable outcry from the rail unions and a general strike. Ironically, in 1991 Guilford obtained permission to abandon what little remained of the original line. The last connection with the company's track at Charlestown, seldom used, was not removed until 1994.

In a further irony, collective bargaining had increased ST labor costs significantly by 1994, so Guilford announced that the bulk of the workforce would be returned to MEC and B&M terms and conditions under a new holding company, Guilford Rail System. The extant ST became by and large merely an owner of locomotives.

Sources: Hilton and Due, *Electric Interurban Railways*, 320; Hilton, "Meets All Trains"; Karr, *Lost Railroads*, 153; Moody and Young, "Six Miles and a Toll Bridge."

36. Portland & Ogdensburg

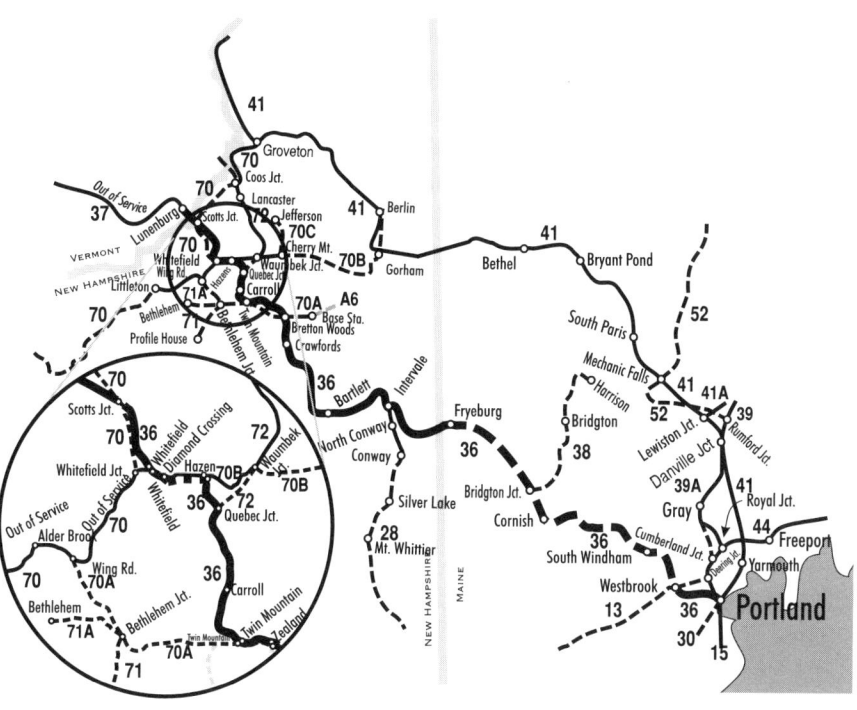

0 Portland, ME	35.5 Hiram (Hiram Bridge) (Hiram Jct.)	84 Crawfords (Crawford Notch)
1 B&M Transfer	42 Brownfield	87 Bretton Woods (Mt. Pleasant House)
4.5 Westbrook-Cumberland Mills (Cumberland Mills)	48.5 Fryeburg, ME	88 Bretton Woods-Fabyan (Fabyans)
10 South Windham	53 Center Conway (Conway Center), NH	
11 Newhall	55.5 Redstone	89 White Mountain House
12.5 White Rock	58 North Conway	91.5 Zealand
15.5 Sebago Lake	60.5 Intervale (Intervale Jct.)	93.5 Twin Mountain
17.5 Smiths Mill	63.5 Glen & Jackson (Glen Sta.)	96 Carroll (Carroll Tank)
19.5 Richville		98.5 Quebec Jct.
23.5 Steep Falls	69.5 Bartlett (Upper Bartlett)	100 Hazens
25.5 Mattocks (East Baldwin)	73.5 Sawyers (Sawyer River)	102 Diamond Crossing
30.5 Cornish (Baldwin)	76.5 Notchland (Bemis)	102.5 Whitefield
32.5 West Baldwin	78 Carrigain	106 Scotts Jct. (Scotts), NH
35 Bridgton Jct.	80 Willey House	108 Lunenburg, VT

36. Portland & Ogdensburg

Built: 1869–75, 1889.

Operators: *Portland & Ogdensburg*, 1874–80; *Maine Central*, 1880–1981; *Guilford*, 1981–84; *Twin State*, 1985–99; *Conway Scenic*, 1995–.

Daily Passenger Trains: *1874:* 6; *1893:* 6; *1908:* 6 (plus Portland–Sebago Lake, 2; North Conway–Fabyans, 2; Intervale–Beecher Falls, 2; Portland–Bartlett, 2); *1920:* 4 (plus Portland–Fabyans, 8); *1933:* 2; *1947:* 2; *1958:* 2. Passenger service ended 1958 (resumed North Conway–Crawfords, 1995; North Conway–Fabyans, 1996).

Abandonment: Westbrook [1 mile north]–NH State Line, 1995; Whitefield–Hazens, ca. 1998.

A charter was granted to the Portland & Ogdensburg RR on February 11, 1867, and the company was organized on January 10, 1869. Portland interests promoted the railroad to bring tourists to the White Mountains and as another route to Canada. Ground was broken in Portland in 1869, but the line was not completed to Bartlett

until the summer of 1873. Progress was slow because of extensive bridging and excavation required by the proposed alignment. High construction costs brought the company to the brink, but it was rescued by the city of Portland which bought company stocks and bonds. Trains ran to Bemis from August 31, 1874, although regular service did not begin until September 14. Bartlett station was a mansard-roofed wooden three-story building that contained offices and a restaurant; a lengthy overall platform canopy was provided to the north of the tracks. A second platform enabled trains to pass. A number of sidings were built, one of which served a turntable and a six-stall roundhouse.

Beyond Bartlett, the alignment was blasted, bridged, and embanked to a summit at Gateway (just before Crawfords), 1,950 feet above sea level, followed by a descent to the Ammonoosuc River valley. The new

In 1992 more than 30 years had passed since any passenger had boarded a train at picturesque Crawfords station. (R. D. Karr)

line served Crawford House Hotel, a resort opened in July 1859 on the site of inns earlier destroyed by fire. A noteworthy trestle was named for local artist Godfrey P. N. Frankenstein (not for Mary Shelley's character). Willey Brook was crossed by an 804-foot, center-braced A-frame, two-span truss, supported at each end by hewn granite piers. The official opening of the P&O took place on August 7, 1875, to a connection with the Boston, Concord & Montreal (former White Mountains RR) line at Fabyans. From there P&O trains operated over BC&M tracks to Scotts Jct., where the P&O built a short connection to Lunenburg, VT. By the time the P&O reached Lunenburg in December 1875, a Vermont company, the Essex County RR, had extended the route to St. Johnsbury, VT, where it connected with other railroads that by the end of 1877 reached Swanton and a connection to Canada. With shareholder consent, the MEC took a lease of the P&O in 1880.

Several independent logging lines brought traffic to the line. During 1877 the Saunders family of Livermore built the Sawyers River line from Sawyers River depot to provide an outlet from their sawmill. This continued in use until the sawmill closed in 1928. From Carroll, the

36. Portland & Ogdensburg

Zealand Valley RR, built by lumber baron J. E. Henry between 1884 and 1886, operated until 1897. The Bartlett & Albany RR operated from 1887 until 1893, using rails and equipment leased from the Eastern RR, to bring lumber to a mill built in 1874. In 1905, the Conway Lumber Company opened a mill in Conway—by 1915 said to be the largest in the United States—and in 1907 constructed the Rocky Branch RR from near Glen Station into Sargents Purchase. Operation of the Rocky Branch ended in 1914 after a fire destroyed part of the rolling stock fleet, although a new line, the East Branch RR, was built and operated from Glen north to Jackson Township between 1916 and 1919.

The MEC accorded considerable importance to the P&O, eventually establishing it as its Mountain Division. In 1889 the MEC built its own line between Fabyans and Scotts Jct., eliminating the need to use BC&M tracks. For many years, the MEC and B&M together ran through trains from Boston via Rollinsford and Intervale to points

These dapper gentlemen posed in front of the Fabyans, NH, depot and the Fabyan House a century ago. (Courtesy Walker Transportation Collection, Beverly Historical Society & Museum)

36. Portland & Ogdensburg 183

north. The MEC erected new station buildings in Queen Anne style at Crawford and Fabyans in 1891. Both featured an octagonal tower and spire, topped by a weather vane. The original buildings were relegated to baggage and freight service. A station was built at Bretton Woods to serve Mt. Pleasant House, a resort replaced in 1902 by the still grander Mt. Washington Hotel, about a mile south of the new station. The Bretton Woods Conference, which set the scene for the post-war World Bank and International Monetary Fund, was held here in 1944. Beginning in 1939, the B&M streamlined unit 6000 ran as the *Mountaineer* from Boston, through Intervale, to Whitefield and beyond.

After World War II passenger traffic, which had declined in the 1920s and 1930s, did not recover. In 1953, the *Mountaineer* became a Budd rail diesel car (RDC), the only such units to operate on the MEC, and this ended permanently on September 5, 1955. Other named express trains, the *North Wind* and *Night White Mountains,* had been introduced by the B&M, but survived only to 1956, when the MEC anticipated the end of passenger service. The final passenger runs between Portland and St. Johnsbury were made on April 26, 1958.

Inspection by MEC President E. S. Miller on August 26, 1974, resulted in a decision to upgrade the Mountain Division, culminating in 1978 when the state of New Hampshire erected a bridge over Highway 302 east of Bartlett to eliminate an awkward grade crossing. Just five years later, however, Guilford, the line's new owner, decided that operation was uneconomical, with as many as three extra locomotives dispatched regularly from Rigby Yard in South Portland to assist freight trains over the hump. The last scheduled through freights departed from both ends on September 2, 1983, and passed each other at Bartlett; a final round trip from Rigby Yard was made the next day to clear sidings.

That was not the end of the road, however. A special train to promote railroad safety to school children ran on October 16, 1983. The line was used again on June 9, 1984, to move an oversize load to a power station at Hiram. Fifteen days later Guilford concluded a long-term lease of the Whitefield–St. Johnsbury segment to the Twin State RR, a new line associated with the Lamoille Valley RR. The final irony came in September 1984 when several ballast trains ran between Rigby Yard and Whitefield after washouts on the B&M's ex-White Mountains line.

Eventually the state of New Hampshire acquired the intrastate right of way as far west as Hazens, and leased the length between Intervale and Hazens to the Conway Scenic RR on July 13, 1994. An inaugural train between North Conway and Bartlett ran on December 17, with scheduled excursion passenger service from May 1995. The first train beyond Bartlett to Crawford Notch ran in spring 1996. Conway Scenic passenger trains run regularly as far west as Bretton Woods–Fabyan, and on occasions to Quebec Jct. and beyond. Between Hazens and just east of the crossing at Whitefield the track has been lifted, and all trains use the parallel ex-B&M line. The Twin State lost its final customer in the fall of 1999, and thus trains no longer regularly operate west of Whitefield, although the tracks remain in place.

Guilford continues operation in Maine at least as far as Westbrook-Cumberland Mills, but notified the state on September 17, 1994, that it had initiated abandonment proceedings for the unused length between Windham and the New Hampshire border. The ICC approved the request on October 12, but the state obtained a temporary stay of execution and eventually purchased the line on December 31, 1996. The state maintains the line, although no trains operate on it.

Sources: Bachelder, *Mountaineer*; Baker, *Formation*, 203; Belcher, *Logging Railroads*; Drury, *Historical Guide*, 386-88; Drury, *Train-Watcher's Guide*, 285-86; Robertson and English, *Century of Railroading*; Potter, *Great American Railroad Stations*, 103-4.

37. St. Johnsbury & Lake Champlain

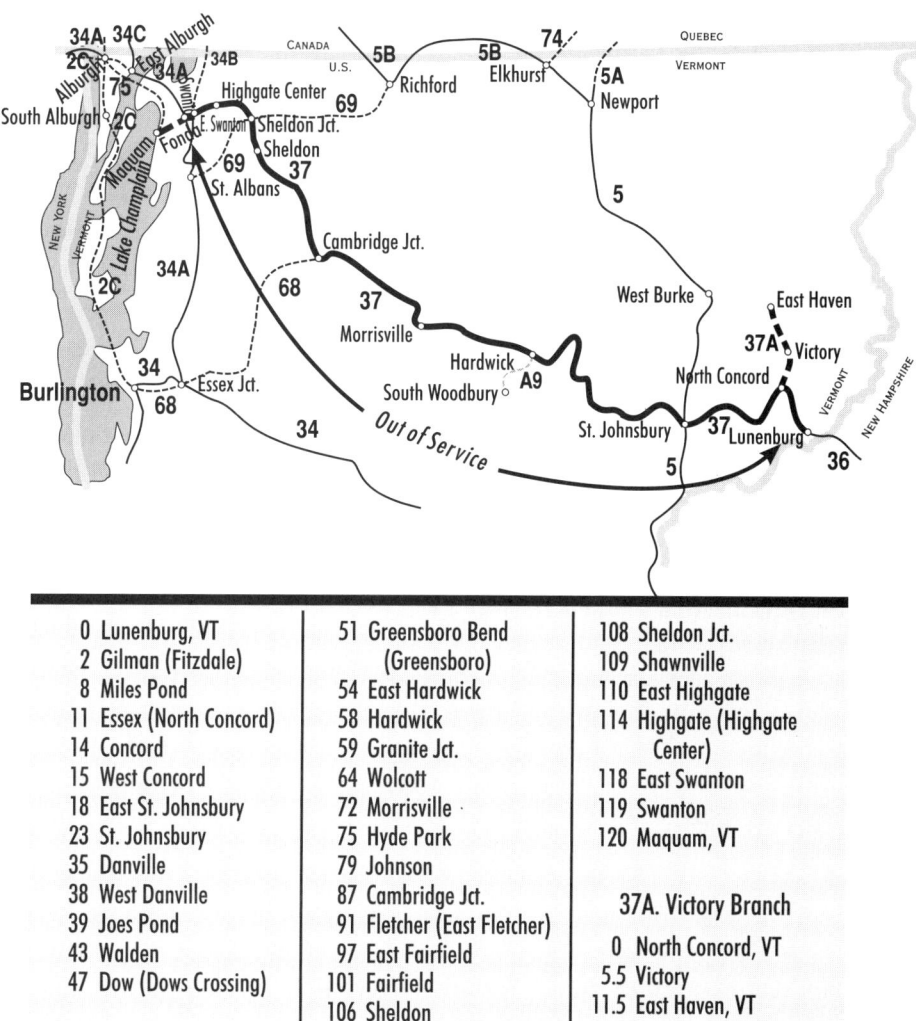

0 Lunenburg, VT	51 Greensboro Bend	108 Sheldon Jct.
2 Gilman (Fitzdale)	(Greensboro)	109 Shawnville
8 Miles Pond	54 East Hardwick	110 East Highgate
11 Essex (North Concord)	58 Hardwick	114 Highgate (Highgate
14 Concord	59 Granite Jct.	Center)
15 West Concord	64 Wolcott	118 East Swanton
18 East St. Johnsbury	72 Morrisville	119 Swanton
23 St. Johnsbury	75 Hyde Park	120 Maquam, VT
35 Danville	79 Johnson	
38 West Danville	87 Cambridge Jct.	**37A. Victory Branch**
39 Joes Pond	91 Fletcher (East Fletcher)	0 North Concord, VT
43 Walden	97 East Fairfield	5.5 Victory
47 Dow (Dows Crossing)	101 Fairfield	11.5 East Haven, VT
	106 Sheldon	

Built: 1869-77, 1880; Victory Branch, 1882.

Operators: *Portland & Ogdensburg VT Division, 1871-80; St. Johnsbury & Lake Champlain, 1880-1948; Maine Central, 1912-67; St. Johnsbury & Lamoille County, 1948-74; Lamoille County,*

37. St. Johnsbury & Lake Champlain

1973-74; *St. Johnsbury & Lake Champlain*, 1974-76; *Vermont Northern*, 1976-77; *Lamoille Valley*, 1978-95; *Twin States*, 1985-99.

Daily Passenger Trains: *1873:* (St. Johnsbury-Concord, 4; St. Johnsbury-Hyde Park, 2); *1893:* 2 (Lunenburg-Swanton; plus St. Johnsbury-Swanton, 2); *1920:* (St. Johnsbury-Swanton, 4; Lunenburg-St. Johnsbury, 4); *1935:* 2 (St. Johnsbury-Swanton, 2; Lunenburg-St. Johnsbury, 2); *1950:* (St. Johnsbury-Swanton 2 [mixed]; Lunenburg-St. Johnsbury, 2). Passenger service ended Swanton-Maquam, 1917; St. Johnsbury-Swanton, 1956; Lunenburg-St. Johnsbury, 1958.

Abandonments: Victory Branch (Victory-East Haven, 1909; North Concord-Victory, 1918); Swanton-Maquam, 1917.

Three companies were organized on February 10, 1867, to continue the Portland & Ogdensburg RR from the New Hampshire/Vermont border westward to complete a through route to Canada. On Christmas Eve, 1867, a groundbreaking ceremony at St. Johnsbury inaugurated work on the Montpelier & St. Johnsbury RR to Danville. A similar ceremony followed on New Years Eve at Swanton for the Lamoille Valley RR, which was to take the line onward to Lake Champlain. The Essex County RR was charged with building east from St. Johnsbury to connect with the P&O at South Lunenburg.

A significant alignment change made by the Montpelier & St. Johnsbury took the right of way north to the south corner of Greensboro and a 270° turn was made to reach and follow the Lamoille River valley. A short stretch of track in St. Johnsbury to serve the Fairbanks scale factory was in service by the end of 1870. Although the Essex County had been the last to start construction, it was the first to operate scheduled service, from the end of January 1872, to Concord. It reached Lunenburg in September 1875 and connected with the P&O before the end of the year. Operation over the Lamoille Valley from St. Johnsbury to Hardwick began on New Years Day, 1872, was extended to Wolcott in October, and to Morrisville on December 31, 1872. Connection with the Burlington & Lamoille RR in Cambridge was not made until July 2, 1877. Through service between St. Johnsbury and Burlington began that day. The last spike was driven ceremoniously at Fletcher in July, and though service from Portland began on July 30.

Although the SJ&LC is now a memory, the Fisher covered bridge over the Lamoille River at Wolcott is still a sight to see. This lattice and girder structure spans 108 feet, and features a continuous lantern roof for escape of steam and fumes. (R. D. Karr)

All three companies operated together as the P&O's Vermont Division, although they remained independent of the rest of the P&O.

The Vermont Division's inability to raise capital, however, precluded construction of several planned stations, many bridges were of a temporary nature, and potential revenue was lost owing to insufficient rolling stock. The P&O itself would not help. Bondholders foreclosed on the three lines in 1879. Following reorganization on January 31, 1880, as the St. Johnsbury & Lake Champlain RR, which took formal control as of July 1, many improvements were made. An extension in 1880 from Swanton to Maquam on Lake Champlain, where a hotel was built, brought the rails to a wharf serving steamboats to Plattsburgh, NY, and Rutland RR steamers. The Boston & Lowell RR obtained control of the line in 1885, although it continued to be operated independently. The SJ&LC retained this status when the B&L was acquired by the Boston & Maine two years later, even though the latter leased the line.

Two mostly-freight branch lines were built off the SJ&LC. The Victory Branch, built in 1882 from North Concord to East Haven, primarily served a privately owned logging railroad. The independent Hardwick & Woodbury RR operated between 1896 and 1937, although a remnant survived in Hardwick until about 1975. The Maquam extension was abandoned in 1917. Above East Haven, the Victory branch was abandoned in 1909; most of the remainder was gone by about 1918, although a short length was in use until the mid-1930s. In 1912 the old Essex County RR between St. Johnsbury and Lunenburg was transferred to the MEC, which operated it as an extension of its Mountain Division (the ex-P&O) to Portland. The Montreal, Portland & Boston RY completed ten miles of track from Sheldon Jct. due north to Franklin in 1882, but the line was never used and eventually was taken up.

On January 1, 1925, responsibility for the SJ&LC was turned over to local management. Severe storms struck the line on November 3, 1927. Many miles of track were washed out, and no trains operated for several days. The covered bridge across the Passumpsic River in St.

Most of the rails of the SJ&LC remain in place, but many grade crossings, like this one at Route 15 in Wolcott, have been paved over. (R. D. Karr)

37. St. Johnsbury & Lake Champlain

Johnsbury was deliberately burned to prevent damage to a highway structure downstream. Trains resumed running on either side of the break on November 9, with limited through service over a temporary bridge until the end of the month. With replacement by a permanent steel bridge, normal service was restored on February 15, 1928. Upon abandonment of the former Burlington & Lamoille line in 1938, a length slightly less than a mile was transferred to the SJ&LC to serve remaining mill customers.

The SJ&LC eventually entered receivership in 1944 and reorganized as the St. Johnsbury & Lamoille County RR on January 24, 1948. In 1950 passenger service was reduced to mixed trains only, and even these ended in 1956, followed two years later by MEC service over the Lunenburg–St. Johnsbury portion. Local customers bought the SJ&LC from the B&M in 1955. They in turn sold it to H. E. Salzberg in 1959, who subsequently conveyed it in 1967 to the Samuel M. Pinsly group, which also acquired parts of the Central Vermont from East Swanton to Fonda Jct. The latter purchase enabled abandonment of a long covered bridge between East Swanton and Swanton. Despite Pinsly's efforts, the line was unsuccessful, and all traffic ended in 1972, with approval to abandon in 1973. The state of Vermont bought the right of way and leased the line to Bruno Loati of Morrisville in the name of the Lamoille County RR. The railroad resumed operation, but changed its name to the St. Johnsbury & Lamoille County in April 1974. Unhappy with the maintenance of the line, the state terminated the lease in October 1976 and transferred it to the Vermont Northern RR, a subsidiary of the Morrison-Knudsen Corporation. Still dissatisfied, the state refused to provide long-term subsidies. With abandonment probable, major shippers formed the Northern Vermont Corporation to take over operation, and incorporated the Lamoille Valley RR to take over operations as of January 1, 1978.

Traffic in the 1980s grew modestly while costs were strictly controlled. Trackage rights were obtained in 1980 for use of the CV's former Missisquoi line to St. Albans in place of facilities at Fonda, in exchange for traffic rights to serve customers in East Swanton. Unfortunately, the connection was severed in 1984 following bridge damage across the river west of Sheldon Jct., caused by a major derailment. That year, the Lamoille Valley formed the Twin State RR to take a long-term lease from the state and the MEC of the eastern section of the P&O between Whitefield and St. Johnsbury. The Twin State began operation on June 26, 1985. East of Sheldon Jct., the Lamoille Valley took over the eastward length of the Missisquoi to Richford on March 7, 1988, although service was provided for only a brief time.

On September 1, 1989, the LV was bought by CSF Acquisitions Corporation (owned by Clyde S. Forbes). After just six years, the company announced its intention to abandon its line between Morrisville and Swanton. The rails west of Johnson had been out of use for many years, with most grade crossings paved over, and a key bridge between Swanton and East Swanton removed. East of Morrisville, traffic over the line to St. Johnsbury ceased in the autumn of 1994. On September 18, 1996, the Surface Transportation Board granted the LV permission to abandon service over the Morrisville-Swanton section, effective October 17. Three weeks before then, however, the petition to abandon was withdrawn, although the lease was not renewed. Accordingly, control reverted to the state on December 31, 1997, followed by surrender of the lease under an agreement made on February 19, 1998. Despite state efforts to find an operator, the line remains out of use. Service on the Twin State RR between St. Johnsbury and Lunenburg dwindled to a single customer, a paper mill at Gilman, which closed on October 1, 1999.

Sources: Bachelder, *Mountaineer*, 6-7; Drury, *Historical Guide*, 285-86, 387; Jones, *Railroads of Vermont*, 2: 111, 224-30; Karr, *Lost Railroads*, 74, 77, 79, 89, 97, 151, 153; Lewis, *Vermont's Covered Bridge Road*; *Railpace*, 15 (Nov.1996): 37; 16 (Nov. 1997): 37; 18 (April 1999): 36.

38. Bridgton & Saco River

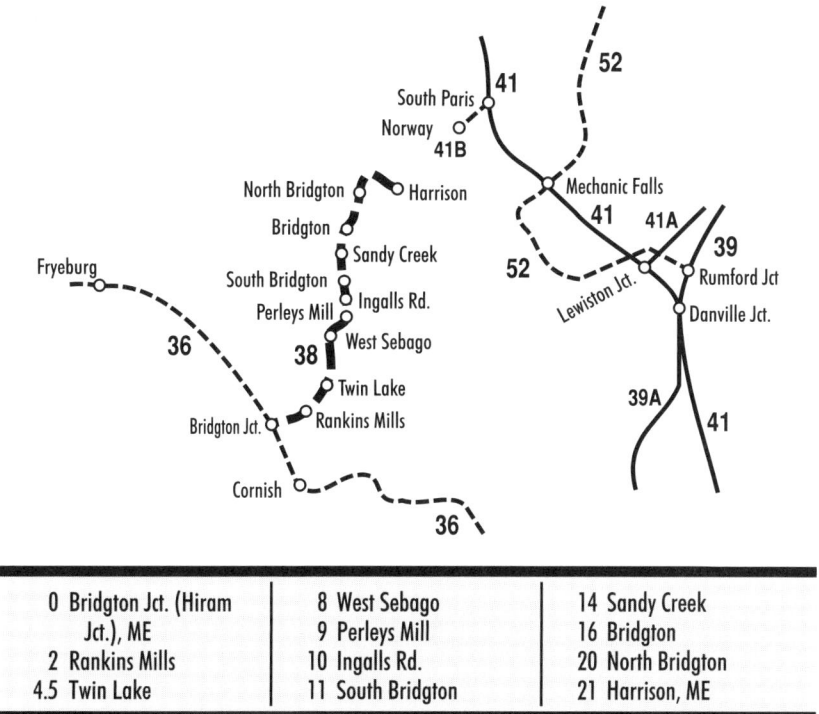

0 Bridgton Jct. (Hiram Jct.), ME	8 West Sebago	14 Sandy Creek
	9 Perleys Mill	16 Bridgton
2 Rankins Mills	10 Ingalls Rd.	20 North Bridgton
4.5 Twin Lake	11 South Bridgton	21 Harrison, ME

Built: 1882-83; 1898.

Operators: *Bridgton & Saco River RR*, 1883-1927; *Bridgton & Saco River RY*, 1927-30; *Bridgton & Harrison RY*, 1930-41.

Daily Passenger Trains: *1893:* 4; *1913:* 6; *1916:* 4; *1919:* 7; *1925:* 2; *1930:* 2 (Bridgton Jct.-Bridgton); *1935:* 4 (Bridgton Jct.-Bridgton); *1938:* 4 (Bridgton Jct.-Bridgton). Passenger service ended 1941.

Abandonments: Bridgton-Harrison, 1930; Bridgton Jct.-Bridgton, 1941.

Bridgton, situated between the foot of Highland (or Dock) Lake and the western shore of Long Lake astride Steven's Brook, was an established resort, but access was restricted in winter. Severe winter weather in 1879 isolated the area for lengthy periods although the Portland & Ogdensburg RR continued to operate. Bridgton businessmen and landowners banded together and promoted a 30-mile

38. Bridgton & Saco River

standard-gauge railroad from the P&O to the Norway Branch RR, which connected with the Grand Trunk RY at South Paris. Such bold ambition was soon tempered by appreciation of the estimated cost. A more practical scheme was developed by George E. Mansfield, the champion of the 2-foot narrow gauge. His report recommended a 16-mile 2-foot-gauge line running north from the main line at Hiram as far as Bridgton.

A charter for the narrow-gauge Bridgton & Saco River RR was obtained on June 29, 1881, with work commencing shortly after. On Tuesday, January 31, 1883, public trains began operation from Hiram to Bridgton. Rolling stock comprised two 0-4-4 Hinkley-built Forney locomotives, two passenger cars, and fifteen freight cars, supplemented around 1886 by a caboose.

Hiram Jct. was renamed Bridgton Jct. in 1888 to obviate confusion with the P&O's nearby Hiram station. A third Forney locomotive was obtained from the Portland Company five years later. On August 3, 1898, a five-mile extension from Bridgton to Harrison involving a long trestle across the head of Long Lake was completed. The railroad was

B&SR no. 2 crosses the Long Lake trestle at Harrison around the time the extension opened in 1898. (Courtesy Walker Transportation Collection, Beverly Historical Society & Museum)

profitable for many years, with lumber and seasonal passengers being its mainstays. When the Maine Central took control on July 24, 1912, independent operation continued, although additional locomotives and freight cars were introduced and some track improvements made. Passengers accounted for most of the line's traffic.

Obvious decline set in after 1920. Local management replaced mixed trains with rail busses, but costs continued to soar. By 1927 the MEC was suggesting abandonment and allowed the company to default on its mortgage payments. A new company, the Bridgton & Harrison RY, controlled by the town of Bridgton, made a successful bid for the line at a receiver's auction on July 1, 1930.

Faced with limited revenue and deferred maintenance, particularly on the Long Lake trestle, the B&H abandoned the Harrison extension on October 30, 1930. Except for excursions and when there was sufficient demand, particularly after snowfalls, trains normally comprised two vehicles rudely converted from road busses. A third was bought from the Sandy River RR in 1936. Car- and train-load traffic continued to be steam-hauled until the end.

Exasperated by continued losses, Bridgton voted October 9, 1939, to sell the line. A deal with a scrap merchant was completed on May 13, 1940. The town obtained permission to abandon the railroad on January 17, 1941, although the final train ran in September.

Sources: Crittenden, *Maine Scenic Route*, 73–86; Hilton, *American Narrow Gauge*, 407; Mead, *Busted & Still Running*; Moody, *Maine Two-Footers*, 25–31, 123–44; Karr, *Lost Railroads*, 85, 103.

39. Maine Central (Original System)

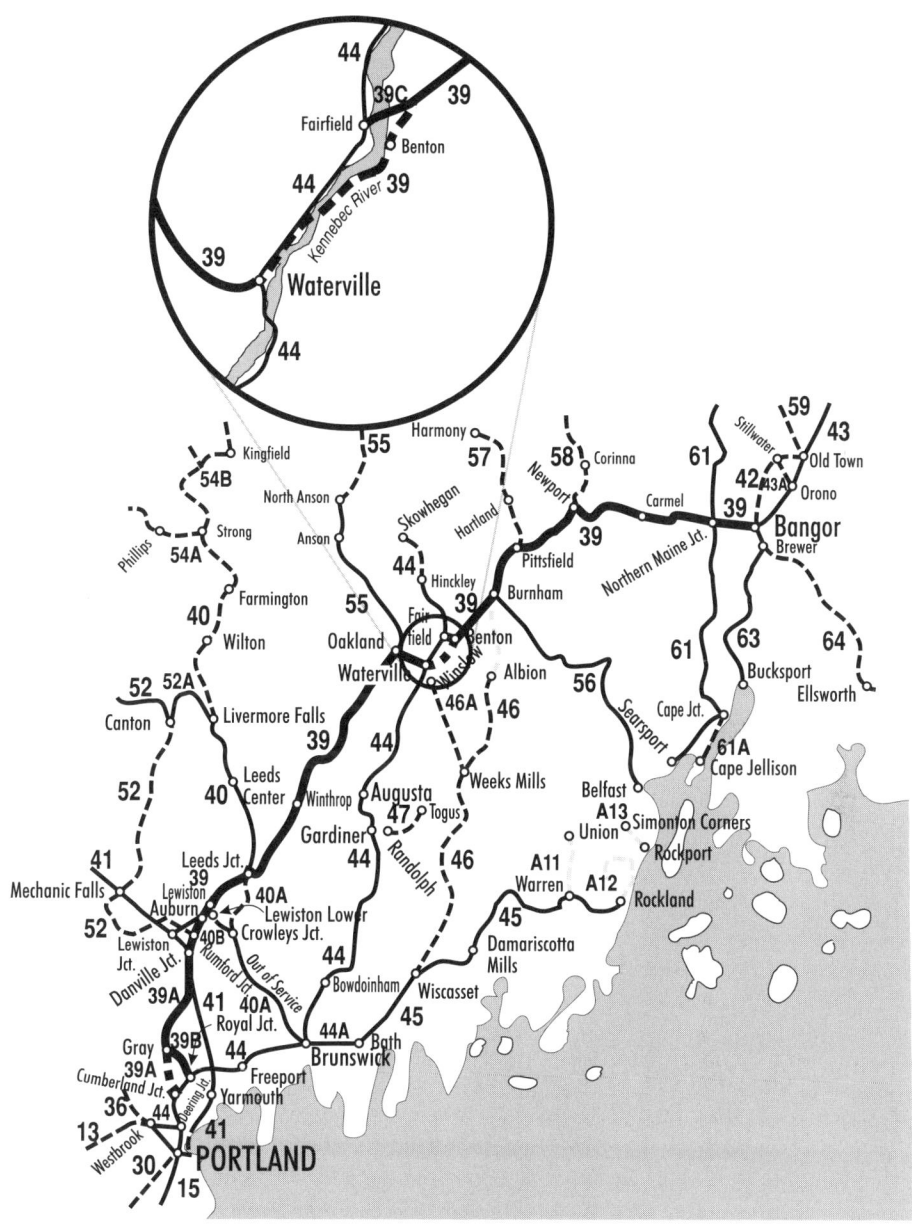

Guilford local freight OT-1 rounds a bend at Hurd Corner, ME, a few miles east of Newport, in July 1993. (R. D. Karr)

39. Maine Central (Original System)

0 Danville Jct., ME	58 Benton (West Benton)	9 Gray
1.5 Rumford Jct. (Poland Spring Jct.)	64 Clinton	11 Porters Mill Rd. [1975 ft. north]
2 Hacketts Switch (Hacketts)	69 Burnham Jct. (Burnham)	12 Wescustogo
	76 Pittsfield Center (Pittsfield)	14 Walnut Hill
5 Auburn	83 Newport (Newport Jct.)	17 Cumberland Jct. (Cumberland), ME
7 Lewiston (Lewiston Upper)	86 East Newport (East Newport [Eastville])	
14 Greene	91 Etna	**39B. Walnut Hill Diversion**
17 Leeds Jct. (Leeds)	94 Damascus	
21 Monmouth	95 Carmel	0 Porters Mill Road [1975 ft. north], ME
23 Annabessacook	100 Hermon Pond	2.5 Walnut Hill
26 Winthrop	103 Hermon Center (Hermon Centre)	6 Royal Jct., ME
30 Maranacook		
32 Readfield	105 Northern Maine Jct.	
40 Belgrade	110 Bangor Union Sta. (Bangor), ME	**39C. Fairfield Diversion**
43 Lakeside		0 Benton [0.5 mi. north], ME
44 North Belgrade (Messalonskee)	**39A. P&K Extension**	1 Fairfield (Kendall Mills), ME
49 Oakland (West Waterville)	0 Danville Jct., ME	
55 Waterville	5 New Gloucester	
	7 Rowes	

Built: 1853–55; P&K Extension, 1871; Walnut Hill Diversion, 1911; Fairfield Diversion, ca. 1918.

Operators: *Androscoggin & Kennebec*, 1848–55; *Penobscot & Kennebec*, 1855–62; *Maine Central*, 1862–1981; *Guilford*, 1981–.

Daily Passenger Trains: *1851:* 4 (Danville Jct.–Waterville); *1873:* Portland–Lewiston, 6; Lewiston–Waterville, 2; Waterville–Bangor, 6; *1892:* Portland–Leeds Jct., 4; Portland–Waterville, 4; Waterville–Bangor, 10; *1912:* Portland–Leeds Jct., 18; Leeds Jct.–Waterville, 12; Waterville–Bangor, 12; *1919:* Portland–Lewiston, 8; Lewiston–Leeds Jct., 6; Leeds Jct.–Waterville, 4; Waterville–Bangor, 13; *1935:* Portland–Leeds Jct., 7; Leeds Jct.–Waterville, 5; Waterville–Bangor, 12; *1950:* Portland–Leeds Jct., 9; Leeds Jct.–Waterville, 5; Waterville–Bangor, 12; *1959:* Portland–Waterville, 2; Waterville–Bangor, 8. Passenger service ended 1960.

Abandonments: Mill Road–Cumberland Jct., 1912; Waterville–Benton [0.5 miles north], 1918.

Headed by a venerable EMD-built GP-35 once owned by the Norfolk Southern, Guilford's Rumford–Portland train RUPO waits to enter the yard at Danville Jct. in June 1999. (R. D. Karr)

A little over a month after the Atlantic & St. Lawrence RR received its charter, another was obtained on March 28, 1845, by a group of Maine businessmen for a link between Danville on the A&SL and the emerging industrial centers of Auburn–Lewiston and Waterville. The charter of the Androscoggin & Kennebec RR did not specify track gauge, but 5-foot 6-inch was the only practical option, since this gauge had been adopted by the A&SL, with which it would connect to reach Portland. Service to Lewiston began in December 1848, a few weeks after the A&SL extended to Danville from Yarmouth. Service to Waterville began December 5, 1849.

To minimize financial risk, the Maine legislature on April 7, 1845, chartered a separate line, the Penobscot & Kennebec RR, to extend the rails to Bangor. Construction was slow and trains did not run through to Bangor until August 1855. Subsequently, the two companies requested permission from the legislature to merge. Consent was given on April 1, 1856, but with a proviso that fares should be equal with those of the competing Kennebec & Portland line. But instead of merging, the A&K leased the Penobscot & Kennebec.

The heated rivalry between the two Portland-Waterville routes forced the Kennebec & Portland into reorganization as the Portland & Kennebec RR in 1862. The legislature repealed the equal fares provision on March 17, 1862, and authorized the merger of the A&K and Penobscot & Kennebec to form the Maine Central RR, which took place that October.

Increasing traffic on the standard-gauge lines (particularly Portland to Boston), the inconvenience and cost of traffic exchanges, and competition from the Grand Trunk RY (as the A&SL had become in 1853) led the MEC into leasing the rival standard-gauge Portland & Kennebec in 1870 and narrowing its own line. The MEC also built a standard-gauge extension from Danville to Cumberland Jct., which required extensive fill and bridging; it was completed in 1871. The MEC designated the line through Auburn-Lewiston the "Back Road" and the ex-P&K route through Brunswick and Augusta became the "Lower Road." From then on, through passenger trains from points south of Portland and beyond Waterville took the Lower Road, leaving the Back Road with local service only. After 1912, however, the seasonal *Bar Harbor Express* used the Back Road, as did some later express trains. When required, the Back Road provided a diversionary route for trains scheduled over the Lower Road.

A major improvement program just before World War I resulted in the Walnut Hill diversion, a new line from a point north of Porters Mill Road in North Yarmouth to Royal Jct., a new connection with the former Portland & Kennebec. The diversion eased grades and curves, and the original alignment between Porters Mill Road and Cumberland Jct. was abandoned.

Around 1917 or 1918 the tracks between Waterville and a point north of Benton were abandoned in favor of using the former Kennebec & Portland line to Fairfield. The MEC built a new connection, including a bridge across the Kennebec River, between the Kennebec & Portland in Fairfield to a point just north of Benton.

For many years until after the First World War the Lower Road was the more important route, as Brunswick and Augusta produced considerably more traffic than Auburn-Lewiston. Still, Auburn and Lewiston had become substantial mill towns by the 1870s. Auburn's 21 factories

A northbound Guilford freight is seen in June 1999 in Dunns Corner, not far from Walnut Hill, on the diversion route built in 1911. (R. D. Karr)

then produced more than 2 million pairs of shoes annually, and in 1917 one factory was making 75 percent of the world's supply of white canvas shoes, most of which were shipped by rail.

A new articulated streamlined train was introduced on April 1, 1935, jointly by the MEC and B&M, on a three-hour express schedule between Portland and Bangor. The first of its kind in the east, the *Flying Yankee* used the Back Road, making only two mandatory intermediate stops at Lewiston and Waterville. Additional flag stops between Lewiston and Bangor were added over the years. During World War II this was replaced by a steam-hauled consist, which continued under diesel power until April 1959. By then, almost all intermediate train stops had been eliminated.

All local passenger service over the Back Road ended after February 6, 1960, following approval by the Maine Public Utilities Commission, although two round trips between Waterville and Bangor and the by then once-weekly *Bar Harbor Express* continued until September 5. The night train from Vanceboro was the last to enter Portland Union Station, just after 6:30 a.m. on Tuesday, September 6, 1960.

After Guilford took over the MEC in 1981, the Back Road became part of its Freight Main Line, and use of the Lower Road was largely discontinued north of Brunswick. Switching and blocking were gradually transferred from Bangor to Rigby Yard in South Portland, and dispatching is now mostly from North Billerica, MA. Several daily through freights are scheduled over the line, some of which turn onto the former Androscoggin RR at Leeds Jct., bound for Rumford.

Sources: Bachelder, *Rumford Rocket*, 6–7; Bachelder, *Special Trains*, 4–16; Baker, *Formation*, 203–04; Drury, *Historical Guide*, 386–88; Kirkland, *Men, Cities & Transportation*, 1: 215; 2: 6.

40. Androscoggin

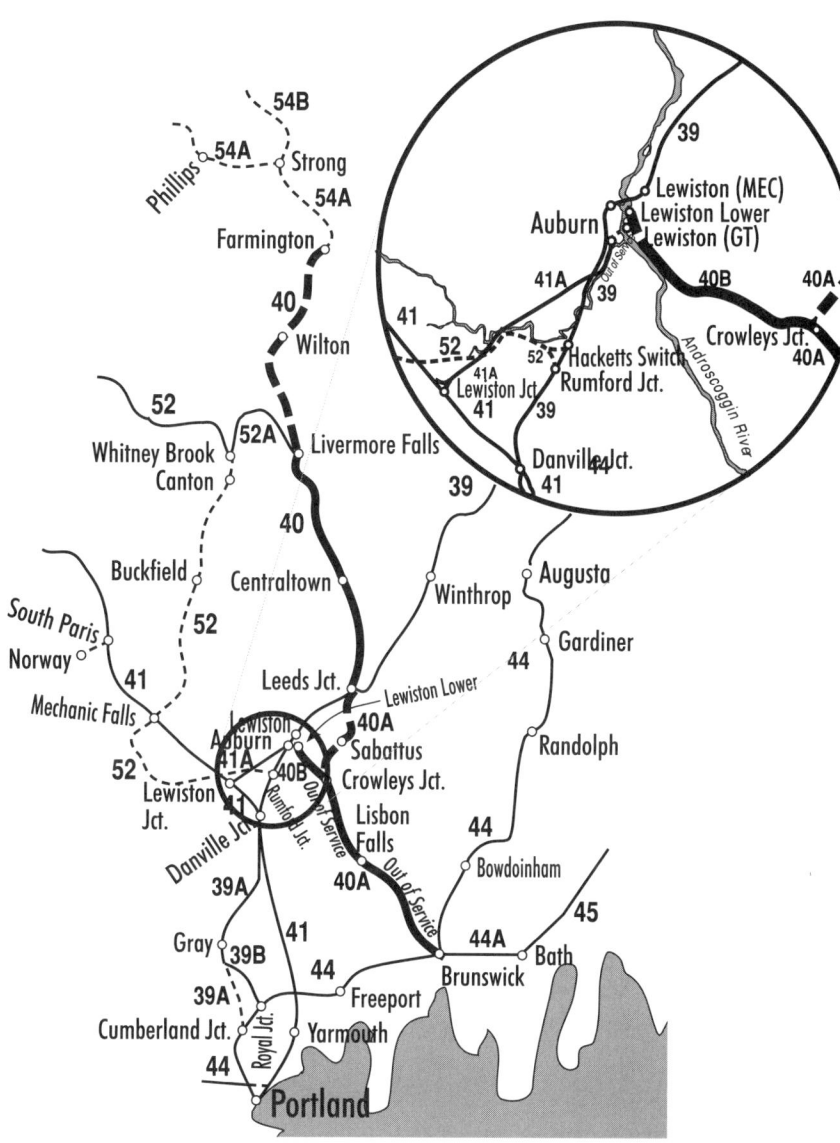

40. Androscoggin

0 Leeds Jct., ME	22 The Bridge (Jay)	14.5 Lisbon
1 Libbys Pit (Highmoor)	25.5 North Jay	18 Lisbon Falls (Little River)
2.5 Curtis Corner	29.5 Wilton	20 Simpsons
7.5 Centraltown (Leeds Center) (Leeds)	31.5 Tyngston (East Wilton)	21.5 Pejepscot Mills (Pejepscot)
9 Androscoggin (Wayne Pond) (Dead River)	36 Westville (West Farmington)	23 Topsham
11 Littleboro (North Leeds)	36.5 Farmington, ME	26 Brunswick, ME
12.5 Stricklands (Stricklands Ferry)	**40A. Brunswick Extension**	**40B. Lewiston Branch**
15 Norlands (East Livermore)	0 Leeds Jct., ME	0 Crowleys Jct., ME
19 Shuy	2 Wales	5 Lewiston Lower (Lewiston), ME
20 Livermore Falls	5 Golders	
	7 Sabattus (Sabbatusville)	
	11.5 Crowleys Jct. (Crowleys)	

Built: 1851–59.

Operators: *Androscoggin*, 1852–70; *Maine Central*, 1870–1981; *Guilford*, 1981– ; *Maine Coast*, 1995–ca. 1997.

Daily Passenger Trains: *1869:* 2 (Brunswick–Lewiston, 4); *1893:* 4 (Brunswick–Lewiston, 10) *1915:* 4 (Brunswick–Lewiston, 12); *1930:* 4 (Brunwick–Lewiston, 6); *1950:* 2. Passenger service ended Leeds Jct.–Crowleys Jct.,1932; Brunswick–Lewiston, 1933; Leeds Jct.–Farmington, 1956.

Abandonments: Leeds Jct.–Crowleys Jct., 1938; Livermore Falls–Farmington, 1982; at Lewiston Lower, 1984.

Like the Androscoggin & Kennebec RR, from which it started at remote Leeds Jct. 11 miles northeast of Lewiston, the Androscoggin RR was built as a 5-foot 6-inch broad-gauge line. Its backers anticipated significant traffic in lumber and quarried stone. By December 1852 the line extended as far as Livermore Falls on the Androscoggin River. This area was an outlet for felled lumber, and later the site of pulp and paper mills. The rails reached North Jay in 1856, East Wilton the following year, and Farmington in June 1859. Quarries at North Jay produced the high quality white granite that many years later would be used in building Grant's Tomb in New York City. Farmington at the time was a small village, but grew rapidly as a railhead for extensive lumber traffic.

At the northern end of the Androscoggin at Farmington, MEC trains met those of the diminutive 2-foot narrow-gauge Sandy River & Rangeley Lakes, as shown in this 1921 scene. (Courtesy Walker Transportation Collection, Beverly Historical Society & Museum)

At first, returns were limited because the Androscoggin & Kennebec RR exploited the Androscoggin's dependency by levying unreasonably high transfer charges. When negotiations for trackage rights to Portland failed, the Androscoggin decided to construct a standard-gauge line southward from Leeds Jct. to the Kennebec & Portland RR at Brunswick, with a branch from Crowleys to Lewiston. Both were completed in 1861. An attempt was made by the A&K to block narrowing of the original line to standard gauge at the same time, but the owners evaded service of a court injunction and performed the work one Sunday in 1861. The case was litigated for three years, but in 1864 the Maine Supreme Court upheld the Androscoggin. Ironically, during the next few years the extension enjoyed satisfactory results, whereas traffic on the original main line failed to produce reasonable returns, resulting in default on bond interest in 1865. After foreclosure by the bondholders a separate company, the Leeds & Farmington RR, was incorporated to acquire the line between those two points, but was immediately leased to the Androscoggin. These arrangements survived just five years. By 1870 the Maine Central RR had committed to major expansion through acquisition of interests in other independent lines, and it leased the Androscoggin from June 29, 1871. The L&F was absorbed in 1874, but the Androscoggin was not sold to the MEC until August 19, 1911.

Traffic grew considerably. From November 1879, the narrow-gauge Sandy River RR connected at transfer sidings in Farmington, and on September 1, 1897, the Portland & Rumford Falls RR opened a link between Livermore Falls and Gilbertville.

Decline set in during the 1920s when passenger receipts fell dramatically, resulting in diversion of trains between Leeds Jct. and Crowleys and closure of that section in June 1932, although it was used for storage of rolling stock until abandoned in 1938. Passenger service between Lewiston Lower and Brunswick ended in 1933, but was continued on the original main line until 1956. North of Livermore Falls the line was closed and abandoned in 1982 and is now a trail.

The MEC obtained permission to abandon the final 0.6 miles of the Lewiston Lower Branch in 1978, but customers agreed to subsidize operation. The arrangement ended in 1982, and Guilford promptly truncated the Lewiston Industrial Track, as it had become known. Track was removed in September 1983. In 1995 Guilford granted trackage rights to the Maine Coast RR to operate the line between Brunswick and Lisbon Falls, but this was short lived. The junction switches at Brunswick were taken out, and in July 1998, Guilford sought permission from the Surface Transportation Board to abandon the line between Lewiston and Brunswick, only to withdraw its application in the summer of 1999. Since then work has been done to reinstate and improve track between Brunswick and Lisbon Falls.

These days, the line from Leeds Jct. to Livermore Falls is single track, operated under radio dispatch west of automatic block signaling territory on the main line to serve Rumford. A daily round trip road freight is run from Rigby Yard to Rumford through Livermore, serving the International Paper and Wausau Mosinee facilities at Rileys and Mead Paper Corp. at Rumford.

Sources: Bachelder, *Rumford Rocket*; Chase, *Maine Railroads*; Karr, *Lost Railroads*, 98, 144, 147; *Railpace* 18 (Dec. 1999): 36.

41. Atlantic & St. Lawrence

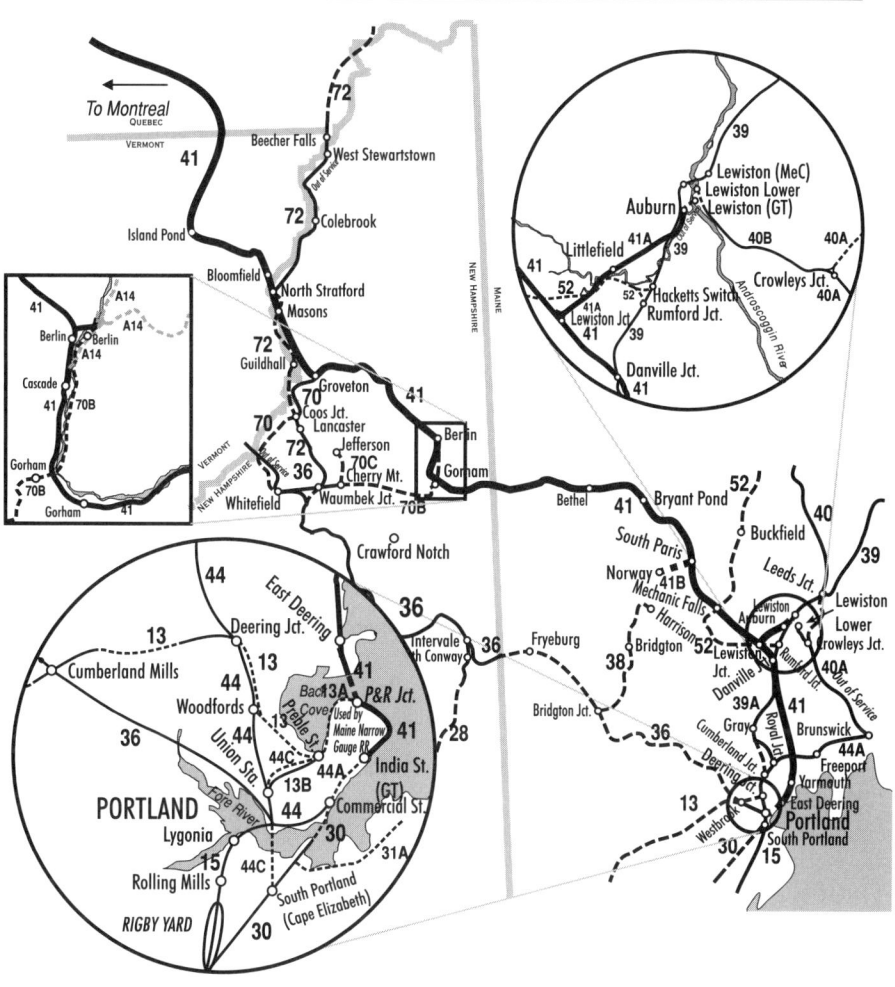

0 Portland GT Sta. (Portland India St.), ME	11.5 Yarmouth
1.5 Back Cove (Portland & Rochester Jct.) (Portland Jct.) (Union Jct.)	12 Yarmouth Jct.
	15.5 Dunns (Dunns Corner) (North Yarmouth)
2.5 East Deering	18.5 Pownal (West Pownal)
5.5 Falmouth	22.5 New Gloucester (Intervale) (Woodman)
9 Cumberland	

25 Cobb (Cobbs Brook)
27.5 Danville Jct. (Danville)
28.5 Hotel Rd. (West Danville)
30 Lewiston Jct.
32 Empire Rd. (East Poland)
36.5 Mechanic Falls

41. Atlantic & St. Lawrence

41 Oxford	98 Berlin (Berlin Falls)	156 Summit
47.5 South Paris	102 Jericho	160 Lake
50 Jacksons Crossing	103 Copperville (Milan)	161 Paradis
53 Snow Falls (Snows Falls)	105 Foggs Siding	165 Norton (Norton Mills), VT
55.5 Bates (West Paris)	109 West Milan	*166 Stanhope, PQ*
62 Bryants Pond (Bryant Pond)	112 Crystal	*297 Montreal, PQ*
65.5 Lockes Mills	114 Percy	
67 South Bethel (Walkers Mills)	116 Stark	**41A. Lewiston & Auburn RR**
70 Bethel	122 Groveton (Groveton Jct.)	0 Lewiston Jct., ME
71 Skillingston	126 Mapleton (Stratford Hollow)	1.5 Littlefield
74 Allens (West Bethel)	130 Masons (Stratford Jct.)	5 Auburn
80 Gilead, ME	134 North Stratford (North Stratford Jct.), NH	5.5 Lewiston, ME
86 Shelburne, NH	135 Bloomfield, VT	**41B. Norway Branch**
88 Leadmine Crossing	142 Wenlock	0 South Paris, ME
91.5 Gorham	145 East Brighton	1.5 Norway, ME
96 Cascade	149 Island Pond	

Built: 1846–53.

Operators: *Atlantic & St. Lawrence*, 1848–53; *Grand Trunk*, 1853–1923; *Canadian National*, 1923–89; *St. Lawrence & Atlantic*, 1989–.

Daily Passenger Trains: *1853:* 4; *1869:* 2; *1893:* 4; *1916:* 10; *1927:* 8; *1930:* 4; *1936:* 2; *1950:* 2; *1960:* 2. Lewiston Branch: *1929:* 8; *1933:* 4; *1936:* 2; *1955:* 2. Norway Branch: *1883:* 14; *1910:* 8; *1926:* 6; *1930:* 4; *1939:* 2. Passenger service ended Norway Branch, 1939; Lewiston Branch, 1956; Portland–Montreal, 1967. Service resumed East Deering–Bethel (seasonal) 1993–97.

Abandonments: Lewiston Branch, 1980 (in Auburn, partially reopened ca.1988); Portland–East Deering [1 mile south], 1988; Norway Branch, 1990 (partially reopened 1997).

When nothing came of the 1834 plan of the Maine Board of Internal Improvements for a statewide transportation infrastructure, Bangor lawyer John Alfred Poor stepped in with his own proposal for a system of railroads that would benefit the state, and the city of Portland in particular. He had a grand vision of rail lines radiating from Portland both to Montreal and northeast to New Brunswick and Nova Scotia, enabling year-round trade with Europe and providing

Bound for Canada, a Canadian National freight passes the restored depot at Gorham, NH, in July 1988. (R. D. Karr)

Montreal with a warm water outlet when the St. Lawrence froze over. By 1842 the completion of the standard-gauge Portland, Saco & Portsmouth RR had opened a route from Portland to Boston using the Eastern RR.

Poor gained sufficient support to petition the Maine legislature in January 1845 for a charter for the Atlantic & St. Lawrence RR. While the matter was being debated in Augusta, Boston interests were before the Montreal Board of Trade presenting a case for a line from their city to Montreal. Poor undertook an epic five-day trip through severe snowstorms to Canada to argue for his Portland route. He succeeded in securing postponement of a vote on February 9, having gained support from Canadian businessmen who would incorporate separately as the St. Lawrence & Atlantic RY. The Maine charter was approved the next day, and a charter for the Canadian company was granted on March 17.

Stock in the Atlantic & St. Lawrence RR was placed on sale in June 1845, and the company was formally organized on September 25. By then about $1 million had been subscribed, almost all by Portland residents, of an estimated $2.5 million capital requirement. In April 1846 the two companies agreed to adopt the 5-foot 6-inch broad gauge used elsewhere in Canada, partly as a means to avoid traffic being siphoned off to Boston. A groundbreaking ceremony took place in Portland on July 4, 1846. Construction began on August 20 and was completed to Yarmouth less than two years later, enabling passenger service to start on July 20, 1848. Costs exceeded estimates, and to continue the second length to Danville, which had been started on November 23, 1846, the company was forced to borrow $113,000. Even this was insufficient but appeal to the city of Portland resulted in a loan of $1 million. The extension opened on November 25, 1848.

Meanwhile the Maine company's Canadian counterpart had started construction from Longueil, across the St. Lawrence from Montreal, in October 1846 and completed its first 15 miles on December 27, 1848. The A&SL continued northward to Mechanic Falls on February 4, 1849, but by then money was again running short and further appeals

Built in 1909 by the Grand Trunk, the bridge across the Androscoggin River on the Lewiston & Auburn RR was converted to an inviting pedestrian and cycling pathway in 1994, as seen in this 1999 view looking into Lewiston from Auburn. (R. D. Karr)

41. Atlantic & St. Lawrence

had to be made to the city of Portland for more funds. Oxford was reached in September 1849 and South Paris on June 8, 1850. Regular service to Bethel commenced in March the following year, extended to West Bethel on June 10, to Gilead some weeks later, and to Gorham on July 23. Groveton, NH, became the terminal on July 12, 1852, and North Stratford followed before the winter snows.

In Canada the SL&A had had its fair share of financial difficulties as well, but had been saved by the government's Guarantee Act of May 30, 1849. The line had reached Richmond on October 15, 1851, and Sherbrooke on September 11, 1852. During the previous summer officials of the two companies had met to determine which of several alignments should be adopted through Vermont. The SL&A agreed to complete 16 miles from the border south to Island Pond. Work northward from North Stratford began in earnest on December 13 and was inspected on February 4, 1853, with introduction of regular service on April 4. The SL&A reached Island Pond on July 11, and through service began one week later. Ten days before, the SL&A had been merged into the Grand Trunk RY, and the A&SL was leased by the GT on August 5. The final link, Victoria Bridge at Montreal, was opened for regular traffic on December 12, 1859.

By the 1870s the broad gauge had become an anachronism. Standard-gauge lines were extending into GT territory; the last straw was the narrowing of the Maine Central lines in 1871. Accordingly, the decision to convert was made in 1873. The entire Portland–Montreal line was converted over a single 12-hour period on Friday night and Saturday morning, September 25–26, 1874. In a further reversal of Poor's policy of isolation, the GT now built connections in Portland with the PS&P and the Boston & Maine. The system also expanded through construction of the standard-gauge Lewiston & Auburn RR from Lewiston Jct. to serve their most heavily industrialized quarters. A charter had been obtained on February 2, 1872, and the GT agreed to lease and operate the line from March 25, 1874, and to provide stations. Passenger service connecting with main line trains began July 13, with freight following after conversion of the main line. For many years some passenger trains ran through to Portland. A second branch, the Norway Branch RR, in which the Town of Norway held two-thirds of the stock, was chartered on April 23, 1879. The GT agreed to build the line and lease it from opening for $1 per annum. Local passenger trains

St. Lawrence & Atlantic symbol freight 293 leaves Danville Jct. for Canada in late May 1999. (R. D. Karr)

were provided until replacement in January 1926 by main line trains making side trips up the branch.

For over sixty years, the GT brought great prosperity to Portland. Immense quantities of grain outstripped the capacity of dockside elevators, several of which were built either by the city or private enterprise and leased to the GT. Around the turn of the century a new stockyard was built in East Deering. Partly to alleviate congestion in Commercial Street, the Union Branch was built by the Portland Union Station Co. along Back Cove to Portland Jct. A 1.5-million bushel capacity grain elevator was completed in 1902. A grand new station at India Street, designed by Spier & Rohns in an eclectic style featuring pink granite and a tall tower, was opened on November 4, 1903.

In 1916 the system returned a considerable profit; but in 1917, with gross revenues at their highest level ever, inflation and a steep rise in operating costs resulted in a huge loss. Coupled with burdensome costs from projects elsewhere, loss of independence was inevitable. The GT was taken over by a Board of Management on May 21, 1920, and on

41. Atlantic & St. Lawrence

January 30, 1923, became a part of the Canadian National Railways. Operation of the A&SL began to decline almost immediately. Canadian political considerations demanded diverting export traffic away from Portland to Saint John and Halifax.

In the spring of 1920, the Warner Sugar Refining Co. of New York City incorporated the New Hampshire Stave & Heading Mill for construction of a facility in North Stratford, NH, which eventually extended over almost 50 acres. A lumber railroad, chartered in Vermont during May, involved about 1.5 miles of spurs and sidings, which were installed under contract by the GT. The 12-mile main line was completed under a separate contract, from about 1500 feet west of the A&SL bridge over the Connecticut River to Lewis in the Yellow Bogs, in the fall of 1921. Trackage rights were exercised over the intermediate length of about 1.5 miles. Two long branches were built toward Lewis Pond, with at least six spurs serving major lumber camps. The line was short-lived. By 1924, demand for barrels had decreased, and although economies were made, the last trains ran during the winter of 1926–27; tracks were removed between August and October. In 1929 the mill was sold to the St. Regis Paper Co., but eventually closed.

By 1930, rail freight to Portland had dwindled. Wharves were sold and the grain elevators abandoned, and other savings measures were instituted. India Street station in Portland lost its prominent tower in 1948; the station was razed at the end of March 1966. Passenger trains, which had been reduced in 1960 from year-round service to a weekends-only train during summers, made their last runs on August 12, 1967.

CN reincorporated the Grand Trunk Corporation in 1970 to take over its operations in the United States but excluded the A&SL. The Norway Branch was truncated to about half its original length in August 1983, the remainder serving a spur to Wilner Wood Products Co. Following the burning of the Back Cove bridge in Portland in January 1984, which cut off CN access to Commercial Street, the entire line was included in a five-year abandonment plan submitted to the state of Maine. For a time the yard and tracks in Commercial Street remained in use by a single CN RS-11 locomotive, switching cars received from Guilford.

The entire line was placed for sale in 1989. The Emons Transportation Group of York, PA, purchased the A&SL for $12 million on May 22, 1989. They have operated the line as the St. Lawrence & Atlantic

RR ever since. Through freights operate each day between Canada and Danville Jct., with connecting local freights to Auburn and East Deering as far south as the burnt Back Cove bridge. (The St. Lawrence & Atlantic has never operated the ex-GT tracks in downtown Portland.) Wilner's plant in Norway closed in November 1991, and with it the remainder of the Norway Branch.

A new multimodal facility on the Lewiston & Auburn, designed to attract containerized freight in addition to feed, lumber, and building products, was constructed in 1994 and helps sustain traffic on the main line. The last mile and a half through Auburn, though, is effectively abandoned, the bridge over the Androscoggin into Lewiston now serving pedestrians and bicyclists. A connection with the Norway branch was restored in 1997 to form a siding at the New England Public Warehouse, and a second multimodal facility opened on the L&A the same year.

Starting in December 1993 the proprietors of a ski resort in Bethel, ME, sponsored the *Sunday River Silver Bullet Ski Express* to run weekends between there and East Deering. In subsequent seasons it also operated daily, but after considerable losses it was discontinued after the 1996–97 season. Part of the line in Portland is used by the 2-foot-gauge Maine Narrow Gauge RR, which began operation in 1994 with locomotives and rolling stock purchased from the erstwhile Edaville RR of Carver, MA.

Sources: Bachelder, *Androscoggin Valley Ltd.*; Jones, *Railroads of Vermont*, 1: 275–91; Judd, Churchill, and Eastman, *Maine*, 314–16; Karr, *Lost Railroads*, 150; Kirkland, *Men, Cities & Transportation*, 1: 208–14, 445, 478; Lewis, *American Shortline Railway Guide*, 225; *Railpace*, 16 (Nov. 1997), 37.

42. Bangor, Old Town & Milford

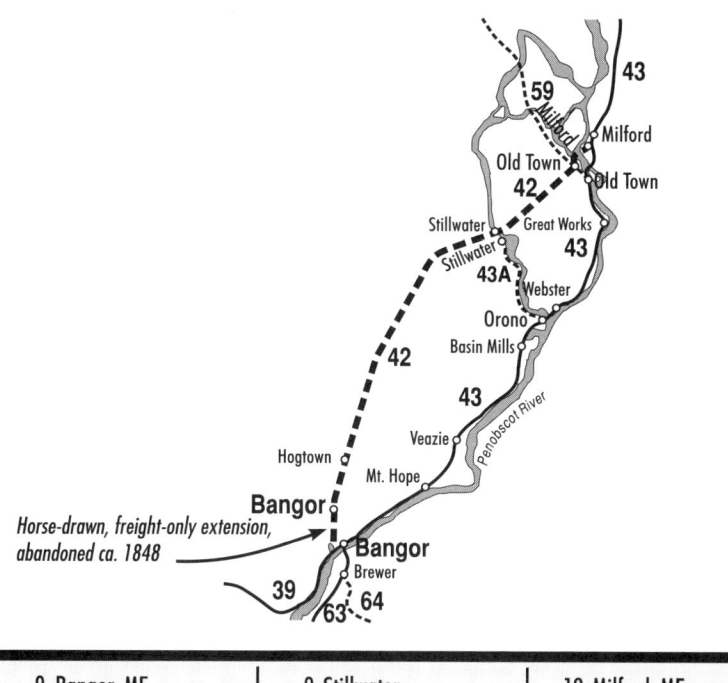

| 0 Bangor, ME | 9 Stillwater | 12 Milford, ME |
| 1 Hogtown | 11 Old Town | |

Built: 1832–55.
Operators: *Bangor & Piscataquis Canal & RR*, 1836–55; *Bangor, Old Town & Milford*, 1855–69.
Daily Passenger Trains: *1837:* 6. Passenger service ended 1869.
Abandonment: 1870.

Exploitation of central Maine lumber resources began in the mid-1700s. Lumber was floated down the Penobscot River from its head at Dolby Pond and down the Stillwater River to mills in Old Town, Orono, Stillwater, and Bangor. Bangor grew rapidly as the head of navigation for large oceangoing craft. Incorporated as a town in 1791, it became a city in 1834 with a population of over 6,000. By then mill proprietors had decided that an alternative to mud roads was required to get their products to the port.

42. Bangor, Old Town & Milford

A railroad charter was obtained in 1832 for the Bangor & Old Town RY for construction of a link between Bangor and Old Town through Stillwater. Work began at once but ended the next year with grading partially completed to Orono. Meanwhile other parties obtained charters, amongst them the Bangor & Piscataquis Canal & Railroad Company, on February 1, 1833. The two companies engaged in fierce rivalry, culminating with the new company purchasing the older one for $50,000. The line was completed during 1836 at a total cost of $354,000, and the first train ran on November 6—the first use of steam traction in northern New England—with formal opening three weeks later. Trains operated daily except Sundays. From the terminal in Bangor, between Howard Lane and Curve Street, an in-street extension was built south to the docks at City Point for horse-drawn freight cars. Operation must have been colorful; the first two locomotives, built by Messrs. Stephenson & Rothwell in England, were of the drop-hook type, with no cut-off—they went forward or in reverse at full speed.

Despite a virtual monopoly on shipment of lumber products from mills upriver, returns were disappointing, and legislative assent to sell

Although abandoned 130 years ago, the right of way of the Bangor, Old Town & Milford survives as a rough bicycle path, shown here in September 1999 near where it crosses Forest Avenue in Orono. (R. D. Karr)

42. Bangor, Old Town & Milford

the line was obtained during 1847. A deal was not struck for two years, ownership finally passing on November 1, 1849, to a new set of investors for just $60,000. At about the same time, the docks extension was abandoned after protest by local citizens, but the remainder was relaid using secondhand 36-pound double-head rail from the New Jersey & Pennsylvania RR. The company posted a good profit in 1853 and, for just the second time in its existence, paid a dividend.

General Samuel Veazie, a prominent local lumberman and banker, entered the scene in 1854, after encouragement by John A. Poor. Veazie bought the railroad and reincorporated it as the Bangor, Old Town & Milford RR on March 14, 1855. The line came to be known locally as the Veazie Railroad. Upgrading of the line with 45-pound T-rails was done to accommodate increased axle loads following purchase of a 4-4-0 Hinkley saddle tank engine from the Old Colony RR. Fulfilling the vision of the line's new name, Veazie managed completion of the two bridges required across the Penobscot River to reach Milford, at the then enormous cost of $110,000. Extension up river was contemplated but no action was taken, perhaps because in 1859 the greatest loss ever was reported.

Veazie died in 1868 and regular trains over his railroad survived him by only one year. With the European & North American RR finally underway, Veazie's heirs negotiated a sale price far in excess of the line's asset value. The E&NA wanted the line because by its purchase competition in the Bangor area would be eliminated, and the construction of the E&NA would be simplified by use of parts of the BOT&M right of way at each end. A recently ordered Hinkley locomotive was included in the deal. Dismantling of the BOT&M was completed by June 1870.

Development in Bangor has obliterated the alignment south of Milford Street, but from there to the northeast a rough bicycle path runs to Stillwater. To Old Town the line has been taken over by Stillwater Avenue (Route 2A). Honoring Veazie, boulders and stone monuments engraved with the letter "V" have been placed by a local historical society to mark the course of Maine's first true railroad.

Sources: Bachelder, *Special Trains*, 5–6; Karr, *Lost Railroads*, 73; Walker, "Bangor, Oldtown & Milford Railroad."

43. European & North American

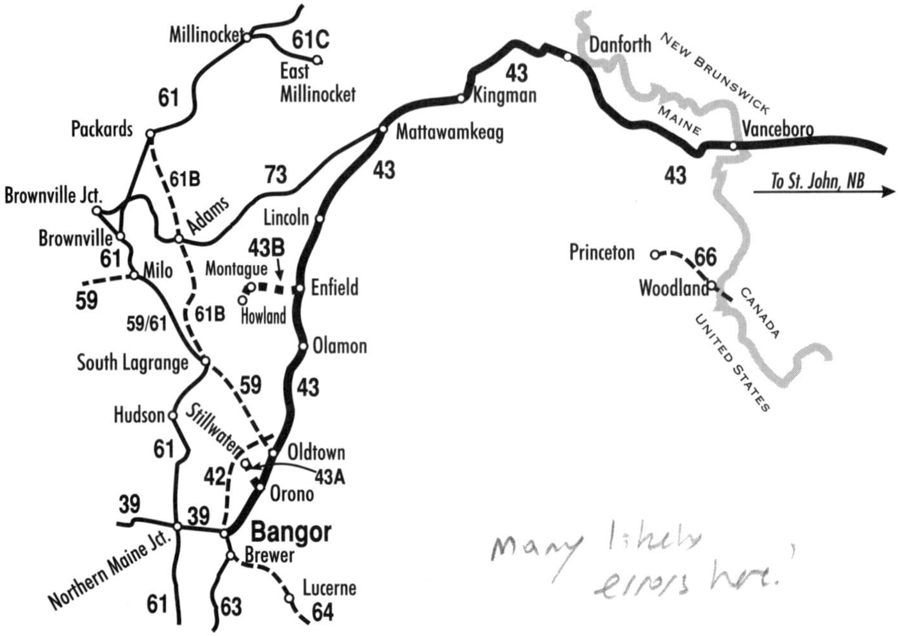

0 Bangor Union Sta. (Bangor), ME
0.5 Exchange St. [MEC Sta.]
1 River Switch (Bucksport Jct.)
3 Mt. Hope
4 Veazie
7 Basin Mills
7.5 Eight Mile Siding
8 Orono
8.5 Webster
11 Great Works
12 Oldtown (Old Town)
13 Milford
18 Costigan
21.5 Greenbush
26.5 Olamon
30.5 Passadumkeag
35 Enfield
40 Pollard Brook (South Lincoln)
44.5 Lincoln
46 Middletown (Lincoln Center)
46.5 North Lincoln (Houstons)
50.5 South Winn (Chamberlains)
55.5 Winn
57.5 Mattawamkeag (Keag)
66 Kingman
68 Drew (Crossuntic) (Sprague)
72.5 Meadow Brook Siding
76 Wytopitlock
78 Herseys
79 Bancroft
88 Danforth
93 Eaton (Jackson Brook)
98 Forest
101 Flag Stop
102 Tomah
106 Wilderness
109 Lambert Lake
115 Vanceboro, ME
121 McAdam Jct., NB
261 Saint John, NB

43A. Stillwater Branch

0 Orono, ME
3 Stillwater, ME

43B. Howland Branch

0 Enfield, ME
2.5 Montague
3.5 Howland, ME

43. European & North American

Built: 1865-71; Stillwater Branch, 1870-71; Howland Branch, ca. 1889, 1907.

Operators: *European & North American*, 1869-82; *Maine Central*, 1882-1981; *Canadian Pacific*, 1887-1988; *VIA Rail*, 1978-82 & 1985-94; *Guilford*, 1981-; *Canadian Atlantic*, 1985-95; *Eastern Maine*, 1995-.

Daily Passenger Trains: *1873:* 4; *1901:* 4; *1915:* 4; *1930:* 4. *1951:* 4; *1960* (Mattawamkeag-Vanceboro): 2; *1970* (Mattawamkeag-Vanceboro): 2; *1980* (Mattawamkeag-Vanceboro): 2; *1990* (Mattawamkeag-Vanceboro): 2. Passenger service ended Bangor- Mattawamkeag, 1960; Mattawamkeag-Vanceboro, 1994.

Abandonments: Stillwater Branch, ca. 1942; Howland Branch, ca. 1963.

The final piece of John A. Poor's vision of a rail system centered on Portland was the European & North American RR. A charter for this broad-gauge line was obtained in 1850, with two purposes in mind: first to connect the Maritime Provinces with Montreal via Portland and Bangor; second, to reduce trans-Atlantic passages between Europe and New York by as much as three days. The scheme languished, however, primarily because agreement could not be reached over the alignment. The southern end, from Portland to Bangor, was completed by the two companies that later formed the Maine Central RR. The first section of the company's Canadian counterpart, the European & North American RY, opened from St. John to Shediac, NB, on August 1, 1860, and to St. Duchene on the Gulf of St. Lawrence by 1864.

That year the city of Bangor approved a loan of $500,000, but it was not used until 1866 when the state of Maine granted 830,000 acres of land to the company to be sold or used as collateral for loans. The company purchased the Bangor, Old Town & Milford RR, using its alignment in Bangor and Milford, but abandoning the route through Stillwater, for which it substituted a branch from Orono to serve various lumber mills that had been the mainstay of the old railroad.

Completion of the main line from Bangor to Olamon in the spring of 1869 was followed by extension to Mattawamkeag in winter the same year. Meanwhile, the Canadian company extended from St. John to St. Croix about May 1870, with a stage connection to the E&NA.

Lavish opening ceremonies for the entire line took place on October 18 and 19, 1871, with Ulysses S. Grant, President of the United States, and General Lord Lisgor, Her Majesty's Governor-General of the Canadian Dominion, presiding. Poor was unable to attend; he had died six weeks earlier.

Poor's death was not the only untimely event. The MEC converted to standard gauge in 1871, creating gauge change difficulties at Bangor, and by 1873, the U.S. economy was in severe recession. The E&NA and the portion of the Canadian company west of St. John had merged as the Consolidated European & North American RY Co. on December 1, 1872. The remainder of the Canadian operation was taken over by the Intercolonial RY, later to become part of Canadian National.

The newly organized E&NA leased the Bangor & Piscataquis RR in 1873 and the Bangor & Bucksport RR upon completion in 1874, but both regained independence by 1879. The E&NA converted to standard gauge in 1877. The Canadian segment was reorganized as the independent Saint John & Maine RY on September 1, 1878, and was leased by the New Brunswick RY from July 1, 1883; the NB was in turn leased to the Canadian Pacific as of July 1, 1890. The MEC leased the E&NA in 1882, with trackage rights granted to the CP over the length from Mattawamkeag to Vanceboro upon opening of the CP's "Short Line" across northern Maine in 1889.

A short freight-only branch was built around 1889 from Enfield to Montague (now West Enfield) to lumber mills on the Penobscot River, and was extended in 1907 to the confluence with the Piscataquis River at Howland. Occasional passenger service was provided by mixed trains, although they were not listed in public timetables and were long gone before closure and abandonment.

From about 1907, possibly earlier, the MEC operated an overnight service with sleeper cars to Halifax, and a daytime trip featuring parlor cars between Boston and St. John, along with local service from Bangor. Additional trains east of Mattawamkeag were run by the Canadian Pacific RY.

In the summer of 1926 a new train was added, the *Pine Tree/Acadian*, from Boston to St. John, running Friday night eastbound and Saturday westbound, carrying through coaches and sleeping cars to Halifax; by 1930 it had become a daily-except-weekends operation.

Old Town station, which has not had passenger service since 1960, as it appeared in September 1999. (R. D. Karr)

The *Gull*, however, provided overnight service daily during summers from about 1926.

So things continued for many years. The last local passenger train was discontinued as of April 25, 1954, and additional stops were added to the *Gull*. MEC passenger trains made their final run between Vanceboro and Bangor September 5, 1960. The CP continued to operate its Montreal–St. John *Atlantic Limited* over the E&NA between Mattawamkeag and Vanceboro until 1978, when the train was taken over by VIA, the Canadian passenger authority. This service lasted until 1982, and was restored in 1985. VIA finally ended it December 1994.

By the 1970s freight was in severe decline. East of Mattawamkeag, the line saw more CP trains than MEC consists, so sale of this section to the CP was negotiated and the deal was signed on December 17, 1974. The MEC maintained traffic rights over the line, although they were used only sporadically. Guilford, which took control of the Bangor–Mattawamkeag segment in 1981, operates up to four trains a day over the line, which it still owns, with principal traffic lumber, paper, and chemicals. In 1988 the CP turned over its portion of the E&NA to the Canadian Atlantic RY. This company operated the line east of Mattawamkeag until 1995 when the Eastern Maine RR, a subsidiary of the Irving Oil Company, took over, and this company continues to operate it today. Inter-modal service from Canada was slated to begin in summer 2000.

Little remains of the Stillwater Branch; the line was truncated short of Bridge Street in Orono about 1948, and the rest was completely out of use by 1953. The alignment has been taken over by State Route 16 as Bennoch Road. West of Enfield Station, some of the Howland Branch to Montague can be walked. The remainder to Howland is occupied by housing and associated roads.

Sources: Bachelder, *Special Trains*, 4-6; Baker, *Formation*, 203; Judd, Churchill, and Eastman, *Maine*, 316-20; Karr, *Lost Railroads*, 106, 122; Kirkland, *Men, Cities & Transportation*, 1: 218-21, 473-74; Zimmermann, *Sunrise Route*, 19-31, 224.

44. Kennebec & Portland

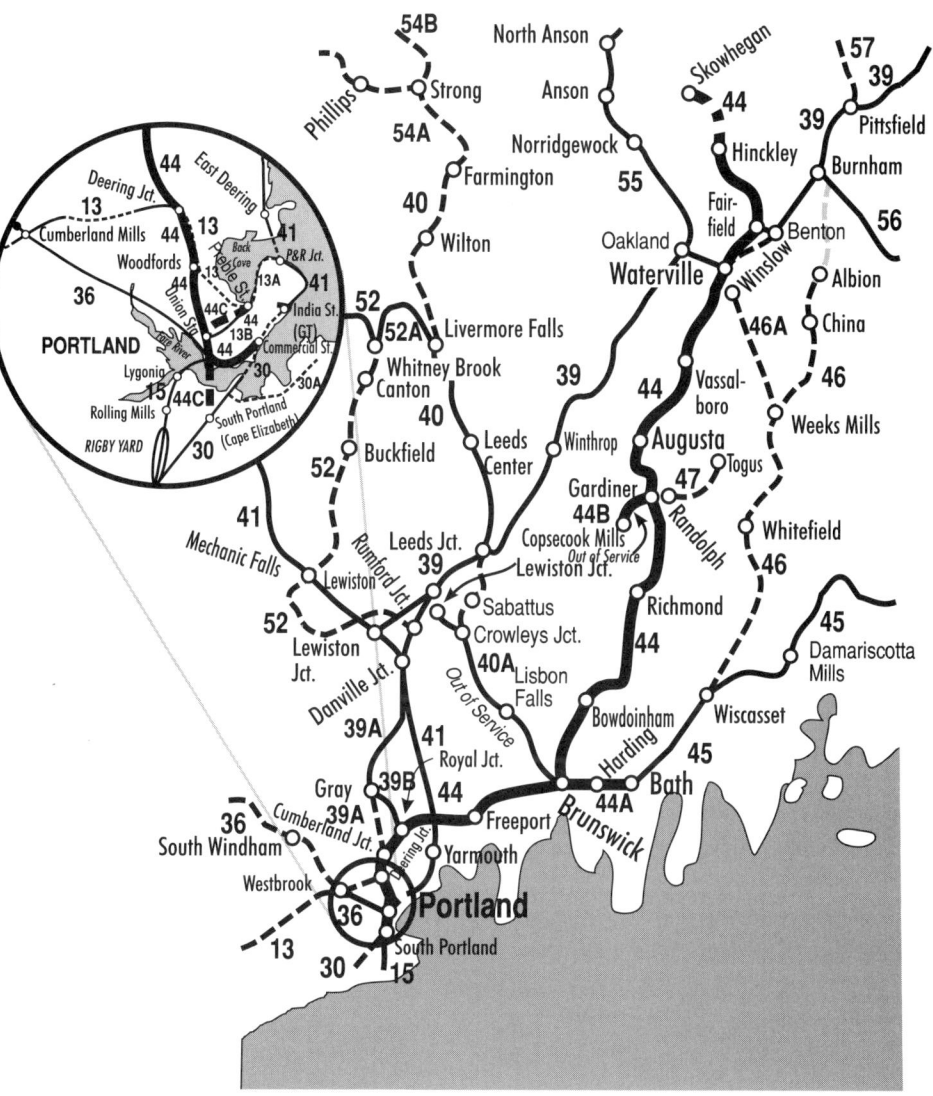

0 Portland, [Commercial St.], ME	46.5 Richmond	95 Hinckley (Pishons Ferry) (Pishons)
2 Portland [Union Sta.]	49 Iceboro	100 Skowhegan, ME
4 Woodfords	50 Dresden	
6 Deering Jct. (Westbrook Jct.) (Westbrook)	54 South Gardiner (Lawrences Mills)	**44A. Bath Branch**
7.5 West Falmouth (Falmouth)	57.5 Gardiner	0 Brunswick, ME
	58.5 North St. Siding	3 Cooks Corner (Cooks)
13.5 Cumberland Center (Cumberland Jct.) (Cumberland)	60 Farmingdale	4.5 Harding (Hardings)
	62.5 Hallowell	6 New Meadows
	63.5 State House Siding	8.5 Bath, ME
15.5 Royal Jct.	64.5 Augusta	
17 Yarmouth (Yarmouth Jct.)	68 Kennebec	**44B. Cobbosseecontee Branch**
	72 Riverside (Sidney) (Seven Mile Brook)	0 Gardiner, ME
22.5 Freeport	75 Vassalboro	2 Copsecook Mills, ME
27.5 Hillside (Oak Hill) (Oakwood)	83 Winslow	
	84 Waterville	
31 Brunswick	87 Fairfield (Kendalls Mills)	**44C. Cape Elizabeth Branch**
33 Topsham	90 Shawmut (Somerset Mills)	0 Portland, [Preble St.], ME
35 Cathance		
39 Bowdoinham	92 Nobles	3 Cape Elizabeth (South Portland), ME
42.5 Harwards (Harwards Rd.)	93 Good Will Farm	

Built: 1847-60; Bath Branch, 1847-49; Cape Elizabeth Branch, ca. 1851; Cobbosseecontee Branch, 1899-1900.

Operators: *Kennebec & Portland*, 1848-64; *Portland & Kennebec*, 1864-70; *Maine Central*, 1870-1981; *Guilford*, 1981-; *Maine Coast*, 1990-.

Daily Passenger Trains: *1869:* Portland-Augusta, 4; Augusta-Skowhegan, 2; Brunswick-Bath, 6; *1893:* Portland-Augusta, 12; Augusta-Waterville, 10; Waterville-Skowhegan, 6; Brunswick-Bath, 12; *1920:* Portland-Waterville, 13; Waterville-Skowhegan, 8; Brunswick-Bath, 14; *1935:* Portland-Waterville, 9; Brunswick-Bath, 6; Waterville-Skowhegan, 2); *1944:* Portland-Waterville, 10; Brunswick-Bath, 6; Waterville-Skowhegan, 1 mixed; *1952:* Portland-Waterville, 9; Brunswick-Bath, 4; 1958: Portland-Waterville, 8; Brunswick-Bath, 4; *1960:* Portland-Waterville, 4. Through passenger service to Skowhegan discontinued 1871. Passenger service ended Waterville-Skowhegan, 1946; Brunswick-Bath, 1959; Portland-Waterville, 1960.

44. Kennebec & Portland

Abandonments: Cape Elizabeth Branch, ca. 1860; in Skowhegan, 1953; Shawmut–Skowhegan, 1971.

A charter was obtained in 1836 for a standard-gauge rail line, the Kennebec & Portland RR, to link Portland with the state capital of Augusta. Nothing happened until the middle of the next decade, after the K&P renewed its own charter in 1846. The new charter included a branch from Brunswick to Bath, a shipbuilding port for two centuries, which ultimately became famous for the Bath Iron Works started by General Thomas Hyde after the Civil War and still constructing warships today.

Construction of the line from the broad-gauge Atlantic & St. Lawrence RR in Yarmouth, 12 miles from Portland, eastward to Brunswick and Bath began in 1847. The A&SL, which had begun operating in 1848, provided access to Portland. The opening of the K&P from Yarmouth to Bath added considerably to local fourth of July festivities in 1849.

Once underway, the K&P proceeded to eliminate the gauge change at Yarmouth and dependency on the A&SL by constructing in 1850 its own route to Portland by way of Deering Jct., where it met the tracks of the struggling York & Cumberland RR. It made arrangements with the latter to use its tracks and share its Portland terminal on Preble Street. The K&P also constructed a link with the Portland, Saco & Portsmouth RR by way of an extension to Cape Elizabeth (today's South Portland), which included a trestle over the Fore River. In 1860 the K&P abandoned and replaced the Cape Elizabeth connection in favor of a link from Woodfords to the PS&P terminal on Commercial Street. A few years later the K&P extended its own line south from Deering Jct., ending its use of the Y&C (soon to be the Portland & Rochester).

With its Portland connection secure, the K&P continued to work on what was to become the main line, north from Brunswick to Augusta. The line northward from Brunswick along the Cathance and Kennebec River valleys was opened to Richmond in January 1851 and to Augusta in 1852. Augusta, although the state capital from 1827, was just a minor center for lumber, the paper industry, textile mills, and shoe manufactures; the 1850 census recorded a population of only 8,225.

The Somerset & Kennebec RR was formed in 1848 to continue the K&P's line from Augusta to Waterville and beyond, in competition with the broad-gauge lines to the west that eventually formed the Maine Central. Augusta depot had been built at Water Street, with sidings on a shelf at the foot of precipitous cliffs on the west bank of the river. Extension required a steeply graded line to the east of the city center. The Somerset & Kennebec opened its line to Waterville and Kendalls Mills, centers of pulp and pulp-fiber manufacturing, in 1855, and to Skowhegan, another mill town, in 1856. The K&P operated the Somerset & Kennebec from its opening under short-term agreements without a formal lease. Extensive lumber reserves were soon exploited, and barge traffic down the Kennebec River disappeared in favor of rail traffic.

Rivalry with the MEC in the early 1860s resulted in the bankruptcy of the K&P, from which the Portland & Kennebec RR emerged in 1864 and leased the Somerset & Kennebec. Six years later, the MEC leased the P&K and the Somerset & Kennebec, preparatory to narrowing its own line and completing its own connection north from Cumberland Jct. in 1871. North of Waterville, the line to Skowhegan was relegated to the status of a branch. The time was ripe for growth; in 1871 the Knox & Lincoln RR extended the Bath Branch via a ferry connection, and in 1874 the MEC absorbed the P&K. In 1888 MEC trains over the P&K began using a new Union Station in Portland shared with the Boston & Maine. Virtually parallel lines were opened by independent companies, which caused some loss of traffic. The Cobbosseecontee Branch was built in Gardiner in 1899–1900 as an industrial track following today's Route 9 and the Cobbosseecontee Stream.

The P&K route via Brunswick and Augusta was known as the Lower Road, and the MEC line through Lewiston became the Back Road. Through passenger trains from points south of Portland and beyond Bangor normally were routed over the Lower Road, leaving the Back Road with local service, although in the twentieth century a few crack express trains did take the latter. When the Lower Road suffered damage from the great floods of March 1936, all through trains were diverted over the Back Road until late summer.

Passenger service entered an inexorable decline from about 1930. Service north of Waterville to Skowhegan, which from July 29, 1935, had comprised a single round trip was further (and somewhat oddly) reduced on October 15, 1937, to a single eastbound mixed train daily with a round trip on Sundays. Service ceased altogether in 1946. En-

44. Kennebec & Portland

suing years saw closure of various ticket agencies. On the Rockland Branch (formerly the Bath Branch and Knox & Lincoln), passenger service ended in April 1959. The *Bar Harbor Express*, along with the two remaining round trips over the Lower Road, ended on Labor Day, 1960.

At Skowhegan, the MEC cut back its operation from the downtown yard to a smaller facility on the west bank of the Kennebec River in 1953. The single-track river bridge continued in use for pedestrians until it was washed away by storms in 1987. Permission to abandon north of Shawmut was obtained in 1971. At about the same time, the Scott Paper Co. began construction of the S. D. Warren mill in Hinckley, and paid the MEC to retain the five miles of intermediate track, which was subsequently reactivated. The remainder of the roadbed to Skowhegan was bought by the state. The last movement over the Cobbosseecontee Branch was made about 1982.

Guilford's Rumford–South Portland symbol freight RUPO turns onto the Kennebec & Portland at Royal Jct., where the Lower Road and Back Road routes diverge. In this September 1999 view the train is coming off the Walnut Hill Diversion of the Back Road; the Lower Road continues to Brunswick straight ahead past the signal. (R. D. Karr)

Guilford, which took over operation of the MEC in 1981, ran the last through train between Brunswick and Augusta in 1986, although there were several moves from each end handling storage cars and small consignments. Through movements were precluded beyond 1987 by a washout at Farmingdale. Permission to abandon the Brunswick–Augusta segment was obtained in 1989, with all remaining rolling stock removed prior to sale of the line in 1991 to the Maine Department of Transportation. Although the state leased the line to the Maine Coast RR, it was not operated.

Meanwhile, the Bath branch east of Harding and the Knox & Lincoln line closed in 1986 and were also sold to the state. Guilford continued for a while to serve a BIW plant at Harding, which was also the Maine Coast RR interchange point. The Maine Coast leased the Maine DoT-owned line from 1990, and nowadays serves the plant from an interchange in Brunswick, billing Guilford for this service.

South from Waterville, the line to Augusta remained in service. Guilford named it the East Augusta Running Track and operated freight trains to several customers in East Augusta. The line from Brunswick to Augusta was reinstated in 1996, when the Maine Coast began operation of about one train per week to deliver cars to a beverage dealer in the western part of Augusta. The bridge across the Kennebec River connecting these two lines remained out of service, and part of the former main line track in Augusta was graveled over for use as a parking lot.

In 1999 the Maine Coast convinced the state and Guilford's East Augusta customers that they would be better served from Brunswick than from Waterville. The Augusta Parking District was forced to remove the gravel, and the state paid to repair the bridge. In February 2000 the Maine Coast ran the first train in years across the Kennebec bridge to East Augusta, although because of a union contract a Guilford crew switches the customers using the Maine Coast train! Guilford sends in the crews by taxi and no longer operates regular service between Waterville and Augusta.

Sources: Bachelder, *Special Trains*, 4, 6, 9, 11–13; Baker, *Formation*, 203–4; ICC Finance Docket no. 18148; Karr, *Lost Railroads*, 124, 130, 146; Kirkland, *Men, Cities & Transportation*, 1: 215–17, 2: 5–6; Peters, *Maine Central*, 14, 15; Poor, *History*, 31; *Railpace* 19 (April 2000): 36.

45. Knox & Lincoln

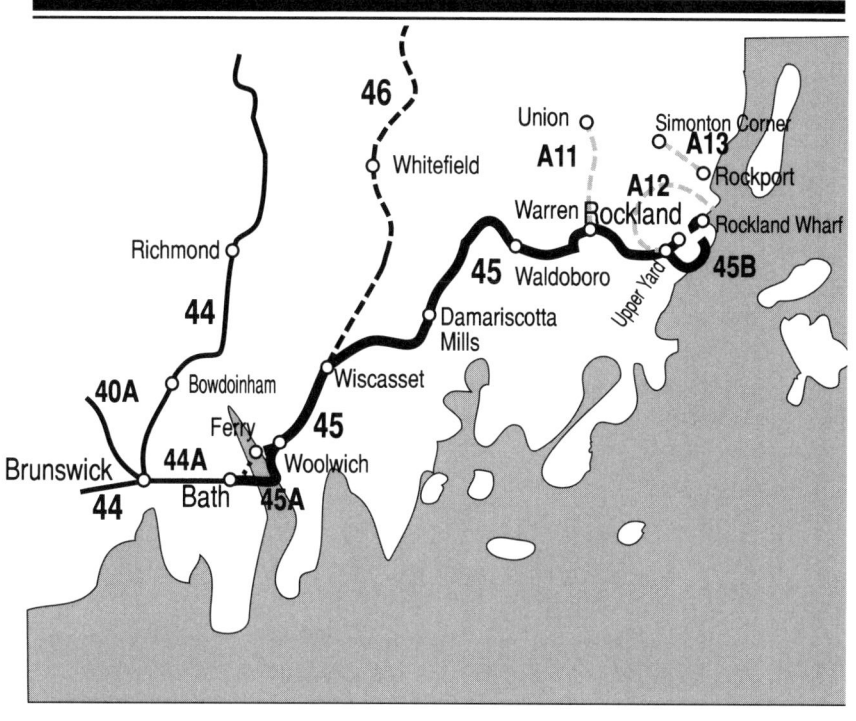

0 Woolwich Ferry, ME	20 Damariscotta Mills	**45A. Bath Extension**
0.5 Woolwich	23.5 Nobleboro	
3 Nequasset	26.5 Muscongus Bay	0 Woolwich, ME
4.5 Wrights	27.5 Glendon	1 Bath, ME
7 Montsweag (Westport)	28 Winslows Mills	
10.5 Wiscasset [Boat Landing]	29.5 Waldoboro	**45B. Rockland Wharf Branch**
	33.5 East Waldoboro	
11 Wiscasset	34.5 Warren	0 Rockland [Upper Yard], ME
14.5 South Newcastle	41.5 Georges River	
16.5 Shattucks Siding	43.5 Thomaston	2 Rockland Wharf, ME
18 Newcastle (Newcastle & Damariscotta)	47 Rockland [Upper Yard]	
	47.5 Rockland, ME	

Built: 1868-76; Bath Extension, 1925-27.

Operators: *Knox & Lincoln:* 1870-91; *Maine Central,* 1891-1981; *Guilford,* 1981-84; *Maine Coast,* 1990-.

45. Knox & Lincoln

Daily Passenger Trains: *1873:* 6; *1893:* 6; *1916:* 6; *1921:* 6; *1935:* 8; *1950:* 6. Passenger service ended 1959 (excursions operated by Maine Coast ca. 1991–).

Abandonment: Rockland Wharf Branch (outer 0.5 miles), before 1940; Woolwich Ferry-Woolwich, ca. 1970.

By the time the Kennebec & Portland RR completed its initial line from Yarmouth to Bath in 1849, plans were underway to extend the rails eastward. A month after the opening ceremonies the Maine legislature chartered the Penobscot & Kennebec to build to Rockland. When it was discovered that the same name had already been granted to another railroad, the legislature renamed it the Penobscot, Lincoln & Kennebec RR. Six extensions of time to build were granted between 1856 and 1868, and in 1864 the name was changed to the Knox & Lincoln RR.

A Maine Coast RR locomotive switches freight at Rockland in August 1992, less than two years after that railroad commenced operating the Knox & Lincoln. (R. D. Karr)

45. Knox & Lincoln

The objectives of the line were Wiscasset on the Sheepscot River, which had once been a major port; Waldoboro, at the head of navigation of the Medomak River and formerly a center for construction of masted steamships; and Rockland, with its nearby limestone quarries. Construction difficulties and costs were significant. With a requirement to maintain navigation for large vessels plying the Kennebec River to wharves upstream of Bath, it was decided to use a track-equipped ferry to avoid the cost of building a bridge to connect with the Portland & Kennebec.

Construction finally began east from just north of Sasanoa Point in Woolwich in the late 1860s and was completed to the Rockland engine house in November 1871. The Maine Central RR offered to purchase the line, but the stockholders—principally the towns through which the line ran—objected on grounds that the MEC was dictating unfavorable terms. In 1883 an alternative bid by a group that offered $1.3 million in bonds and $200,000 in cash was accepted, but the deal fell through when it became apparent that traffic could not justify such an outlay. A two-mile branch to the wharves at Rockland was built around this time. Land was acquired in 1886 for a new terminal at Union Street in the center of Rockland; new facilities were opened the following year. The company struggled on independently for another eight years, with a small upturn following construction of the Lime Rock RR, but agreement was finally reached in 1891 for lease by the MEC. Two years later additional traffic in limestone developed following construction of the independent Georges Valley RR (later Knox RR) north from Warren. Eventually a major cement manufactory, a minor steel fabrication factory, and a food cannery in Rockland provided further traffic.

The K&L was merged with the MEC during 1901, and it was operated in conjunction with the MEC's Bath Branch as the Rockland Branch to provide service between Brunswick and Rockland. In Rockland, the MEC commissioned Coolidge & Shattuck to design a new station, completed in 1918. During the 1950s it was remodeled for use as municipal offices.

In 1925 work began on the Carlton two-deck drawbridge, sponsored jointly by the state and the railroad, to obviate the inconvenient ferry across the Kennebec River. The bridge was opened on October 24, 1927, and carried eight passenger trains on weekdays, two of which originated in or terminated at Brunswick, although by 1931 through trains (as opposed to through cars on the *Bar Harbor*) to and from

Portland and places to the south were no longer operated. Flood damage to the Lower Road in the spring of 1936 resulted in reinstatement of through trains from Portland to Rockland, although these arrangements ended in 1937. Through trains to and from Portland were reinstated about 1940.

After World War II passenger traffic on the Rockland Branch slumped. Through coaches to and from Boston ended in the spring of 1957 as the Boston & Maine progressively introduced Budd-built rail diesel cars (RDCs), although the MEC continued to operate two round trips between Portland and Rockland daily, with one on Sundays. From January 18, 1959, the K&L had only a single round trip daily except Sundays, and that ended on April 4, 1959.

Guilford closed the line in 1984 three years after it took control of the MEC. Negotiations during abandonment proceedings resulted in a lease-purchase agreement by the Maine Department of Transportation. The Maine DoT selected a new short haul operator, the Maine Coast RR, to resume operation of the K&L, along with part of the MEC's Bath Branch east of Harding, for a period of five years beginning October 26, 1990. Headquarters were established in Waldoboro. The lease was subsequently renewed. Maine Coast trains now operate from Rockland to Brunswick, and from Brunswick to Augusta. Traffic comprises mainly cement, coal, volcanic ash, lime, pearlite, lumber, and LP gas. Passenger excursions are also operated. The outer half-mile of the Rockland Wharf Branch had been abandoned before 1940. Part of the rest was abandoned in the 1980s but restored in the late 1990s.

Sources: Bachelder, *Rumford Rocket*, 9; Baker, *Formation*, 203; Cornwall and Smith, *Names First*, 96; Karr, *Lost Railroads*, 86; Kirkland, *Men, Cities & Transportation*, 1: 487; Lewis, *American Shortline Railway Guide*, 152; Peters, *Maine Central*, 14, 15.

46. Wiscasset, Waterville & Farmington

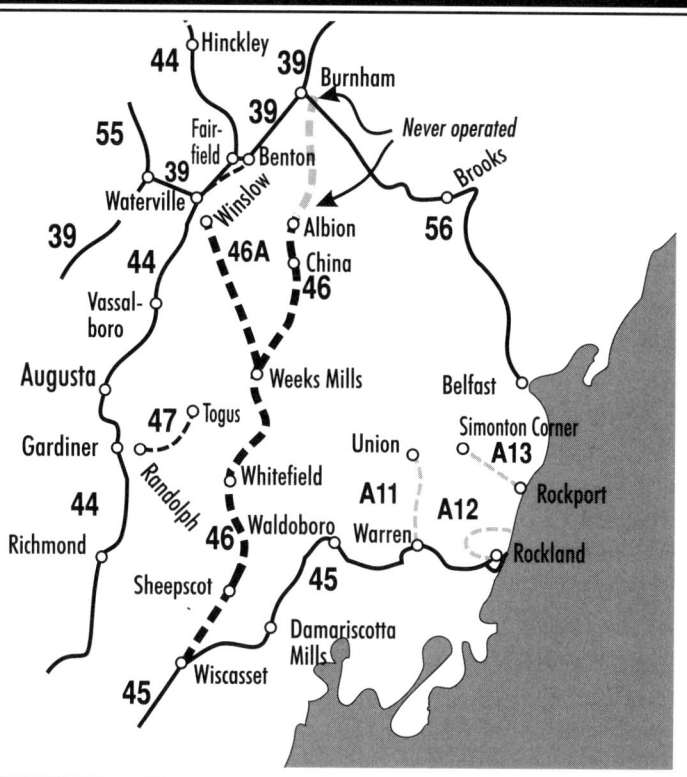

0 Wiscasset, ME	24 Windsor	**46A. Waterville Branch**
5 Sheepscot	28 Weeks Mills	
7.5 Alna Center	31 Newells Corner (Pigeon Plains)	0 Weeks Mills, ME
9 Head Tide		3 South China
13 Whitefield	32 Palermo	4 China Lake
15.5 Prebles (Nigger Meadow)	34 Coles Corner	5 Clarks
	38 China	6 East Vassalboro
17 North Whitefield	40 South Albion (Johnson Brook)	11.5 North Vassalboro
18 Ezarys		15 Winslow, ME
20 Coopers Mills	43.5 Albion, ME	
23 Maxcys (Maxys Mills)		

Built: 1894–95; Waterville Branch, 1898–1902.

Operators: *Wiscasset & Quebec*, 1895–1901; *Wiscasset, Waterville & Farmington RR*, 1901–06; *Wiscasset & Farmington RY*, 1907–33.

46. Wiscasset, Waterville & Farmington

Daily Passenger Trains: *1895:* 4; *1901:* 2 (plus Wiscasset–Weeks Mills, 2); *1903:* Wiscasset–Winslow, 2; Weeks Mills–Winslow, 4; Weeks Mills–Albion, 2; *1916:* 2 (plus Wiscasset–Weeks Mills, 2); *1930:* 2. Passenger service ended Waterville Branch, 1909; Wiscasset–Albion, 1933.

Abandonments: North Vassalboro–Winslow, 1913; Weeks Mills–North Vassalboro, 1915; Wiscasset–Albion, 1934.

Wiscasset is a small warm-water port on the west bank of the Sheepscot River. Local interests promoted it in the 1850s as an alternative to Portland and surveyed possible rail routes, preferring a route to Augusta via Togus, for connection with the Kennebec & Portland RR. After obtaining a charter on April 15, 1854, the Kennebec & Wiscasset RR company was unable to raise sufficient capital. The charter was revived and amended several times. On February 14, 1873, the company became the Wiscasset & Moosehead Lake RR, and later the Wiscasset & Quebec RR, which envisaged a 241-mile line into Quebec province.

WW&F 0-4-4T locomotive no. 3 crosses the standard-gauge MEC tracks at Wiscasset in 1923. Note the ball signal and the very young "crew member"! (Courtesy Walker Transportation Collection, Beverly Historical Society & Museum)

46. Wiscasset, Waterville & Farmington

A new survey for a 2-foot narrow-gauge line was sponsored in 1892 by R. T. Rundlett and W. D. Patterson for an alignment from Wiscasset to Pittsfield, which would entail a grade crossing of the Belfast & Moosehead Lake RR at Burnham. The company was organized, with Rundlett as President and Patterson as secretary/treasurer. Work began in June 1894 and was completed to Weeks Mills on March 1, 1895, to Palermo on July 24, to China on September 24, and to Albion on November 4, 1895. Rundlett proposed that the Kennebec Central extend its line from Togus to the W&Q at Coopers Mills and also suggested a dual-gauge line between Weeks Mills and Waterville. The MEC declined, and with an apparent hatred of the narrow gauge, took every step possible to prevent the W&Q from crossing the B&ML at grade about half a mile east of Burnham. The Maine Railroad Commission authorized a temporary diamond, to be replaced by a bridge on or before July 1, 1898; but with about half of the track laid on the 11.75 miles north toward Burnham, the cost of piling in bogs east of the Sebasticook River proved prohibitive and work on the W&Q ceased abruptly. Track was left in place but never used.

Instead, two companies were incorporated: the Waterville & Wiscasset RR to build from Weeks Mills through South China to Waterville, and the Franklin, Somerset & Kennebec RR to take the line on through Oakland, Belgrade, Smithfield, Rome, and Mercer to Farmington, where connection would be made with the Sandy River RR. Most of the proposed right of way was acquired in 1898 and most of the work on the W&W was completed by late 1899. Cost of servicing its debt bankrupted the W&Q on July 1, 1900. Receivers continued to operate the Wiscasset–Albion length but arranged sale of the W&Q and its subsidiaries on March 29, 1901, to the Wiscasset, Waterville & Farmington RR.

The new company had been incorporated on February 5 with offices in Waterville. Leonard Atwood, an inventor living in Farmington, was elected president and pressed on with the extension, commencing track laying near New Sharon and awarding a contract for bridging the Kennebec River between Winslow and Waterville. The alignment would have required a flat crossing in Farmington, to which the MEC and Sandy River lines objected. On June 26, 1901, the Railroad Commissioners upheld these objections, sealing the fate of the proposed extension.

Work on the former W&W continued, using track recovered from New Sharon and new 65-pound rail. A small workshop was built at Winslow. A safety certificate was issued on June 9, 1902, enabling opening as a branch.

Financial results were disappointing and the company, whose entire assets and income had been mortgaged on June 30, 1902, entered receivership on October 7, 1905. A second reprieve was granted on December 4, 1906, when the assets were bought for $93,000 by Carson D. Peck, owner of a chain of New England retail stores. Reorganized as the Wiscasset, Waterville & Farmington RY on January 1, 1907, the railroad implemented strict economies, which produced marginal profits for a few years. Principal traffic was lumber, with some movements of potatoes and grain, supplemented by a contract for conveyance of mail; tonnage and revenue had entered serious decline, however, by Peck's death in April 1915. The Winslow branch north of Vassalboro had been abandoned in the summer of 1913, and the remainder above Weeks Mills followed in early 1915. Thereafter the company ran a daily mixed train, with freight largely milk, from Albion to Wiscasset, and another round trip from Wiscasset to Weeks Mills, supplemented as required. On December 14, 1925, the company was sold for $60,000 to a cooperative of local farmers who struggled with it. Trips to Weeks Mills ended in 1930. These savings measures were insufficient and, for the fourth time, bankruptcy was declared later in the year.

S. J. Sewall, a prior associate of Peck, and H. P. Crowell were appointed receivers on November 30, 1930. Less than a month later the company was taken over by Frank W. Winter, who managed to restore minimum profitability. Lumber traffic continued, as did the mail contract, but most remaining traffic was lost to trucks. The principal engine shed was severely damaged by fire in 1931, taking with it two of the line's five locomotives. Receivership was entered yet again on December 31, and the next year the company was sold to Winter's son-in-law, Malcolm Philbrook. The transfer was purely nominal as Winter continued as manager. Winter bought the assets of the Kennebec Central in January 1933 and transferred both its locomotives to the WW&F. Commission inspectors ordered work on both engines and on the timber trestle quay at Wiscasset. These costs were beyond the means of the railroad, and a decision was made to close the line immediately after completion of current lumber contracts.

A WW&F mixed train pulls into the Wiscasset yard after a stop at the MEC interchange circa 1930. (Hugh Boutell, courtesy Walker Transportation Collection, Beverly Historical Society & Museum)

At 7:33 a.m. on June 15, 1933, with the lumber stockpile reduced by half, the morning train from Albion, hauled by a KC locomotive on one of its first outings, jumped the track at a broken rail south of Whitefield. Both the train crew and the company left the train where it was. Following approval for abandonment the tracks were foreclosed by a creditor in November 1934 and removed shortly thereafter. The remaining assets of the WW&F were scrapped in 1937.

During the 1990s the Wiscasset, Waterville & Farmington Railway Museum, based at the site of the former Sheepscot station, rebuilt a short section of the line and constructed replicas of the station, engine house, and maintenance facilities. It now operates excursion trains in summers using diesel power, and late in 1999 it acquired its first operating steam locomotive. Volunteers from the museum are restoring the surviving depot at Albion, and, using volunteer labor, the museum plans to extend the track along more of the old right of way.

Sources: Crittenden, "Wiscasset, Waterville & Farmington Railway"; Hilton, *American Narrow Gauge Railroads*, 413-14; Jones and Register, *Two Feet to Tidewater*; Moody, *Maine Two-Footers*, 7-12, 167-92; *Railpace* 17 (Nov. 1998): 39; Thurlow, *WW&F Two-Footer*; Wiggin, *Big Dreams*.

47. Kennebec Central

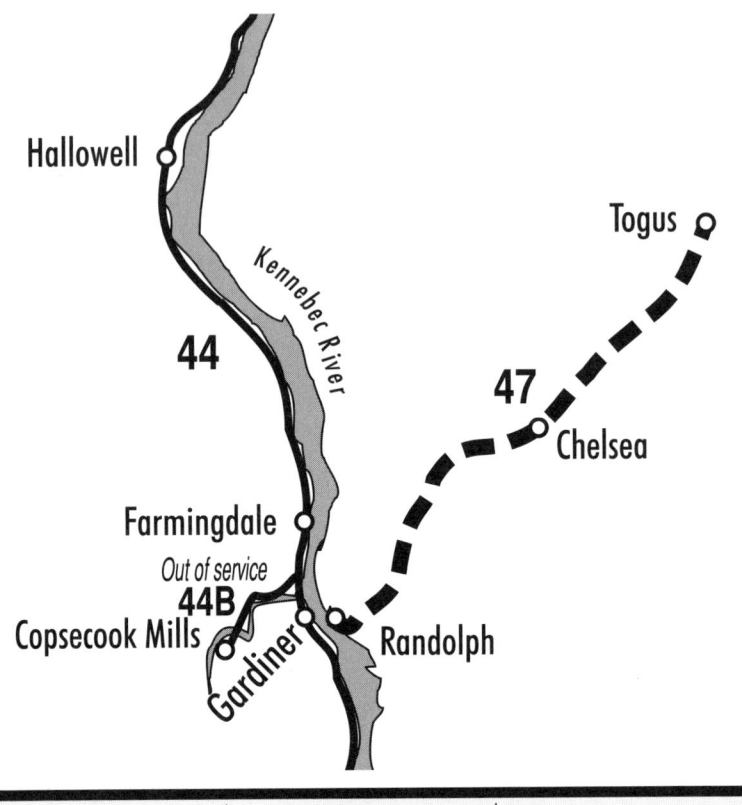

| 0 Randolph, ME | 5 Togus (National Soldiers |
| 3 Chelsea | Home), ME |

Built: 1889-90.
Operators: *Kennebec Central,* 1890-1929.
Daily Passenger Trains: *1893:* 8; *1915:* 10 *1919:* 8; *1925:* 8.
Abandonment: 1929.

Togus would have had a station on the standard-gauge Kennebec & Wiscasset RR, proposed in 1854 to link the Kennebec & Portland RR at Augusta with the port of Wiscasset, if the scheme had not failed. By the late 1880s, the National Soldiers' Home at Togus of-

47. Kennebec Central

fered potential for a line from the Kennebec River. Capital requirements were to be minimized by adopting 2-foot gauge and starting from Randolph on the east bank of the Kennebec River, which was navigable by barges as far as the town. The alignment chosen ran across easily graded wetlands through Chelsea.

Articles of Association for the Kennebec Central RR were approved on September 12, 1889, and the company was organized on October 3. Construction using 25-pound rail began almost immediately, with formal opening ceremonies on July 7, 1890, although outstanding minor work delayed scheduled service until the 23rd. Small passenger stations were provided. At Randolph the freight yard featured several widely-spaced sidings to facilitate access by road vehicles as the line had no connections with other railroads. Several sidings were laid at Togus, including a spur leading directly to the Home's boiler house. Rolling stock, which initially comprised two Forney 0-4-4 locomotives acquired new in 1890 and 1891, a collection of vacuum-braked passenger cars, and some non-fitted freight cars, was serviced in a small workshop at Randolph.

During construction consideration was given to a ten-mile extension to China village at the head of China Lake, but the proposal was rejected because of limited traffic potential. After the similarly-gauged Wiscasset & Quebec RR began construction in 1894, an alignment about eight miles long was surveyed for a connection at Coopers Mills; given the Maine Central's antipathy to the W&Q, nothing more was done.

Throughout the line's existence freight was its mainstay, principally coal for the Home brought in by barge to Randolph or transferred by dray from the MEC depot in Gardiner. Less-than-carload traffic was also handled. For most of its life, passenger traffic was significant, generally inbound veterans and visitors to Home residents, boosted by leisure journeys to sports and musical events held on the Home's extensive grounds. Annual ridership was extremely variable, however, peaking at 71,699 in 1900–01, compared with 57,920 the year before. The opening of a trolley route from Augusta to Togus in 1901 caused further instability in passenger traffic during the second decade of operation. The number of rail travelers ranged between 49,000 and 63,000, although 70,845 were recorded in 1909–10, according to changes in the number of Home residents, veterans' family demographics, and the vagaries of winters in Maine. A rapid decline in passenger numbers started in 1912, sinking to 28,923 in 1919 before stabilizing. Despite this, the company recorded modest profits, enabling replacement of the original locomotives with Forneys obtained from the Bridgton & Saco River RR in 1922 and one from the Sandy River & Rangeley Lakes RR in 1926.

The end came suddenly in 1929 when the federal government awarded the contract for coal business to truckers. Operations ceased on June 29. Assets were retained in expectation of a revival, but following the onset of the Great Depression the locomotives were conveyed to the Wiscasset, Waterville & Farmington in January 1933, and general dismantling of the line followed that year.

At present, embankments which carried the line to the Home passenger depot and coaling stage remain north of Hallowell Road, neatly preened. Southward, much of the line has returned to wetlands but it can be walked as far as Hankerson Road west of Chelsea, beyond which the alignment has been largely taken over by Collins Road and housing development.

Sources: Crittenden, *Maine Scenic Route*, 103-11; Hilton, *American Narrow Gauge Railroads*, 409; Moody, *Maine Two-Footers*, 1-5, 155-66; Wiggin, *Big Dreams*, 40-41.

48. Clarendon & Pittsford

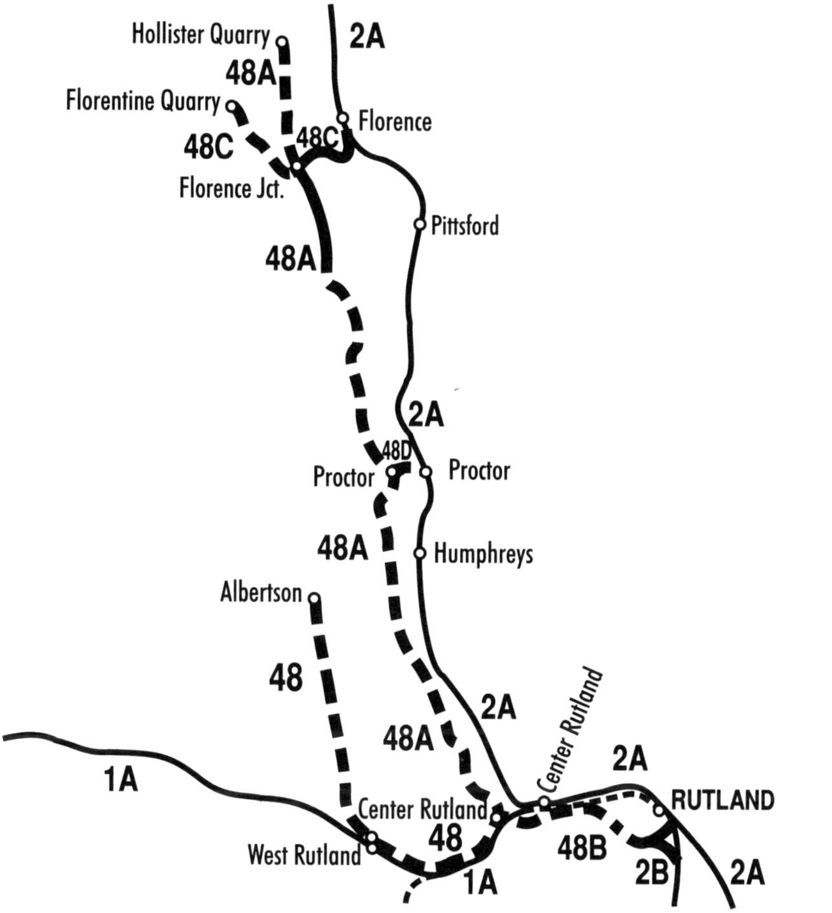

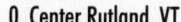

0 Center Rutland, VT
1 West Rutland
3 Albertson, VT

48A. Hollister Branch

0 Center Rutland, VT
4.5 Proctor
8 Florence Jct.
10 Hollister Quarry, VT

48B. Pittsford & Rutland RR

0 Rutland, VT
2 Center Rutland, VT

48C. Brandon & West Rutland RR

0 Florence, VT
1 Florence Jct.
2 Florentine Quarry, VT

48D. Proctor Connection

0 Proctor, VT
0.5 Proctor [CV], VT

Clarendon & Pittsford's 44-ton Whitcomb locomotive no. 10 is shown at Center Rutland, VT, in 1964. (Courtesy Walker Transportation Collection, Beverly Historical Society & Museum)

Built: 1885–1909.

Operators: *Clarendon & Pittsford*, 1886–1972; *Brandon & West Rutland*, 1909–11; *Vermont*, 1972– ; *Otter Valley*, ca. 1977–80.

Daily Passenger Trains: None.

Abandonments: Center Rutland–Albertson, 1988; Pittsford & Rutland RR (Rutland [0.4 miles west]–Center Rutland, 1938); Hollister Branch (Hollister Quarry–Florence Jct. [0.4 mi. north], 1938; Center Rutland–Proctor, Florence Jct [0.4 mi. north]–Florence Jct., 1977; Proctor–south of Florence Jct., ca. 1980); Brandon & West Rutland RR (Florence Jct.–Florentine Quarry, ca. 1977).

On September 10, 1885, the Vermont Marble Co. obtained a charter for the Clarendon & Pittsford RR to haul quarried stone from Proctor to West Rutland. The line opened in stages between 1886 and 1888. Connection was made with the Delaware & Hudson RR (former Rutland & Washington) in West Rutland. A separate company, the Pittsford & Rutland RR, built a line from Center Rutland to Rutland in 1890 to connect with the Bennington & Rutland line; it was leased from the outset by the C&P. The independent Brandon & West

48. Clarendon & Pittsford

Rutland RR, conceived in 1893, was not organized until May 1901, and did not complete its two-mile line from Florence to Florentine Quarry until 1909. Demand for stone increased when the first high-rise buildings were being constructed. The Proctor line was extended to Hollister in 1903, followed by a line to Albertson in 1908. To economize on operations, the separate lines were absorbed and the B&WR and the P&R were purchased in 1911. There was never scheduled public passenger service, although quarry workers were conveyed from about 1912 to 1925 between Proctor and Florence and also to West Rutland. Passengers were also permitted to ride the freights upon payment of a nominal sum, and occasional excursions were run. In 1938, the Hollister line was cut back to about 0.4 miles north of Florence Jct., to serve a single quarry. Most of the P&R was sold to the Rutland RR at the same time, which used the eastern half mile to provide freight service to some customers in Rutland for many years (part of the line remains in use even now); the rest was abandoned.

Over the next three decades there were only minor changes to the system, although maintenance declined. After the Vermont RY commenced operation over parts of the former Rutland RY, the marble company offered to sell its railroad assets. A deal was made in 1972, although the C&P remained a nominally independent company. Under the Vermont RY the length between Center Rutland and Proctor was redundant and was abandoned in 1977. Quarries at the northern end could be served by switchers off the main line, while those at the southern end were accessible from the D&H. During the next three summers the Otter Valley RR operated tourist trains over three miles of trackage between Proctor and Florence Jct. Ironically, the now largely abandoned C&P lends its name today to the former Rutland & Washington line, which was purchased from the D&H by the Vermont RY in December 1983.

Nothing now remains of the original C&P, except for the section of the former B&WR between Florence and Florence Jct., the wye in Rutland, and a few spurs and sidings. A huge OMYA plant south of Florence Jct. provides the only traffic; parts of the Florentine and Hollister lines survive for car storage and switching at the facility.

Sources: Bachelder, *Green Mountain Flyer*, 12, 17–20, 28–31; Drury, *Historical Guide*, 378; Jones, *Railroads of Vermont*, 1: 228; Jones, Maxfield, and Gove, *Vermont's Granite Railways*; Karr, *Lost Railroads*, 97, 136, 150; Lewis, *American Shortline Railway Guide*, 64.

49. Woodstock

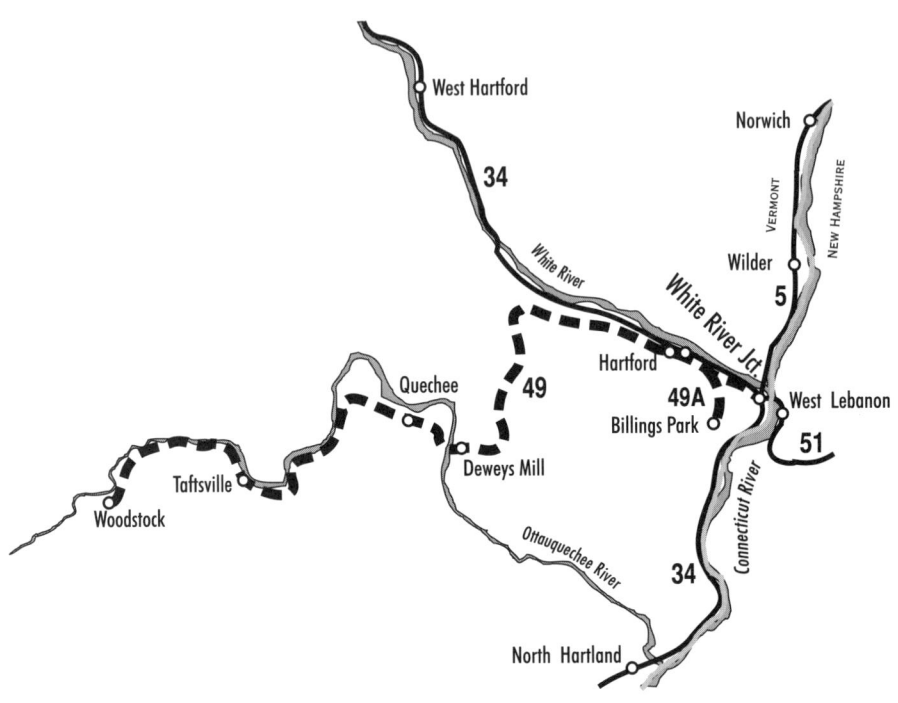

0 White River Jct., VT 1.5 Hartford 4 Deweys Mills 6 Quechee	10 Taftsville 13.5 Woodstock, VT	**49A. Fair Grounds RR** 0 Hartford, VT 0.5 Billings Park, VT

Built: 1874-75; Fair Grounds RR, 1890.

Operators: *Woodstock*, 1875-1933; *Central Vermont* (Fair Grounds RR), 1890-1928.

49. Woodstock

Daily Passenger Trains: *1877:* 4; *1893:* 6; *1906:* 8; *1920:* 4; *1931:* 2. Passenger service ended 1933.

Abandonments: Fair Grounds RR, 1928; White River Jct.–Woodstock, 1933.

Woodstock was a minor mill town when, on October 20, 1863, a charter was obtained for a rail link with the Connecticut River and Vermont Central lines at White River Jct. A line running generally westward along the west branch of the White River was envisaged, but surveys were not completed, and work did not commence until 1874, when exploitation of local lumber began. The Woodstock RR opened almost a year later. Charters for extension beyond Woodstock, to Rutland, were obtained by other companies but none were viable. By 1890 the company was bankrupt but emerged from receivership as the Woodstock RY.

That year, an oddity came along in the form of the Fair Grounds RR. It was built independently and opened on September 1 to carry traffic to and from the annual Twin State Fair. Operation of trains from White River Jct. for just one week a year entailed reversal at Hilton, east of Hartford, to access the line. The owners of the line contracted with the Central Vermont RR to provide service, as the Woodstock RR had insufficient rolling stock.

Throughout its existence the Woodstock company remained independent, fulfilling common carrier obligations by running mixed trains. Lumber and other wood products eventually accounted for most of the outbound freight, together with farm goods, supplemented by inbound and outbound miscellaneous traffic, but the line was always a marginal operation. Introduction of higher axle weight locomotives required several improvements, chief among them the replacement in 1911 of the Quechee Gorge bridge in Hartford. Replacing a slender trestle, the new structure featured bents supported by riveted lattice-frame vertical and horizontal members sprung from an arch. Such investment could not be sustained. After 1920 inbound coal and fertilizer traffic exceeded outgoing tonnage, and the line's modest prosperity ended. The Twin State Fair, which had not been held between 1901 and 1906, was discontinued for good after the summer of 1928, so the Fair Grounds RR was abandoned and dismantled.

The proud crew of the Woodstock's locomotive A. G. Dewey *pose for a photo shortly after the engine was delivered. (Courtesy Walker Transportation Collection, Beverly Historical Society & Museum)*

By the early 1930s all hope of a future had gone. Sale of the line was not a reasonable possibility, since both the Central Vermont and Boston & Maine with which it connected had fallen on hard times during the Great Depression. Closure took place in 1933, and permission to abandon was obtained almost immediately.

The Quechee Gorge Bridge still exists, converted to carry U.S. Route 4. For those who care to walk the trail that passes beneath it, the elevations are a delightful reminder of Edwardian engineering, although proportions have been marred by replacement of the original superstructure with prefabricated welded steel bents and stringers and a concrete deck. Woodstock station and freight house may still be seen.

Sources: Mead, *Over the Hills*; Karr, *Lost Railroads*, 14, 87; Jones, *Railroads of Vermont*, 1: 271-74; 2: 336-48.

50. White River

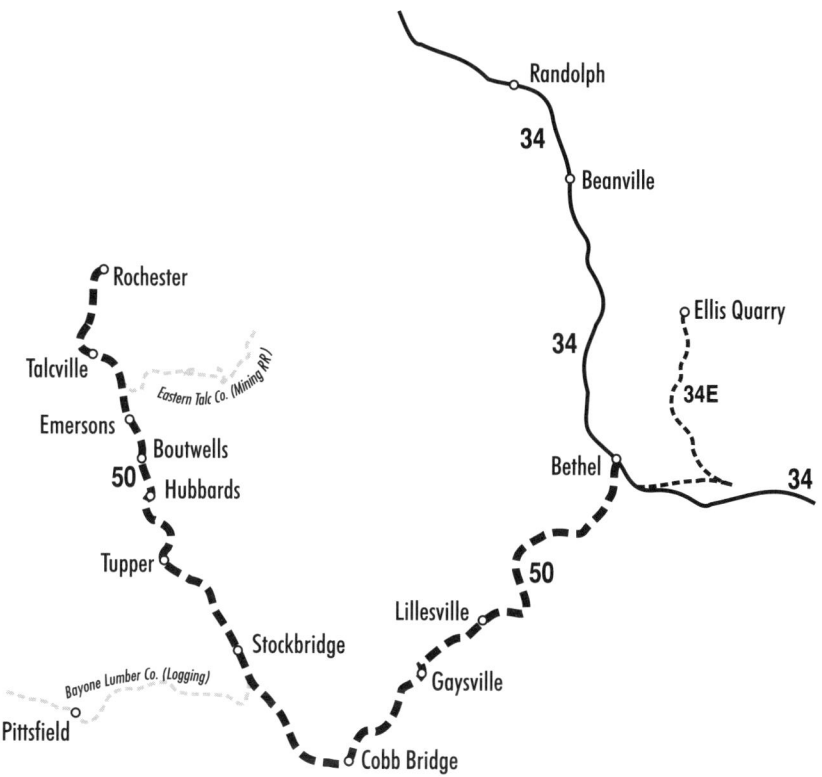

0 Bethel, VT	11 Stockbridge	16 Emersons
4 Lillesville	12 Tupper	18 Lower Rochester
5 Gaysville	14 Hubbards	(Talcville)
8 Cobb Bridge (Riverside)	15 Boutwells	19.5 Rochester, VT

Built: 1899–1900.
Operators: *White River Valley*, 1900–02; *White River*, 1902–33.
Daily Passenger Trains: *1903:* 2; *1914:* 8; *1926:* 4; *1933:* 2. Passenger service ended 1933.
Abandonment: 1933.

Much of Rochester, VT, must have turned out to see the White River RR operate its first train to their town in 1900. (Courtesy Walker Transportation Collection, Beverly Historical Society & Museum)

The White River Valley RR obtained a charter from the Vermont Commissioners on June 30, 1896. The proprietors had in mind an electric line that would carry lumber from the Rochester area to Bethel on the Central Vermont main line, but they almost immediately faced problems raising money for construction. The scheme languished for several years until the company was organized on December 27, 1898, and construction began in June 1899. Funds for completion were still hard to come by, and work ceased in 1900. The railroad had opened as far as Rochester, operating under steam power. Bankrupt, the company was reorganized as the White River RR on November 21, 1902, with headquarters in Rochester.

At Bethel, the WR built platforms adjacent to the CV station but at a different height, with a stair and subway connection. With the exception of Gaysville and Stockbridge, all intermediate stations were flag stops. The Eastern Talc Co. built a quarry line with several spurs from north of Emersons, and a logging line was constructed by the Bayonne Lumber Co. from south of Stockbridge to Pittsfield and beyond.

Lack of maintenance caused the Vermont Railroad Commissioners to order closure in September 1906. Under new management, which

50. White River

included E. S. French, later President of the Boston & Maine, the line reopened during 1907. The ensuing decade was the heyday of the line, with considerable growth in passenger, quarried stone, and agricultural traffic. By the 1920s highway competition and declining demand for stone took their toll. The Great Storm of 1927 washed out several parts of the line, and freight service was not reinstated until September 1928. Passenger accommodation was not again provided until January 1, 1929, and then by mixed trains, but this ended in 1932. Freight service ceased in 1933.

Permission to abandon was obtained the following year. Subsequently, most of the alignment was used for roads, among them State Highway 100 north of Stockbridge. Apart from a length of about one mile southwest of Gaysville to Cobb Bridge, the entire alignment can be driven over, but there are few traces that a railroad once existed.

Sources: Cornwall and Smith, *Names First*, 127; Jones, *Railroads of Vermont*, 2: 327; Karr, *Lost Railroad*, 88.

51. Northern

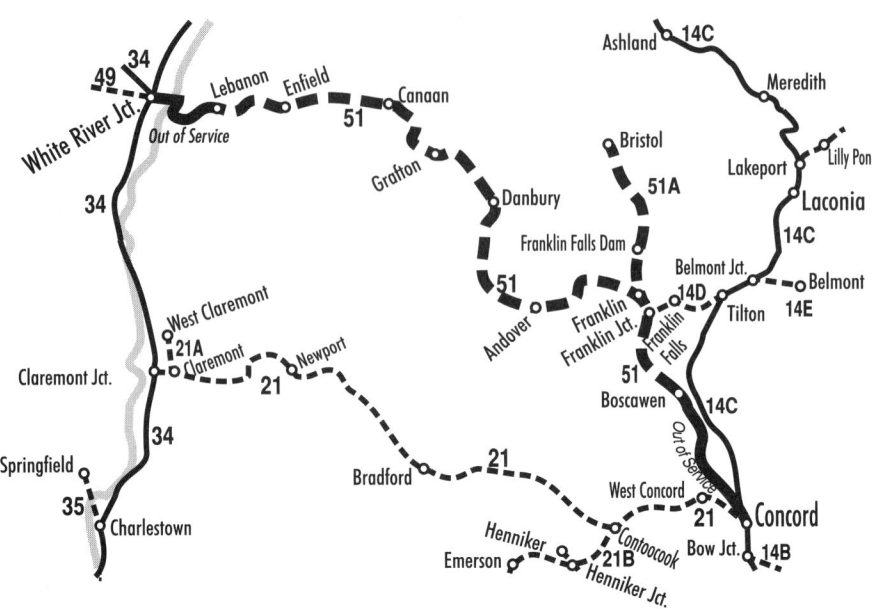

0 Concord, NH	32 West Andover (Gale)	69 Westboro (West Lebanon), NH
7 Penacook (Fisherville)	35 Converse (South Danbury)	70 White River Jct., VT
10 Boscawen	39 Danbury	
14 Gerrish (North Boscawen)	44 Grafton	**51A. Franklin & Bristol RR**
16 Webster Place	46 Grafton Center (Cardigan)	0 Franklin, NH
17 Franklin Jct.	52 Canaan	*2 Franklin Falls Dam*
19 Franklin	57 Pattee (West Canaan)	5 Oakdale Park
21 Webster Lake	59 Enfield	8 Hill
23 Webster Place	61 Mascoma (East Lebanon)	10 Blakes
25 Halcyon (East Andover)		13 Profile Falls
29 Andover	65 Lebanon	15 Bristol, NH
31 Potter Place		

Built: 1845-47; Franklin & Bristol RR, 1847-48.

Operators: *Northern*, 1847-84, 1887; *Boston & Lowell*, 1884-87; *Boston & Maine*, 1888-1983; *Guilford*, 1983-92.

Daily Passenger Trains: *1851:* 4 (Franklin-Bristol, 2); *1869:* 6 (Franklin-Bristol, 2); *1897:* 10 (Franklin-Bristol, 4); *1919:* 10 (Franklin–Bristol, 4); *1935:* 10 (Franklin–Bristol, 2 [mixed]); *1950:* 8; *1960:* 4. Passenger service ended Franklin–Bristol, 1936 (mixed); Concord–White River Jct., 1965.

Abandonments: Franklin & Bristol RR (Franklin Falls Dam–Bristol, 1937; Franklin–Franklin Falls Dam, 1940); Boscawen–Westboro, 1992.

The Christmas season of 1844 must have been a gratifying time for the New Hampshire legislature, for on December 27, it granted charters to both the Cheshire and the Boston, Concord & Montreal RRs, and amended the Northern RR charter of June 18. Each company selected Concord as a stepping-off point for potentially lucrative traffic from the north and northwest, particularly northern New York and Quebec. The objective of the Northern was the Connecticut River at the White River, where the planned Vermont Central and Connecticut & Passumpsic Rivers lines would join. The surveyors placed the alignment along rivers and streams, but in the northwest corner of Enfield township, a deviation was made to accommodate the locally very prominent and politically influential Shaker colony west of Lake Mascoma.

Daniel Webster, unquestionably the greatest of American orators, observed at opening ceremonies at Lebanon in 1847 that the Northern connected "the home of my adoption [Boston] with the home of my nativity [Franklin] and my Alma Mater [Dartmouth College in Hanover]." Mills in Boscawen and Lebanon provided most of the traffic. The Shaker community in Enfield built a half-mile bridge of stone-filled wooden cribbing to export lumber and flannel for the New York market from its highly profitable Shaker Mills Company, as well as packaged seed; the bridge was destroyed by the great hurricane of 1938. The Northern also took over operation of the Franklin & Bristol RR, which had operated independently for less than a year, fed by textile mills and agriculture.

The Northern and VC arranged their schedules for convenient connections or through cars. As early as November 1852, the two companies advertised Boston–Montreal service via the Boston & Lowell, Concord, Northern, VC, Vermont & Canada, and the Champlain & St. Lawrence. North of White River Jct., the Connecticut & Passumpsic Rivers had a connection with Montreal over the standard-gauge Massawippi Valley RR to Sherbrooke, PQ, and the broad-gauge Grand

Trunk beyond from 1870; in 1873 a second but standard-gauge throughout connection was made over the Missisquoi & Clyde Rivers RR and South Eastern RY. Thus the Northern became an important route for almost its entire life. After 37 years of independent operation it was leased to the Boston & Lowell RR in 1884, and it became part of the Boston & Maine system in 1887.

A new junction station was constructed south of Franklin to accommodate the Franklin & Tilton RR. That line was leased from opening in 1892 by the Concord & Montreal to keep out the B&M.

Nothing remarkable happened until 1925 when, on September 27, busses operated by the B&M Transportation Co. replaced passenger trains over the Franklin & Bristol line, apart from a single round trip mixed train. In the fall of 1927, a named passenger train, the *Red Wing* from Boston to Montreal, was diverted from the former BC&M route. It included a combined sleeper/parlor car, *Fernie*, bought from the Soo Line, which had used it on its Chicago-Twin Cities service, featuring an open verandah at the tail end. The *Red Wing* and *Alouette* were operated in conjunction with the Canadian Pacific, which contracted for three E8A diesel locomotives, the sole example of that type to be bought by a Canadian operator.

Parts of the Franklin & Bristol had been built in the flood plain of the parallel Pemigewasset River. Storms on March 17, 1936, washed out several sections of the track bed and operation ceased. The B&M applied to abandon the entire F&B, but the ICC on October 19, 1936, gave permission to discontinue operations only. The Army Corps of Engineers had requested that the line remain in situ pending finalization of flood control design work to include a dam across the Pemigewasset River near the falls to create the Franklin Falls Flood Control Area and Reservoir. Once design work had been completed, the ICC on September 24, 1937, permitted the B&M to abandon the line. The 10.3 miles north of Franklin Falls Dam site to Bristol were taken up and what was left became an industrial spur, for which abandonment procedures were not required. Materials for constructing the dam were brought in by rail, so the southern 2.5 miles of the F&B remained in use to the dam site until 1940.

The B&M and Central Vermont jointly funded a new station at White River Jct. in 1937 to replace the original facility, which had

The initial ten-mile stretch of the Northern out of Concord, although not legally abandoned, has not seen trains in many years, as this June 1999 view attests. (R. D. Karr)

The depot at Franklin Jct., NH, as it appeared in the days of B&M steam. (Courtesy Walker Transportation Collection, Beverly Historical Society & Museum)

burned in 1911, and its temporary replacement, also destroyed by fire in March 1935. Several stations and ticket agencies were closed between 1941 and 1955.

Something of a resurgence occurred from October 31, 1954, following abandonment of the former BC&M main line between Plymouth and North Haverhill, NH. The *Alouette* was re-routed via White River Jct., joining the *Ambassador* and *Cannon Ball*. By 1957, passenger trains generally comprised Budd rail diesel cars (RDCs), with the exception of the *Red Wing*, which was discontinued after October 25, 1959. Passenger service continued until January 3, 1965, although the final northbound run of the *Alouette* took place the next day. There is a story, perhaps apocrypha, that its return trip from Wells River on January 5 had to be replaced by busses hired by the CP. Through freight trains continued for some years, generally one daily round trip, but

51. Northern

ended some time before September 1982. One of the reasons for the Northern's longevity was its usefulness as a route for high and wide traffic, until a tunnel at Bellows Falls was enlarged about 1980. The New England Southern RR obtained trackage rights over 6.6 miles to serve a lumber yard at Penacook, but the line was out of use by 1990.

Guilford obtained permission to abandon between Boscawen and Lebanon during 1992. When it sold the line to the state of New Hampshire in July 1995, it retained ownership of the track and began removing it in 1996. Guilford continued operation to Westboro until the track was embargoed in 1997. Pressure from legislators and potential shippers in 1999 prodded Guilford into selling the three miles between White River Jct. and Lebanon to the state. In May 2000 the Claremont Concord RR agreed to operate the line for five years. The largest customer is expected to be Twin State Sand & Gravel, who will ship aggregate from its pit near White River Jct. to a processing plant in West Lebanon.

Sources: Bachelder, *Alouette*, 5, 34–36; Baker, *Formation*, 101, 142–43, 146; Drury, *Historical Guide*, 366; Heffernan and Stecker, *New Hampshire*, 92; Karr, *Lost Railroads*, 91, 102, 152; Kirkland, *Men, Cities & Transportation*, 1: 165, 2: 436; *Railpace* 18 (Oct. 1999): 36.

52. Portland & Rumford Falls

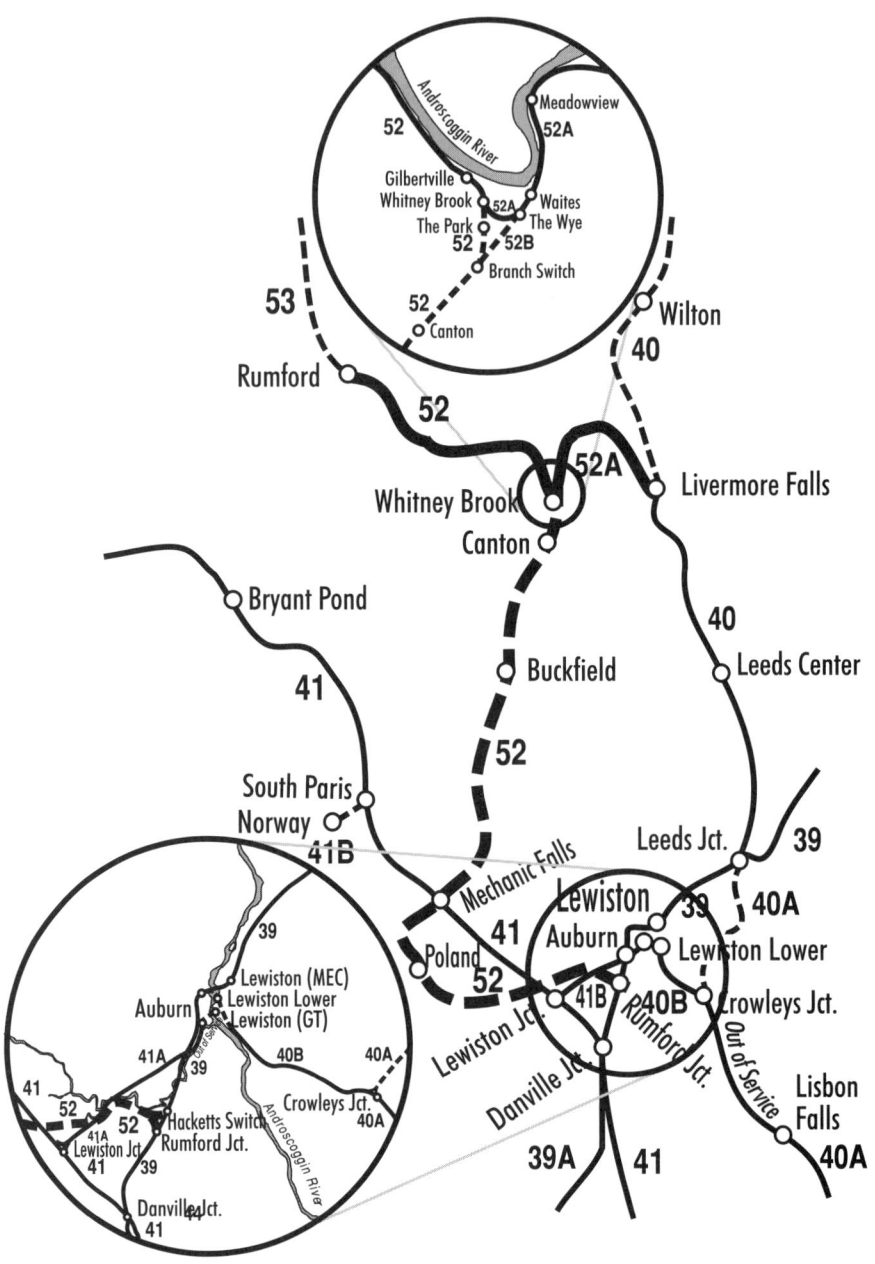

52. Portland & Rumford Falls

0 Rumford Jct., ME	37 Branch Switch	1 Waites
4 Elmwood	37.5 The Park	2.5 Meadowview
6 Riccars (Poland Springs)	38 Whitney Brook	4.5 Sawyers
8 Poland	38.5 Gilbertville	5.5 Rileys
11.5 Mechanic Falls	43 Worthley (East Peru)	7.5 Jay Bridge
16 West Minot (Minot)	45 Peru	9 Chisholms Mills
20 East Hebron (Hebron)	48 Dixfield (West Peru)	10 Livermore Falls, ME
25 Buckfield	52.5 Rumford, ME	
29.5 East Sumner (Sumner)		**52B. Whitney Brook Wye**
31.5 Hartford (Hartford Center)	**52A. Livermore Falls Branch**	0 Branch Switch, ME
36.5 Canton	0 Whitney Brook, ME	0.5 The Wye, ME
	0.5 The Wye	

Built: 1849–96.

Operators: *Buckfield Branch*, 1850-56; *Portland & Oxford Central*, 1862-73; *Rumford & Buckfield Falls*, 1879-90; *Portland & Rumford Falls*, 1890-1907; *Maine Central*, 1907-81; *Guilford*, 1981-.

Daily Passenger Trains: *1868:* 2 (Mechanic Falls–Sumner); *1893:* 4 (Mechanic Falls–Rumford); *1912:* 6 (Canton–Livermore Falls, 4); *1916:* 4 (Canton–Livermore Falls, 4); *1930:* 6 (Canton–Livermore Falls, 2); *1932:* 2 (Leeds Jct.–Rumford, 2); *1951:* 2 (Livermore Falls–Rumford). Passenger service ended Rumford Jct.–Whitney Brook, 1951; Livermore Falls–Rumford, 1955.

Abandonments: Rumford Jct.–Whitney Brook, Whitney Brook Wye, 1952.

Following the incorporation of the Atlantic & St. Lawrence RR in 1845 and commencement of construction the year following, interested citizens of Buckfield set about planning a connection to it at Mechanic Falls on the Androscoggin River. By early 1847 some $17,000 had been pledged, and the Maine legislature granted a charter to the Buckfield Branch RR to build from Mechanic Falls to Canton, authorizing the then enormous share capital of $500,000.

Subscriptions to stock were opened on March 30, 1848, and a call produced sufficient capital to commence grading between Buckfield and Mechanic Falls; a groundbreaking ceremony was held at Buckfield on October 31, 1848. The first rails of this broad-gauge line were not laid at Mechanic Falls until August 13, 1849, by which time earlier enthusiasm had waned, together with hopes for early completion of the line northward to the Androscoggin River. Further calls on stock were largely ignored, so completion as far as Buckfield required a loan of $35,000. One F. O. J. Smith, envisioning use of the route to make connections at Canton with steamboats plying the Androscoggin to Rumford, granted a mortgage to the line, which enabled completion as far as Buckfield in 1850. A formal opening ceremony was held on Tuesday, January 8, but drifting snow precluded operation until Friday, January 11.

The stockholders' lack of enthusiasm proved correct, for at the end of the first financial year construction had stalled at Sumner and revenues barely covered operating costs. At the Buckfield Branch's annual meeting on April 12, 1851, a plea was made for additional subscriptions, but only $14,000 was raised. Smith took advantage by foreclosing his loan; having acquired the company, he immediately set about extending the line to Canton and beyond to Lake Anasagunticook and west to Rumford.

In March 1853 Smith commissioned the Androscoggin Navigation Co. to provide steamboat service from Canton to Rumford. In June 1854 the railroad had reached Sumner but disgruntled landowners demanded full settlement for property acquired; Smith could not afford to pay them, so they retaliated by removing rails and placing obstacles on the track. To add to his worries, a specially-built steamer capsized after hitting a rock east of Peru in 1854. Despite Smith's appeals to local communities, subscriptions were not forthcoming. Work on the railroad slowed and had all but ceased by October 1855. The Buckfield Branch was forced into receivership in September 1856 and operation was suspended.

Relieved of many of his obligations, Smith incorporated the Portland & Oxford Central RR, which obtained a charter in 1857 to complete the line from Sumner to Canton together with rights to acquire the Buckfield Branch. Pleas to and votes by towns to subscribe capital resulted in nothing until 1862. That year the P&OC resumed operation of the original line under new management headed by A. R. Morrill of the Maine Central. A decade of almost continual legal and financial problems ended with completion of the route from Sumner to Hartford in 1868 (although the June 1869 *Official Guide* shows service to Sumner only) and to Canton in 1870. The MEC was approached in 1871 in hopes it would purchase or lease the line, but

52. Portland & Rumford Falls

nothing came of it. A court order closing the P&OC took effect in November 1873, with Smith appointed receiver.

Led by the Hon. George D. Bisbee, a new company, the Rumford Falls & Buckfield RR, petitioned to take over the tracks of the P&OC and to revive its authority to construct to Gilbertville. When the charter was granted, the promoters acquired Smith's interests, converted the line to standard gauge, and resumed service to Canton by 1879. The extension to Gilbertville was completed by the spring of 1884.

Under the guidance of Hugh Chisolm, the owner of a large paper mill in Rumford, the Portland & Rumford Falls RR was incorporated in 1890 to build from Gilbertville to Rumford Falls, and in November leased the RF&B. Its own line was opened on August 1, 1892, although the terminal at Rumford was not finished until Friday, May 26, 1893, with full service commencing the next Monday. The station's architecture was typical of the period although on a grander scale. The timber-framed and clad building, which contained many extremely large offices and expansive waiting rooms, featured a 60-foot belvedere and clock and fully canopied platforms.

The P&RF embarked on two schemes to break the Grand Trunk monopoly on transfer traffic at Mechanic Falls by providing direct connections with the MEC. First to be built was a line south and east from Mechanic Falls across the GT to the MEC at Rumford Jct., south of Auburn, which opened on February 12, 1894. The second extension, which followed the south bank of the Androscoggin River from Canton and Whitney Brook to Chisholms Mills, near Livermore Falls, opened on September 1, 1897. It included a short section of track connecting a point called The Wye on the new branch with a point on the old main line just north of Canton, forming a large wye. A short extension to Livermore Falls that provided a connection with the MEC (the former Androscoggin RR) followed in 1899. Ultimately, it was this link that brought about the demise of the original main line.

A period of prosperity began, and the proprietors, noting the expansion of lumbering operations in northern Oxford County, the construction of mills across the river at Rumford, and the success of the Sandy River RR, determined to extend the line northward. A separate company, the Rumford Falls & Rangeley Lakes RR, was organized in September 1894, and the first section opened on September 1, 1895. To connect with it, the P&RF built a bridge over the Androscoggin River and a spur to the waterfront, for a total length of 1.4 miles.

Independent operation of the P&RF ended in 1907 when the owners agreed to a lease by the MEC. Fire destroyed the Rumford terminal on March 19, 1913. A more humble, but not cheap, brick and stone structure was built on the connecting line just south of the river. The P&RF survived World War II intact, to be merged into the MEC in September 1946, but was an obvious candidate for economies in the 1950s. The MEC decided to consolidate traffic by using the Livermore Falls branch rather than the circuitous route through Mechanic Falls. Track between Rumford Jct. and Poland was out of service by April 1951 and the line south of Canton was closed and abandoned in 1952. All passenger service on the remainder of the P&RF ended in 1955.

The status of the line was reduced progressively in ensuing years. Guilford retained the segment from Livermore Falls to Rumford as a 44-mile unsignaled branch under radio dispatch arrangements. Nowadays, a daily round trip freight runs from Rigby Yard in South Portland to serve International Paper at Rileys station in Jay and the Mead facilities in Rumford, with sidings and switching facilities at Rileys (for up to 120 cars) and others at Worthley and Dixfield. Switchers work over the line from Rumford, Dixfield, and Rileys. In spring 1997, work to improve track at Rumford was completed to enable the use of six-axle locomotives.

Sources: Bachelder, *Rumford Rocket*; Guilford, *Working Timetable*, 89-91; Hutchinson, *Rumford Falls & Rangeley Lakes*; Karr, *Lost Railroads*, 110.

53. Rumford Falls & Rangeley Lakes

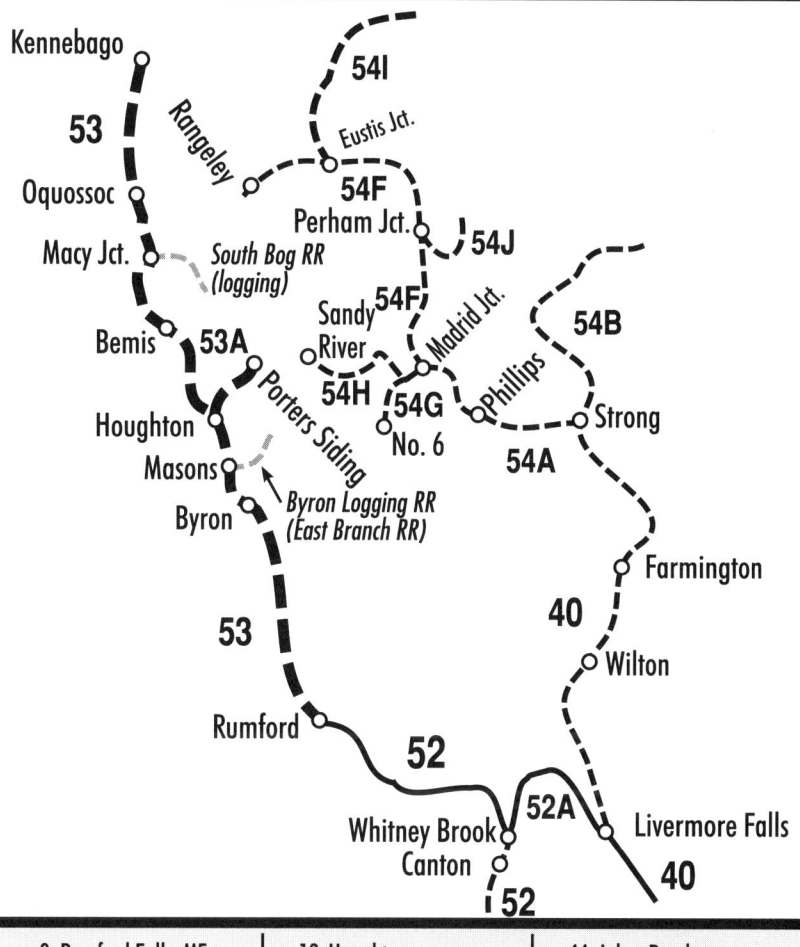

0 Rumford Falls, ME	18 Houghton	44 Johns Pond
1 Porters	22 Ten Degree	46.5 Kennebago, ME
3 Hale	23.5 Summit	
5 Mitchells	26.5 Bemis	**53A. Houghton Branch**
6 Frye	32 Welchs	
8 Chapman	35 Macy Jct.	0 Houghton, ME
9 Reeds Mill	33.5 South Rangeley	2.5 Thurstons Siding
9.5 Roxbury	36 Oquossoc	4.5 Porters Siding, ME
11 Hop City	37 Kamankeag (Indian	
14 Byron	Rock)	
15.5 Masons (Mendearth)	39 Realty	

53. Rumford Falls & Rangeley Lakes

Built: 1894–1912; Houghton Branch, 1896.

Operators: *Rumford Falls & Rangeley Lakes*, 1895–99; *Portland & Rumford Falls*, 1899–1907; *Maine Central*, 1907–1936.

Daily Passenger Trains: *1899:* 2 (Rumford–Bemis); *1912:* 4 (Rumford–Oquossoc); 1915: Rumford–Oquossoc, 2; Bemis–Kennebago, 2; *1916:* Rumford–Oquossoc, 2; Oquossoc–Kennebago, 2; *1930:* 2; *1935:* 2 (Rumford Falls–Oquossoc). Trains to Kennebago did not operate daily. Passenger service ended Oquossoc–Kennebago, 1933; Rumford–Oquossoc, 1935.

Abandonments: Houghton Branch, 1905; Rumford–Kennebago, 1936.

Conceived as an extension of the Portland & Rumford Falls RR by that company's proprietors, the Rumford Falls & Rangeley Lakes RR was chartered and organized in September 1894 to build a standard-gauge line north into Franklin County, primarily for lumber and quarry traffic. What the proprietors appeared to have overlooked was the cost of using a standard-gauge line primarily for logging, as compared with the more economical narrow-gauge Sandy River & Rangeley Lakes network to the east. Construction, beginning in 1894 from the mills at Rumford, involved the Portland & Rumford Falls RR. An upgraded 1.4-mile spur to the river was built to an impressive three-span bridge, which featured two 45-foot lattice girders, a 283-foot through center pin truss, a 406-foot wooden trestle, and a filled causeway. The first section, to Byron, opened in July 1895, although work was not completed until August. On September 1, 1895, the line was completed to Houghton, and opening celebrations were held on October 5, with an excursion from Lewiston–Auburn. At least one freight siding was provided at each station, and a two-stall engine shed was built at Houghton. Stone for track ballast was quarried by the contractor from a site about 1.5 miles north of Byron.

Meanwhile, work commenced in May 1895 to extend the line to Bemis on Mooselookmeguntic Lake. A few miles were available for use by December, but full opening was not possible until May 1896. Extensive facilities at Bemis included a turntable and roundhouse, and a short manually-operated narrow-gauge track from the station to Upper Dam Wharf for conveyance of baggage.

53. Rumford Falls & Rangeley Lakes

Blanchard & Twitchell, a logging company based in Milan, NH, built the Byron Logging RR (known as the East Branch RR) in only 12 weeks, opening it from a point south of Houghton in November 1896. One month later, the RF&RL completed the Houghton Branch northwest to Township E to serve Mavor Brothers Houghton Logging RR. These logging lines closed in 1902 and 1905 respectively.

The P&RF bought a controlling interest in the RF&RL in 1899, but separate operation continued. Rangeley Lake remained for a while an elusive target, but South Rangeley was eventually reached in 1901 and Oquossoc on September 1, 1902. A short spur was built from the South Rangeley station on to a wooden pier. About 1.5 miles below South Rangeley a junction was made by the South Bog RR, another logging line opened in 1901 and operated until 1906. At Oquossoc, a turntable recovered from Rumford was installed beyond the station on the west side of the line, serving another two-stall engine shed and several short freight spurs.

In April 1907 the MEC, which by then was operating trains beyond Rumford, agreed to lease the RF&RL. Anticipating this agreement, the RF&RL auctioned off its locomotives on April 14. With cash in hand, the board of directors sought to extend the line through even remoter parts of Franklin County and across the Canadian border to Lac Megantic. A charter for the Rangeley Lakes & Megantic RR was obtained on March 12, 1909, but capital was not forthcoming. A revised charter was issued on March 16, 1911, and a survey of the proposed alignment was approved on February 20, 1912. Construction commenced but work ceased in December 1912 at Kennebago, where humble facilities comprised a loop and neck, with a grounded passenger/baggage car— formerly Portland & Rumford Falls clerestory No. 51—as the station building.

After the Portland & Rumford Falls RR built a new station on the connecting line south of the Androscoggin River in 1913, Porters station was closed. The Maine Central bought nearly all of the RL&M's stock. Regular traffic north of Oquossoc ceased in July 1933, although occasional pulpwood trains used the line until August 1935. The Kennebago Bus Co. obtained consent to use a gasoline-engined double-truck, 20-seat railbus on an REO frame, which could haul a limited number of freight cars as needed. One daily passenger train between Rumford and Oquossoc continued to operate until November 1935, but the line became seasonal from November of that year. When the great floods of March 1936 carried away the bridge across the Androscoggin River the MEC decided that cost of replacement was unjustified and so convinced the ICC to permit abandonment of the line.

Demolition commenced in spring 1937. P&RF locomotive no. 159, an elderly 2-6-2 with three-axle tender, was transferred on temporary track panels sequentially laid and removed across the road bridge at Rumford. Among the last rites of the RF&RL, in late summer no. 159 was cut up in Rangeley Place, Rumford. The railbus survived several ownerships, eventually to become an exhibit at Clark's Trading Post in Lincoln, NH.

Sources: Hutchinson, *Rumford Falls & Rangeley Lakes*; Karr, *Lost Railroads*, 91, 92.

54. Sandy River & Rangeley Lakes

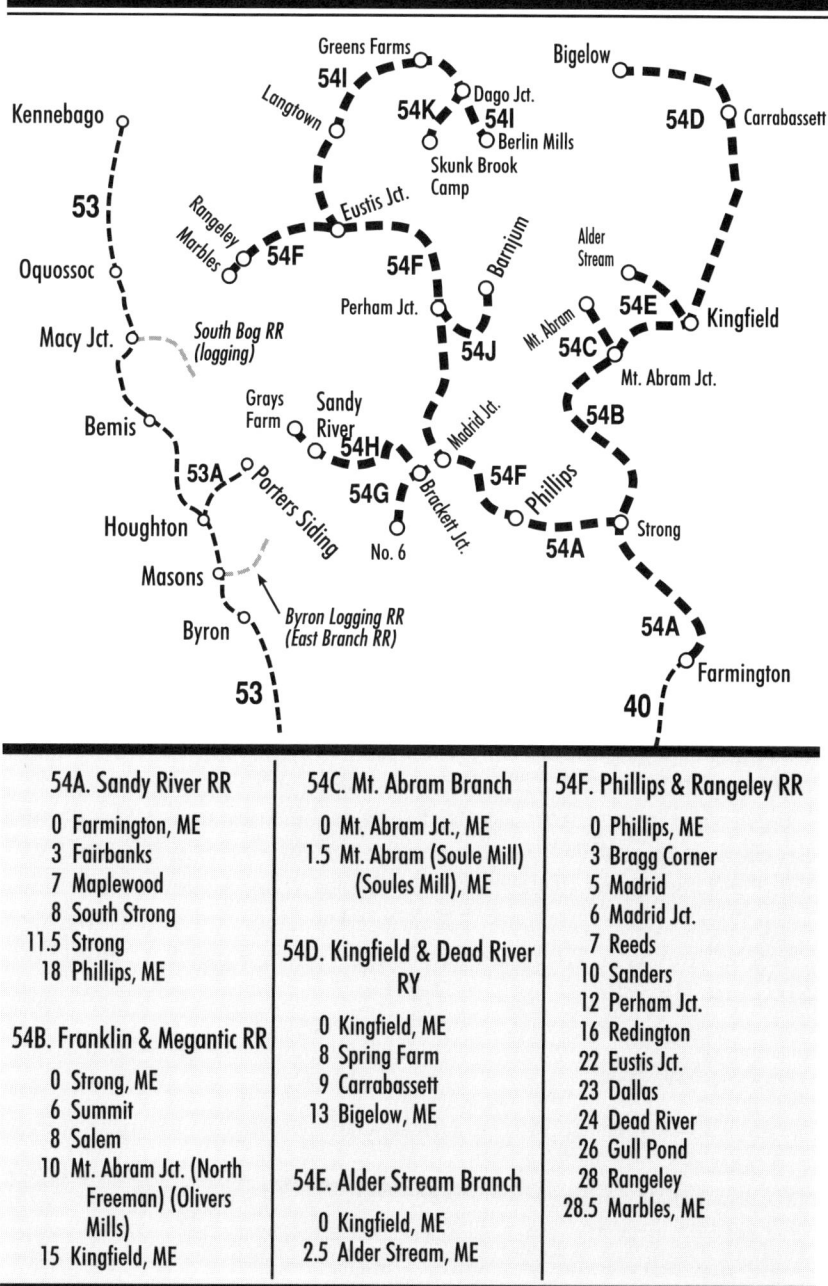

54A. Sandy River RR

- 0 Farmington, ME
- 3 Fairbanks
- 7 Maplewood
- 8 South Strong
- 11.5 Strong
- 18 Phillips, ME

54B. Franklin & Megantic RR

- 0 Strong, ME
- 6 Summit
- 8 Salem
- 10 Mt. Abram Jct. (North Freeman) (Olivers Mills)
- 15 Kingfield, ME

54C. Mt. Abram Branch

- 0 Mt. Abram Jct., ME
- 1.5 Mt. Abram (Soule Mill) (Soules Mill), ME

54D. Kingfield & Dead River RY

- 0 Kingfield, ME
- 8 Spring Farm
- 9 Carrabassett
- 13 Bigelow, ME

54E. Alder Stream Branch

- 0 Kingfield, ME
- 2.5 Alder Stream, ME

54F. Phillips & Rangeley RR

- 0 Phillips, ME
- 3 Bragg Corner
- 5 Madrid
- 6 Madrid Jct.
- 7 Reeds
- 10 Sanders
- 12 Perham Jct.
- 16 Redington
- 22 Eustis Jct.
- 23 Dallas
- 24 Dead River
- 26 Gull Pond
- 28 Rangeley
- 28.5 Marbles, ME

54G. Madrid RR	7 Grays Farm, ME	54J. Barnjum Branch
0 Madrid Jct.		0 Perham Jct., ME
2 Brackett Jct.	54I. Eustis RR	3.5 Barnjum, ME
5.5 No. 6, ME	0 Eustis Jct., ME	
	6 Langtown	54K. Skunk Brook Branch
54H. Madrid Branch	10 Greens Farm (Stratton Jct.)	0 Dago Jct., ME
0 Brackett Jct., ME	12 Dago Jct.	2 Skunk Brook Camp, ME
3.5 Madrid Village	14 Berlin Mills, ME	
5 Sandy River		

Built: Sandy River, 1878-79; Franklin & Megantic, 1883-84; Kingfield & Dead River, 1893-99; Phillips & Rangeley, 1889-91; Madrid, 1902-03; Eustis, 1903-04; Skunk Brook Branch, ca. 1904; Barnjum Branch, 1912.

Operators: See text for operators before 1908. *Sandy River & Rangeley Lakes*, 1908-32, 1933-35.

Daily Passenger Trains: *1893:* Sandy River, 6; Phillips & Rangeley, 4; Franklin & Megantic, 2: *1912:* Farmington-Rangeley, 6; Strong-Bigelow, 4; *1915:* Farmington-Rangeley, 2; Farmington-Phillips, 4; Strong-Rangeley, 2; Strong-Bigelow, 4; *1916:* Farmington-Marbles, 2; Strong-Rangeley, 2; Farmington-Phillips, 4; Strong-Kingfield, 4; Kingfield-Bigelow, 6; *1931:* Farmington-Phillips, 4; Strong-Carrabassett, 4.

Abandonments: Eustis RR (Greens Farm-Berlin Mills, 1909; Langtown-Greens Farm, 1919; Eustis Jct.-Langtown, 1932); Skunk Brook Branch, 1909; Mt. Abram Branch, Alder Stream Branch, 1922; Kingfield & Dead River RY (Carrabassett-Bigelow, 1926; Kingfield-Carrabassett, 1935); Madrid RR, Madrid Branch, Barnjum Branch, Phillips & Rangeley RR, 1932; Sandy River RR, Franklin & Megantic RR, 1935.

Sandy River RR

Samuel B. Cushman, in association with others with lumber interests in Franklin County, originally sought extension of the MEC north of Farmington along the Sandy River. Rejection of this plan was inevitable given the costs of applying MEC construction standards to what would be for many years a logging line. The organizers turned to George E.

Canoes await the passengers who will depart from the SR&RL train that has just arrived at Marbles Station at the Rangeley Lakes House Hotel in 1916. (Courtesy Walker Transportation Collection, Beverly Historical Society & Museum)

Mansfield, whose 2-foot-gauge Billerica & Bedford RR in Massachusetts had recently been constructed at low cost. Mansfield spoke at public meetings in several Maine communities during March 1878. Enthusiasm led to incorporation of the Sandy River RR on April 29, and Mansfield was appointed superintendent on June 1.

Surveys between Farmington and Phillips estimated the construction cost at $27,000. Although considerably cheaper than a standard-gauge line, the outlay represented a sum of over $10 for each local resident. Even so, the town of Phillips immediately approved a bond issue contingent on completion of the line by November 30, 1879, and groundbreaking took place soon after. The somewhat meandering route was completed on November 20, 1879. Rolling stock came from the B&B (which had failed after only six months), including two Hinkley-built Forney locomotives converted to wood firing. Transfer sidings with the MEC were laid at Farmington and a workshop was provided at Phillips. With the line in operation, Mansfield resigned in September 1880 to go to the Bridgton & Saco River RR.

In the next few years consideration was given to extending the line to Gardiner at the navigable head of the Kennebec River, thus attracting the attention of Gardiner lumber merchants Josiah Maxcy and Weston Lewis. They secured a majority interest in July 1892 when the narrow-gauge system was struggling for survival on diminished lumber traffic and low-return agricultural products. The planned extension died, although the idea was revived some years later by the Wiscasset & Quebec RR.

Franklin & Megantic RR

Promotion of a second 2-foot-gauge line, from Strong to Kingfield, was led by S. W. Sargent. Under a charter issued on July 1, 1883, grading of the Franklin & Megantic RR began in 1884. Capital was not im-

Sandy River RR workers Raymond Phillips and George Hodgman pose with engine no. 3 at Kingfield in 1906. (Courtesy Walker Transportation Collection, Beverly Historical Society & Museum)

mediately forthcoming and the track was not substantially completed until December 10. Onset of a severe winter delayed operation to spring 1885. There were no intermediate communities except logging camps. The company owned two locomotives and a fleet of flat cars. A spur to Mt. Abram was built about 1889 but closed in 1899. Dwindling receipts required extension to the north, for which the Kingfield & Dead River RR subsidiary was incorporated in 1893. Even so, by 1896 the F&M was delinquent on debt payments and entered receivership, emerging in 1897 as the Franklin & Megantic RY, which Maxcy and Lewis bought. The Mt. Abram branch reopened in 1907, the same year that the Alder Stream branch was built.

Kingfield & Dead River RY

In June 1893 the F&M board resolved to extend northward along the Carrabassett River from Kingfield to Bigelow. The Kingfield & Dead River RY was set up as a subsidiary and completed the line the following summer. There were no intermediate communities other than lumber camps. The company owned no rolling stock, motive power and other equipment being provided by the F&M. Sandy River vehicles worked through under an exchange agreement. Upon reorganization of the F&M in 1897 the subsidiary was effectively disowned. Maxcy and Lewis bought it at a receiver's auction on August 2, 1898.

Phillips & Rangeley RR

Chronologically the third narrow-gauge main line in the Rangeley region was the Phillips & Rangeley RR, promoted by Calvin Putnam and Henry P. Closson and chartered on April 17, 1889. Although both promoters had extensive lumber interests in Somerset County and hauling timber was intended to be the chief business of the line, they also hoped that a connection with the Sandy River RR in Phillips would bring passenger traffic to Rangeley Lakes. The line opened to Dallas, midway between Redington Mill and Rangeley, in April 1890. Completion to Rangeley, delayed until the spring thaw, was celebrated on June 10, 1891.

When costs exceeded expectations, shareholders on October 21, 1891, elected Arthur Sewall, president of the Maine Central, as chairman. Management of the P&R remained in Phillips, although the reg-

Phillips & Rangeley Lakes no. 1 takes water from this strange-looking water tower at Sanders in the 1890s. (Courtesy Walker Transportation Collection, Beverly Historical Society & Museum)

istered office was now the MEC headquarters in Portland. Results continued to be extremely disappointing, and in 1897 Putnam wrested control from the MEC. Three proposals for extensions were then made, each to be constructed by subsidiaries. Of them, the seven-mile Rangeley RR from Rangeley Lake to the Rumford Falls & Rangeley Lakes RR at Oquossoc failed to obtain a charter; the others were the Madrid and Eustis RRs. The P&R declared bankruptcy on January 30, 1905, and receivers took over on February 1. Beyond Rangeley a spur sponsored by John G. Marbles was built during 1906 to serve his waterfront Rangeley Lakes Hotel. Receivership ended on June 8, 1908, with sale at auction of the P&R and Madrid to the Sandy River & Rangeley Lakes RR.

Madrid RR

On April 29, 1902, the Madrid RR received a charter for a line to be built southwestward from the P&R at a point in Phillips Township, now Madrid Jct., along the Sandy River South Branch to a lumber camp in Weld Township known simply as No. 6. Safety certification was obtained on May 11, 1903. The Madrid on July 1, 1902, had obtained approval for a branch through Madrid village, and work was completed at the same time.

From the outset the P&R provided rolling stock and operated the Madrid, and on April 5, 1904, it leased the line. A year later both railroads were in receivership. In 1911 the SR&RL built an extension to Grays Farm (known as Littlefields from 1912).

Eustis RR

The Eustis Railroad obtained a charter on April 29, 1903, and built from Dallas on the P&R through Langtown to the south branch of the Dead River. Safety certification was obtained on May 9, 1904, as far as Greens Farm in Coplin. Extension to Berlin Mills in Stratton was certified on May 24, 1904, and to Stratton on Flagstaff Lake in June. Al-

Phillips & Rangeley locomotive no. 2 working the logging yard at Camp 6 in Madrid. (Courtesy Walker Transportation Collection, Beverly Historical Society & Museum)

though operated by the P&R, the company owned three 0-4-4 Baldwin-designed Forney locomotives and several flat cars which were freely exchanged with other lines. Several logging branches were built into Eustis Township. Even though the Eustis joined the P&R in receivership in 1905, it remained profitable for almost two years under P&R management. The SR&RL leased the Eustis in 1908 but on such unfavorable terms that operation ceased in 1909. On August 24, 1911, the SR&RL bought the assets of the Eustis at auction.

Sandy River & Rangeley Lakes RR

To consolidate their narrow-gauge acquisitions, Maxcy and Lewis incorporated the Sandy River & Rangeley Lakes RR on January 30, 1908. In 1911 the company had some $240,000 in unsold shares, which enabled the MEC to take control on August 31. During the fol-

By 1934, shortly before service ended forever, all passengers were carried either by railbusses or mixed trains, such as those shown here at Strong depot, with SR&RL engine no. 24. (Courtesy Walker Transportation Collection, Beverly Historical Society & Museum)

54. Sandy River & Rangeley Lakes 271

lowing year a new branch in Madrid Township was constructed to Barnjum, south of Mecham Hill. Several logging branches were built and dismantled in ensuing years. Traffic peaked in 1919, but that year the Eustis north of Langtown was abandoned. As local roads improved, highway competition began to take its toll, and the railroad was burdened with heavy debts.

Fire severely damaged the Phillips shop and rolling stock in 1923. Immediate return of the SR&RL to local management resulted in receivership on July 1, under Maxcy (controlling finance) and Herbert S. Wing of Kingfield (superintending operations). Passenger trains, some of which had featured the unique *Rangeley* parlor car, were replaced by mixed consists and gasoline rail busses in 1926. All operations ceased on July 8, 1932, and a petition to abandon was submitted. The Maine Transportation Commissioners sustained an objection by the Lawrence Plywood Company, however, and service resumed from Farmington to Phillips and Carrabassett on April 17, 1933. Apart from these segments, the remainder of the SR&RL was dismantled during autumn 1934 and sold on May 18, 1935, eventually becoming assets of H. E. Salzberg.

On appeal, the Maine Supreme Court decided in favor of abandonment on June 28, 1935, and the last train ran on June 30. The track was removed and sold the next summer. Some of the rolling stock of the SR&RL ended up at the Edaville RR museum in Massachusetts, and much of this was eventually transferred to the Maine Narrow Gauge RR & Museum in Portland in 1994.

Sources: Cornwall and Farrell, *Ride the Sandy River*; Crittenden, *Maine Scenic Route*; Crittenden, "Sandy River,"; Hilton, *American Narrow Gauge*, 410-13; Moody, *Maine Two-Footers*, 12-25, 55-122, 197.

55. Somerset

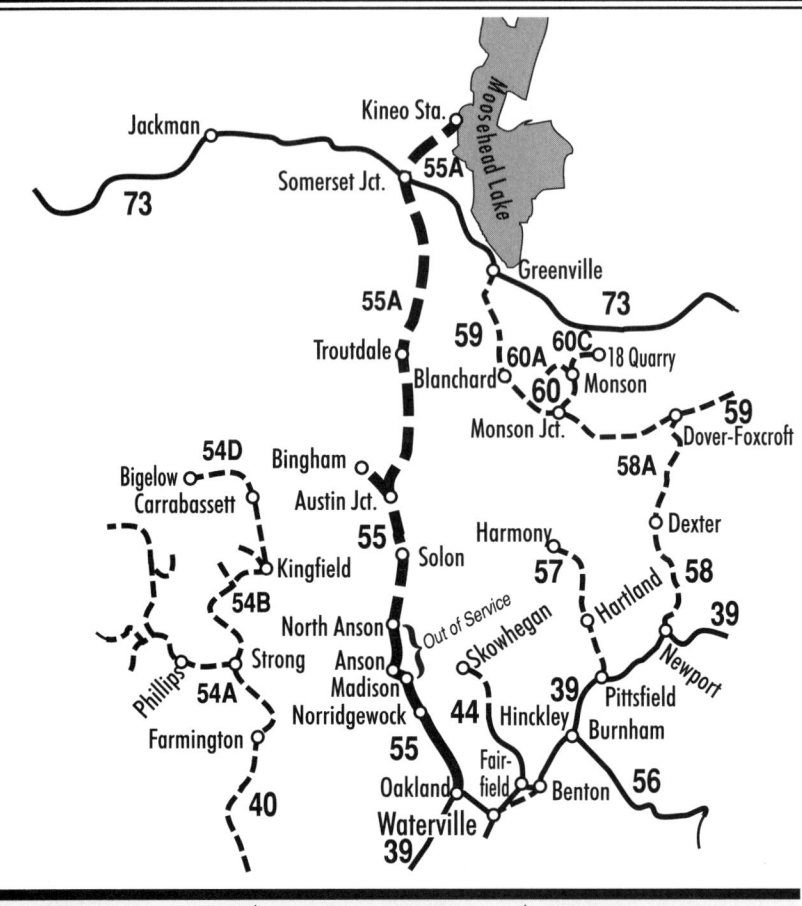

0 Oakland, ME	40 Austin Jct.	16.5 Bakers
3 Hoxies	41 Bingham, ME	20 Troutdale (Mosquito)
5.5 Otis Hill		24.5 Lake Moxie
7 Beluga	**55A. Kineo Extension**	29.5 Forsythe
10.5 Bangs		33.5 Moores
13 Norridgewock	0 Austin Jct., ME	36 Indian Pond
21 Madison	1 Bingham Heights (Moscow)	39 Misery
21.5 Anson	8 Deadwater	40.5 Marrs
25.5 North Anson	11 Dimmick	45.5 Somerset Jct.
30.5 Embden	12 Lake Austin (Bald Mountain)	51.5 Kineo Sta. (Rockwood), ME
33.5 Caratunk		
34 Solon		

55. Somerset

Built: 1873-90; Kineo Extension, 1904-07.
Operators: *Somerset*, 1873-1911; *Maine Central*, 1911-81; *Guilford*, 1981-.
Daily Passenger Trains: *1878:* 2; *1907:* 4; *1929:* 4; *1932:* 2. Passenger service ended 1933.
Abandonments: Kineo Extension, 1933; North Anson- Bingham, 1979.

When the Somerset & Kennebec RR failed to extend beyond Skowhegan after 1857, the Somerset RR obtained a charter in 1860 to build a line northward from either the S&K or the Androscoggin & Kennebec RR at Waterville. The aim was to exploit traffic in dairy products, lumber, paper and pulpwood, and consignments of locally-made shoes from Norridgewock; textiles and paper from Madison; and products from the extensive saw, grist, and fulling mills in Anson, which was also a significant agricultural center. North Anson was eventually to provide considerable traffic in quarried slate schist.

Lack of funding prevented a start, and the charter languished, although revived in 1866, 1868, and 1871. After the Androscoggin & Kennebec—by then the Maine Central—had been converted to standard gauge, construction of the Somerset began in Oakland, opening to Madison in 1873 and to North Anson in January 1874. A one-mile spur to a quarry near Dodling Hill was also built from Norridgewock. Despite its good prospects, the company barely managed to pay dividends, and as a result planned extensions to the north failed to attract capital. By the early1880s the line went bankrupt, but re-emerged in 1883 as the Somerset RY. Work on an extension to Bingham commenced in 1888; Embden was reached that year, Solon in 1889, and service to Bingham started in 1890.

The company was insolvent by the early 1900s and agreed to sell out in August 1904 to the Kennebec Valley RR, which subsequently reverted to the Somerset name. In order to exploit lumber resources and resort traffic in 1904, the Somerset built an extension north from Austin Jct., a point about a mile south of the end of the main line at Bingham. The extension opened to Deadwater on February 22, 1905, to Landers in 1906, and to Rockwood, on the shores of Moosehead Lake, on March 4, 1907. The terminal at Rockwood was named Kineo

The deck of the Somerset Railroad's bridge across the Carrabasset River at North Anson has been covered to permit use by all-terrain vehicles, snowmobiles, and bicycles. Nature is gradually taking over the remnants of a switch in this view from July 1999. (R. D. Karr)

Station after a large resort, Mt. Kineo House, located a mile away at Mt. Kineo on a peninsula on the other side of the lake.

The large cash surplus which the Somerset accumulated attracted the MEC, which acquired stock control in 1907. On July 1, 1911, the independent company was merged, together with acquisition of Mt. Kineo House, which eventually became part of MEC's SamOset subsidiary. Generally, through trains to and from Kineo Station in the summer months ran direct and did not serve Bingham; the rest of the year, they reversed at Bingham and did not call at Bingham Heights. For many years the MEC ran lengthy Pullman trains to Kineo Station, some of which, during the summer months, included through sleepers and parlor cars from Boston and New York. At the terminal a ferry took customers on to the Mt. Kineo resort.

Competition from more accessible resorts and the economic impact of the Great Depression brought about closure of the line to Kineo Station. Approval to abandon was given on July 22, 1933. Passenger ser-

55. Somerset

vice to Bingham continued until September 24, when a certificate issued by the Public Utilities Commission was received that approved a bus route to replace passenger service over the entire line from Oakland. Mt. Kineo House was razed by the MEC in 1938.

Freight sustained the remainder of the line for another forty-five years. Bingham lost all service in 1979 when freight runs were cut back to quarries at North Anson. The line then passed to Guilford, which maintains it as its Madison Running Track, conveying traffic to and from Madison Paper Industries. Beyond there the line is out of service; the bridge across the Kennebec River still stands, and the overgrown rails extend to just less than a mile north of North Anson. The Carrabassett River bridge is covered and used unofficially as a trail. North of Bingham most of the route is a dirt track that can be driven over by an ordinary family car, although there is a gap at Indian Pond where the Kennebec River has been dammed. The arch bridge at Somerset Jct. remains, as do station buildings at Bakers and Troutdale.

Sources: Baker, *Formation*, 209; Cornwall and Smith, *Names First*, 113; Harlow, *Steelways*, 320; Karr, *Lost Railrods*, 88, 138; Peters, *Maine Central*, 14-15.

56. Belfast & Moosehead Lake

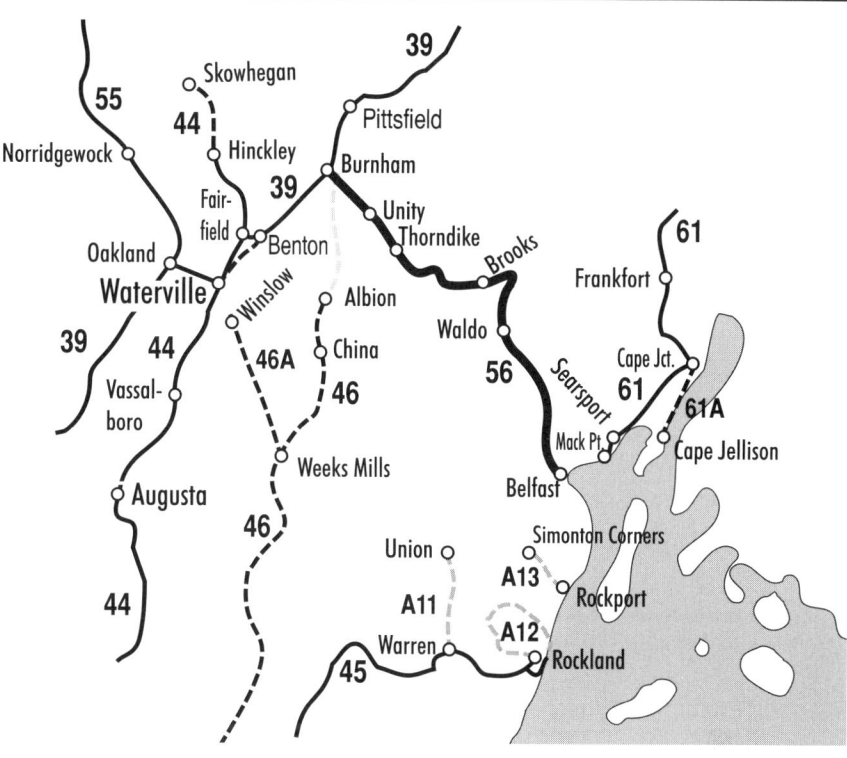

0 Belfast, ME	14 Forbes	29.5 Winnecook
2.5 City Point	19 Knox	33 Burnham Jct., ME
8 Waldo	22 Thorndike	
12.5 Brooks	25.5 Unity	

Built: 1867-70.

Operators: *Maine Central*, 1871-1926; *Belfast & Moosehead Lake*, 1926-.

Daily Passenger Trains: *1893:* 6; *1912:* 6; *1935:* 4; *1950:* 4 (2 mixed). Passenger service ended 1960. Excursions introduced 1987.

Abandonments: None.

> *B&ML General Electric 70-tonner no. 51 pulls a mixed train out of Burnham Jct. in 1952. (Albert L. Thomas, courtesy Walker Transportation Collection, Beverly Historical Society & Museum)*

56. Belfast & Moosehead Lake

Chartered in Maine and incorporated on February 28, 1867, the Belfast & Moosehead Lake RR was the first of many schemes designed to promote Atlantic ports other than Portland for exportation of the huge stands of timber north of the original Maine Central line. Construction of the section between Belfast and Burnham commenced in 1867, but progress was slowed during negotiations for a lease by the MEC. The city of Belfast subscribed to a majority of company stock so the line could be completed on December 23, 1870, but it was not formally opened.

Earlier that year, the MEC had acquired control of the Portland & Kennebec RR; not wanting to operate what would have been essentially a lumber operation, the MEC objected to an extension of the B&ML into Somerset County. Plans for extension north of the MEC were dropped when a lease agreement was reached, and regular operation of the B&ML by the MEC began in May 1871. Passenger service was provided from the outset. The Belfast terminal was located on Common Street, together with an engine shed, and a freight-only spur branched off just north of the station and ran roughly parallel with Front Street to serve several wharves. Apart from lumber to Belfast, principal inbound traffic comprised coal, chicken feed, fertilizer, vegetables, and tin cans to serve the sardine processing market. Outbound trains hauled processed ocean and chicken products, as well as shoes manufactured in Belfast.

The MEC operated the line for over 50 years until traffic fell away in the 1920s; the lease was terminated on January 2, 1926. Local management continued operating the line using worn steam locomotives for over four decades until the company adopted diesel power. The first diesel-hauled train ran in 1946 using a GE 70-ton locomotive, and the last steam-powered train ran in December 1948. By then, the fleet comprised four diesel locomotives; a fifth was bought in April, 1951. Until Purdue, Tyson, and Arkansas came on the scene, Waldo County was probably the country's most prolific chicken production center and provided much business for the B&ML. Despite the relatively small population—in 1980 total population of the seven townships served by the line was only 11,071, of which more than half was in Belfast—passenger service survived until March 9, 1960. A contract to convey mail ended at the same time, and with it operation of the last short-line railroad post office car. By about 1970, the line had just one

56. Belfast & Moosehead Lake

major customer, a feed mill at Thorndike, where a new engine shed was constructed to reduce the amount of dead-heading from Belfast.

With few freight customers, the company began running summer passenger excursions in 1987. Virtually all freight, which apart from chicken feed largely comprised lumber, coal, and soybean oil, had ended by 1990. A few years later, however, the railroad managed to woo the Crowe Rope Company away from the Maine Coast RR. Crowe now receives about 100 carloads a year of plastic pellets, which are transferred to trucks for delivery to several local Crowe plants.

In 1992 the city of Belfast sold its B&ML shares to private owners, on condition that the city might require the railroad to relocate away from the waterfront. Passenger operations are run from both Belfast and Unity, some trips out of the latter place using a Swedish-built steam locomotive and consist. Sometime after passenger excursions began, a cruise vessel—the *Voyageur*—was introduced to ply the mouth of the Penobscot River. In 1996 the company built a new pier extending 180 feet into the harbor at Belfast to avoid use of public piers by the *Voyageur*.

Sources: Bachelder, *Androscoggin Valley Ltd.*, 32; Baker, *Formation*, 203, 209; Lewis, *American Shortline Railroad Guide*, 35; *Railpace*, 15 (Oct. 1996): 37.

57. Sebasticook & Moosehead

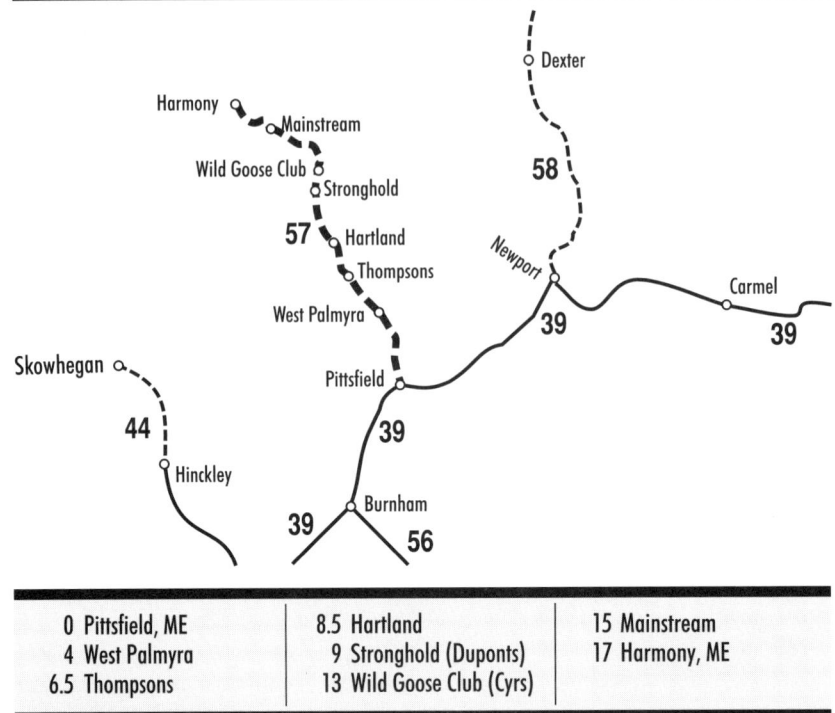

0 Pittsfield, ME	8.5 Hartland	15 Mainstream
4 West Palmyra	9 Stronghold (Duponts)	17 Harmony, ME
6.5 Thompsons	13 Wild Goose Club (Cyrs)	

Built: 1886–1912.

Operators: *Sebasticook & Moosehead*, 1886–1911; *Maine Central*, 1911–81.

Daily Passenger Trains: *1887:* 6 (Pittsfield–Hartland); *1901:* 4 (Pittsfield–Hartland); *1912:* 6 (Pittsfield–Mainstream); *1914:* 4; *1920:* 4 (1 mixed); *1926:* 2 (mixed); *1932:* 2 (mixed). Passenger service ended 1949.

Abandonments: Hartland–Harmony, 1966; Pittsfield–Hartland, 1983.

Proposals for a line extending north from the Maine Central through Wellington to Greenville on Moosehead Lake were first made in the early 1880s. A charter was granted to the Sebasticook & Moosehead RR in 1886, although with opening of the Bangor & Piscataquis to Greenville in 1884, the scheme was hopelessly optimis-

57. Sebasticook & Moosehead

tic. Construction commenced immediately, and the line was opened to Hartland during 1887. There was no local industry and the population was small, so the line was almost entirely dependent on lumber. Some grading was done to extend the line beyond Hartland, but rails were not laid.

Legislative approval was obtained in 1891 for building through Harmony to Athens, with a time extension granted in 1895, along with authority to grade through Wellington to Monson Jct., but these lines were never constructed. Four years later, the impecunious company entered receivership, although the line managed to struggle on to reach Mainstream in January 1901. Traffic receipts dwindled as lumber stocks were depleted. Ever optimistic, two more extensions were authorized in 1907: north from Mainstream to the Canadian Pacific RY at Elliotsville and south from Pittsfield to the Wiscasset, Waterville & Farmington RR at Albion. Nothing was done to build them.

From 1912 until 1966 the Sebasticook & Moosehead ended here in Harmony, ME. By July 1999 little sign of the railroad remained. (R. D. Karr)

The company lingered on independently until 1911, when stockholders approved merger with the MEC, largely through exchange of stock. In an attempt to make something of the line, the MEC built and opened the final few miles beyond Mainstream to Harmony in 1912. Thereafter, although lumber continued to be a significant contributor to receipts, the line also conveyed outbound agricultural and mill products, and inbound coal, feedstuff, and other goods associated with a rural economy.

Through the decades the area's population declined, the 1980 census recording a total of just over 5,300 heads in the four townships served by the line. With the population shrinking and construction of State Routes 152 and 164 by the 1920s, passenger traffic declined rapidly. By 1930 trains had generally been reduced to mixed consists, with additional scheduled freight-only trips to Hartland. By 1938 only Hartland and Harmony were ticket agencies. Further highway improvements brought about the end of the single mixed consist on April 24, 1949. Mills sustained freight traffic for many years, but the Hartland–Harmony length was taken out of use in 1963. Permission to abandon this section was obtained in 1966. Service over the remainder continued, almost as if the line had been forgotten, until negotiations started for Guilford's eventual purchase of the MEC. It ended before the deal was completed, with permission to abandon received in 1983.

Sources: Chase, *Maine Railroads*; Karr, *Lost Railroads*, 124, 146; Moody, *Maine Two-Footers*; Peters, *Maine Central*, 14–15; Whitney, *Monson*, 9.

58. Dexter & Newport

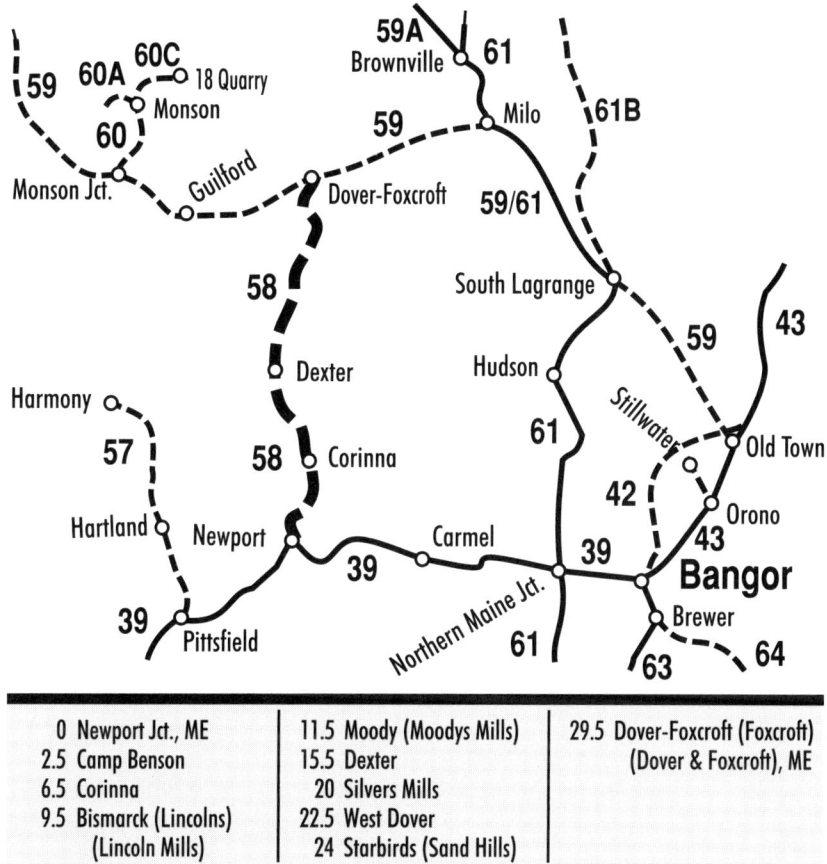

0 Newport Jct., ME	11.5 Moody (Moodys Mills)	29.5 Dover-Foxcroft (Foxcroft)
2.5 Camp Benson	15.5 Dexter	(Dover & Foxcroft), ME
6.5 Corinna	20 Silvers Mills	
9.5 Bismarck (Lincolns)	22.5 West Dover	
(Lincoln Mills)	24 Starbirds (Sand Hills)	

Built: 1868-69; 1888-89.
Operators: *Maine Central*, 1869-1981; *Guilford*, 1981-90.
Daily Passenger Trains: *1893:* 6; *1915:* 4. Passenger service ended ca. 1933.
Abandonment: 1990.

In 1868 several lumber companies operated in Penobscot County north of Newport. Corinna was noted for dairy products and potatoes. Dexter, which already had two wool mills, would eventually become famous for boot and shoe manufacture, and has today a world-wide reputation for production of classic American shoe products. With Maine Central backing, the Dexter & Newport RR was promoted to connect the two towns. Construction began that year from Newport and was operated under lease by the MEC from opening on December 1, 1868 (although no mention of it appears in the *Official Guide* for June 1869).

A charter was obtained in 1888 in the name of the Dexter & Piscataquis RR to extend the line from Newport to Dover-Foxcroft. The alignment avoided wetlands as much as possible, while serving intermediate lumber mills. The principal purpose of the line, which was completed in 1890, was to divert freight away from the Bangor & Piscataquis RR. The original terminal in Dexter was retained as a freight depot, and a new passenger station was built at a slightly higher level nearby. The D&P was also leased from the outset by the MEC; both companies were absorbed in December 1939.

Mill traffic sustained the line for many years, although traffic dwindled in the early years of the twentieth century. Passenger trains were withdrawn as part of a 1930s economy program. Freight traffic diminished following mill closures and highway competition, but the line survived another fifty years. Trains ceased to operate in 1986, and a petition to abandon was submitted to the ICC. The state of Maine lodged routine objections, but was unwilling or unable to purchase the right of way. Approval was given by the ICC in 1990, and the tracks were torn up. Four years later, however, Maine bought the right of way and adopted it as a recreational trail.

One curious memento of the railroad age survives in Dover-Foxcroft. To the west side of the former right of way, at the station site, there sits a former Budd buffet-lounge sleeper car built in 1949; formerly belonging to the New York Central and later Amtrak, it now houses the studio of radio station WDME.

Sources: Baker, *Formation*, 209; Cornwall and Smith, *Names First*, 35, Karr, *Lost Railroads*, 151.

59. Bangor & Piscataquis

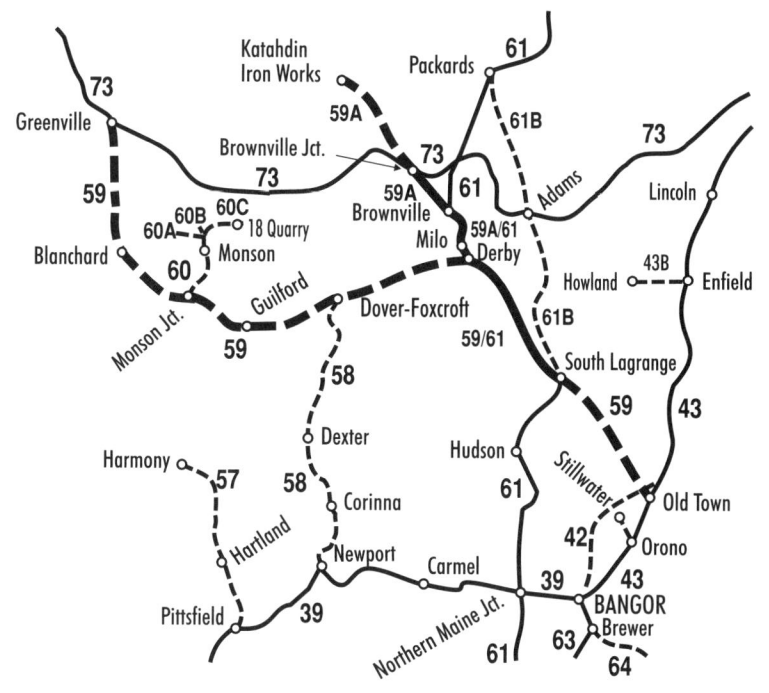

0 Old Town, ME	45 Lows Bridge	**59A. Katahdin Iron Works Branch**
4 Pea Cove	49 Sangerville	
8 Alton	50.5 Guilford	0 Derby (Milo Jct.)
14 South Lagrange	55 Abbot Village	1.5 Milo
17.5 Lagrange	57 Monson Jct.	4.5 Brownville
20.5 Parkers (Boyd Lake)	60 Kingsbury	8 Brownville Jct.
29 Derby (Milo Jct.)	61 Parrot	17 Katahdin Iron Works, ME
34.5 South Sebec	64 Blanchard	
39.5 East Dover	66 Quarry	
42.5 Dover-Foxcroft (Dover & Foxcroft)	71 Shirley (Shirley Mills)	
	76 Greenville, ME	

Built: 1864–84.

Operators: *Bangor & Piscataquis*, 1869-73; *European & North American*, 1873-76; *Bangor & Piscataquis*, 1876-92; *Bangor & Aroostook*, 1892–; Katahdin Iron Works Branch: *Bangor & Katahdin*

59. Bangor & Piscataquis

Iron Works, 1881-87; *Bangor & Piscataquis*, 1887-92; *Bangor & Aroostook*, 1892-.

Daily Passenger Trains: *1880:* 2; *1890:* 2 (Derby-Katahdin Iron Works, 2); *1916:* Old Town-South Lagrange, 2; Derby-Greenville from Northern Maine Jct., 2; *1931:* 2 (South Lagrange-Greenville, from Bangor, 2; Derby-Brownville Jct., 2); *1954:* 2 (Derby-Greenfield, mixed). Passenger service ended Brownville Jct.-Katahdin Iron Works, 1922; Old Town-South Lagrange, 1933; Derby-Greenville, 1958.

Abandonments: Brownville Jct.-Katahdin Iron Works, 1922; Old Town-South Lagrange [0.55 mile south], 1933; Guilford (mill yard)-Greenville, 1962; Derby-Guilford (mill yard), 1964.

The twin village of Dover-Foxcroft sits astride the Piscataquis River. It was there to which the Bangor & Piscataquis RR planned a line from Old Town on the Penobscot River, principally for movement of lumber. The company, which was incorporated on March 5, 1861, adopted broad gauge, in keeping with the Penobscot & Kennebec RR, which had reached Bangor in 1855, and the proposed European & North American RR.

Construction from Old Town through Derby to Dover was completed on December 14, 1869, and a charter revision enabled extension to Guilford on December 20, 1871. The line was leased by the E&NA in 1873, and an extension to Abbot opened on December 12, 1874. Shortly after the lease was relinquished on November 2, 1876, the B&P converted to standard gauge. An extension to Blanchard opened on May 7, 1877. Construction of several large trestles to the north delayed opening to Greenville on Moosehead Lake until July 14, 1884. In 1892, the Bangor & Aroostook leased the B&P and merged it on April 1, 1899.

A small iron ore mining operation in what is now Katahdin Iron Works Township began around 1830. A tram road was built from the south side of Silver Lake to Derby, on the Piscataquis River, as early as 1836, using oxen for motive power. Large deposits of bog iron ore were discovered at the foot of Ore Mountain in 1843, followed by attempts at exploration and major commercial exploitation by the Maine Iron Company. A settlement at Silver Lake, named Smithville in honor of the principal promoter, succeeded, along with a hotel there, but the

Much of the former B&P can be driven by ordinary automobile. The long radius of this curve south of Greenville, shown in July 1999, suggests its railroad origins. (R. D. Karr)

company failed. The Katahdin Iron Works Co. (named for Mt. Katahdin, some 35 miles to the north) took over, but also foundered in 1856. An attempt at revival during the Civil War by the Piscataquis Iron Works Co. also failed, and was succeeded by the Bangor & Katahdin Iron Works Co. on January 24, 1876. The company chartered the Bangor & Katahdin Iron Works RY a month later, but construction of the first section, from Milo Jct. to Brownville, did not begin until June 13, 1881. About six miles had been built along the route of the old tram road by December 1881, and the entire line to the mines and furnaces of the Katahdin Iron Works was completed on July 19, 1882.

The B&P leased the line in 1887. High quality pig iron was produced in charcoal-fired furnaces, but the Bessemer process took business away to Pennsylvania and Illinois. Mining ceased in 1890, but stockpiles of ore continued to be processed and shipped until 1899. The Bangor & Aroostook, which had taken over the lease of the branch in 1892, absorbed it on November 6, 1901. The initial 4.5 miles of the branch between Derby and Brownville were incorporated into the BAR main line, and the next section to Brownville Jct. was used to connect with the Canadian Pacific; but the last nine miles served only the iron works settlement.

Several attempts to reopen the mines came to naught. The Silver Lake Hotel was promoted as a resort and hunting lodge until it burned in 1913. Closure of the ironworks had been followed by departure of the majority of residents, and traffic over the branch was minimal. Because there was no practical access by other means, passenger trains continued to operate, but these eventually ended in 1922 with the abandonment of the branch from just north of Brownville Jct. Effectively isolated for much of the year, the former hotel proprietor persuaded the railroad to leave the tracks intact and obtained permission to operate a Model T Ford fitted with flanged wheels over it. After he died in 1929, his widow, Sara Grey, continued this operation as part of a postal route until 1933, when the county completed a surfaced road. The track was removed during 1934.

The section of the B&P between Old Town and South Lagrange was reduced in status to a branch in 1905, upon opening of the BAR's Northern Maine Seaport RR. Passenger service continued until abandonment of the segment in 1933. By the 1950s the line between Derby and Greenville was marginal, since Brownville Jct. had become the pri-

With Moosehead Lake in the background, a BAR train pulls into Greenville station to pick up passengers in 1896. (Courtesy Walker Transportation Collection, Beverly Historical Society & Museum)

mary interchange with Canadian Pacific. Passenger service, which had been provided exclusively by mixed trains since the 1930s, was kept up until 1959, by which time it had outlived virtually all similar branch line operations. The line west of the Guilford mill yard closed in 1959 and was abandoned three years later. In 1964 the yard itself and the line from Derby was also abandoned. In Monson, Blanchard, Shirley, and Little Squaw Township, the alignment is now dirt or local roads, although a short section appears to exist as a siding at Greenville station. The length between South Lagrange and Brownville is part of the BAR main line, and the segment between Brownville and Brownville Jct. connects with the ex-CP Canadian American RR, now operated in conjunction with the BAR.

Sources: Angier and Cleaves, *Bangor & Aroostook*; Bachelder, *Rumford Rocket*, 19, 45–46; Baker, *Formation*, 203; Bangor & Aroostook Railroad, *Bangor & Aroostook*; Cornwall and Smith, *Names First*, 6; Karr, *Lost Railroads*, 80, 88, 119, 122.

60. Monson

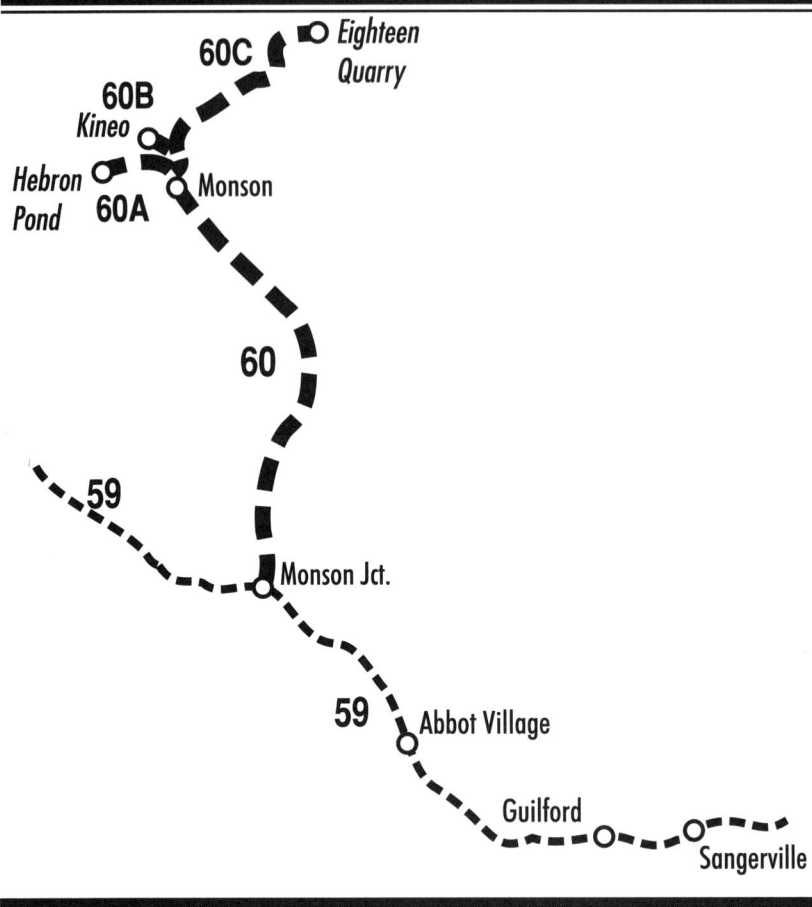

| 0 Monson Jct., ME
6 Monson, ME

60A. Hebron Branch
0 Monson, ME | 1 Hebron Pond, ME

60B. Kineo Branch
0 Monson, ME
0.5 Kineo, ME | **60C. Eighteen Quarry Branch**
0 Monson, ME
4 Eighteen Quarry, ME |

Built: 1883; Eighteen Quarry Branch, 1909.
Operators: Monson, 1883–1943.
Daily Passenger Trains: *1883:* 2; *1893:* 4; *1919:* 8; *1925:* 4; *1935:* 4. Passenger service ended 1938.

60. Monson

Abandonments: Eighteen Quarry Branch, 1922; remainder, 1944.

Monson, on Lake Hebron, was bypassed to the south by the Bangor & Piscataquis RR because surveys and estimates demonstrated relative ease of construction along contours of the Piscataquis River valley. Local businessmen petitioned unsuccessfully for a standard-gauge line running north from the B&P to Monson village for slate traffic, and south to Athens.

With support from business interests in Portland and Lowell, MA, a charter was obtained on March 18, 1881, for the Monson & Athens RR to build a 2-foot-gauge line—the first not under George E. Mansfield's tutelage—between those two townships. Difficulties raising capital resulted in reorganization and a new charter the following year as the Monson RR, although the Monson & Athens name appears to have been used for a few more years. The backers decided to focus their efforts on building the length between Monson and the B&P. Contracts for the line included building two short branches beyond Monson to serve Monson Slate Co. quarries, and construction commenced in the spring of 1883. Work was sufficiently complete to enable running of an inaugural train on Saturday, September 4, but scheduled service did not begin until mid-October.

Track consisted of 50-pound rail on rough-hewn timber ties, and the line used stub switches featuring stock rails plated on the underside and driven against the leads from "harp" frames, to avoid the costs of machined switch blades. Two Hinckley 14-ton 0-4-4 Forney wood-burning locomotives supplied power; most freight cars were designed for slate traffic, while a Laconia-built combination passenger/baggage car was used for passengers.

Financial returns were disappointing, requiring mortgage of the assets in 1884. H. A. Whiting had been appointed president in March 1883, with J. F. Kimball as treasurer, both associated with the Monson Slate Co.; W. L. K. Esterbrooke was named superintendent. A northward extension to Greenville was considered briefly in 1885; the advent of the Sebasticook & Moosehead RR, which also proposed to run to Greenville, may have been a factor in rejection of this plan. Similarly, the failure that year of a proposed Athens & Skowhegan RR ended any prospect of extension south of Monson Jct.

Superintendent Estabrooke died in 1904 and was succeeded by H. E. Morrill. After the railroad recorded losses for several years,

Everything about the Monson was diminutive, including its engine house in Monson, shown here in August 1936. (Hugh G. Boutell, courtesy Walker Transportation Collection, Beverly Historical Society & Museum)

Monson Slate, which was entirely dependent on the line, took over in 1908. Beyond Monson, a freight-only line of about four miles known as the "Eighteen Quarry Branch" was constructed in 1909. Around this time a siding was constructed near the North Guilford Road grade crossing to serve the Portland-Monson Slate Co. quarry. A freight shed was built there in 1912.

Both original locomotives were converted to coal-firing in 1912. To meet the needs of expansion, an additional locomotive, much larger than its predecessors, was obtained from Vulcan in 1913, and another—no. 4 in the company's list, and somewhat smaller—in 1918. Number 4 replaced the original no. 2, which was scrapped. All three remaining locomotives were damaged by a fire in the Monson engine house on November 3, 1919. An unsuccessful attempt was made to convert no. 1 to a snowplow, although it lingered on at Monson until demise of the company in 1943.

Early morning and late evening passenger trains were withdrawn on Monday, October 10, 1921; the Eighteen Quarry Branch was closed the next year. The Monson remained profitable for some years, but by the mid-1930s demand for slate roofing had declined, and traffic became insufficient to require a scheduled train.

By the time Superintendent Morrill retired on September 1, 1938, the Monson's owners were considering transfer of traffic to highways. All passenger services were withdrawn as of November 1, and thereafter freight trains ran on an "as required" basis. Morrill's successor, Paul Jackson, made additional cost reductions but they did not satisfy the owners. The company declared bankruptcy in 1943, and both the quarries and the railroad were embargoed. Without waiting for permission to abandon, the receivers arranged for dismantling of the companies' assets during the winter of 1943-44.

The last survivor of the New England two-foot narrow gauge lines, the Monson Railroad Co. was dissolved in 1945. The two remaining locomotives eventually went to the Edaville RR in Massachusetts, but many years later returned to Maine to work at the Maine Narrow Gauge RR tourist line in Portland.

Sources: Crittenden, *Maine Scenic Route*, 87-93; Hilton, *American Narrow Gauge*, 409-410; Jones, *Two Feet to the Quarries*; Jones and Register, *Two Feet to Tidewater*; Karr, *Lost Railroads*, 108; Moody, *Maine Two-Footers*, 32-40, 145-153; Whitney, *Monson*.

61. Bangor & Aroostook

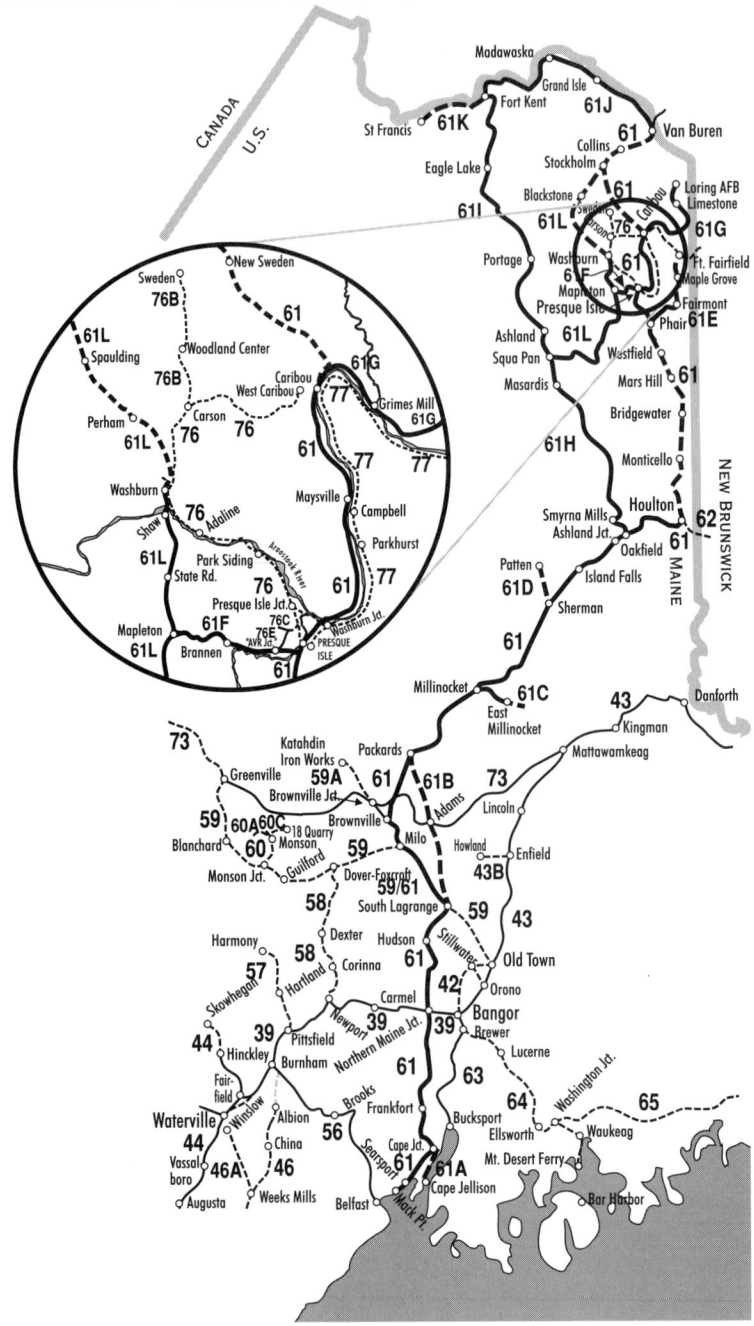

61. Bangor & Aroostook

0 Mack Point, ME	160 New Limerick (New Limenfoir)	**61D. Patten & Sherman RR**
1 Searsport	167 Houlton	0 Patten Jct., ME
2 Kidders	173 Littleton	5.5 Patten, ME
2.5 Stockton Springs (Stockton)	177 Monticello	
5 Cape Jct.	182 Harvey	**61E. Ft. Fairfield Branch**
7.5 Sandy Point	187 Bridgewater	0 Phair
11 Prospect	191 Robinson	4 Easton
16.5 Frankfort	195 Mars Hill	7 Fairmount
20 Winterport	199 Westfield	9.5 Maple Grove
24 Arey	205 Phair	13.5 Ft. Fairfield, ME
26.5 Hampden	211 Presque Isle	
29 South Switch	219 Maysville	**61F. Mapleton Branch**
29.5 Northern Maine Jct.	225 Caribou	0 Presque Isle, ME
35 North Bangor	235 New Sweden	2 "AVR Jct."
38 Glenburn	240 Jemtland	4 Brannen (Lombards)
45.5 Hudson	242 Stockholm	7.5 Mapleton, ME
50.5 Bradford	243 Stockholm Jct.	
54 South Lagrange	248 Collins	**61G. Aroostook Northern RR**
57.5 Lagrange	251 Watson (Canibas)	0 Caribou, ME
61 Parkers (Boyd Lake)	259 Van Buren, ME	4 Grimes Mill
66.5 Derby (Milo Jct.)		7 Murphy Rd.
67 Milo	**61A. Cape Jellison Branch**	9 Houghtonville
71.5 Brownville	0 Cape Jct., ME	10 Goodrich
82.5 Schoodic	0.5 Cape Jellison, ME	11 Morrow Rd.
86.5 Packards		12 East Rd.
90.5 West Seboois	**61B. Medford Cut-Off**	13.5 California Rd.
94.5 Long A (Ingalls)	0 South Lagrange, ME	15 Long Rd.
98 Perkins	9.5 Medford	16 Limestone
99.5 Norcross	17 Adams	19 Loring AFB, ME
105 Millinocket	22 Rand Cove	
110 Grindstone	28 Packards (Packard), ME	**61H. Ashland Branch**
120 Davidson		0 Ashland Jct., ME
126 Stacyville	**61C. Schoodic Stream Branch**	1.5 Smyrna Mills
130 Sherman (Sherman-Patten)	0 Millinocket, ME	6 Dudley
131 Patten Jct.	5 Gilbert	10 Shorey (Hillman)
136 Crystal	8 Dolby (Dolby Rips)	12 Weeksboro
140 Island Falls	9 East Millinocket	15 Little Canada
142 Dyer Brook	*10 (end of track), ME*	16 Howe Brook
149 Oakfield		20 St. Croix
150 Ashland Jct.		24 Hawkins (Prides Mill)
156 Ludlow		26 Griswold

33 Masardis
37.5 Squa Pan
43.5 Ashland, ME

61I. Fish River Branch

0 Ashland, ME
1.5 Sheridan
11.5 Portage
16.5 Nixon
17.5 Buffalo
24.5 McNally
28.5 Winterville
35 Eagle Lake
39.5 Wallagrass
73.5 Soldier Pond
82 Ft. Kent, ME

61J. Van Buren Extension

0 Ft. Kent, ME
9.5 St. Luce
11.5 Frenchville
19 Madawaska
21.5 Fournier
23.5 St. David
28.5 Grand Isle
31.5 Lille
34 Notre Dame
37.5 Parent
39.5 Violette
42.5 Keegan
44 Van Buren, ME

61K. St. Francis Branch

0 Ft. Kent, ME
2 Ft. Kent Village

7 Ledges
9 Wheelock
12 St. John
17 St. Francis, ME

61L. Mapleton Cut-Off

0 Squa Pan, ME
10 Walker
18 Mapleton
21.5 State Rd.
24 Shaw
26 Washburn
30.5 Perham
33.5 Spaulding
36 Hanford
42 Blackstone (Westmanland)
48 Stockholm Jct. (Stockholm), ME

Built: 1891-99; 1905, 1924; Ft. Fairfield Branch, 1894; Patten & Sherman RR, 1895-1901; Ashland Branch, 1896; Aroostook Northern RR, 1897; Fish River Branch, 1902; Cape Jellison Branch, 1905; Schoodic Stream Branch, 1906-07; Medford Cut-Off, 1907-08; St. Francis Branch, 1909; Van Buren Extension, 1909-10; Mapleton Branch, Mapleton Cut-Off, 1910.

Operators: *Bangor & Aroostook*, 1894-.

Daily Passenger Trains: *1916:* Northern Maine Jct.-Van Buren, via Ft. Kent, 2; via Medford Cutoff, 2; Northern Maine Jct.-Caribou, 2; Northern Maine Jct.-Greenville, 2; Houlton-St. Francis via Ashland Jct. and Squa Pan, 2; Squa Pan-Van Buren via Mapleton, 2; Mapleton-Presque Isle, 4; Phair-Ft. Fairfield, 8; Caribou-Limestone, 6; Northern Maine Jct.-Searsport, 4; Sherman-Patten, 6; Millinocket-East Millinocket, 4; *1931:* Northern Maine Jct.-Ft. Kent via Van Buren, 2; Northern Maine Jct.-Van Buren, 2; Northern Maine Jct.-Derby (thence Greenville), 2; Oakfield-Ft. Kent via Squa Pan, 2; Squa Pan-Van Buren via Mapleton, 2; Mapleton-Caribou, 2; Phair- Caribou, 4; Phair-Ft. Fairfield, 4; Caribou-Limestone, 2; Sherman-Patten, 4; Millinocket-East Millinocket, 4; *1948:* Northern Maine Jct.-Van Buren via Ft. Kent, 4; Oakfield-St. Francis, 2 via Ft. Kent; Squa

The scrap heap is the destination for these BAR steam locomotives shown leaving Northern Maine Jct. in 1950. (Courtesy Walker Transportation Collection, Beverly Historical Society & Museum)

Pan-Van Buren via Mapleton, 2; Phair-Ft. Fairfield, 2; Caribou-Limestone, 6; Millinocket-East Millinocket, 4; *1954:* Northern Maine Jct.-Van Buren, 4; *1960:* Northern Maine Jct.-Van Buren, 2. Passenger service ended Medford Cutoff, 1931; Searsport-Bangor, 1933; Ft. Kent-Van Buren, 1948; Squa Pan-Stockholm and Presque Isle-Mapleton, 1951; all remaining except Northern Maine Jct.-Van Buren, 1954; Northern Maine Jct.-Van Buren, 1961.

Abandonments: Schoodic Stream Branch (East Millinocket-end of track, 1922); Cape Jellison Branch, 1925; Monticello-Bridgewater, 1975; Medford Cut-Off, 1977; Caribou-Stockholm, 1979; Houlton-Monticello, 1980; Collins-Van Buren, 1982; Bridgewater-Phair, 1984; Mapleton Cut-Off (Blackstone-Stockholm Jct., 1986; Washburn-Blackstone, 1991); Stockholm Jct.-Collins, 1986; Patten &

Sherman RR, ca. 1996; Ft. Fairfield Branch (Fairmount–Ft. Fairfield, 1997); St. Francis Branch (Ft. Kent [0.4 miles west]–St. Francis), 1997.

By the 1880s, only the major towns of Houlton and Presque Isle in rural Aroostook County enjoyed train service provided over branches operated by the New Brunswick & Canada RY. Albert Burleigh of Houlton promoted the Bangor & Aroostook RR to fill the void with a line from the European & North American at Mattawamkeag to Van Buren, but the enormous cost of the proposal delayed incorporation of the company until February 1891. A charter issued on March 13 included the novel provision of a 15-mile wide "monopoly" corridor. To reduce cost, the BAR leased the Bangor & Piscataquis RR effective April 1, 1892. The B&P provided a route between Old Town (only 12 miles from Bangor via the E&NA) and Brownville. Work began immediately on a line from Brownville to Houlton and beyond to Caribou and Van Buren.

Construction took longer than anticipated. Ground conditions and the severe winter of 1892–93 presented difficulties, and it was not until Christmas Day, 1893, that a symbolic opening ceremony took place in Houlton. Regular service between Bangor and Houlton began in January 1894. Extension through to Caribou was finished in December, along with a branch to Ft. Fairfield. That same year a 3,600-foot industrial siding was built from Island Falls depot to the town center, and an additional 700-foot spur to a paper mill was added in 1900. A long branch from a junction east of Oakfield to Ashland opened in 1896. Stockholders questioned such rapid expansion when the main line was incomplete, but they were apparently placated by Burleigh's pledge of his personal assets, the purchase of the B&P line on April 1, 1899, and completion to Van Buren on November 23. Burleigh's family continued to promote other lines in the region, notably the Aroostook Northern RR from Caribou to Limestone, which was leased by the BAR on completion in November 1897, and the Fish River RR, completed to Eagle Lake in November 1902 and to Ft. Kent in December, and leased from December 14. The Burleighs also promoted the Patten & Sherman RR, organized in 1895 and leased on opening in 1901. On November 6, 1901, the Bangor & Katahdin Iron Works RR was purchased.

61. Bangor & Aroostook

In order to provide an alternative to its connection with the MEC at Old Town, where capacity was limited, the BAR obtained a charter in December 1904 for the the Northern Maine Seaport RR for a line from South Lagrange southward to the MEC at Northern Maine Jct. west of Bangor, and onward to a new deep-water port at Cape Jellison in Stockton Springs. BAR trains ran from Northern Maine Jct. into Bangor using trackage rights over the MEC. The opening was celebrated on November 27, 1905. The next year, BAR interests organized the Schoodic Stream RR to build from Millinocket to Medway; the BAR operated it on opening in January 1907 from Millinocket to about a mile beyond East Millinocket, although Medway itself was never reached. The Medford Cut-off, which reduced grades as well as shortened the route, was approved in April 1907 and opened the following December.

The first challenge to the BAR's corridor monopoly occurred with the grant of a charter to the Aroostook Valley RR in 1909. Appeals to the courts and Maine Railroad Commissioners failed to stop construction of this rival. Partly in an unsuccessful attempt to stifle the new line, the BAR built branches from Van Buren to St. Francis, from Squa Pan

A northbound BAR freight passes through South Lagrange in July 1992. (R. D. Karr)

St. Francis, at the end of a 17-mile branch from Ft. Kent, was the farthest outpost of the BAR. (Courtesy Walker Transportation Collection, Beverly Historical Society & Museum)

to Stockholm, and from Mapleton to Presque Isle between 1909 and 1911. In 1915 a bridge (under the auspices of the Van Buren International Company) was built across the St. John River to connect with what would soon become Canadian National RYs. The Northern Maine Seaport company was absorbed on October 30, 1919. An extension was proposed from St. Francis along the St. John River to Allagash and then south to Seboois; maps indicate that some work may have been done, but the line was never completed.

The wharves at Cape Jellison were destroyed by fire in November 1924. Insurance proceeds were used to replace them with more spacious facilities at Mack Point, which became the zero milepost for the BAR's main line, although it never saw passenger service. Permission to abandon the Cape Jellison Branch was obtained the next year.

Passenger service on branch lines declined in the 1930s. First to go on June 30, 1931, were the remaining mixed trains on the former B&P's Old Town line, followed by those on the Northern Maine Seaport line from July 1, 1933. Busses provided substitute service for the Patten & Sherman line from late 1934 and for the Mapleton Branch from spring 1939, although passenger trains resumed on both lines during the 1942–43 winter and spring; the Mapleton Branch reverted to train service as of April 1945. Further economy measures after about 1931 included discontinuation of many passenger stops, a process that accelerated after World War II. A curiosity of the BAR is that it never operated scheduled Sunday passenger trains.

Freight traffic during this period comprised potatoes and potato by-products, lumber, and shipments of paper from mills at Millinocket, East Millinocket, Madawaska, and various other locations. In 1946 the BAR extended the former Aroostook Northern line within Limestone to reach the south side of Loring Air Force Base. This was the railroad's final significant construction. All trains were diesel-hauled from 1952. The daily limited service to Caribou, named the *Aroostook Flyer* in 1931, survived until replaced by busses on November 25, 1957.

During 1959 the BAR and Maine Central jointly petitioned the Maine Public Utilities Commission for permission to end all passenger service, which on the BAR since 1954 had only been operated between Bangor and Van Buren. The commission, however, required the BAR to continue operation of one train each day (except Sunday) for a year between Northern Maine Jct. and Caribou, with three mandatory stops. The Maine Supreme Court overruled the commission on appeal by the MEC, and passenger services on that railroad ended September 6, 1960. The BAR, however, decided to continue passenger operations to fulfill a contract with the Postal Service for two round trips between Northern Maine Jct. and Caribou. Intermediate stops were made at Millinocket, Sherman (southbound only), Houlton, and Presque Isle, with taxi service between the southern terminal and Bangor. If that was not enough to give regular passengers dyspepsia, a note appeared in the October 30, 1960, timetable indicating that boxed lunches could be ordered for delivery to the southbound train at Houlton. Hungry passengers bound northward were left to their own devices. Passenger service finally ended on September 4, 1961.

An attempt was made to diversify into non-rail investments through formation of a holding company, the Bangor & Aroostook Corporation, which merged with the Punta Alegre Sugar Corporation on October 1, 1964, to form Bangor Punta Alegre. The railroad, now a burden on the consolidated accounts, was sold to the Amoskeag Co., headed by former New Haven RR president Frederick C. Dumaine, Jr., on October 2, 1969. Abandonments began in 1971, starting with the segment of the main line between Monticello and Bridgewater, which had seen just 125 car loads that year. A business recession resulted in closure of the remainder of the original main line between Houlton and Phair and from Presque Isle to Van Buren in the 1980s. The line's staple freight of potatoes and potato byproducts had largely disappeared by then, leaving mostly paper, forest products, coal, and oil.

Further decline brought about sale of the entire BAR to Iron Road RYs on March 17, 1995. The new owners were interested in developing rail service from Maine and southern New Brunswick over the original Canadian Pacific route through northern Maine. Over the past few years they have been successful, although part of the Ft. Fairfield Branch has been closed, with permission to abandon between Fairmount and Ft. Fairfield given in October 1997. The former Patten & Sherman line and the St. Francis Branch have also recently been abandoned.

Sources: Angier and Cleaves, *Bangor & Aroostook*; Armstrong, *Railfan's Guide*, 11-12; Bachelder, *Special Trains*; Baker, *Formation*; Bangor & Aroostook Railroad, *Bangor & Aroostook*; Karr, *Lost Railroads*, 80, 88, 119, 122, 133, 136-38, 142, 148, 152; Lewis, *American Shortline Railway Guide*, 31; *Railpace* 16 (Dec. 1997): 37.

62. New Brunswick & Canada

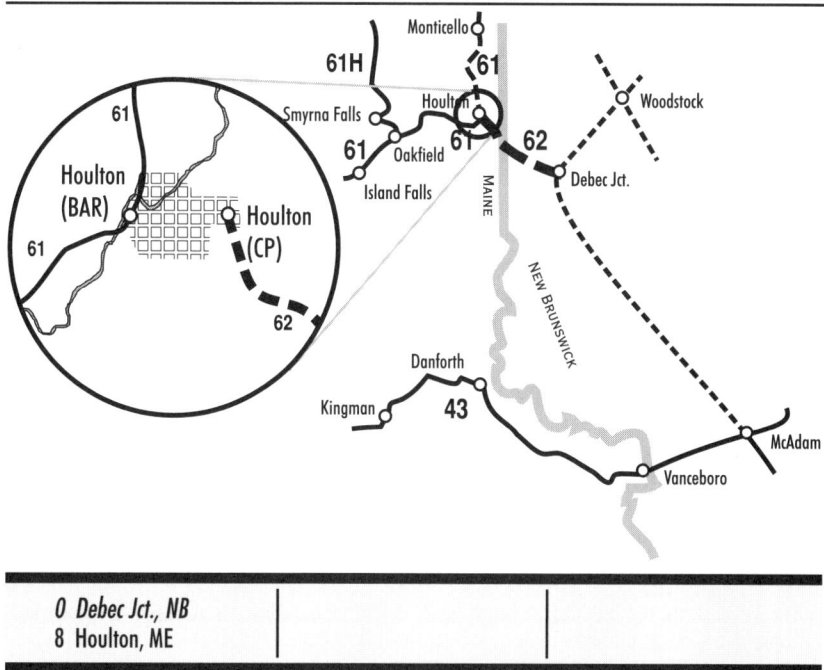

0 Debec Jct., NB		
8 Houlton, ME		

Built: 1870.

Operators: *New Brunswick & Canada*, 1870-82; *New Brunswick*, 1882-90; *Canadian Pacific*, 1890-1987.

Daily Passenger Trains: *1873:* 2; *1892:* 10; *1916:* 6; *1938:* 4; *1942:* 2; *1948:* 4. Passenger service (mixed) ended 1949.

Abandonment: 1989.

Houlton, ME, was the birthplace of the Bangor & Aroostook RR, but the town, originally a lumber and later an agricultural center, was put on the railroad map in 1870 by a branch of the New Brunswick & Canada RY. Originating with an 1835 charter for the St. Andrews & Quebec RY, the NB&C inherited twenty route miles of broad-gauge track extending north from the Bay of Fundy. A lengthy extension to Debec, NB, through McAdam was finished in 1862, followed in 1866 by a branch from Lawrence to St. Stephen, NB, across the St. Croix River from Calais, ME, served by the Calais & Baring RR

(St. Croix & Penobscot after 1870). The main line reached Woodstock, NB, in 1868 where interchange was available from 1873 with the 3-foot-6-inch-gauge New Brunswick RY. Lumber and other Maine products were exported across the border.

When construction of the European & North American RR neared completion, NB&C proprietors saw merit in its line as a feeder route, and accordingly in 1870 built a branch from Debec across the international border to a terminal in Houlton, ME. The length in Maine, incorporated as the Houlton Branch RR, was operated from opening in conjunction with the Canadian portion by the NB&C.

For a short while, the NB&C main line served as a broad-gauge connector between the standard-gauge E&NA (which had been narrowed in 1877) and the narrow-gauge New Brunswick RY. The NB&C converted to standard gauge in 1879. In 1882 the New Brunswick RY leased the NB&C, and takeover by the Canadian Pacific ensued in 1890. The Houlton Branch RR was operated under lease until the end. Originally traffic had been predominantly lumber, but with the depletion of timber, farm products—principally potatoes and potato byproducts such as starch—became the mainstay of outbound traffic. Traffic was seriously reduced when the BAR reached Houlton in January 1894.

Until after World War II both the CP and the BAR benefitted from an increase in traffic spawned by agricultural growth, and additional sidings were installed at Houlton. Busses had replaced summer passenger trains in 1936; remaining passenger service was provided by mixed trains from 1943. After these ended in 1949, freight trains continued to trundle along deteriorating and increasingly overgrown track. Regular freight service ended in 1987, and a petition to abandon was approved by the ICC two years later.

Sources: Hilton, *American Narrow Gauge*; Karr, *Lost Railroads*, 88, 151; Zimmermann, *Sunrise Route*, 224.

63. Bucksport & Bangor

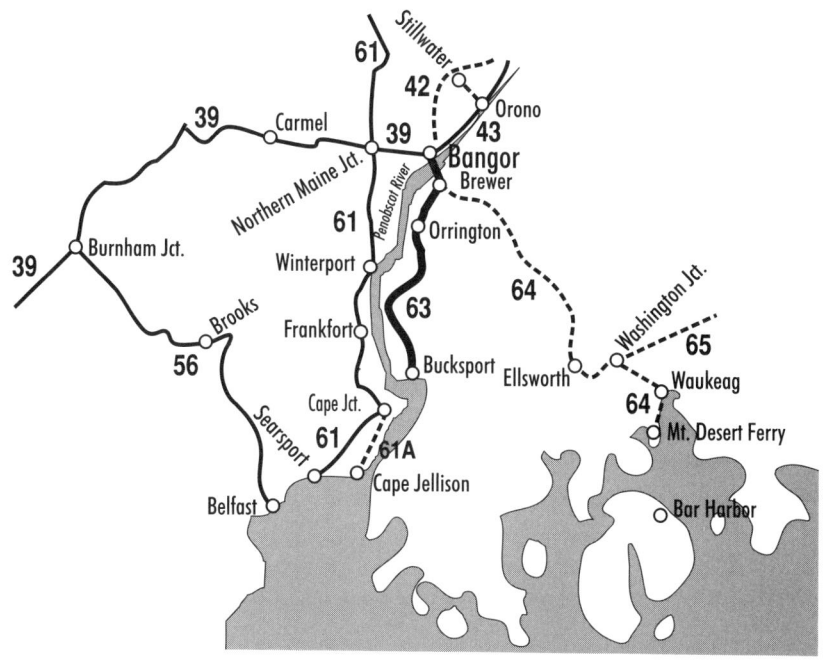

0 Bangor (Bangor Union Sta.), ME	4.5 Sobins	12.5 Bucksport Center (Winterport Ferry)
0.5 Calais Jct.	5 Pierces (Pierces Crossing)	14.5 Chipmans
1.5 Brewer Jct. (Brewer)	5.5 Orrington	16 Meddo
2 South Brewer (Brewer Village)	8 South Orrington (Mill Creek)	17.5 Bucksport, ME
4 North Orrington (Freemans)	10 Hinks (Hinks Landing)	
	11.5 North Bucksport	

Built: 1873-74.

Operators: *European & North American*, 1874-79; *Bucksport & Bangor*, 1879-80; *Eastern Maine*, 1882-83; *Maine Central*, 1883-1981; *Guilford*, 1981-.

Daily Passenger Trains: *1893:* 6; *1916:* 4; *1924:* 6; *1931:* 4; *1936:* 2 (mixed). Passenger service ended Bucksport-Brewer Jct., 1936; Brewer Jct.-Bangor, 1957.

Abandonments: None.

A Guilford freight pulls out of the Bucksport paper mill in July 1992. (R. D. Karr)

Bucksport was a prosperous small port by the mid-1850s, as reflected in its 1817 renaming from Buckstown. R. P. Buck, a local businessman, promoted a short broad-gauge line from the European & North American RR at Bangor, and on February 1, 1873, along with several associates, secured a charter for the Bucksport & Bangor RR. Subscriptions to shares were slow in coming, compelling the board of directors in late 1873 to negotiate a five-year lease by the E&NA, which would operate the line with its own equipment. Construction costs in Bangor were relatively high because of the need to build a high-level, sharp-radius curve to minimize land acquisition and an 810-foot Howe-truss bridge across the Penobscot River. The line opened on December 12, 1874.

The following year the board resolved to convert the B&B to standard gauge at the same time as the E&NA, but the conversion of both lines was delayed until September 12, 1877, by the E&NA's receivership. After the E&NA's lease expired on October 1, 1879, control reverted to Buck and Stewall B. Swazey, as trustees, who had already declared the B&B bankrupt. The next step was a lease by L. L. Lincoln of Augusta, former Superintendent of the Maine Central RR First Division, who certainly brought new ideas to the company. Lincoln had in

63. Bucksport & Bangor

mind extension of the line eastward, either through Ellsworth to Sullivan or directly to Bar Harbor. With a view to lowering costs, he took the curious step of arranging another conversion of the line, this time to 3-foot gauge, even though 2-foot was promoted elsewhere in Maine. Work was done over the weekend of October 9-10, 1880. Track costs were minimal—the rails were simply respiked to existing ties—but the cost of purchasing new rolling stock was high.

Traffic growth did not meet expectations, and Lincoln commenced negotiations with the Maine Central, which was leasing and operating the E&NA. B&B shareholders were exasperated, and Lincoln resigned in the face of their vitriol. Reincorporation of the line as the Eastern Maine RR on February 1, 1882, did not improve matters. Effective May 1, 1883, the MEC leased the former B&B, and reconversion to standard gauge was completed within weeks.

Fish and goods transferred from ships in Bucksport provided most of the freight traffic in relatively small loads. Passenger trains were infrequent and began to be replaced by busses in February 1930; three round trips were operated by the SamOset, the MEC's hotel and bus company subsidiary, the first such replacement on the MEC. Mixed trains now provided the only rail passenger service. These ended in 1936, a few years after all MEC road operations were transferred to the Maine Central Transportation Co. The same year, Eastern Maine shareholders agreed to merger with the MEC.

For a number of years less-than-carload traffic was often handled in a combination car in place of a caboose. One such car was advertised until 1935. Bucksport station at McDonald Street was closed in 1935, although the line continued to serve quay sidings until a dry goods store and warehouse on Main Street closed in the 1950s.

Presently, Guilford regards the B&B as an unsignaled freight line, with operation featuring a daily round trip from Portland to Calais Jct. and Bucksport, conveying mainly chemicals inbound to the Champion International paper mill at Bucksport and pulp and paper products outbound, supplemented by petroleum products. Local switchers also operate from Bangor to Bucksport as required. Bucksport station, now owned by the local historical society, has been restored.

Sources: Bachelder, *Special Trains*, 33-35; Fisher, "Locomotives," 72; Hilton, *American Narrow Gauge*, 407-8; Potter, *Great American Railroad Stations*, 77; Zimmermann, *Sunrise Route*.

64. Maine Shore Line

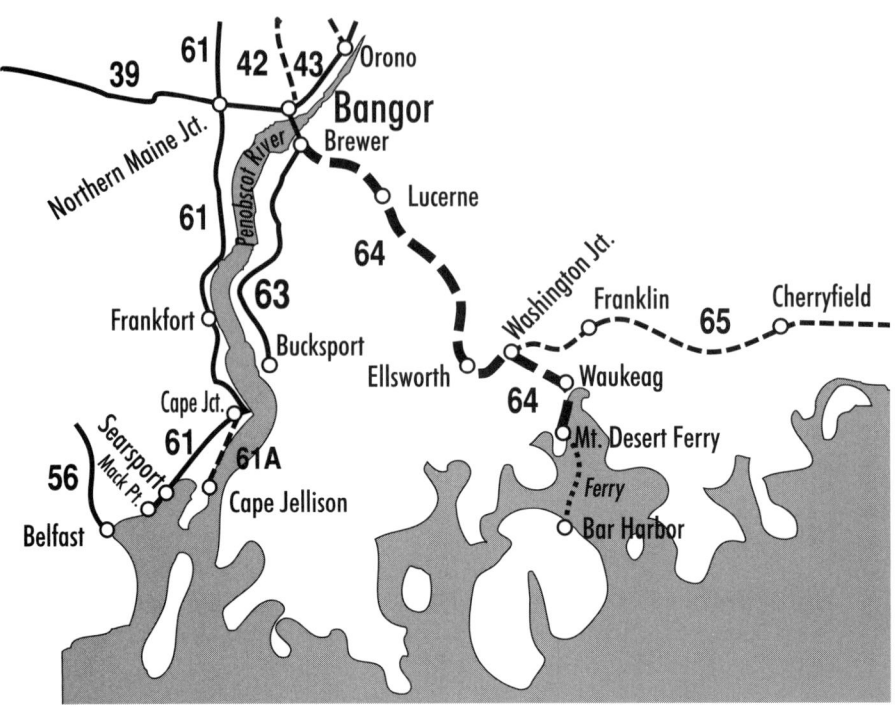

0 Brewer (Brewer Jct.), ME	18 Green Lake	38 Hancock
11 Holden	23 Nicolin	40 Waukeag
12 Egerys Mill (McKenzies)	28 Ellsworth Falls	42 Mt. Desert Ferry, ME
14 Lake House	30 Ellsworth	
15 Lucerne-in-Maine (Phillips Lake)	32 Washington Jct.	
	35 Franklin Rd.	

Built: 1882-84.

Operators: *Maine Central*, 1884-1981; *Guilford*, 1981-84.

Daily Passenger Trains: *1893:* 8; *1919:* 10; *1935:* 4 (Brewer-Washington Jct); *1950:* 4 (Brewer-Washington Jct). Passenger service ended Waukeag-Mt. Desert Ferry, 1934; Washington Jct.-Waukeag, 1938; Brewer-Washington Jct., 1957.

64. Maine Shore Line

Abandonments: Waukeag–Mt. Desert Ferry, 1938; Washington Jct.–Waukeag, 1959; Brewer–Washington Jct., 1985.

Both the Maine Shore Line and Washington County RRs originated with the Bangor & Calais RR company, chartered in August 1871 and incorporated in May 1872. Prolonged debate on the route stalled the start of construction. Bangor eventually voted to purchase stock in April 1873, with the caveat that the subscription support a line from Bangor only to Ellsworth. Later that year, Eastport offered to subscribe, provided that it would be the eastern terminal. Meanwhile, boosters in both Bucksport and Castine promoted their communities as the terminal. Bucksport was selected, since a through route to Portland could be constructed, with the possibility of lease by the Eastern RR.

While talk continued, the B&C completed a survey from Ellsworth to East Machias between January and July 1873. The line would never be built, however, for two other companies had entered the scene. One, the Bucksport & Bangor, was completed in 1874. The charter for the second, the Eastport & Calais, lapsed before it was built, but on March 4, 1881, the legislature issued a charter to the Maine Shore Line RR for a line between Ellsworth and Calais, with the right to build an extension to Bangor if the B&B did not exercise its rights to connect with the proposed line. The MEC—lessor of the B&B from 1883—agreed to lease the MSL. An amendment to the charter allowed construction of branches within the towns it passed though. The line was completed to Ellsworth in 1883, and the rest of the route, to Mt. Desert Ferry, about a mile from Hancock Point, during 1884.

The first 25 miles offered few traffic prospects except a mill near Holbrook Pond at East Holden. The area was sparsely populated and primarily farm land. Ellsworth, on the Union River, was the only significant community, its economic base having changed from lumber and shipbuilding to leather goods and other small industries before arrival of the railroad. MEC steamers, the *Sappho* and *Sebenoa*, plied Frenchman Bay providing a half-hourly service between Mt. Desert Ferry and Bar Harbor. Plans to extend the MSL eastward died, but were taken up a decade later by the Washington County RR.

New England's first limited train, the summer-only *Boston & Mount Desert* (subsequently renamed the *Bar Harbor Express*) was introduced in June 1887. Comprising five 70-foot Pullmans and one baggage car, it made the journey from Boston in 8¾ hours. Run in both 1888 and 1889, with time reduced to 7¾ hours, the final trip was made in October of the third season.

When the Washington County RR opened in 1893, the line to Mt. Desert Ferry became a branch. In June 1906 a new limited was introduced from New York to Mt. Desert Ferry. Unnamed in the schedule, it at first ran over the Boston & Maine's Worcester, Nashua & Portland Division, but in 1911 it was diverted via Lowell, South Lawrence, and Dover and named the *State of Maine Express*. In June 1917 service was extended to Washington, DC. Several other trains from the south conveyed through coaches, many including sleepers.

Road improvements and increasing competition from automobiles caused a decline in the line's fortunes. Mt. Desert Narrows had been crossed by a highway bridge as early as 1884, but major improvement was made in April 1931 with the building of a causeway between Trenton and Thompson Island (incidentally forming Oldhouse Cove). Ferry service ended, and thereafter service beyond Ellsworth to Mt. Desert Ferry was provided exclusively by mixed trains, with the limited

Between 1884 and 1931 passengers departed from trains here at Mt. Desert Ferry to board steamboats to and from Bar Harbor across Frenchman Bay. (Courtesy Walker Transportation Collection, Beverly Historical Society & Museum)

Nearly 15 years after abandonment, most of the rails are intact on the Maine Shore Line, as shown in this view at Ellsworth Falls in September 1999. (R. D. Karr)

trains from Bangor to Ellsworth six times weekly from June through September, and bus service between Ellsworth and Bar Harbor. In a burst of optimism, a new *Bar Harbor Express* from Philadelphia and New York was added four times weekly in 1932, temporarily reduced to twice weekly in 1933.

In 1934 all mixed trains ceased and the length between Waukeag and Mt. Desert Ferry closed, although permission to abandon was not obtained until 1938. Service patterns over the remainder were not altered substantially until most seasonal trains, including the limiteds, were suspended in 1943 and 1944. The *Bar Harbor Express* returned to Ellsworth in 1946, with reduced frequency. To maintain pre-war running times, they were almost always powered by one of the MEC's two 4-6-4 steam locomotives. By 1955 this train had been reduced to twice weekly, and on November 25, 1957, all passenger service ended. The remainder of the original line beyond Washington Jct. was abandoned in 1959, although a short section at the junction was retained as a spur.

The MSL south of Brewer to Washington Jct. was necessarily retained for freight service, but this ended some years later after Guilford bought the MEC. After closure during 1984 and permission to abandon a year later, the state of Maine acquired it, along with the former Washington County. The state continues to maintain the unused right of way today. When Ellsworth High School was built on part of the right of way, the state reportedly built a bypass to retain the line. Recent proposals to restore service from Bangor to Washington Jct., then over the Washington County to Calais, have gained support from Maine's government.

Sources: Bachelder, *Special Trains*, 6-16, 23-24, 33-34; Dublin, *Some Classic Trains*, 40-43; Karr, *Lost Railroads*, 98, 116, 148; Zimmermann, *Sunrise Route*, 71-197.

65. Washington County (Maine)

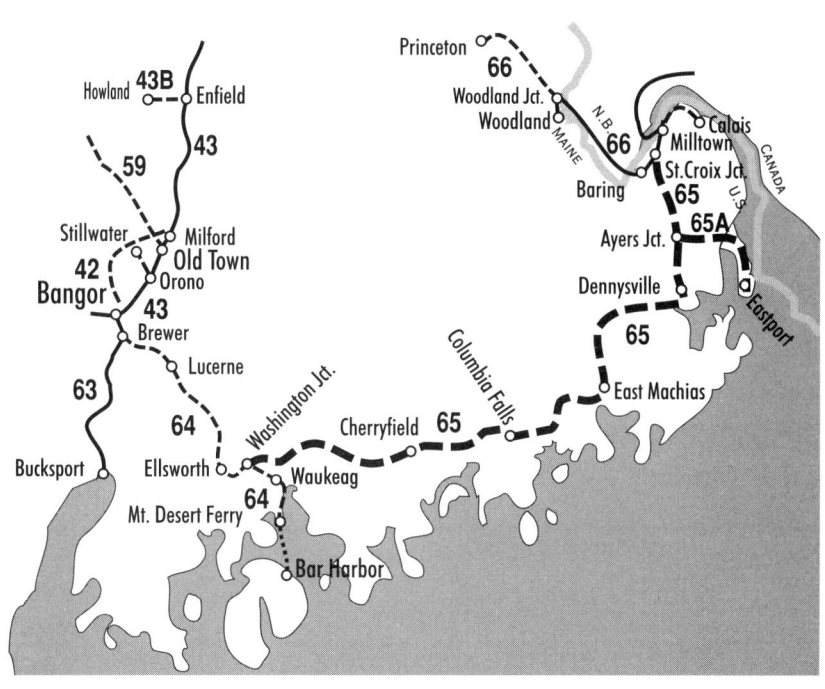

0	Washington Jct., ME
8	Eastbrook
9.5	Franklin
13	Hannas
15	Schoodic
17	Tunk Lake (Tunk Pond)
19.5	Goodwins
22	Stovers
24.5	Unionville
28.5	Lynchs
29	Cherryfield
30	Fryes
32.5	West Harrington
34.5	Harrington
37.5	Plummers
38.5	Columbia (Addison)
40	Wards
41.5	Columbia Falls
42.5	Matthews
43.5	Indian River
46	Jonesboro
51	Watts
53.5	Whitneyville
56	Hilltop
57	Machias
60	Machiasport
61.5	East Machias
62.5	Gardners
63	Jacksonville
69	Ellis
75	Marion
79	Dennysville
86	Ayers Jct. (Eastport Jct.)
89	Charlotte
98.5	St. Croix Jct., ME

65A. Eastport Branch

0	Ayers Jct. (Eastport Jct.), ME
3.5	Pembroke
8.5	Perry
11	Pleasant Point
13	Quoddy
15.5	Eastport, ME

Ayers Jct., where the Eastport Branch joined the main line of the Washington County, in 1908. (Courtesy Walker Transportation Collection, Beverly Historical Society & Museum)

Built: 1896-98.

Operators: *Washington County*, 1898-1904; *Maine Central*, 1904-81; *Guilford*, 1981-84.

Daily Passenger Trains: *1900:* 6 (Eastport Jct.-Eastport, 10); *1919:* 4; *1935:* 4; *1950:* 4. Passenger service ended Eastport Branch, 1938; Washington Jct.-Calais, 1957.

Abandonments: Ayers Jct.-Eastport, 1978; Washington Jct.-St. Croix Jct., 1985.

Colonel Joseph Norton Greene, an engineer and contractor for the Grand Southern RY in Canada, along with others, on March 7, 1893, obtained a charter for the Washington County RR to build eastward from the Maine Shore Line RR, followed by company incorporation in July 1894. The WC was given power to lease other lines, and separate legislation permitted it to lease or purchase the St. Croix & Penobscot RR. Authority to construct the line expired on January 28, 1895, but an extension was obtained. The alignment was changed from the original surveyed route between Franklin and Cherryfield and from Charlotte and Calais to obviate costly bridges in Franklin, and to reduce mileage at the eastern end to avoid Robbinston.

Most of the construction work took place in 1897 and 1898. The Eastport branch required the building of three long trestles: 900 feet

65. Washington County (Maine)

between Quoddy and Carlows Island, 700 feet to reach Pleasant Point Bar, and another of similar length to reach hard ground southwest of Perry. The state commissioners approved the grade crossings in July 1898, and regular service from Calais to Eastport began on July 15, although a certificate was not issued to legalize operations until October 8. Washington Jct. to Cherryfield and Marion to Eastport Jct. were approved on November 22, and from Machias to Marion on December 6. The final section, Cherryfield to Machias, received formal approval on December 17, and a special inaugural train ran on Christmas Day. The Washington County began calling itself the "Sunrise Route." Eastport service generally operated to and from the junction, making connections with main line trains.

High maintenance costs and repair of several washouts in February, March, and May of 1900, followed by accidents and management problems, took their toll. By 1903 it was apparent that the company would default on bond payments, which had been largely underwritten by the county. Foreclosure proceedings began in the U.S. Circuit Court in Portland on May 29, culminating in a single bid at auction by one of the directors, F. W. Whitridge. After the line was reorganized as the Washington County RY, the Maine Central took control in 1904 and had bought all of the stock by June 1905, although the line continued to be operated separately until it was absorbed by the MEC in 1911.

Lumber and processed fish were the line's mainstay, but by the 1950s the WC's fortunes were in severe decline. Passenger service on the Eastport Branch had ended in 1938. Eastport had lost most of its fish processing facilities and had become an area of high unemployment. Operation of freight trains over the branch continued into the 1970s, gradually declining. Abandonment was delayed until 1978 because the Passamaquoddy tribe claimed title to the land occupied by the alignment across their reservation. The tracks were eventually dismantled in 1980.

Trains continued for a few more years over the rest. Passenger service between Bangor and Calais ended on November 25, 1957. Principal freight customers were Georgia-Pacific at Woodland and International Paper at a lumber farm near Cherryfield, supplemented by pulpwood from Columbia Falls and Dennysville, the latter also providing outbound grain traffic. But the costs of maintaining such a long route were excessive. Guilford encouraged Georgia-Pacific to route traffic via the Canadian Pacific from Calais/St. Stephen and the former European & North American to Mattawamkeag. In June 1985, with abandonment virtually inevitable, International Paper announced its intention to close the Cherryfield facility and obtain lumber from Mattawamkeag and Dover-Foxcroft. Regular freight service was reduced to a once-weekly round trip, supplemented for a few weeks by two trains for clearing a lumber stockpile at Cherryfield. Guilford then closed the line and sought permission to abandon, leaving behind a MEC PS-1 box car near the Machias freight house, where it remains today. The Maine Department of Transportation stepped in, obtaining a mortgage for the line on August 19, 1985.

Hopes that the state could find a short-line operator were not realized. Most of the grade crossings were paved over, and part of the track around Harrington was damaged by a logging company. The Maine DoT in 1994 proposed scrapping some track east of Cherryfield, the proceeds to be used to help fund the restoration of Portland-Boston passenger service and other projects, but citizen protests helped kill this scheme.

In recent years three sets of interests have vied for funds to use on the corridor east of Ellsworth. The Eastern Maine Railroad Development Commission, sponsored by local businesses, hopes to realize a multimodal facility at Ayers Jct. to truck goods between there and a new pier in Eastport. Various active and would-be short-line operators have proposed freight or passenger operations east of Ellsworth: early in 1997, the New England Southern RR submitted a proposal to the Maine DoT to operate gravel trains to Cherryfield; another proposition involved operation of steam-hauled tourist trains over a length north of Acadia National Park; but the most imaginative proposal came from a dentist based in Woodstock, VT, who suggested that bulk commodity users support operation of a rail-based mobile clinic. In contrast, trail advocates maintain that rail use of the corridor is impractical and that the tracks should be replaced by a recreational path. As a possible compromise, the Maine DoT has been working on a rail-with-trail scheme. The governor and legislature have yet to agree on plans for the future use of the Washington County.

Sources: Bachelder, *Special Trains*, 6; Karr, *Lost Railroads*, 136, 148; Peters, *Maine Central*, 8, 15; Zimmermann, *Sunrise Route*, 139-223.

66. St. Croix & Penobscot

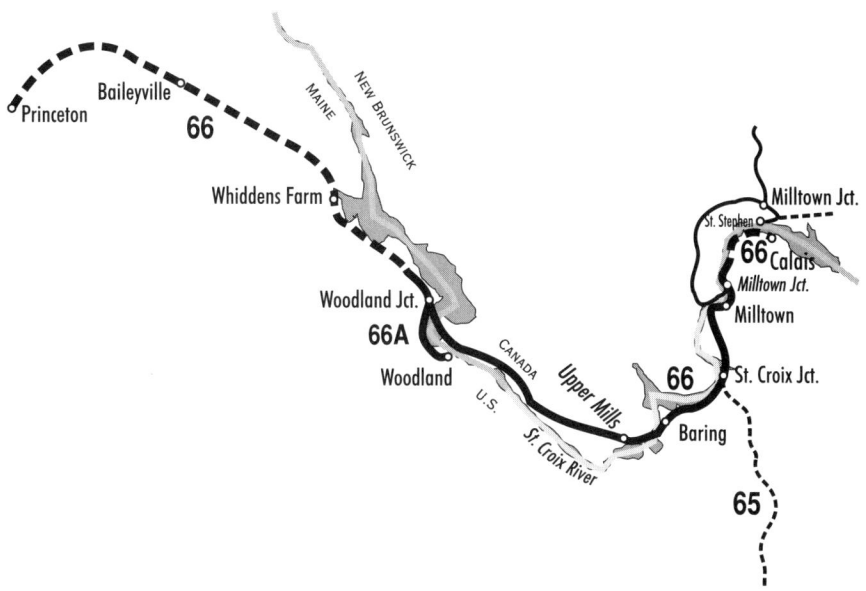

0 Calais, ME	6 *Upper Mills, NB*	21 Princeton, ME
1.5 *Milltown Jct.*	10 Woodland Jct. (Spragues Falls), ME	
2 Milltown (Salmon Falls)		66A. Woodland Branch
3.5 St. Croix Jct.	13 Whiddens Farm	
5 Baring, ME	17 Baileyville	0 Woodland Jct., ME
		2 Woodland, ME

Built: 1835-57; Woodland Branch, 1906.

Operators: *Calais*, 1839-41; *Calais & Baring*, 1849-70; *Lewys Island*, 1857-70; *St. Croix & Penobscot*, 1870-98; *Washington County*, 1898-1911; *Maine Central*, 1911-81; *Guilford*, 1981-.

Daily Passenger Trains: *1893:* 2; *1900:* 2; *1912:* 2; *1925:* 2 (mixed); *1933:* 2 (mixed); *1945:* 2 (Calais-Woodland, mixed). Passenger service ended Woodland Jct.-Princeton, 1933; Calais-Woodland, 1946.

Abandonments: Woodland Jct.-Princeton, 1935; in Calais, 1984.

A MEC mixed train pulls into Princeton station, at the end of the St. Croix & Penobscot. The station still survives, although modified. (Courtesy Walker Transportation Collection, Beverly Historical Society & Museum)

A charter, the first in Maine, was obtained in 1832 for the Calais RY, to be built between Calais and Salmon Falls (later Milltown). Nothing was done, but the charter was renewed on July 25, 1835, for another three years. An extension to Baring was surveyed in 1836 but not built. Grading was eventually completed in 1837, but track—wooden beams with a nailed iron surface—was not laid until yet another charter renewal was granted in 1838. Horses pulled the trains when the two-mile line opened in 1839.

While considerable quantities of lumber were conveyed, the limitations of horse-drawn traction made the line uneconomical, and in 1841 operations ceased, and the company was unsuccessfully put up for sale. Six years later the Calais & Baring RR proposed to revive the line and adopt steam power. Incorporated in 1848 but not chartered until July 1849, the C&B began running trains in the spring of 1851, and completed the line to Baring in July.

The Lewys Island RR was chartered in 1854 to extend the line from Baring in order to exploit large lumber stands along the St. Croix River. Construction began the next year, and was completed in 1856. In Baring the alignment crossed the St. Croix River into New Brunswick and recrossed into Maine at Spragues Falls to reach Baileyville on Grand Falls Flowage, and then Princeton on Lewy Lake. Freight had to be transferred at Baring to the C&B.

Unfortunately, the two companies could not come to terms on interchange costs, and in 1862 the Lewys Island defaulted on its mortgage, which was held by the city of Calais. The city took over operation until 1870, when the C&B purchased the line. That year the depot at Calais was razed by a fire, which destroyed a considerable area of the city. The C&B was reincorporated as the St. Croix & Penobscot RR and obtained a new charter which authorized extension to the European & North American RY. Depression in the lumber industry, beginning in 1874, precluded implementation of this plan, and the idea was never again seriously considered.

Until 1898 the St.C&P was isolated from other railroads. That year the new Washington County RR acquired the St.C&P in order to reach Calais. Some realignment was undertaken to ease curves and gradients east of Milltown. In 1905, after the Maine Central gained control of the Washington County, the St. Croix Paper Co. constructed a mill west of the river, in the district later known as Woodland. A branch was built to serve the New Mill, as it was known; an associated dam project required a short relocation of the main line. The branch junction had a wye to enable through passenger trains to and from Princeton to operate via Woodland.

The former St.C&P became part of the MEC in 1911, when the latter absorbed the Washington County. The MEC improved a short branch across the river at Union Mills near Milltown and constructed a connection with the New Brunswick & Canada RY, which had built a line around St. Stephen.

There followed 15 halcyon years. The line reached its zenith in 1926, but decline set in starting with the closure of Baileyville station; Princeton was barely hanging on. In 1929 just one daily (except Sunday) mixed train remained. North of Woodland Jct. the line was taken out of service on July 24, 1933, and officially abandoned two years later, the wye being retained to switch and turn cars and locomotives. North of the junction, the initial 0.75 miles of track became an industrial spur that remains in use today. The mixed train to Woodland made its last run in the summer of 1946.

With abandonment of the Washington County on August 19, 1985, the branch became isolated from the rest of the Guilford system. It had been leased by Georgia-Pacific, successors of the St. Croix Paper Co., to keep it running, but Guilford resumed operation later that year and used it as an experiment in negotiating labor agreements through its Springfield Terminal RY subsidiary to reduce operating costs. All traffic was conveyed to and from the Canadian Pacific at Milltown.

Traffic ceased on December 31, 1994, when the CP's Canadian Atlantic subsidiary abandoned all service east of Sherbrooke. A week or so later, operations resumed with lease of the Canadian Atlantic lines in New Brunswick by J. D. Irving's New Brunswick Southern RY. Calais yard still interchanges inbound sodium chlorate in covered hoppers, acid, and kraft pulp, and sends about 15-20 cars outbound daily with plywood substitutes and flakeboard. Two switchers are used, maintained locally, since the branch is far removed from the rest of Guilford's operations. The former roundhouse at Milltown Jct. is in use as a warehouse, and the brick station at Calais survives.

Sources: Bachelder, *Special Trains*, 6; Karr , *Lost Railroads*, 88; Peters, *Maine Central*, 14; Zimmermann, *Sunrise Route*, 90-197; 207 ICC 41 (1935).

67. Montpelier & Wells River

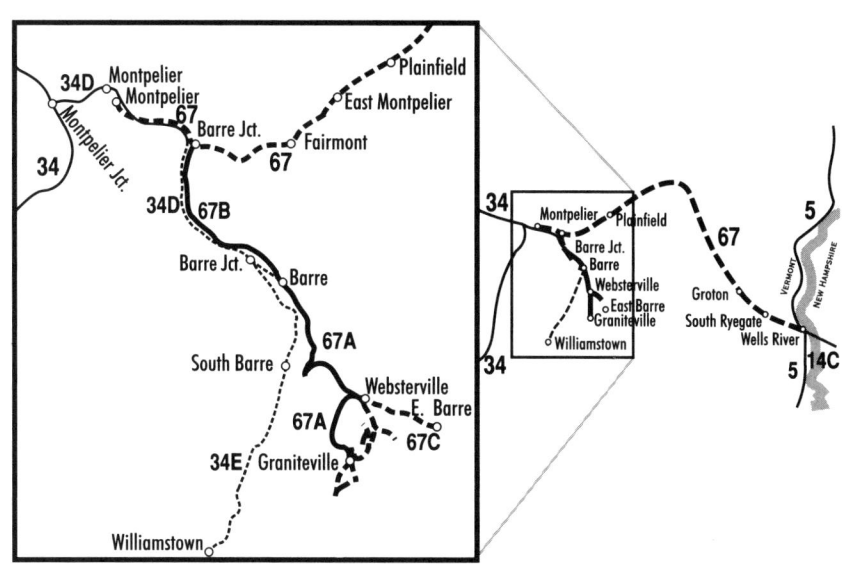

0 Montpelier, VT	22 Lakeside	3 Graniteville, VT
2 Barre Jct. (Barre Transfer) (Coffeehouse Jct.)	23 Rickers	
	29.5 Groton	**67B. Barre Branch RR**
4 Fairmont	33 South Ryegate	
5.5 East Montpelier	35 Boltonville	0 Barre Jct., VT
9 Plainfield	38 Wells River, VT	5.5 Barre, VT
14 Marshfield		
15 Edgewater	**67A. Barre RR**	**67C. East Barre & Chelsea RR**
17 Lanesboro		
20 Rocky Point	0 Barre, VT	0 Websterville, VT
	2 Websterville	1.5 East Barre, VT

Built: 1872–94.

Operators: *Montpelier & Wells River*, 1873–1944; *East Barre*, 1892–93; *East Barre & Chelsea*, 1893–95; *Barre*, 1888–1913; *Barre & Chelsea*, 1944–57; *Montpelier & Barre*, 1957–80; *Washington County*, 1980–99; *New England Central*, 1999; *Vermont*, 1999–.

Daily Passenger Trains: *1894:* 6 (Montpelier-Barre, 18); *1904:* 6 (Montpelier-Barre, 12); *1916:* 8 (Montpelier-Wells River, 8); *1922:* 4;

1933: 2; *1950:* 2. Passenger service ended Barre-Websterville-East Barre, 1922; Barre Jct.-Barre, 1928; Montpelier-Wells River, 1956.

Abandonments: Websterville-East Barre, 1937; Barre Jct.-Wells River, 1956; Montpelier-Barre Jct., 1958.

For such a short line, the history of the Montpelier & Wells River RR is remarkably complex. It owed its conception in 1867 to proposals for a link between the Vermont Central RR at Montpelier and the Connecticut & Passumpsic Rivers/Boston, Concord & Montreal lines at Wells River. Quarry traffic was intended to be its mainstay. Progress was slow, and the line did not open until November 1873. The M&WR entered receivership in 1875, but the original proprietors were able to reorganize in 1877.

In 1875 the Central Vermont had leased a newly-built railroad through Montpelier to Barre, and extended it south to Williamstown in 1888, which gave the CV access to the rich quarry country south of Barre. To compete, the M&WR sponsored two new lines. The first, the Barre RR, obtained a charter early in 1888; by the end of the year it had opened a line from a connection with the CV in Barre to Websterville, and by the spring of the following year it had completed its line to Graniteville. The Barre RR featured 5 percent grades, some of the steepest of any conventional railroad, switchbacks at South Barre and Websterville, and a number of quarry branches and spurs to Upper Graniteville and Foxville on the Washington-Orange County border, and to Upper Websterville just west of East Barre. The Barre RR used small industrial-design saddle-tank locomotives for both its freight and passenger trains.

In 1888 the M&WR obtained a charter for the Barre Branch RR to connect its main line from a point called Coffeehouse Jct. (later Barre Jct.) in Montpelier to the Barre RR in Barre. It leased the Barre Branch, which closely paralleled the CV's line to Barre, on opening in June 1889. The M&WR also leased a portion, less than two miles, of the Barre RR in Barre in 1894.

On September 3, 1892, the East Barre RR opened a 1.7-mile line east from Upper Websterville to East Barre. When reorganized in 1893 as the East Barre & Chelsea RR, it envisaged a southward extension of about 12 miles, but these plans were put aside when it was leased by the Barre RR in 1895. By 1896 the Barre RR was operating 27 miles of track, including quarry spurs and sidings. Although the Barre RR was

An M&WR passenger train is shown at Montpelier on a cold winter's day in February 1936. (Courtesy Walker Transportation Collection, Beverly Historical Society & Museum)

under common ownership with the M&WR, the two railroads were run separately.

In 1911 the Boston & Maine bought control of both the M&WR and the Barre RR, although both lines retained their nominal independence. Two years later the Barre and East Barre & Chelsea RRs were merged as the Barre & Chelsea, and the Barre Branch company became part of the M&WR. Passenger service on the Barre & Chelsea ended in 1922. The B&M turned management over to local interests in 1926. M&WR passenger service south of Barre Jct. ceased on May 29, 1928.

Ironically, the Barre & Chelsea bought the M&WR in December 1944. Operating economies were made through conversion to diesel traction, using three 600 h.p. B-B switchers acquired from Alco between 1944 and 1949. Less than ten years passed before the company petitioned the ICC for permission to abandon owing to losses operating the "main" line between Montpelier and Wells River, which bore 40 percent of the company's operating cost but produced merely 5 percent of total revenue. When consent was given to abandon the former main line between Barre Jct. and Wells River in 1956, Samuel Pinsly bought the remaining assets, including two locomotives; the Montpelier & Barre RR, incorporated on November 13, 1956, took them over in 1957.

The next year the M&B purchased the Central Vermont line from Montpelier Jct. to Barre and abandoned the parallel M&WR segment. Operations over the remainder continued until 1980, when the M&B obtained permission to abandon. The state of Vermont bought the right of way and immediately leased it to the Washington County RR, a consortium of local shippers. Operation commenced on November 17, 1981. In 1990 the operating company was sold to CSF Acquisitions, the owner of other Vermont and New Hampshire short lines.

Bombardier of Canada established a railroad rolling stock assembly plant in Barre in 1981, where commuter and intercity rail, rapid transit, and light rail cars have been built. In early September 1997 the Washington County undertook extensive track realignment in Montpelier, subsidized by the state, to accommodate a riverfront park.

Disaster struck the railroad in the small hours of June 28, 1998, when the engine house at Montpelier burned to the ground, apparently a victim of arson. The line's two Alco S-1 locomotives, dating from 1944 and 1949, were destroyed, along with track equipment and road vehicles. Ironically, the timber-framed structure had previously replaced a building that had burned in February 1907. On February 2, 1999, the Washington County assigned its lease to the New England Central RR, who operated the line only until September 8. The state then made an interim agreement with the Vermont RY for continued operation, under which the company receives a weekly subsidy.

Sources: Drury, *Historical Guide*, 198-99; Jones, Maxfield, and Gove, *Vermont's Granite Railways*; Karr, *Lost Railroads*, 93, 113, 115; Lewis, *American Shortline Railway Guide*, 275; *Railpace*, 16 (Nov.1997): 37; 17 (Aug. 1998): 38.

68. Burlington & Lamoille

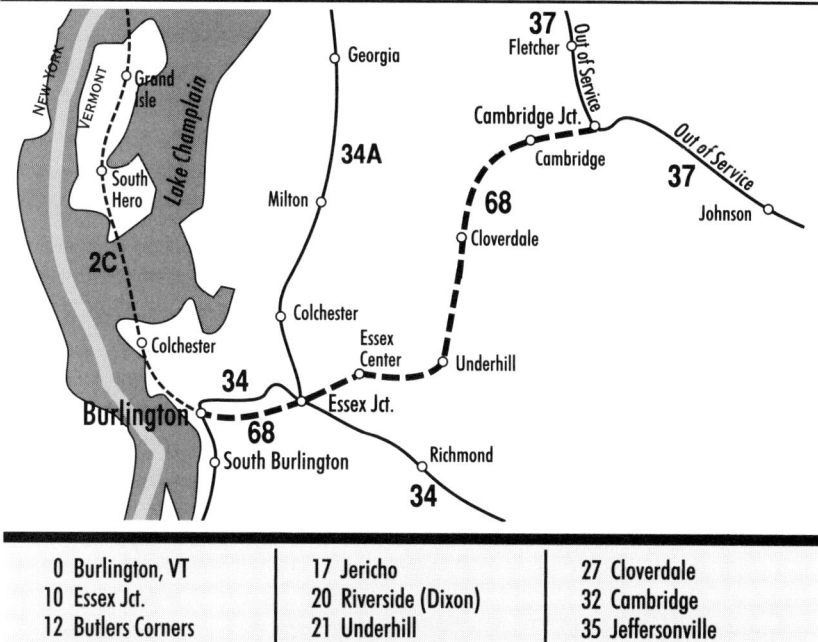

0 Burlington, VT	17 Jericho	27 Cloverdale
10 Essex Jct.	20 Riverside (Dixon)	32 Cambridge
12 Butlers Corners	21 Underhill	35 Jeffersonville
13 Essex Center	25 North Underhill	35.8 Cambridge Jct., VT

Built: 1876-77.

Operators: *Burlington & Lamoille*, 1877-89, *Central Vermont*, 1889-1938.

Daily Passenger Trains: *1893:* 6 (Essex Jct.-Cambridge Jct.); *1919:* 6 (Essex Jct.-Cambridge Jct.); *1935:* 2 (Essex Jct.-Cambridge Jct., mixed); *1938:* 2 (Essex Jct.-Cambridge Jct., mixed). Passenger service ended Burlington-Essex Jct., 1889; Essex Jct.-Cambridge Jct., 1938.

Abandonments: Burlington-Essex Jct., 1889; Essex Jct.-Cambridge Jct., 1938.

Finding justification for the Burlington & Lamoille RR is difficult. With the ongoing war between the Central Vermont RY and the Rutland RR, with which the new line would connect, the only potential beneficiary was the Lamoille Valley RR, a forerunner of the St. Johnsbury & Lake Champlain RR. The line was completed in 1877

The crew of the Burlington & Lamoille's locomotive Taunton *posed for this photograph, probably around the time the line opened in 1877. (Courtesy Walker Transportation Collection, Beverly Historical Society & Museum)*

and opened on June 30, with regular service from July 2, just prior to completion of the LV to Swanton. Apart from Burlington and South Burlington, the line served an essentially rural area. It is surprising that the line was not leased by the CV, although the two railroads developed a friendly working relationship, notwithstanding the fact that west of Essex Jct. the B&L competed with a CV branch. Agricultural products to and from sparsely populated farmlands barely sustained the line, so there were virtually no returns for shareholders. Threatened by territorial incursions by the Maine Central and Boston & Maine systems, the CV did finally lease the B&L in 1889 and immediately abandoned the length between Burlington and Essex Jct. Survival of the remainder until 1938, with just one mixed train in each direction, is remarkable. Upon abandonment that year, just under one mile of track at Cambridge Jct. was transferred to the SJ&LC to serve a mill.

There are no traces of the B&L west of Essex Center, although roads north of Burlington International Airport are built on the alignment. Eastward, to Riverside, parts of the alignment are visible from State Highway 15. Trails and minor roads occupy some of the rest in Underhill and Cambridge. Former stations at Essex Center, Jericho, Underhill, Cambridge, and Jeffersonville survive as private residences.

Sources: Bachelder, *Mountaineer,* 7; Baker, *Formation,* 227; Jones, *Railroads of Vermont,* 2: 116–26; Karr, *Lost Railroads,* 75, 97.

69. Missisquoi

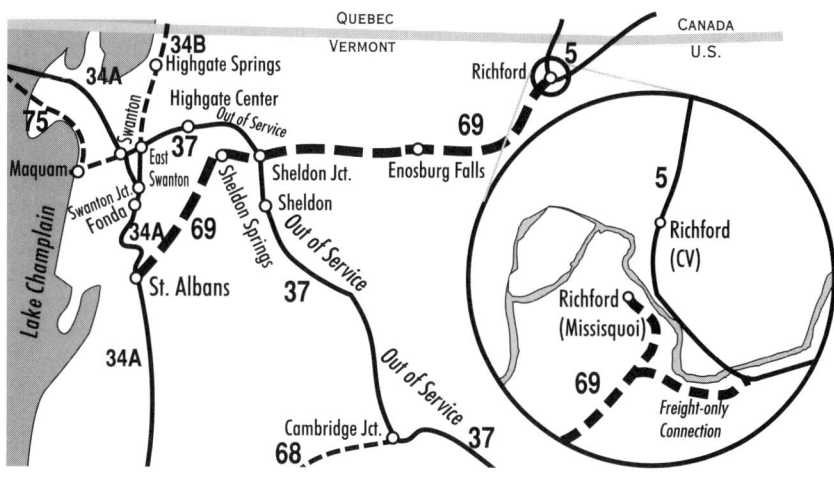

0 St. Albans, VT	10 Sheldon Jct. (Sheldon)	19 Enosburg Falls
5 Greens Corner (East Swanton)	12.5 North Sheldon	21 North Enosburg
8.5 Sheldon Springs	13.5 East Franklin Rd. (South Franklin)	24 East Berkshire
		27.5 Richford, VT

Built: 1870-73.

Operators: *Vermont Central*, 1873-77; *Missisquoi*, 1877-86; *Missisquoi Valley*, 1886-88; *Central Vermont*, 1888-1990; *Lamoille Valley*, 1983-85, 1988-89.

Daily Passenger Trains: *1876:* 2; *1882:* 2; *1884:* 2; *1893:* 5; *1916:* 6; *1919:* 4; *1924:* 6; *1928:* 2; *1936:* 2. Passenger service ended 1938.

Abandonments: St. Albans-Sheldon Jct., 1990; Sheldon Jct.-Richford, 1992.

On November 14, 1867, the Missisquoi RR was incorporated to build a line from St. Albans east to Richford. The company planned to use parts of the virtually moribund St. Albans & Richford Plank Road dating from 1851, with the Vermont Central proposing to take over the plank road's debts. The road company was subsequently purchased by the Vermont & Canada, a subsidiary of the VC, for $30,000.

The Missisquoi began construction in 1870, proceeding eastward from a junction with the VC in St. Albans. By early summer about nine miles had been graded to just beyond Sheldon Springs, and track had been laid as far as Greens Corner. Progress was slowed by bridging of the Missisquoi River at Sheldon Springs; the eastern junction at Richford, where it connected with the newly-built South Eastern RY, was not made until late June 1873. On July 1, 1873, the day of opening, the VC leased the company. The VC's financial difficulties resulted in termination of the lease on November 15, 1877. Bondholders took control, completing the passenger and freight facilities that previous management had been unable to afford.

On November 4, 1883, Edmond Ellis, a South Eastern RY brakeman with a grudge against the Missisquoi, threw a switch to route the daily eastbound passenger train onto a spur at Enosburg. In the wreck that followed, the water tower was displaced, the locomotive plunged into the river, and both the engineer and fireman died. Ellis was arrested, tried, and convicted for his heinous crime.

The Missisquoi was reorganized as the Missisquoi Valley RR on December 24, 1886. The Central Vermont leased the MV on June 30, 1888, and purchased it on April 15, 1899, designating it the Missisquoi Valley Division and later just the Richford Branch. For many years the Quaker Oats mill at Richford (later owned by the H. K. Webster Co.) was the prime source of traffic. The station at North Enosburg suffered fire damage in 1904, followed in 1906 by the burning of Richford Station, which was rebuilt in pseudo-Queen Anne style, featuring a hipped roof and a bay window housing the signal post. Fire also damaged South Franklin station in 1910.

In the mid-1920s, weekday service was reduced to just six passenger trains, a daily milk train, and one through and one local freight. From 1924 to 1927 the CV experimented with a battery-electric car, which was claimed to have a range of 100 miles on full charge. After three years the car was converted to gas-electric power. By the early 1930s passengers were conveyed by mixed trains, and all passenger service ended on November 11, 1938.

After World War II, service was reduced to a single round-trip freight on weekdays and Saturdays only, serving the Webster facility at Richford, customers in Enosburg, and a pulp and paper mill in Sheldon

69. Missisquoi

Springs. In the late 1970s escalating operating expenses led to increased charges that Webster considered unreasonable, so mill traffic was diverted to trucks.

An attempt was made to attract traffic back to the line, with several improvements made including rail welding at several locations. On June 29, 1984, however, part of a CP/Guilford consist, diverted because of a washed-out bridge on the Connecticut River line at Wells River, VT, derailed at the Missisquoi River bridge just west of Sheldon Jct. After recovery of the train, a severely damaged bridge span was removed. The CV claimed that the rear four cars, which were Guilford's, had been inadequately maintained and improperly loaded. The dispute was arbitrated by the Association of American Railroads, which concluded that Guilford was indeed at fault and responsible for damages. Guilford refuted the findings, and the CV brought suit at the U.S. District Court in Rutland. Arbitration decisions were upheld, with $600,000 in damages, but Guilford has repeatedly appealed the decision. West of Sheldon Jct., the CV continued to service the Missisquoi Pulp & Paper Mill at Sheldon Springs from St. Albans, as required. The mill operators switched to trucks in 1990, and permission to abandon the truncated branch was obtained later that year. Dismantling had commenced by the winter.

After the derailment the CV discontinued service over the section east of Sheldon Jct. The Lamoille Valley RR restored service on March 7, 1988, but lack of traffic shortly brought operations to an end again, this time permanently. Approval to abandon was given in 1992. Most of the right of way is now a bicycle trail.

Sources: Jones, *Central Vermont*; Jones, *Railroads of Vermont*, 2: 64–70; Karr, *Lost Railroads*, 151, 153–54.

70. White Mountains

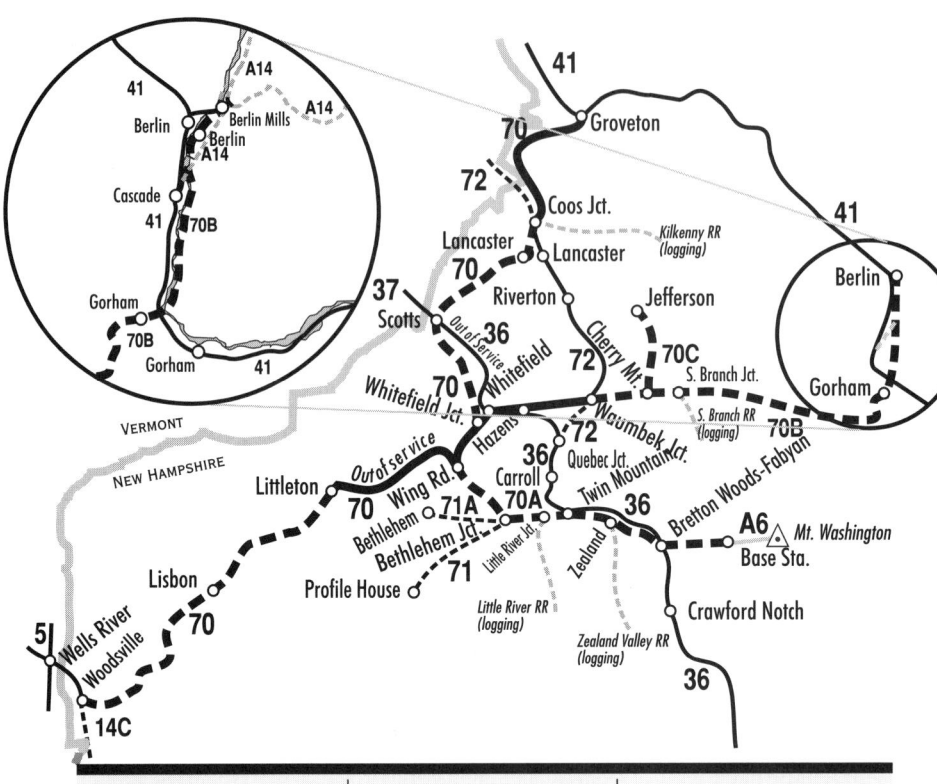

0 Woodsville, NH	38 Mountorne (South Lancaster)	5 Bethlehem (Bethlehem Jct.) (Pierces Bridge)
1 White Mountain Transfer	43 Lancaster	8 Little River Jct.
4 Bath	44 Coos Jct. (Maine Central Transfer)	9 Twin Mountain
10 Lisbon		11 Zealand (Zealand Transfer)
12 Sugar Hill	49 Northumberland (Northumberland Falls)	12 Bretton Woods (White Mountain House)
15 Gale River (North Lisbon) (Barrett)		
18 South Littleton	53 Groveton (Northumberland)	14 Fabyan (Bretton Woods-Fabyan)
20 Littleton	54 Groveton Jct., NH	20 Base Sta., NH
21 Apthorp		
23 Alder Brook	**70A. Mount Washington Branch**	**70B. Whitefield & Jefferson Branch**
26 Wing Rd.		
29 Whitefield Jct.	0 Wing Rd., NH	0 Whitefield Jct., NH
34 Scotts		
36 Dalton		

70. White Mountains

0.5 Whitefield	15 Bowman	30 Berlin Mills, NH
3 Hazen	18 Appalachia (Randolph)	
5.5 Waumbek Jct. (Jefferson Jct.) (Cherry Pond)	19 Randolph (Glen Rd.)	**70C. Waumbek Branch**
	20.5 Mt. Madison Springs (Mineral Springs) (Gorham Mineral Spring)	0 Cherry Mountain, NH
8 Cherry Mountain (Jefferson) (Meadows)		1 Thayers Mills
10 Highlands		3.5 Jefferson, NH
12 Boy Mountain	23.5 Gorham	
12.5 South Branch Jct.	29 Berlin	

Built: 1848-95.

Operators: *Boston, Concord & Montreal,* 1853-84, 1887-89; *Boston & Lowell,* 1884-87; *Concord & Montreal,* 1889-95; *Boston & Maine,* 1895-1983; *Maine Central,* 1948-77; *North Stratford,* 1977-89; *Guilford,* 1983-89; *New Hampshire & Vermont,* 1989-99. Waumbek Branch: *Johns River,* 1870-79, then as for the main line.

Daily Passenger Trains: *1868:* 2 (Woodsville-Littleton); *1893:* 4 (Lancaster-Groveton, 8; Wing Rd.-Fabayan, 4); *1907:* 4 (Lancaster-Groveton, 6; Whitefield Jct.-Berlin, 6; Wing Rd.-Fabyan, 4); *1919 (summer):* 3 (Lancaster-Groveton, 4; Wing Rd.-Bretton Woods, 9; Whitefield Jct.-Berlin, 3; Wing Rd.-Woodsville, 11; Cherry Mountain- Jefferson, 6; Bethlehem Jct.-Base Sta., 2); *1936:* Woodsville-Whitefield, 4; Whitfield Jct.-Berlin, 4, Wing Rd.-Bretton Woods, 2; *1958:* Woodsville-Berlin, 2. Passenger service ended Waumbek Branch, 1921; Mt. Washington Branch (Bretton Woods-Base Sta., 1931; Wing Rd.-Bretton Woods, 1938); Whitefield Jct.-Coos Jct, 1932; Coos Jct.-Groveton, 1938; Woodsville-Berlin, 1961.

Abandonments: Waumbek Branch, 1925; Mt. Washington Branch, 1938; Whitefield Jct.-Lancaster., 1941; Coos Jct.-Lancaster, ca. 1980; Whitefield & Jefferson Branch (Waumbek Jct.-Berlin, 1996); Woodsville-Littleton, 1996.

On December 24, 1848, the White Mountains RR was chartered to build a line from Groveton, NH, where it would meet the broad-gauge Atlantic & St. Lawrence RY then under construction, southward to Lancaster and on to the Connecticut River where it would connect with the proposed Boston, Concord & Montreal RR. Track gauge was not specified, but standard was selected in view of construction of other lines to or in the Connecticut River valley. The

A B&M shuttle train from Fabyans, with an open observation car, conveys passengers to the Mt. Washington Cog RY at Base Station at the beginning of the 20th Century. (Courtesy Walker Transportation Collection, Beverly Historical Society & Museum)

Boston, Concord & Montreal agreed to lease the line, enabling the WM to open from Wells River to Littleton, along the Ammonoosuc River, on August 1, 1853; Lancaster, however, was not reached until 1870.

Extension to Groveton and the Grand Trunk RY (the former A&SL) followed in 1872. A year later the BC&M bought the WM and considered expansion. With the Portland & Ogdensburg RR then a reality, a branch line was completed in stages between 1872 and 1876 from Wing Road through Fabyan to the Mt. Washington Cog RY at Base Station. As of 1879, Bethlehem Jct. became a transfer station with the Profile & Franconia Notch RR, and several logging lines provided traffic for the BC&M in the years that followed. One of these was A. L. & W. G. Brown Company's narrow-gauge Johns River RR, which gradually expanded from the vicinity of Whitefield to Jefferson Station (later Cherry Mountain) in 1870. Growth in resort traffic led to this line's incorporation as the Whitefield & Jefferson RR in 1878, when it was rebuilt to standard gauge. Opened as a common carrier in July 1879, the W&J was leased by the BC&M, and passenger trains were introduced.

The BC&M was in turn leased by the Boston & Lowell RR on July 1, 1884, although the arrangement was declared invalid by the New

Hampshire courts in 1889. The BC&M then merged with the Concord RR to form the Concord & Montreal RR. The C&M immediately set about extending the W&J to Gorham and Berlin in 1892, which involved a substantial trestle over both the GT and the Androscoggin River. Through service to Berlin started on June 10, 1893. In 1895 the C&M opened the 3.5-mile Waumbek Branch, named for the Waumbek House hotel that it served in Jefferson. The South Branch RR, built by the Brown's Lumber Co. opened in 1897 and was operated as a B&M spur from 1903 to 1906, with log trains to Berlin Mills. From about 1905, the WM and Grand Trunk lines were indirectly connected by the Berlin Mills RY near Cascade.

Summers-only service on the Waumbek Branch ended on June 27, 1921, and the line was abandoned shortly thereafter. Last passenger trains to Base Station ran on August 31, 1931, with complete closure in June 1932. That same year the B&M acquired trackage rights over the MEC between Whitefield and Fabyan and from Waumbek Jct. to Coos Jct. This enabled the B&M to discontinue use of the WM between Wing Road and Fabyan and from Whitefield Jct. to Lancaster, although legal abandonment of these segments did not occur until years later. The B&M retained the use of its own station at Bretton Woods until 1941. In 1948 the MEC acquired trackage rights over the WM between Coos Jct. and Groveton, and used these until 1977 to access its Upper Coos line. Passenger service declined significantly during the 1950s and ended altogether with a final round trip between Woodsville and Berlin on December 2, 1961, using a Budd rail diesel car (RDC).

What remained of the WM became part of Guilford in 1983. The line east of Woodsville was deemed unprofitable. The New Hampshire & Vermont RR, a subsidiary of CSF Acquisitions, acquired it under a ten-year lease-purchase agreement from Guilford effective November 21, 1989. In April 1993 Guilford granted the NH&VT trackage rights between Woodsville and White River Jct. for direct connection with the Central Vermont.

The NH&VT discontinued operations west of Littleton in 1995 when the bridge between Woodsville and Wells River, VT, was condemned and Guilford decided not to repair it, making it impossible for the NH&VT to reach White River Jct. The NH&VT received permission to abandon the Woodsville–Littleton and Waumbek Jct.–Berlin segments in 1996. It subsequently sold the entire line from Woodsville to Berlin to the state of New Hampshire, which removed the bridge

New England's last remaining ball signal still guards the diamond at Whitefield where the White Mountain's Whitefield & Jefferson branch (left) crosses the Maine Central, as shown here in August 1998. (R. D. Karr)

over the St. Lawrence & Atlantic RR, enabling the latter to haul double stack container cars. The NH&VT discontinued operations between Whitefield and Littleton around 1997, and to date no one has come forward with an offer to operate this segment. The track between Woodsville and Littleton was removed early in 1997, and that between Waumbek Jct. and Berlin a few months later. From Woodsville to Littleton the line is now a dirt trail. The sections between Coos Jct. and Groveton and from Whitefield to Waumbek Jct. were operated by the NH&VT to service a mill in Gilman, VT, until the fall of 1999 when the mill closed.

Sources: Bachelder, *Androscoggin Valley Ltd.*, 37–51; Belcher, *Logging Railroads*, 18–22, 235; Hilton, *American Narrow Gauge*, 445; Karr, *Lost Railroads*, 80, 81, 97; Lewis, *American Shortline Railroad Guide*, 36, 180; *Railpace*, 15 (Oct. 1996): 37; 16 (Aug. 1997): 37, (Nov. 1997): 37; 18 (Feb. 1998): 37.

71. Profile & Franconia Notch

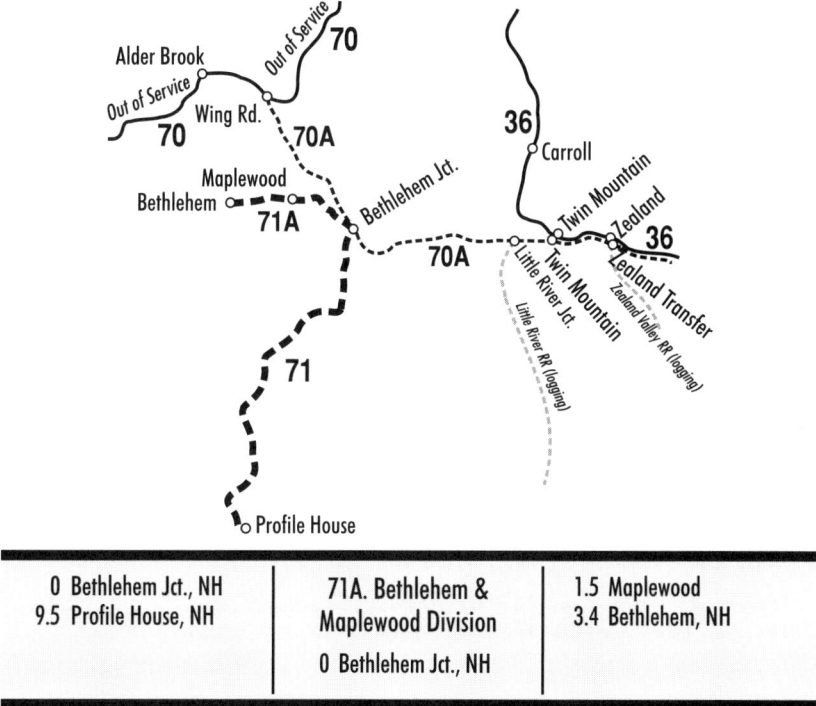

0 Bethlehem Jct., NH	71A. Bethlehem &	1.5 Maplewood
9.5 Profile House, NH	Maplewood Division	3.4 Bethlehem, NH
	0 Bethlehem Jct., NH	

Built: 1879; Bethlehem & Maplewood Division, 1881.

Operators: *Profile & Franconia Notch*, 1879-93; *Concord & Montreal*, 1893-95; *Boston & Maine*, 1895-1924.

Daily Passenger Trains: *1891:* 14 (Bethlehem Jct.-Maplewood, 14); *1919:* 9 (Bethlehem Jct.-Bethlehem, 14); *1923:* 11 (Bethlehem Jct.-Bethlehem). Passenger service ended 1920 (Bethlehem Jct.-Profile House); 1924 (Bethlehem Jct.-Bethlehem).

Abandonments: Bethlehem Jct.-Profile House, 1921; Bethlehem & Maplewood Division, 1925.

Fresh air and escape from urban life attracted those who could afford to vacation in the White Mountains range served after 1803 by the Tenth New Hampshire Turnpike. Despite their remoteness, several inns had developed into hotels by the 1850s, and after the Civil War a number had become splendid resorts for the well-to-do.

North of the resort area the White Mountains RR was the first to serve the area when it opened its main line from the Connecticut River to Littleton in 1853. That year Profile House was built on Profile Lake. Twenty years later the proprietors of the Profile House resort, Charles H. Greenleaf and Richard Taft, promoted a railroad connection but were unable to secure a branch from the WM (by then a part of the Boston, Concord & Montreal RR) which was then extending from Wing Road in Littleton to the base of Mt. Washington. Between 1874 and 1878 the Gale River Lumber Company had operated a logging railroad out of Pierce's Bridge on the Ammonoosuc River.

Greenleaf and Taft incorporated the Profile & Franconia Notch RR on July 11, 1878, to reconstruct the now-closed logging line between their resort and Pierce's Bridge, where it would connect with the BC&M. A 3-foot narrow-gauge line was built and completed on June 25, 1879, at a cost of about $125,000, including rolling stock. The average gradient was 1.5 percent but the ruling grade was 2.2 percent on the three-mile climb through the foothills of Bickford Mountain to the Pemigewasset River. Two Hinkley 4-4-0s provided power.

Greenleaf and Taft proposed a 31-mile extension of the line southward along the river valley to the BC&M at Plymouth to provide an alternative route from Boston. Their plans were thwarted by the Pemigewasset Valley RR, which planned a branch from the BC&M through Lincoln and along the river valley to Fabyans. Progress was slow, and the PV eventually petered out in Lincoln. The P&FN did succeed in opening a three-mile branch to Bethlehem in July 1881. To minimize cost, grading work was limited, and as a result there were several tortuous curves and a ruling gradient of 3.2 percent, which proved too much for the Hinkleys. An 0-6-0 tank engine, with better weight distribution for increased adhesion, was therefore purchased.

Despite operation only during the summer season, the system produced an annual profit of over $8,000. The C&M bought the P&FN for $280,000 in 1893, operating it as two separate branches from Bethlehem Jct. To eliminate one change of trains by passengers from Maine Central trains, the C&M laid a third rail east along its track from Bethlehem Jct. to a point called Zealand Transfer, where P&FN trains made a connection with the MEC. Following lease of the C&M by the Boston & Maine in 1895, the P&FN was converted to standard gauge after the 1896 summer season.

71. Profile & Franconia Notch

Maplewood station, shown here in the narrow-gauge era, survives today in dilapidated condition surrounded by woods. (Courtesy Walker Transportation Collection, Beverly Historical Society & Museum)

Both branches of the P&FN remained prosperous until the First World War, but trucking and automotive competition thereafter sealed their fate. Profile House lost its line in September 1920, with permission to abandon in July 1921; a twist of fate saw the hotel destroyed by fire in August. Bethlehem continued to receive rail service until the autumn of 1924, but the branch was abandoned in 1925. The tracks were removed the following year.

Sources: Crouch, "Narrow Gauge to the Notch"; Hilton, *American Narrow Gauge*, 445; Karr, *Lost Railroads*, 80, 81; Mead, *Up Country Line*; Wood, *Turnpikes*, 201-04.

72. Upper Coos

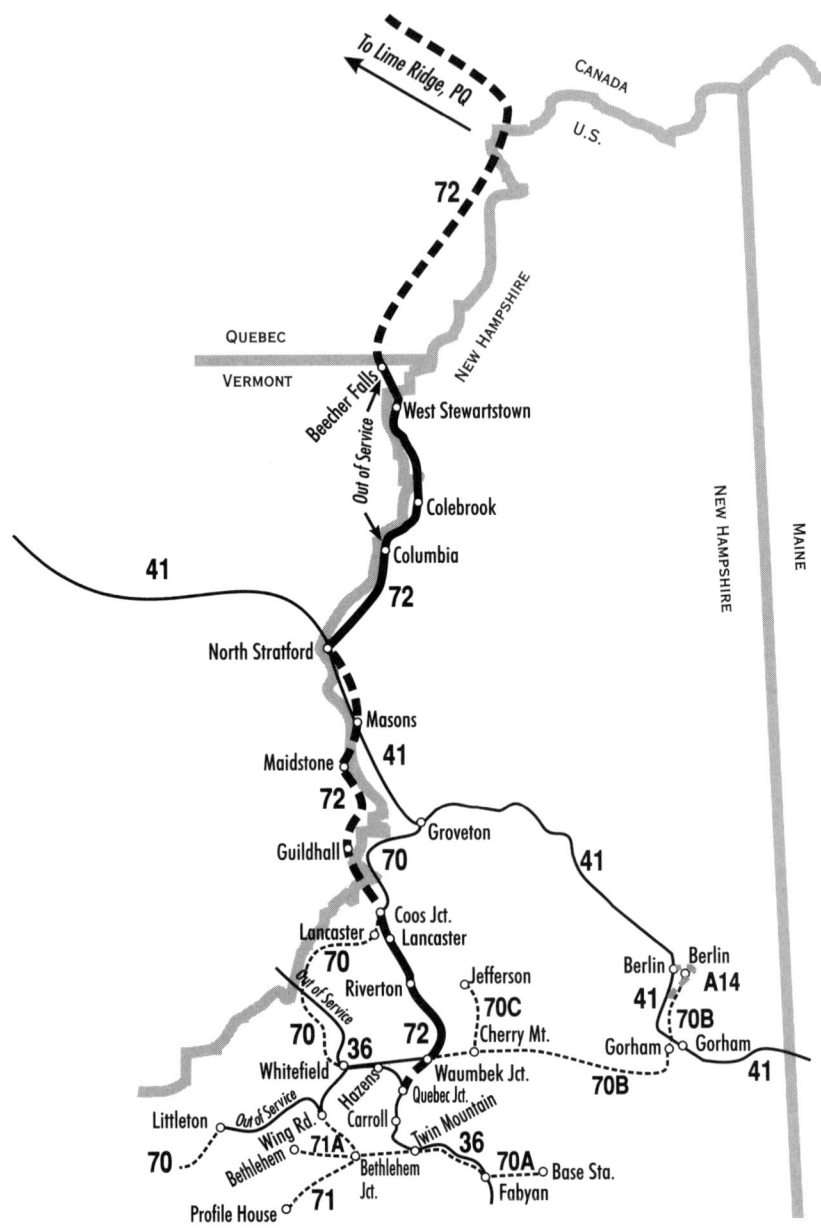

72. Upper Coos

0 Quebec Jct., NH	24.5 Maidstone, VT	51 Piper Hill
2.5 Waumbek Jct. (Jefferson Jct.)	27.5 Masons, NH	53.5 West Stewartstown, NH
	32.5 North Stratford Jct. (North Stratford)	55 Beecher Falls, VT
5 Baileys (Starr King) (Jefferson)		55.5 Hereford (Comins Mill) PQ
	35.5 Eatons	
8 Riverton	36 Georges	91 Cookshire Jct.
12 Lancaster	39 Cones (Columbia House)	104 Dudswell Jct.
13 Coos Jct. (C&M Jct.), NH	41.5 Columbia Bridge	108 Lime Ridge, PQ
18 Guildhall, VT	43.5 Columbia Valley	
20.5 Stevens	45.5 Colebrook	

Built: 1888-91.

Operators: *Upper Coos,* 1888-90; *Maine Central,* 1890-1981; *Guilford,* 1981-89; *North Stratford,* 1977-89; *New Hampshire & Vermont,* 1989-99; *New Hampshire Central,* 1993-.

Daily Passenger Trains: *1890:* 2 (North Stratford Jct.-Lime Ridge; plus 4 North Stratford Jct.-Beecher Falls); *1919:* 2 (plus 2 Quebec Jct.-Beecher Falls); *1933:* 2 (Lancaster Falls, mixed); *1943:* 2 (Lancaster-West Stewartstown). Passenger service ended north of Beecher Falls, 1925; Quebec Jct.-Lancaster, 1933; Lancaster-North Stratford, 1948; North Stratford-Beecher Falls, 1955.

Abandonments: Beecher Falls-Lime Ridge, 1925; Coos Jct.-North Stratford, 1948; Quebec Jct.-Waumbek Jct., 1977.

Associates of George Van Dyke promoted a trans-border railroad to link Van Dyke's extensive lumber holdings in Vermont and Quebec, as well as sawmills on the Connecticut River in both Vermont and Massachusetts, with the Boston, Concord & Montreal RR. Three charters were required in the United States and one act in Canada. The first charter was issued in Vermont on November 14, 1882, for the Coos Valley RR for a line just over 12 miles along the Connecticut River between Brunswick (north of where Maidstone station would be) and Guildhall. On August 28, 1883, New Hampshire granted a charter to the Upper Coos RR, enabling extension from Guildhall to Coos Jct., where it would connect with the BC&M (ex-White Mountains RR) just north of the BC&M station, then continue northward to Colebrook and on to West Stewartstown. A Canadian counterpart, the Hereford Branch RY, was incorporated on June 23, 1887—and reincorporated as Hereford RY on May 4, 1888—to

Looking south at Colebrook, NH, on a hot July day in 1999. The wait for a train will be a long one, since the New Hampshire Central no longer operates this far north. (R. D. Karr)

take the line on to Cookshire, PQ; Vermont issued a charter to another Upper Coos RR for just over one and a half miles of track in the remote area between Beecher Falls and the Canadian border to connect with the Hereford. Work commenced immediately. The Upper Coos operated its first trains between a Grand Trunk connection at North Stratford and West Stewartstown on September 15, 1888, although regular service did not commence until November.

Meanwhile, construction of the 34-mile Hereford RY was finished to Cookshire in December 1888, with regular service commencing in January 1889. After entering Canada the Hereford briefly recrossed into a remote area of New Hampshire, then swung back into Quebec. There were no stations or customers on this isolated 0.75-mile-long U.S. section. A connection with the Canadian Pacific RY was made at Dudswell in November, and Lime Ridge became the northern end of the line about six months later.

72. Upper Coos

Eventually, it was decided to extend the Upper Coos south from Coos Jct. to a junction with the Portland & Ogdensburg RR at what became Quebec Jct. in Carroll. The North Stratford-Coos Jct. section finally opened in late February 1891, and the length between Coos Jct. and Quebec Jct. in May. On May 1, 1890, the two Vermont corporations were leased to the Upper Coos of New Hampshire, which in turn was leased the same day to the Maine Central, along with the Hereford.

Traffic was almost entirely lumber and finished products from local mills, particularly products from a furniture manufacturer (later Ethan Allen) in Beecher Falls. As an international route, the line had small potential. By 1920 only two through passenger trains were operated, the 8:45 a.m. departure from Portland, which took four hours to reach Lime Ridge from Quebec Jct.—at an average speed of 27 mph—and an even slower return train.

In 1925 the MEC abrogated its lease of the Hereford RY and stopped operations on October 31. The company was acquired by the Canadian Pacific, which abandoned 14 miles of track north of the international border. The Upper Coos length in Vermont north of Beecher Falls closed in 1926. Mixed trains between Lancaster and Beecher Falls provided all remaining passenger service as of June 26, 1933; MEC passenger trains no longer ran south of Lancaster. In 1941, the B&M abandoned the former BC&M between Whitefield Jct. and Lancaster and began running trains to Groveton over the Berlin line to Waumbek Jct. and over the MEC/Upper Coos to Coos Jct., retaining the southward length to the depot in Lancaster as a spur.

Following lengthy negotiations the MEC acquired trackage rights over the B&M from Coos Jct. to Groveton and over the Grand Trunk to North Stratford. The last trains over the Upper Coos between Coos Jct. and North Stratford ran on December 31, 1948, and tracks were removed shortly thereafter.

In April 1955 the last remaining passenger service, the mixed train between North Stratford and Beecher Falls, ended. The Beecher Falls Manufacturing Co./Ethan Allen Furniture Co. was then served by just a daily MEC trip from Bartlett via Quebec Jct., conveying mainly pulpwood and furniture outbound, with small amounts of agricultural traffic inbound. Although trucks had taken most of the traffic, as in so many cases, flooding helped kill the line. Minor flood damage sustained in 1972 was repaired, but after storms in June and July 1973 the MEC embargoed the line above North Stratford and petitioned for abandonment on July 24, 1973. After a year of appeals, the railroad made repairs and resumed operation to Beecher Falls on November 19, 1974. In June 1976 the MEC finally obtained permission to abandon the line north of North Stratford, with the state of New Hampshire purchasing the right of way. The last MEC run was on February 17, 1977, and on March 23 a new short-haul operator, the North Stratford RR, began operating the Upper Coos between Waumbek Jct. and Beecher Falls. The track between Quebec Jct. and Waumbek Jct. was removed that year.

Despite an annual subsidy of $70,000, by 1986 the North Stratford operated only as required, and track maintenance was minimal. Poor track conditions led to the line being embargoed on March 9, 1989. By then, the company had just one full-time employee. Six months later the state agreed to closure.

The section of the Upper Coos between Waumbek Jct. and Coos Jct. was leased by the New Hampshire & Vermont RR on November 21, 1989, forming part of its route from Woodsville to Groveton, under a lease-purchase agreement with Guilford negotiated by CSF Acquisitions. Since the fall of 1999 the NH&VT has had no regular customers, but it still provides the only rail connection for the Conway Scenic RR at Hazens

On June 2, 1993, the line between North Stratford and Columbia was leased by the New Hampshire Central RR, primarily to serve gravel pits in Columbia. Traffic comprises mainly quarry products, lumber and salt. Just north of North Stratford, a modern maintenance facility was built, which overhauls rolling stock for several other short line operators.

Sources: Allen, "Maine Central in Northern New Hampshire"; ICC Finance Docket no. 28553; Jones, *Railroads of Vermont*, 2: 43–48, 149–51; Karr, *Lost Railroads*, 85, 109; Lewis, *American Shortline Railway Guide*, 180.

73. Canadian Pacific

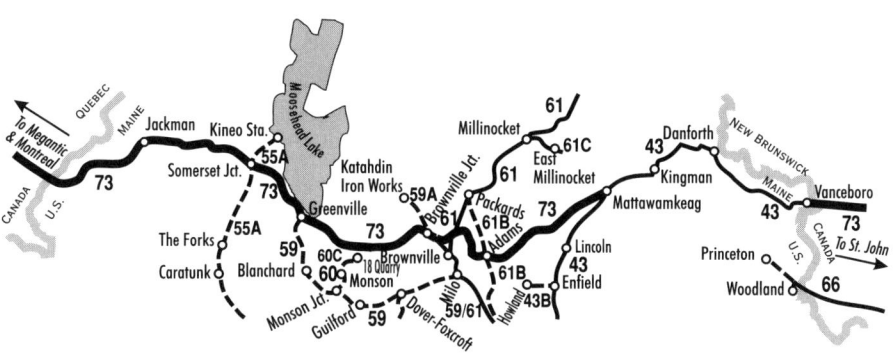

0 McAdam Jct., NB	120 Moores Camp	166 Mackamp
6 Vanceboro, ME	123 Onawa	170 Long Pond
62 Mattawamkeag	126 Bodfish	175 Blair
63 Kirby	127 Camp 12	179 Jackman
66 Craigville	132 Morkill	182 Attean Landing
69.5 Chester (Pea Ridge)	136 Kyleton	184 Attean
75.5 Woodard	139 Greenville (Greenville Jct.)	187 Elmer
79.5 Gilford		190 Boston Ranch
83.5 Seboois	142 Harfords Point	191 Holeb
90 Hardy Point	143 Squaw Brook	198 Keough
95.5 Lake View	149 Moosehead	200 Skinner
100 Knights	154 Somerset (Somerset Jct.)	203 Lowelltown, ME
105 Brownville Jct.	157 Tarratine	*207 Boundary, PQ*
109 Williamsburg	158 Askwith	*222 Megantic, PQ*
114 Barnard	161 Brassua	
118 Benson	162 Brassua Sta.	

Built: 1875–89.

Operators: *Canadian Pacific*, 1885–1988; *Canadian Atlantic*, 1988–95; *Canadian American*, 1995– (Megantic-Brownville); *Eastern Maine*, 1995– (Brownville–McAdam Jct.).

Daily Passenger Trains: *1892:* 2; *1920:* 4; *1933:* 4; *1939:* 4; *1956:* 2; *1960:* (3 days weekly); *1968:* 2; *1980:* 2. Passenger service ended 1982; restored, 1985–94.

Abandonments: None.

73. Canadian Pacific

On February 15, 1881, royal assent was given to a Canadian government bill which authorized the Canadian Pacific RY to construct a trans-continental line "to any point at navigable water on the Atlantic seaboard." In spring 1883 the Canadian parliament had awarded the CP an annual cash subsidy of $186,000 for twenty years to meet interest on construction capital. George Stephen (later Baron Mount Stephen), chairman of the CP, considered locating the line's Atlantic terminal in Portland, and visited there in October 1883, but abandoned this idea when the Maritime provinces protested.

The CP purchased two lines in Quebec, diverted another, and decided on St. John, NB, as its terminal. It would reach the Maritime provinces by way of two intermediate sections across Maine: from Megantic to Mattawamkeag, a line chartered in 1883 as the International RY of Maine; and from there to Vanceboro via trackage rights over the European & North American (operated by the Maine Central). From Vanceboro to St. John, trackage rights were obtained over two Canadian lines, the St. John & Maine (former E&NA RY) and the St. John Bridge & Railway Extension Co. of 1885. Both lines had been leased to the New Brunswick RY, in which Stephen had had a lengthy personal interest. Canada's prime minister, Sir John A. Macdonald, also offered trackage rights over the Intercolonial RY between St. John and Halifax.

The mileage of the CP between Montreal and the Maritimes was considerably less than the rival Intercolonial's, so it became known as the "Short Line." Construction contracts were awarded in autumn 1883, and work between Megantic and Boundary was completed in 1885 and beyond to Holeb in 1886, although this section was not used until mid-September 1888 when the line was finished as far as Greenville. Construction of two major trestles east of Greenville across Wilson Stream and a 1200-foot structure 130 feet above low water across Ship Stream in Onawa, as well as the stabilization of bogs east of Schoodic Lake, delayed overall completion of the line; the last rail was not laid at Packards Brook, about 12 miles east of Brownville, until December 10, 1888. A formal opening ceremony was held on June 2, 1889.

A mixed train, known as the "Scoot," was operated between Megantic and Brownville Jct. from opening; two express trains, the *Eastern* and the *Western*, were introduced in 1893. On January 1,

In July 1999 a Canadian American freight eastbound for Brownville emerges from the twilight near Greenville, ME. (R. D. Karr)

With Alco/MLW RS-3s in the lead, a Canadian Pacific freight crosses Onawa Trestle in August 1959. (Russell F. Munroe, courtesy Walker Transportation Collection, Beverly Historical Society & Museum)

1912, the CP leased the Dominion Atlantic RY in Nova Scotia, which included the Yarmouth steamer service across the Bay of Fundy, and accelerated trans-Atlantic steamer sailings run first by the Allan Line and then by the White Star Line, whose fortunes sank with the *Titanic* in April 1912.

By the 1930s the Short Line had lost many connections. Two round-trip passenger trains, operated overnight, continued until about 1955. The *Atlantic Limited* was introduced in 1956 between Montreal and St. John. Diesel traction did not appear until mid-1958, and steam locomotives continued in use until 1960. Owing to remoteness of many communities it served, the mixed "Scoot" continued to run between Brownville and Holeb, even during strikes in 1950 and 1957, until around 1968, when it became a freight-only train. The CP bought the former E&NA line east of Mattawamkeag to Vanceboro from the MEC in 1974, although the latter retained trackage rights.

VIA Rail Canada was formally incorporated on January 12, 1977, as a subsidiary of the CN, and took over CP passenger staff and rolling stock on September 29, 1978. VIA operated the line's last passenger

73. Canadian Pacific

train, the *Atlantic Limited*, between Montreal and the Maritimes until June 1, 1982, then revived it in 1985. The train survived until December 17, 1994, when it was once more terminated, this time apparently for good. This marked the end of scheduled passenger train service in Maine, apart from excursions.

After rejection of a proposal to abandon, the CP set up the Canadian Atlantic RY on September 1, 1988, to take over all lines east of Megantic. Despite initial enthusiasm, the rail unions would not accept the relaxation of work rules and reduction in wages deemed necessary by management until 1992.

In November 1994, while a second petition to abandon was under consideration, Iron Road Railways, which was negotiating the purchase of the Bangor & Aroostook, agreed to buy the Canadian Atlantic between Brownville Jct. and Sherbrooke, PQ. At about the same time J. D. Irving, a Canadian oil company, bought the line east of

Two Canadian Pacific freights meet on an icy winter's day at Jackman, ME, in February 1963. (Alan L. Thomas, courtesy Walker Transportation Collection, Beverly Historical Society & Museum)

Brownville Jct. Iron Road completed its deal in March 1995 at the same time as it acquired the BAR, and operated the line west of Brownville Jct. as the Canadian American RR, integrating its operations with the BAR. Irving set up two subsidiaries to operate its lines, the Eastern Maine RY for the tracks in the U.S. and the New Brunswick Southern RY for the portion in Canada.

Sources: Booth, *Railways of Southern Quebec*; Dorman, *Statutory History*; Drury, *Train-Watcher's Guide*, 232-34; Lamb, *History of the Canadian Pacific*; Macdonald Papers; Nett, "Canadian Pacific's Maine Line."

74. Orford Mountain

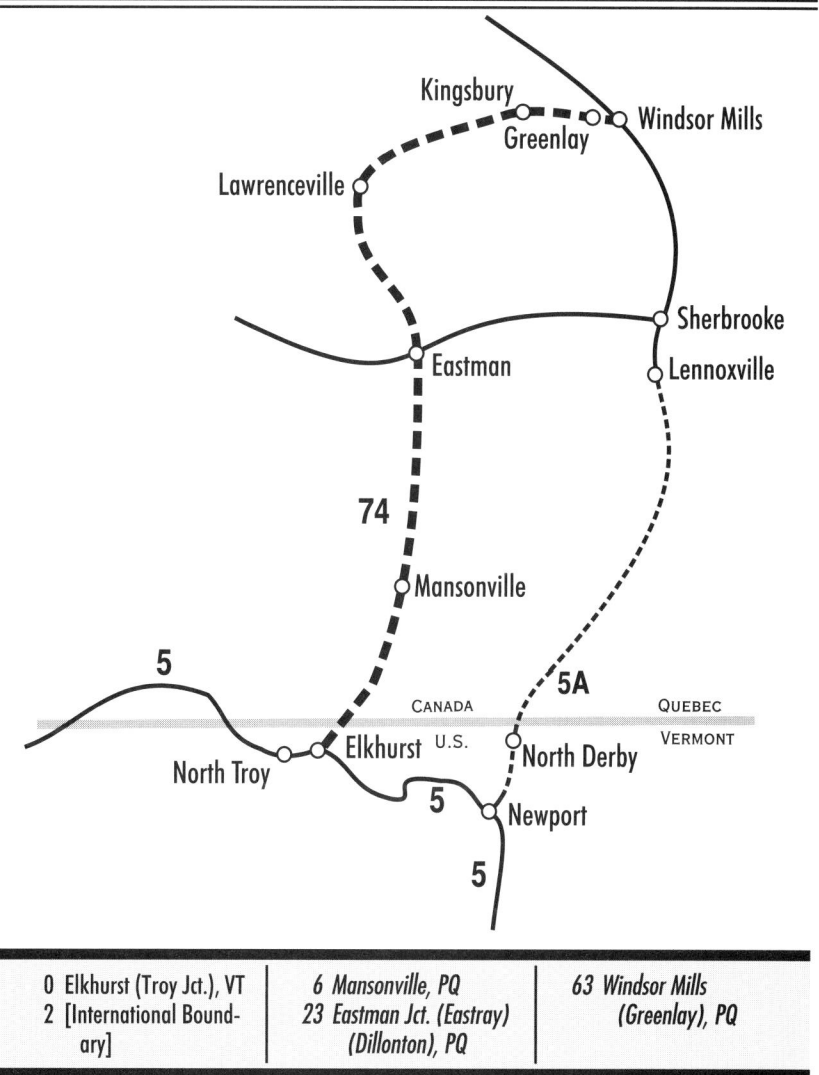

| 0 Elkhurst (Troy Jct.), VT
2 [International Boundary] | 6 Mansonville, PQ
23 Eastman Jct. (Eastray)
(Dillonton), PQ | 63 Windsor Mills
(Greenlay), PQ |

Built: 1889–1910.

Operators: *Orford Mountain*, 1889–1910; *Canadian Pacific*, 1910–65.

Daily Passenger Trains: *1910:* 4; *1916:* 2; *1931:* 2.

Abandonments: Elkhurst–Eastman Jct.,1936; Canadian segments in 1941, 1946, and 1965 (see text).

On July 12, 1888, the Orford Mountain RY was chartered to build a line between the Quebec towns of Eastman and Lawrenceville, utilizing previously graded land and structures from the former Missisquoi Valley RY, a defunct line which had sought to develop the Missisquoi and Black Rivers area of eastern Quebec. The backers of the Orford Mountain hoped the Canadian Pacific would quickly buy them out. Work began in late 1889, and the ten-mile line was completed on October 31, 1891. The last spike was driven on a 16-mile extension from Lawrenceville to Kingsbury on December 1, 1893. The company recorded a profit of just $11 for the year ended June 30, 1894.

In October 1905 the line was extended another ten miles to Greenlay, a village on the St. Francis River opposite Windsor Mills, PQ, on the Grand Trunk RY. Less than two years later the OM began building a southward extension from Eastman through Mansonville, to link with the CP's South Eastern RY at North Troy, VT. Optimism was soon overcome by financial plight, and on January 10, 1910, the OM was leased by the CP, on condition that the southern extension be completed. The CP established a subsidiary, the Midland Railway Company of Vermont, to extend the line south across the border to North Troy. Work started immediately, and the line was finished in the summer of 1910. The connection was made in North Troy at a point 0.6 miles eastward of the CP station known as Elkhurst or Troy Jct., and CP passenger trains from Windsor Mills terminated at the North Troy depot.

The Vermont connection survived on minimal traffic for just over a quarter century. It was virtually useless as a through route. With no traffic to and from intermediate locations, the Midland was the first part of the Orford Mountain to close, along with the length to Eastman, on April 1, 1936. The section from Kingsbury to Greenlay shut down on December 23, 1941, followed on December 15, 1949, by a 12.7-mile section from Valcourt to Kingsbury. The remaining 14 miles between Eastman and Kingsbury were abandoned on April 30, 1965.

Sources: Booth, *Railways of Southern Quebec*, 1: 110; 2: 74, 79, 80; Dorman, *Statutory History*; Jones, *Railroads of Vermont*, 1: 159; Lamb, *History of the Canadian Pacific*, 97.

75. Lamoille Valley Extension

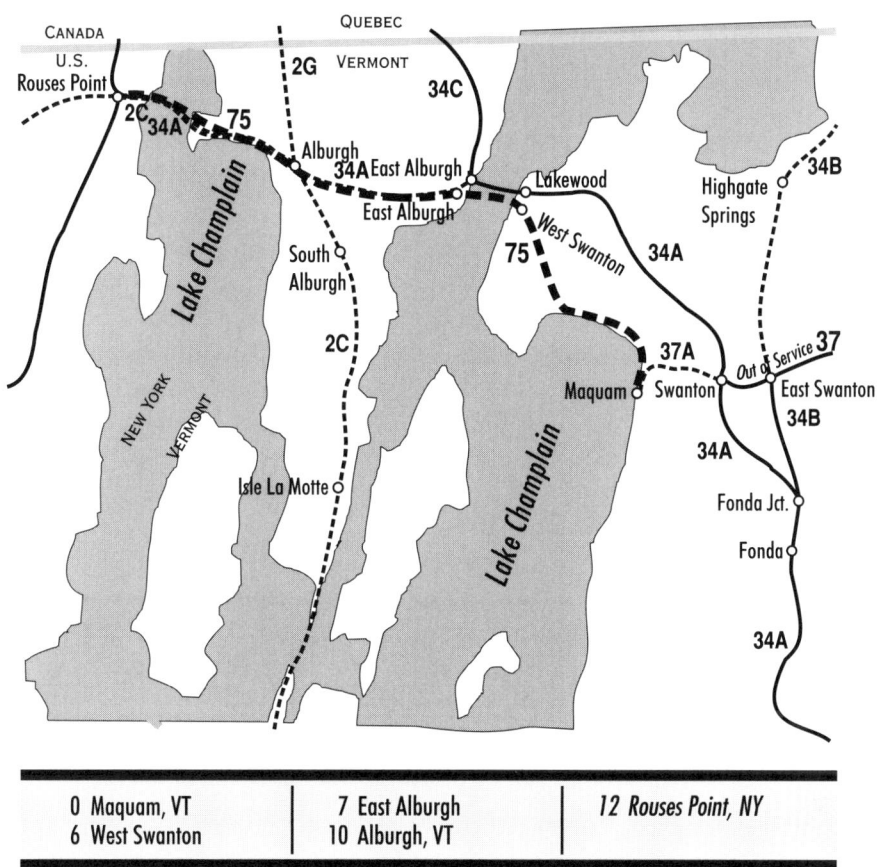

| 0 Maquam, VT | 7 East Alburgh | 12 Rouses Point, NY |
| 6 West Swanton | 10 Alburgh, VT | |

Built: 1883–84.
Operators: *Ogdensburg & Lake Champlain*, 1883–84.
Daily Passenger Trains: None.
Abandonment: 1888.

A charter was obtained on October 25, 1872, by Horace Fairbanks and nine other directors of the Ogdensburg & Lake Champlain RR for a connecting line between the O&LC at Rouses Point, NY, and the proposed Portland & Ogdensburg RR, then under construction to Swanton, VT. At the time, however, the OL&C was under lease to the Vermont Central (succeeded by the Central Vermont in 1873), which did not want competition with its own line to Rouses Point.

Shortly after the P&O opened in 1877, the Vermont portion was placed in receivership and reorganized as the St. Johnsbury & Lake Champlain RR, and financial problems caused the CV to relinquish its lease of the O&LC. William H. Vanderbilt of the New York Central helped provide money to expand the O&LC. In 1880 the SJ&LC completed a line from Swanton to Maquam to connect with the proposed LVE, and grading of the line from Maquam to Rouses Point finally began on February 28, 1883. Work across mainly flat farm country and swampland included a trestle at East Alburgh across the confluence of Missisquoi Bay and Lake Champlain and another over the main channel of the lake between West Alburgh and Rouses Point. West of the village of Alburgh, a grade crossing of the CV line was required. Trains were operated by the O&LC from November 27, 1883, although regular service did not commence until New Year's day. The O&LC took a formal lease of the LVE.

Incensed by this competitive threat, the CV surreptitiously acquired a controlling interest in the O&LC by the summer of 1884; at the O&LC annual general meeting on June 18 the directors were replaced by a new board controlled by the CV. At the next board meeting on July 1, the Ogdensburg & Lake Champlain canceled its lease of the LVE, which brought about immediate closure of the line. In order to prevent revival by either the St. Johnsbury & Lake Champlain or Rutland, the CV moved to tear up the tracks of the LVE, although work was delayed by a court injunction on grounds that the CV could not petition for abandonment of a line that it did not own. The CV therefore purchased the stock of the LVE, and the company was absorbed on December 7, 1887, enabling abandonment of the unused line early in 1888. Dismantling took even less time than construction. Surprisingly, a great deal of the LVE can be traced today.

Sources: Gardner and More, "Lamoille Valley Extension"; Jones, *Central Vermont*; Jones, *Railroads of Vermont*, 2: 225–26; Karr, *Lost Railroads*, 74–75.

76. Aroostook Valley

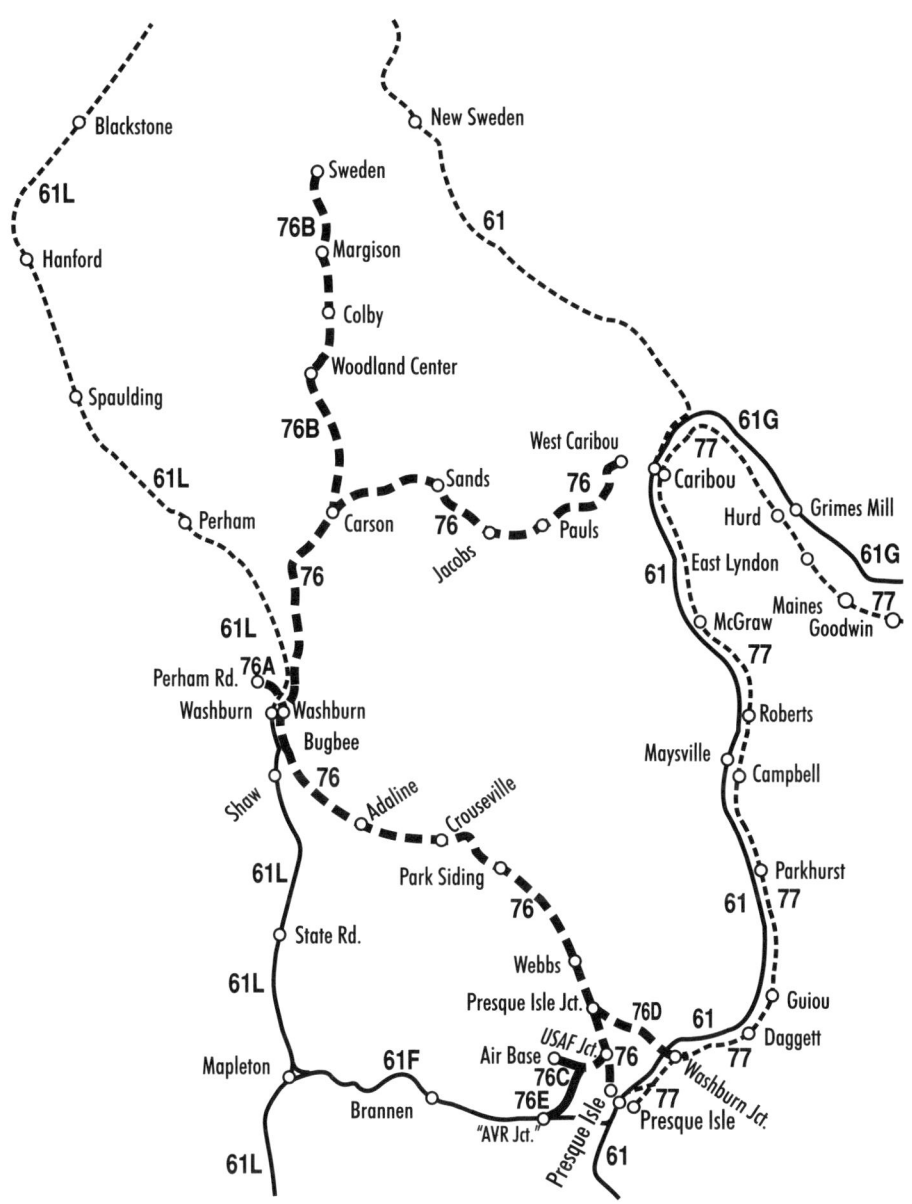

76. Aroostook Valley

0 Presque Isle, ME	76A. Wade Branch	76C. USAF (Skyway) Branch
0.5 West Presque Isle (Dyer St.)	0 Washburn, ME	0 USAF Jct. (Skyway Jct.), ME
1 USAF Jct. (Skyway Jct.)	0.5 Perham Rd., ME	1 "BAR Jct."
2 Presque Isle Jct.		2 Air Base (Skyway Industrial Park), ME
3 Webbs	76B. Sweden Branch	
5.5 Park Siding	0 Carson, ME	
7 Crouseville	3.5 Woodland Center	76D. CP Branch
8.5 Adaline	4.5 Colby	
12 Bugbee	6 Margison (Margison Crossroad)	0 Presque Isle Jct., ME
13 Washburn		2 Washburn Jct., ME
17 Carson	7.5 Sweden (Sweden Siding), ME	
19 Sands		76E. BAR Connection
21 Jacobs		
23 Pauls		0 "BAR Jct.," ME
24 West Caribou, ME		2 "AVR Jct.," ME

Built: 1909-12; Wade Branch, CP Branch, 1910; Sweden Branch, 1911-12; USAF Branch, 1941; BAR Connection, 1992.

Operators: *Aroostook Valley*, 1910-96; *Bangor & Aroostook*, 1996-.

Daily Passenger Trains: *1910:* 22 (Presque Isle-Washburn); *1916:* 8 (Presque Isle-Sweden, 4); *1928:* 8 (Carson-Sweden, 6); *1939:* 6. Passenger service ended 1946.

Abandonments: Presque Isle (Dyer St.) terminal, 1946; Carson-Sweden, 1978; Wade Branch, before 1984; Park Siding-West Caribou, 1987; Presque Isle Jct.-Presque Isle (Dyer St.), 1993; Presque Isle Jct.-Washburn Jct., 1993.

Presque Isle was served by an extension of the Canadian-backed Aroostook River RR from 1881, but not until 1894 was an outlet available to the domestic U.S. system via the Bangor & Aroostook RR. Meanwhile lumber and paper interests led by Arthur R. Gould had leased large forested tracts around Washburn and promoted a line to serve them. They submitted articles of association for the Aroostook Valley RR to the Maine Railroad Commissioners on June 24, 1902, for a largely street-running electric line. Despite objections from the BAR that the proposed line infringed on its 15-mile-wide corridor rights, a charter was granted on July 1, and the AVR was incorporated the next day; a branch from Washburn to Wade was also approved. A suit brought by the BAR delayed surveys, but an align-

76. Aroostook Valley

ment was approved on May 6, 1903. Junctions were to be provided with the BAR and the Aroostook River RR. The municipalities of Presque Isle and Washburn were significant shareholders, and the Canadian Pacific, lessor of the Aroostook River, guaranteed AVR bonds. Construction from Presque Isle to Washburn began in the spring of 1909.

The line was mainly single track with six intermediate passing loops, equipped with trolley wire supplied at 1200V d.c. from a hydroelectric generating plant (owned by Gould) at Aroostook Falls, through a substation at Mason Hill in Washburn. A car shed was provided at West Presque Isle. Two 46-foot Brill passenger cars were acquired. With repeated changes to the alignment, all but 0.75 miles in Washburn, along Presque Isle Street, were in private rights of way. Grades were easy and generally favored the heavier southbound trains. A junction was built with the Aroostook River yard in Presque Isle, but only transfer sidings were provided at each end with the BAR. The line officially opened on July 1, 1910, and shortly after, 0.9 miles of the proposed Wade Branch were completed to a gravel pit.

When an application was filed in 1911 to extend from Washburn to Sweden (located within the town of New Sweden), the BAR objected as a matter of course, but was overruled. Ease of construction enabled scheduled services to commence on December 9. The remainder was completed January 25, 1912. Some months later, the AVR petitioned to extend from Carson to Caribou. On June 29 approval was again granted despite BAR objection. Upon completion, the 24 miles from West Presque Isle to Caribou became the main line, and the Carson–Sweden length became a branch, although initially through trains were provided from Presque Isle to both Caribou and Sweden.

For expanded passenger operations two 56-foot cars were purchased from Wason; six rigid-frame two-axle open cars were also obtained from the Boston Elevated RY to meet summer demand. One freight train operated each weekday over the entire system. Outbound traffic comprised principally potatoes, starch, lumber, and hay; inbound, the line conveyed significant quantities of grain, flour, fertilizer, and other traffic. Packages and parcels were carried by an express car and also in passenger car baggage compartments. At more than $60,000, annual freight revenues generally amounted to double that of passenger receipts.

Aroostook Valley electric car no. 71 crosses the Aroostook River in 1930. (George E. Cantara, courtesy Walker Transportation Collection, Beverly Historical Society & Museum)

Apart from construction of several spurs serving warehouses, the AVR had reached its full extent by 1916. Gould, however, promoted a separate company, the Quebec Extension RR, to build from Washburn westward to Lac Frontière on the Canadian border. This grandiose scheme, estimated to cost around $5 million, failed to gain approval of the Railroad Commissioners despite a substantial sum pledged by London bankers through the CP. Gould sold his controlling interest in the AVR upon entering the U.S. Senate on November 1, 1926, but became president of the company, which position he retained until his death in July 1946.

When the BAR monopoly ended in the early 1920s the AVR built a direct connection with the BAR at Washburn and the street-running section was diverted westward to a private right of way. A branch in Presque Isle to the U.S. Air Force base northwest of the city center was completed in November 1941.

76. Aroostook Valley

In July 1945 two new GE 44-ton diesel-electrics were introduced to replace two electric locomotives dating from the opening of the main line. A third locomotive came in June 1946, but passenger cars were withdrawn on August 7 and replaced by busses. Electric traction equipment was subsequently dismantled. The city of Presque Isle bought the land occupied by the BAR interchange sidings and the river crossing, converted the former to a parking lot, and removed the bridge superstructure.

Careful economic management sustained the company for over 20 years, but its mainstay traffic—potatoes—was eroded by truck competition and by increased production in the western states, particularly Idaho. Some years after World War II much of the Presque Isle air base became the Northern Maine Regional Airport, and a major part became the Skyway Industrial Park. The park eventually provided the majority of AVR traffic. By 1978, however, declining returns led to the closure of the Sweden branch. In 1980 the Arbox III Corporation, a subsidiary of the freight car leasing company TTX, acquired control of the railroad. The new owners closed the main line north of Park Siding through Washburn to West Caribou in February 1982. Flooding of the St. John River in spring 1987 damaged the CP bridge at Perth-Andover, NB, and CP service to Presque Isle ceased.

To maintain an outlet to the main line network, the BAR installed a short connection with the CP sidings in Presque Isle, enabling the AVR to reach the BAR by way of the ex-CP track between Washburn Jct. and Presque Isle. In 1992 the AVR built a new connection from the Skyway Industrial Park to the BAR's Mapleton Branch, which enabled it in 1993 to close and abandon the line between Presque Isle Jct. and Washburn Jct. Despite Presque Isle's promotion of the industrial park's multimodal facilities, the AVR was unable to sustain interchange traffic. When all remaining operations on the AVR ceased in May 1996, the outer part of the Skyway Branch and the new BAR connection, both now operated by the BAR, became the only surviving portions of the AVR.

Sources: Day, *Aroostook Valley Railroad*; Heseltine and Robertson, *Aroostook Valley Railroad*; Melvin, "Aroostok Valley Railroad"; Karr, *Lost Railroads*, 135, 142, 154; Lewis, *American Shortline Railroad Guide*, 24.

77. Aroostook River

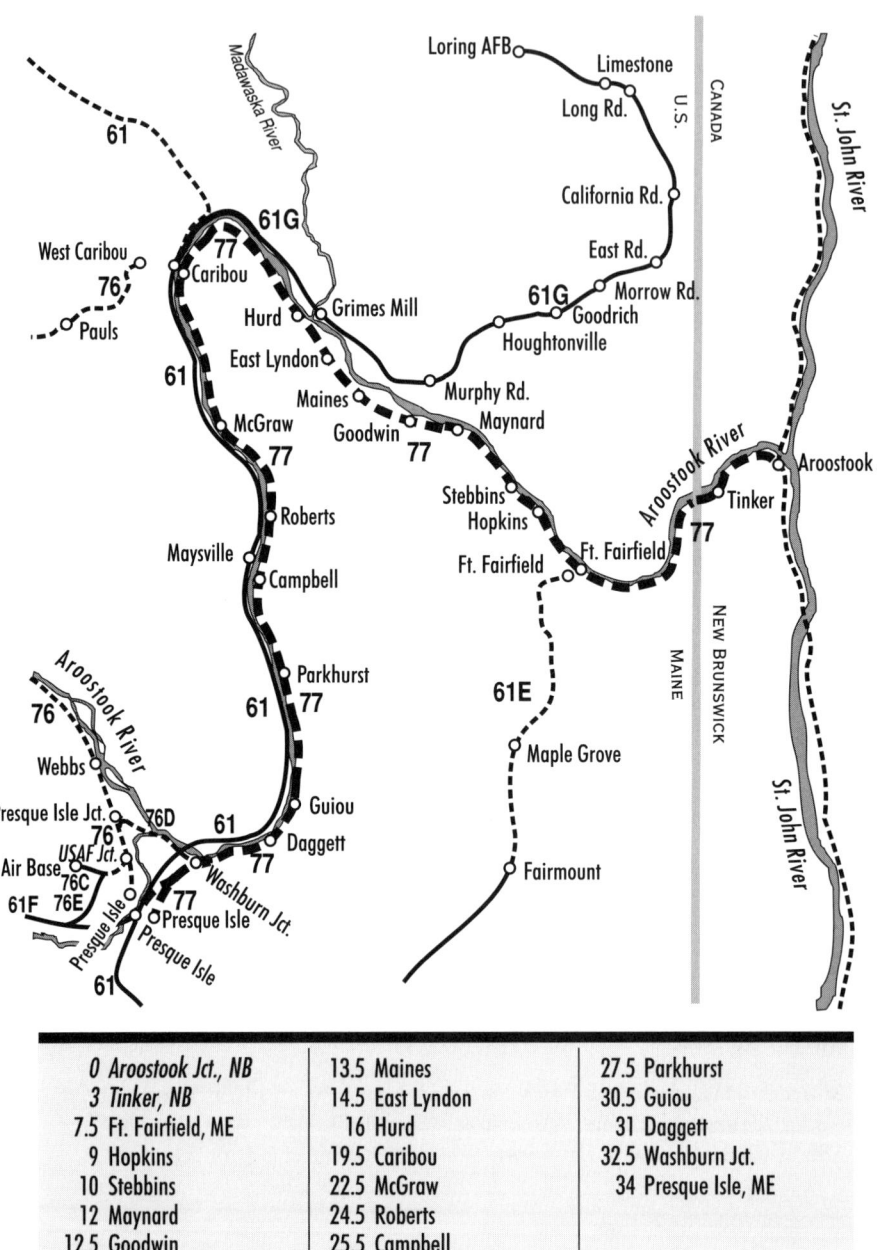

0 Aroostook Jct., NB	13.5 Maines	27.5 Parkhurst
3 Tinker, NB	14.5 East Lyndon	30.5 Guiou
7.5 Ft. Fairfield, ME	16 Hurd	31 Daggett
9 Hopkins	19.5 Caribou	32.5 Washburn Jct.
10 Stebbins	22.5 McGraw	34 Presque Isle, ME
12 Maynard	24.5 Roberts	
12.5 Goodwin	25.5 Campbell	

77. Aroostook River

Built: 1874–81.
Operators: *New Brunswick*, 1875–90; *Canadian Pacific*, 1890–1987; *Aroostook Valley,* ca. 1989–92.
Daily Passenger Trains: *1893:* 4; *1916:* 4; *1931:* 2; *1936:* 2; *1938:* 2. Passenger service ended ca.1940.
Abandonment: 1989 (Washburn Jct.–Presque Isle operated by Aroostook Valley RR, ca. 1989–92).

A charter was granted in 1870 to the New Brunswick RY to build a line between Gibson, NB, opposite Fredericton on the St. John River, to Rivière-du-Loup on the St. Lawrence River in Quebec. It managed construction of 64 miles of railroad as far as Woodstock using 3-foot-6-inch-gauge track in 1873 and another 100 miles to Edmundston opposite Madawaska, ME, in 1878. Its principal traffic was lumber. In 1874 the company resolved to build a branch to Ft. Fairfield in northeastern Maine to exploit the rich potential for softwood traffic. A subsidiary was chartered and incorporated in Maine as the Aroostook River RR. Work was completed in 1875 from Aroostook Jct., southeast of Four Falls, NB, along the Aroostook River to Ft. Fairfield, ME, and it was extended to Caribou the following year. Further extension to Presque Isle had to wait until the AR widened its line to standard gauge in 1881. The Canadian Pacific RY leased the New Brunswick RY and its AR subsidiary in 1890. The Bangor & Aroostook RR, which had arrived in Presque Isle in 1894, continued in a parallel line along the other side of the Aroostook River to Caribou.

From 1910 traffic was exchanged with the Aroostook Valley RR, which had built a two-mile link to the AR at Washburn Jct. Principal traffic became potatoes, other agricultural staples, and miscellaneous goods. Passenger service declined over time, and had ended by the time the U.S. entered World War II.

By the 1980s the line had become a marginal operation, and when the bridge over the St. John River was washed out in the spring of 1987 the line closed. To maintain interchange with the Aroostook Valley, the BAR built a short spur to the AR yard in Presque Isle, facilitating ICC approval of abandonment of the AR in 1989.

Sources: Heseltine and Robertson, *Aroostook Valley Railroad*, 20, 62; Hilton, *American Narrow Gauge*, 407; Lavallee, *Narrow Gauge Railways*, 18–19, 95; Karr, *Lost Railroads*, 151.

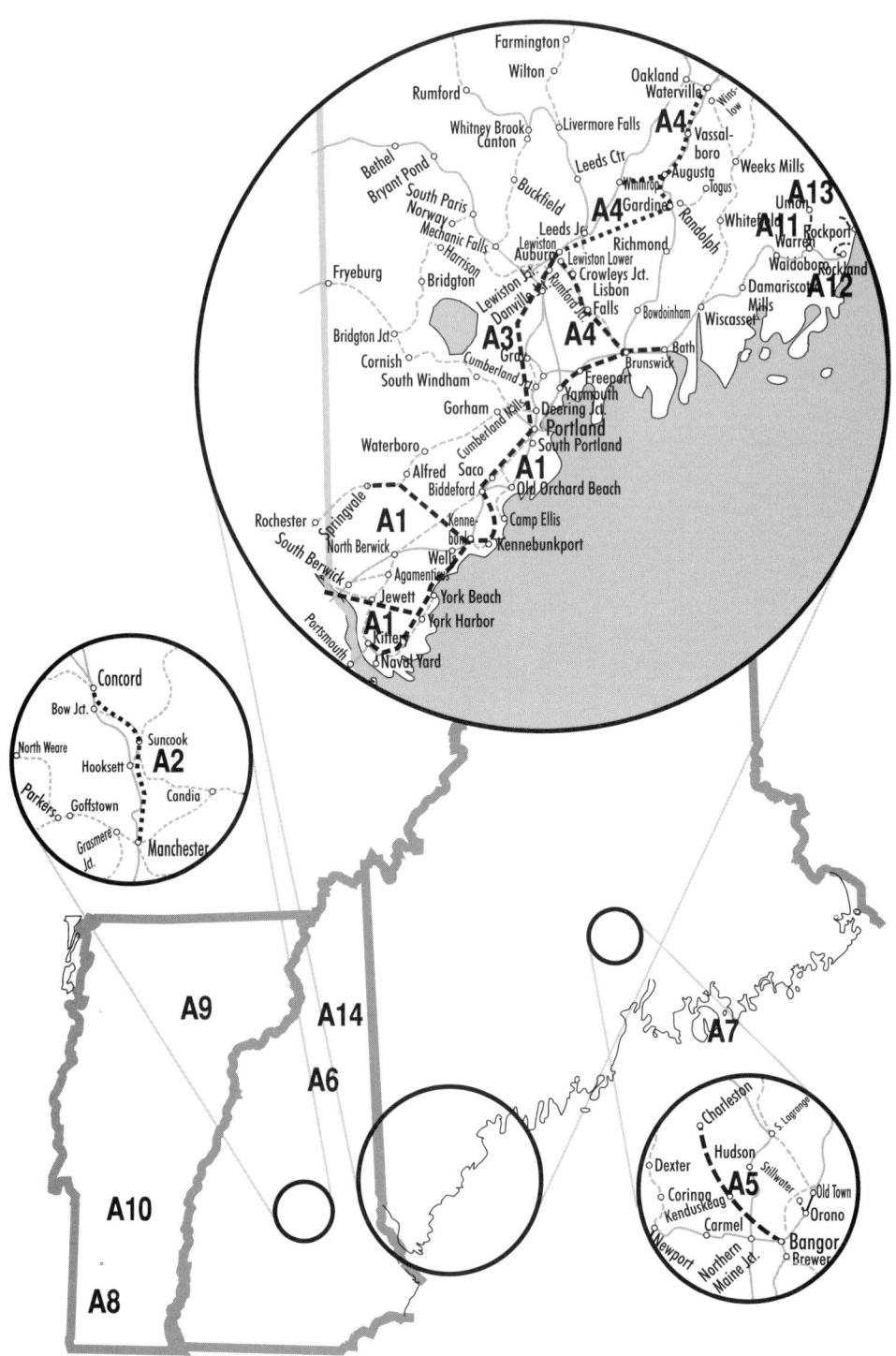

Appendix
Other Lines

In addition to the dense network of common carrier railroads in northern New England, cheap hydroelectric power from its abundant rivers and large supplies of lumber and stone contributed to this region becoming home to a large number of streetcar systems and scores of independent logging, quarry, and industrial railroads. Although small independent railroads occasionally were chartered as common carriers to ease their approval by regulatory bodies, most never operated advertised passenger trains.

Most electric lines were built primarily to carry passengers, but several became interurban lines or were constructed to convey parcels and less-than-carload traffic. Some exchanged freight cars with main lines. The most important interurban lines are described in this appendix, together with two cog mountain lines built in the region, a few of the more interesting non-logging industrial railroads, and one unusual Vermont logging line. The numerous other logging lines are fully described by C. Francis Belcher in his *Logging Railroads of the White Mountains* (1980) and Douglas M. Rice in *Log and Lumber Railroads of New England* (1982).

A1. Atlantic Shore Line

Built: 1893–1923.
Operated: 1893–1949.

By the turn of the century, several trolley lines in greater Portland had combined to form the Portland RR Co. with ambitions of serving communities to the south. A line reached Saco from South Portland in July

1902, and a branch from it to Old Orchard Beach opened in June 1903. During 1900, the Atlantic Shore Line RY was incorporated to create an interurban link to the Boston & Maine RR west of the region. It began with construction of a line from Biddeford south to Kennebunk in 1904, and was extended through Wells to York Beach in 1907, where connection was made with the Portsmouth, Dover & York Beach RY, a line completed in 1903 and merged into the ASL in 1906. Other cross country lines, largely rural, were built. One ran from Cape Porpoise on the coast northeast of Kennebunkport through Arundel and Kennebunk to Springvale on the Mousam River; another ran from Kittery to South Berwick, connecting with the local system in Dover, NH.

By 1907, most of these companies had been merged into the ASL, which sought to increase interchange car load traffic with the B&M. Sidings were built with the B&M's Worcester, Nashua & Portland line at Springvale, and a ferry service was operated between Kittery and Portsmouth. In 1910 the ASL failed and was reincorporated on January 1, 1911, as the Atlantic Shore RY. Operation continued in receivership until takeover by York Utilities Corporation in 1922. The new owner's first act was to introduce a new largely passenger alignment through Sanford to Springvale to ease congestion on the former main line.

Changes were costly and came too late. Passenger demand had declined because of bus competition and much of the seasonal traffic on the coastal routes was lost to the automobile. Operation between Kennebunk and York Beach ended in 1924, and during the next year tracks between Town House, Kennebunkport, and Cape Porpoise carried their last cars. By the end of 1927, cars operated only between Sanford and Springvale. They survived another twenty years until 1947, when passenger cars were replaced by bus service and the remaining 2.2 miles of line became, in effect, an industrial spur. In 1949 Samuel M. Pinsly bought the spur along with the B&M's WN&P line under the ægis of the Sanford & Eastern RR, converted it to diesel power, and removed the electric traction equipment. The branch provided the S&E with its primary shipper, the Goodall-Sanford mills. When they closed in 1961, the track was abandoned.

Sources: Cummings, *Atlantic Shore Line*; Hilton and Due, *Electric Interurban Railways*, 323; Robertson, *Remember the Portland Trolleys*, 11.

Appendix: Other Lines 363

A2. Concord & Manchester Electric Branch (B&M)

Built: 1901-02.
Operated: 1902-33.

In addition to the Springfield Terminal RY, the Boston & Maine took another foray into the electric traction business in 1901, with a 17-mile line between the growing industrial cities of Concord and Manchester. Intended to obviate potential competition, the Concord & Manchester Electric Branch was constructed generally in accordance with main line standards, although there were several short gradients of up to 10 percent. Some sections were in private rights of way. An unusual feature was that the line shared the covered bridge across the Merrimack River with the single-track Suncook Valley branch. Passenger cars were equipped for multiple-unit control on the Sprague system, although this was rarely used.

The line opened on August 11, 1902. By 1903 the B&M had acquired the Concord Street RY and merged it with the C&M, and by the 1920s most traffic was generated by the Concord city network. Busses, the automobile, and the Great Depression all took their toll. Indeed, the B&M replaced the system with busses and a local parcel delivery system. Last cars ran on Friday, April 29, 1933.

Sources: Cummings, *Capital City Streetcar Days;* Cummings, *Granite State Interurban*; Hilton and Due, *Electric Interurban Railways* 324.

A3. Portland-Lewiston Interurban

Built: 1910-14.
Operated: 1914-33.

Industrial growth in Auburn and Lewiston, twin cities astride the Androscoggin River, prompted promotion of a high speed electric line to Portland, chartered and organized in 1907 as the Portland, Gray & Lewiston RR from the MEC in Portland through West Falmouth, Gray, and New Gloucester. It was not a promising venture. Work began in 1910 only after W. Scott Libbey and Henry M. Dingley, who had interests in the Lewiston & Auburn Electric Light Co., took over and personally guaranteed financing. The line was not completed until 1914, by which time Libbey had passed away, and the Androscoggin Electric Co., as successors to the L&AELC, took over and renamed it the Portland–Lewiston Interurban RR. On completion, the MEC promptly removed connections at both ends and refused to interchange freight.

The line was built to classic interurban electric railway standards, with its own 50-foot private right of way. Although initial operations comprised mostly express service, with stops only at the more important road intersections, an order issued in 1915 by the Maine Public Utilities Commission required the company to operate more local cars. Limited trains were allowed 80 minutes in the timetable, an average speed of about 23 mph; locals were allowed an additional 20 minutes. Trains were never mixed; freight was hauled by separate box motor cars. The company was among the first to use a contact wire shoe, beginning in 1917, and it adopted the air horn in 1931 to replace whistles.

Losses were recorded from 1931 on. Despite economy measures, a decision to close the line was made two years later. Final trains ran on June 29, 1933, the nineteenth anniversary of opening.

Sources: Cummings, "Portland–Lewiston Interurban"; Hilton and Due, *Electric Interurban Railways*, 319–20.

A4. Lewiston, Augusta & Waterville Street RY

Built: 1897–1905.
Operated: 1898–1940.

Lewiston and Auburn shared economic growth based on production of textiles and leather goods but were linked by mediocre roads until the advent of streetcar systems in the first decade of the twentieth century. On April 3, 1907, an unbuilt electric line, the Auburn, Mechanic Falls & Norway Street RY was renamed the Lewiston, Augusta & Waterville Street RY. By 1910 the LA&W owned or controlled a network of street railways that connected Lewiston with Waterville, Augusta, Brunswick, Bath, and Yarmouth, where it met the Portland streetcar system.

Less-than-carload traffic was conveyed, with some interchange to and from coastal steamers. Individual freight cars were also handled over short distances from spurs to the Maine Central at various locations. The rapid pace of acquisition brought the company down in 1919, although it was reorganized as the Androscoggin & Kennebec RY. Through cars to Portland ceased, but otherwise the system remained intact until 1928, when the branch from Augusta to Winthrop closed. The Brunswick–Yarmouth main line was abandoned in 1929. All lines east of Sabattus closed on August 1, 1932, followed on May 15, 1937, by the length east of Lisbon Falls to Bath. Apart from Lewiston–Lisbon Falls, replacement bus services operated from the end of 1940. Most rail assets were sold for scrap at auction on January 10, 1941, although new owners did not close the last section between Lewiston and Lisbon Falls until September 1, 1941.

Sources: Hilton and Due, *Electric Interurban Railways*, 323-24; Robertson, *Remember the Portland Trolleys*, 11.

A5. Penobscot Central

Built: 1898–1901.
Operated: 1899–1930.

Railroad construction before 1890 left an unexploited area of Maine of about 30,000 square miles north and east of the Maine Central lines and west and south of the Bangor & Piscataquis. Local interests promoted a line to run north from the MEC in Bangor, with hopes that towns to be served would provide assistance. Such help was not forthcoming, primarily because there were no major sources of traffic on the proposed route, and possibly because of antipathy from the new Bangor & Aroostook RR. Nevertheless, the Penobscot Central RY pushed forward and opened from interchange sidings in Bangor to Corinth in 1899. The original car had a gasoline engine and generator powering batteries, which supplied traction energy. That experiment was short-lived. Construction costs were minimized by tolerating grades as steep as 10 percent. Clearances on one steep Bangor street were so tight that standard mechanical or link-and-pin couplings between locomotives and cars could not be used, requiring an unconventional bar and shackle arrangement.

After electrification in 1901, an extension was built from Corinth to Charleston. The Bangor Railway & Electric Company took over in 1906, following foreclosure and reorganization. For many years the line enjoyed significant revenues from its freight interchange with the MEC, particularly potatoes, since the area was not served by a steam railroad. Still, the communities it served were small, so the line could not generate enough traffic to make passenger trains viable. All service ceased on April 30, 1931.

Sources: Heseltine, "Additional Maine Narrow Gauge"; Hilton and Due, *Electric Interurban Railways*, 148, 323.

A6. Mt. Washington (Cog)

Built: 1866–69.
Operated: 1868–.

At 6,288 feet, Mt. Washington is the tallest peak in New England. The U.S. Weather Service station at the summit, reached by the circuitous Washington Summit Road from the present Route 16, recorded the world's highest wind velocity, gusts registering 231 mph, in 1934. From the peak on a clear day it is possible to see all six New England states, but in winter the slopes are intractable.

The road to the summit from the east had been completed from the Pinkham Turnpike (now Route 16) by the Mt. Washington Summit Road turnpike company in August 1861. After the Civil War several inns and hotels west of the mountain, served by the Tenth New Hampshire Turnpike (now Route 302), were refashioned into lavish resorts for the well-to-do. Sylvester Marsh of Fabyan House promoted a rack railroad that would climb the western slopes. At first ridiculed, Marsh, over a period of almost 15 years, produced models and obtained patents for a cog mechanism. Construction of the line started in May 1866. To connect with it, Marsh obtained a charter in 1867 for the 5.9-mile Mt. Washington Turnpike (now Base Road).

For a rise of 2,528 feet, the average grade was 1 in 4 or 25 percent, although the ruling or maximum grade was just under 37.5 percent. Consists comprised single passenger cars propelled to the summit by wood-burning locomotives of a standard Baldwin type, with a raised firebox and boiler to ensure water coverage of the crown throughout the ascent and descent.

Fabyan was reached by the Boston, Concord & Montreal's White Mountains RR from Wing Road in 1874. Less than a year later the Portland & Ogdensburg also reached Fabyan from the east. In an attempt to keep out the competition, the BC&M completed an extension to Base Station on July 6, 1876, and bought control of the cog railway and the turnpike. After the B&M leased the Concord & Montreal, the successor to the BC&M, in 1895, the cog railway eventually passed to the B&M, who deeded the turnpike to the state in 1905 and much later sold the cog railway to private interests in 1939.

The MWR survives as one of New England's most popular tourist attractions. Its trains, which operate from early May to October, often run at capacity. Steam power is still used on all runs, including two locomotives the railroad built in its own shops in the 1970s and 1980s.

Sources: Drury, *Historical Guide*, 369; Wood, *Turnpikes*, 221-22; Worthen, "Steep but Slow."

A7. Green Mountain (Cog)

Built: 1883.
Operated: 1883-90.

From the late nineteenth century, Maine vied with New Hampshire for seasonal resort traffic. Mt. Desert Island—large parts of which are now included in Acadia National Park—for years attracted the rich, as a place where worldly cares could be left far away. Green Mountain (now Cadillac Mountain), with its splendid scenic vistas, was a tourist attraction with potential to rival Mt. Washington in New Hampshire.

From the south end of Eagle Lake, a 1.1-mile cog line, the Green Mountain RR, was constructed in 1883 to the summit using Marsh's patents developed for the Mt. Washington line. It was operated in summer seasons only, and proved to be a real attraction in the first few years. However, the island resorts were nowhere near the scale of those in the White Mountains. Before the decade was out, returns were minimal; lack of profits brought about its demise at the end of the 1890 season. The line was torn up a few years later. The company's two locomotives were sold in 1895 to the Mt. Washington RY, where they operate to this day.

Sources: Burt, "Mount Desert's Mountain Railway"; Hale, "Cadillac's Old Green Mountain Railway"; Morison, *Story of Mount Desert Island*; Shaughnessy, "Rails to the Sunrise."

Green Mountain Railway locomotive no. 1, Mt. Desert, pushes an open car toward the summit of Cadillac Mountain during its second season of operation in 1884. Built cheaply, the line was worn out by the time of its discontinuation in 1890. No. 1 went to the Mt. Washington Cog RY in 1895, where she is still at work today as locomotive no. 4, the Summit. (Courtesy Walker Transportation Collection, Beverly Historical Society & Museum)

A8. Bennington & Glastenbury

Built: 1872-73.
Operated: 1873-91.

According to Vermont records, the standard-gauge Bennington & Glastenbury RR was chartered in 1872 to bring freight, primarily but not exclusively lumber, to the Vermont Central RR at Bennington, after that company had taken over the Bennington & Rutland line. At its peak, the B&G extended about nine miles, plus spurs and branches, and also operated passenger service comprising one round trip on weekdays. Depletion of lumber stock resulted in closure and abandonment in 1890 or 1891, with Bennington & Rutland trains continuing to run as far as a mill in Woodford as late as 1891. Parts of the alignment were used by the Bennington & Woodford Electric RR streetcar system between 1895 and 1898.

Sources: Bailey, "Some Old Trails," 56; Jones, *Railroads of Vermont*, 1: 48.

A9. Hardwick & Woodbury

Built: 1895-96.
Operated: 1896-ca.1975.

The independent Hardwick & Woodbury RR opened in 1896 as a common carrier hauling freight, mainly granite, from readily accessible quarries owned by the Fletcher Granite Co. in Woodbury, over a length of 8.8 miles to the St. Johnsbury & Lake Champlain RR at Granite Jct. Climbing steep grades, the main line featured a number of switchbacks. The outer terminal, known later as Quarry Station, had earlier been called Woodbury and South Woodbury. Over several years the main line was extended and various branches were constructed. Rudimentary passenger service was provided, one mixed train daily except Sundays departing from Hardwick around 7:00 a.m. and returning around 4:00 p.m., for an average speed of about 3 mph over the ten-mile line. The last statement of passenger traffic receipts in 1921 showed a grand total of two dollars! With closure of the quarries in 1934, most of the line was abandoned and tracks were removed in 1937. About 1.2 miles in Hardwick was retained as a spur over which operation continued well into the 1970s to serve a feed mill. Today the mill is gone, but the siding still exists, albeit buried under dirt and blacktop.

Sources: Jones, *Railroads of Vermont*, 1: 224-230; Shaughnessy, *Rutland*.

A10. Manchester, Dorset & Granville

Built: 1903.
Operated: 1903-18.

Child of the Norcross-West Marble Company (which became part of the Vermont Marble Company in 1913), the Manchester, Dorset & Granville RR had dreams of extending over 100 miles from the Rutland to the Clarendon & Pittsford and to the Central Vermont. It only managed to complete six miles of line from the Rutland's Manchester Center Depot to quarries at Dorset in 1903. The line provided some passenger service, up to four round trips daily using a combine car, until it was closed and abandoned in 1918. These days, some of the quarries it once served are flooded and used as swimming holes.

Sources: Jones, Maxfield, and Gove, *Vermont's Granite Railways*; Karr, *Lost Railroads*, 79; Shaughnessy, *Rutland*.

A11. Georges Valley

Built: 1893.
Operated: 1893–1940.

The Georges Valley RR was built in 1893 from Warren, on the MEC's Knox & Lincoln line, as a common carrier, although its main purpose was to carry limestone quarried east of South Union at Crawford Pond. In 1895, it operated three daily round-trip mixed trains. For years it eked out a marginal existence hauling rock and passengers. The threat of closure forced the biggest shipper, the Knox Lime Company, to take over in 1918, and reincorporate the line as the Knox RR, a wholly-owned subsidiary, in mid-1919. Two daily round-trip mixed trains were scheduled in 1925, but by 1930 there was just one. Common carrier status was abrogated in 1932 and most of the line abandoned. Part of the line survived as an industrial spur until 1940.

Sources: Cornwall and Smith, *Names First*, 43, 57; Karr, *Lost Railroads*, 86.

A12. Lime Rock

Built: 1889.
Operated: 1889–1942.

The nine-mile Lime Rock RR in Rockland was a humble standard-gauge affair, connected with the Knox & Lincoln RR to convey quarried limestone. Seven grade crossings and 11 bridges and trestles, ranging in length from 74 to 322 feet, made the line relatively expensive to construct and maintain. Although chartered as a common carrier, passengers were not conveyed. Demand declined significantly after the Rockland, Thomaston & Camden Street RY opened, but the line survived until May 23, 1942.

Sources: Cornwall and Smith, *Names First*, 60; 217 ICC 509 (1936).

The Manchester, Dorset & Granville operated this combine, but hauling marble was the line's chief business. (Courtesy Walker Transportation Collection, Beverly Historical Society & Museum)

A13. Rockport

Built: 1886.
Operated: 1886–96.

In 1886 the Rockport RR obtained a charter for a common carrier line to bring limestone from quarries at Simonton Corners to kilns at Rockport on West Penobscot Bay. With no connection intended with any other line, 3-foot gauge was chosen to reduce land acquisition and operating costs.

Track was lightweight 25-pound rail spiked directly to ties. Two Hinkley 0-4-4ST locomotives, three bogie cars, and a fleet of two-axle side-dump cars were acquired. The ten directors on the company board—all stockholders in lime burning at Rockport—considerably outnumbered the line's three full-time employees.

During the first several years, three round trips were operated on weekdays. Heavy trains often stalled on the steep grades, and derailments owing to instability on the lightweight track were frequent. The line operated for only a decade. Traffic plummeted after opening of the Rockland, Thomaston & Camden Street RY, an electric operation which served new quarries in Camden. In 1896, its final year of operation, the Rockport reported hauling 700 tons of freight with a revenue of only $406.

After operations ceased, the line was left intact, the locomotives shedded, and other rolling stock left exposed to the elements, perhaps in hope of a revival that never came. The two locomotives were reportedly buried under waste lime and were scrapped upon rediscovery in 1934. Formal abandonment followed in 1937, although track was not dismantled until the wartime demand for steel. The fate of other rolling stock is unknown, but the cars may lie under water in the quarries.

Sources: Heseltine, "Additional Maine Narrow Gauge," 47; Hilton, *American Narrow Gauge*, 410; Karr, *Lost Railroads*, 92, 107; Moody, "Rockport Railroad."

A14. Berlin Mills

Built: ca. 1893.
Operated: 1893–.

The Berlin Mills RY originated as a logging line, the Success Pond RR, built in 1893 to haul lumber to the saw mills at Berlin, NH. The Success Pond ceased operation in 1907, but its trackage in Berlin became the nucleus of the Berlin Mills RY. This short line was always owned and operated by the pulp and wood-processing mills in Berlin as an industrial road. In November 1997 it was leased by the St. Lawrence & Atlantic RR, with which it connects.

Sources: Belcher, *Logging Railroads*, 40–48; Melvin, "Last Day"; *Railpace* 17 (Jan 1998): 37.

Bibliography

Albert, Dave, and George F. Melvin. *New England Diesels.* Omaha: Cockle, 1975.

Alexander, Edwin P. *Down at the Depot: American Railroad Stations from 1831 to 1920.* New York: Bramhall House, 1970.

Allen, C. F. H. "The Maine Central in Northern New Hampshire." *Railway & Locomotive Historical Society Bulletin,* no. 99 (1958): 42-54.

Angier, Jerry, and Herb Cleaves. *Bangor and Aroostook: The Maine Railroad.* Littleton, MA: Flying Yankee Enterprises, 1986.

Armitage, Merle. *The Railroads of America.* Boston: Duell, Sloan and Pearce-Little Brown, 1952.

Armstrong, Jack. *Railfan's Guide to New England.* Adams, MA: Armstrong, 1987.

Bachelder, J. Leonard. *The Alouette.* Ward Hill, MA: Massachusetts Bay Railroad Enthusiasts, 1997.

——. *Androscoggin Valley Limited.* Ward Hill, MA: Massachusetts Bay Railroad Enthusiasts, 1997.

——. *Green Mountain Flyer.* Ward Hill, MA: Massachusetts Bay Railroad Enthusiasts, 1988.

——. *The Half-Century Limited: Celebrating 50 Years of Rare Mileage.* Ward Hill, MA: Massachusetts Bay Railroad Enthusiasts, 1984.

——. *The Mountaineer.* Ward Hill, MA: Massachusetts Bay Railroad Enthusiasts, 1997.

——. *The Rumford Rocket.* Ward Hill, MA: Massachusetts Bay Railroad Enthusiasts, 1984.

——. *Special Trains Operated from Bangor, Maine, to Bucksport and Mattawamkeag via the Maine Central Railroad and From Northern Maine Junction to Searsport and Brownville Junction via the Bangor and Aroostook Railroad, July 27–28, 1985.* Ward Hill, MA: Massachusetts Bay Railroad Enthusiasts, 1985.

———. *State of Maine Branches*. Ward Hill, MA: Massachusetts Bay Railroad Enthusiasts, 1985.

———. *The Strawberry Banke Limited*. Ward Hill, MA: Massachusetts Bay Railroad Enthusiasts, 1984.

Bailey, Harold Leslie. "Some Old Trails of the Iron Horse." *Vermonter* 45 (March 1940): 54-66.

Baker, George Pierce. *The Formation of New England Railroad Systems*. Cambridge: Harvard, University Press, 1937.

Bangor & Aroostook Railroad. *The Bangor & Aroostook: 75 Years*. Bangor: Bangor & Aroostook Railroad, 1966.

Barnum, Louise N. *Atkinson: Then and Now*. [Atkinson, NH?]: Atkinson Historical Society, 1975.

Baughan, Peter E. *A Regional History of the Railways of Great Britain: Vol. XI, North and Mid Wales*. Newton Abbot, England: David & Charles Ltd., 1980.

Beauregard, Mark W. *Railroad Stations of New England Today: Vol. 1, The Boston & Maine Railroad*. Flanders, NJ: Railroad Avenue Enterprises, 1979.

Belcher, C. Francis. *Logging Railroads of the White Mountains*. Boston: Appalachian Mountain Club, 1980.

Blaisdell, Paul H. *Three Centuries on Winnipesaukee*. 2d. ed. Somersworth, NH: New Hampshire Publishing Co., 1975.

Booth, J. Derek. *Railways of Southern Quebec*. 2 vols. West Hill, ON: Railfare, 1982.

Boston and Maine Railroad. *Corporate History of the Boston and Maine Railroad (System), Including Owned, Leased and Controlled Lines as of Dates of Valuation June 30, 1914.* n. p., ca. 1915.

———. *Timetables*, various dates.

———. *What New Hampshire Offers Businessmen in the Way of Business Opportunities*. Concord, NH: Boston & Maine Railroad Information Bureau, 1909.

Bradlee, Francis B. C. *The Boston and Lowell Railroad, the Nashua and Lowell, and the Salem and Lowell Railroad*. Salem, MA: Essex Institute, 1918.

———. *The Boston and Maine Railroad: A History of the Main Road, with Its Tributary Lines*. Salem, MA: Essex Institute, 1921.

———. *The Eastern Railroad: A Historical Account of Early Railroading in Eastern New England*. 2d. ed. Salem, MA: Essex Institute, 1922.

Carman, Bernard D. *Hoot, Toot & Whistle: The Story of the Hoosac Tunnel & Wilmington Railroad*. Brattleboro: Stephen Greene Press, 1963.

Burt, Frank H. "Mount Desert's Mountain Railway." *Appalachia*, no. 96 (December 1943): 434-40.

Cavalier, Julian. *Classic American Railroad Stations.* San Diego: Barnes, 1980.

Chase, Edward E. *Maine Railroads: A History of the Development of the Maine Railroad System.* Portland, ME: Huston, 1926.

Cobb, Chandler & Leslie C. Shaw. "Dover, New Hampshire: A Pictorial Essay." *B&M Bulletin,* 11, No.1 (Fall 1981): 10-23.

Cornwall, L. Peter, and Jack W. Farrell. *Ride the Sandy River.* Edmonds, WA: Pacific Fast Mail, 1973.

Cornwall, L. Peter, and Carol A. Smith. *Names First—Rails Later.* Stamford, CT: Arden Valley Group, 1989.

Crittenden, H. Temple. *The Maine Scenic Route: A History of the Sandy River & Rangeley Lakes Railroad.* Parsons, WV: McClain Printing Co., 1966.

———. "Sandy River & Rangeley Lakes R.R. System." *Railway & Locomotive Historical Society Bulletin,* no. 37 (1935): 15-32.

———. "Wiscasset, Waterville & Farmington Railway." *Railway & Locomotive Historical Society Bulletin,* no. 57 (1942): 114-35.

Crouch, H. Bentley. "Narrow Gauge to the Notch." *B&M Bulletin* 5, no. 4 (Summer 1976): 19-28.

Crouch, H. Bentley, and Harry A. Frye. "Worcester, Nashua & Portland: Part 1, The Phantom Division; Part 3, All Those Branches." *B&M Bulletin* 9 (Summer 1979): 5-14; (Winter 1979-80): 21-33.

CRSS Constructors, Inc. *Maine Department of Transportation: Portland to Boston Passenger Rail Service Reports to Federal Transit Administration.* Arlington, VA: CRSS Constructors, 1995-97.

Cummings, O. R. *Atlantic Shore Line Railway: Its Predecessors and Its Successors.* Warehouse Point, CT: Connecticut Electric Railway Association, 1957.

———. *Capital City Streetcar Days: the Concord & Manchester Electric Branch, the Concord Electric Railways and Predecessors, 1878–1933.* Forty Fort, PA: Cox, 1996.

———. *A Granite State Interurban: The History of the Concord & Manchester Electric Branch of the Boston & Maine Railroad.* Bulletin no.12. Chicago: Electric Railway Historical Society, 1954.

———. "Portland-Lewiston Interurban." *Transportation* 10 (May 1956): 1-28.

Day, Richard L. *Aroostook Valley Railroad Company.* Bulletin 65. Chicago: Central Electric Railfan's Association, 1946.

Della Penna, Craig. *Great Rail-Trails of the Northeast: The Essential Outdoor Guide to 26 Recreational Biking Trails and Their Railroad History.* Amherst, MA: New England Cartographics, 1995.

DeLorme Mapping. *Maine Atlas and Gazetteer.* 15th ed. Freeport, ME: Delorme Mapping, 1991.

———. *New Hampshire Atlas and Gazetteer.* 9th ed. Freeport, ME: Delorme Mapping, 1988.

———. *Vermont Atlas & Gazetteer.* 8th ed. Freeport, ME: Delorme Mapping, 1988.

DiFalco, Francis J. "The Milford-Bennington Railroad: An SW900 and Ten Hoppers Add up to Rock-Solid Success." *Railfan & Railroad* 12 (March 1993): 52-55.

Dorman, Robert. *Statutory History of Steam and Electric Railways of Canada.* Ontario: Government of Canada, 1937.

Drury, George H. *Guide to Tourist Railroads and Railroad Museums.* Railroad Reference Series no. 13. Waukesha, WI: Kalmbach, 1995.

———. *The Historical Guide to North American Railroads.* Railroad Reference Series no. 3. Waukesha, WI: Kalmbach, 1992.

———. *The Train-Watcher's Guide to North American Railroads.* Railroad Reference Series no. 11. 2d ed. Waukesha, WI: Kalmbach, 1992.

Dubin, Arthur D. *Some Classic Trains.* Milwaukee, WI: Calmat, 1964.

Eugley, Arthur R. "An Eastern Route Photo-Essay: Death of a Railroad." *B&M Bulletin* 18, no. 1 (1991): 20-33.

Fisher, Charles E. "Locomotives of the Maine Central Railroad." *Railway & Locomotive Historical Society Bulletin*, no. 55 (1941): 64-72; no. 56 (1941): 87-97.

Gardner, John L., and Robert W. Moore. "Lamoille Valley Extension." *Ambassador* 9, no. 1 (1999): 6-13.

Guilford Transportation Industries. Systems Map. Billerica, MA: Guilford Transportation Industries, [ca. 1994].

———. *Working Timetable No. 3.* Billerica, MA: Guilford Transportation Industries, 1992.

Hale, Richard W., Jr. "Cadillac's Old Green Mountain Railway." *Down East* 3 (July 1957): 40-43.

Hancock History Committee. *The Second Hundred Years of Hancock, New Hampshire.* Canaan, NH: Phoenix, 1979.

Harlow, Alvin F. *Steelways of New England.* New York: Creative Age Press, 1946.

Hartnett House. *Maine City & Town Atlas.* Freeport, ME: Hartnett House, 1987.

Bellows Falls, VT, where the Rutland and Central Vermont met, was a busy place in 1912. (Courtesy Walker Transportation Collection, Beverly Historical Society & Museum)

Harwood, Herbert H., Jr. "Railroad Stations" in *Built in the U.S.A.: American Buildings from Airports to Zoos*, ed. Diane Maddex. Washington, DC: Preservation Press, 1985.

Heffernan, Nancy C. and Ann P. Stecker. *New Hampshire: Crosscurrents in its Development*. Grantham, NH: Tompson & Rutter, 1986.

Heseltine, Charles D., "Additional Maine Narrow Gauge Railroads." *Narrow Gauge Society Newsletter* 2, no. 1 (1972).

Heseltine, Charles D., and Edwin B. Robertson. *Aroostook Valley Railroad*. Westbrook, ME: Robertson Books, 1987.

Hilton, George W. *American Narrow Gauge Railroads*. 2d. ed. Stanford, CA: Stanford University Press, 1990.

———. "Meets All Trains: Springfield Terminal Is the Last of Electric Passenger Lines in Vermont." *Trains* 6, no. 10 (1946): 48-49.

Hilton, George W., and John F. Due. *The Electric Interurban Railways in America*. Stanford, CA: Stanford University Press, 1964.

Hoisington, Richard A., and E. Robert Hornsby. "The Amesbury and Merrimac Branches—And Never the Trains Shall Meet." 2 pts. *B&M Bulletin* 10 (Spring 1981): 9-26; (Summer 1981): 7-12.

Hurd, D. Hamilton. *History of Rockingham and Strafford Counties, New Hampshire.* Philadelphia: Lewis, 1882.

Hutchins, John C. *The Blueberry Express: A History of the Suncook Valley Railroad.* Littleton, MA: Flying Yankee Enterprises, 1985.

Hutchinson, Doug. *The Rumford Falls & Rangeley Lakes Railroad.* Dixfield, ME: Partridge Lane, 1989.

Jager, Ronald and Grace Jager. *New Hampshire: An Illustrated History of the Granite State.* Woodland Hills, CA: Windsor, 1983.

Joint New England Railroad Committee. *Report of the Joint New England Railroad Committee to the Governors of the New England States.* [Cambridge, MA: University Press], 1923.

Jones, Robert C. *The Central Vermont Railway.* 6 vols. Silverton, CO: Sundance, 1981-82.

——. *Railroads of Vermont.* 2 vols. Shelburne, VT: New England Press, 1993.

——. *Two Feet Between The Rails.* 2 vols. Silverton, CO: Sundance, 1979-80.

——. *Two Feet to the Quarries: The Monson Railroad.* Burlington, VT: Evergreen, 1998.

Jones, Robert C., W. J. Maxfield, and W. G. Gove, *Vermont's Granite Railways.* Boulder, CO: Pruett, 1987.

Jones, Robert C., and David L. Register. *Two Feet to Tidewater: The Wiscasset, Waterville & Farmington Railway.* Boulder, CO: Pruett, 1987.

Judd, Richard W., Edward A. Churchill, and Joel W. Eastman, eds. *Maine: The Pine Tree State from Prehistory to the Present.* Orono, ME: University of Maine Press, 1995.

Karr, Ronald Dale. *Lost Railroads of New England.* 2d. ed. Pepperell, MA: Branch Line Press, 1996.

——. *The Rail Lines of Southern New England.* Pepperell, MA: Branch Line Press, 1995.

Kirkland, Edward C. *Men, Cities and Transportation: A Study in New England History, 1820-1900.* 2 vols. Cambridge: Harvard University Press, 1948.

Kistler, Thelma M. *The Rise of Railroads in the Connecticut Valley.* Smith College Studies in History, vol. 23, nos. 1-4. Northampton, MA: Smith College, 1938.

Kyper, Frank. "The Saco Branch: B&M's Longest—and Forgotten—'Branch' in Maine." *B&M Bulletin* 20, no.3 (1995): 7-11.

Lamb, William Kaye. *History of the Canadian Pacific Railway.* New York: Macmillan, 1977.

Lavallee, Omer. *Narrow Gauge Railways of Canada.* Montreal: Railfare, 1972.

Lawry, Nelson H. "It's Government Work: A Long Bridge, a Shipyard Railroad, and a Sunken Pacific." *Railfan & Railroad* 14 (December 1995): 40-43.

Lenk, Walter E. "The Birth of the Boston & Maine Railroad: March 15, 1833 to January 1, 1842." *B&M Bulletin* 1, no. 4 (June 1972); 2, no. 1 (September 1972).

Lewis, Edward A. *American Shortline Railway Guide.* Railroad Reference Series no. 7. Waukesha, WI: Kalmbach Books, 1991.

——. *Vermont's Covered Bridge Road: The Story of the St. Johnsbury & Lamoille County Railroad.* Strasburg, PA: Baggage Car, 1974.

Macdonald, Sir John A. Papers. National Archives of Canada.

Maine Department of Transportation. Rail Transportation Directorate. Unpublished files, 1984-97. Augusta, Maine.

——. *Historical and Archeological Resources Report.* Augusta, ME: Maine Deppartment of Transportation, 1993.

——. Maps. Augusta, ME, 1985-96.

Mead, Edgar T. *"Busted and Still Running": The Famous Two-Foot Gauge Railroad of Bridgton, Maine.* Brattleboro, VT: Stephen Greene Press, 1968.

——. *Over the Hills to Woodstock: The Saga of the Woodstock Railroad.* Brattleboro, VT: Stephen Greene Press, 1967.

——. *Through Covered Bridges to Concord: A Recollection of the Concord & Claremont Railroad.* Brattleboro, VT: Stephen Greene Press, 1970.

——. *The Up-Country Line: Boston, Concord & Montreal Railroad to the New Hampshire Lakes and White Mountains.* Brattleboro, VT: Stephen Greene Press, 1985.

Melvin, George. "The Aroostook Valley Railroad." *Railfan & Railroad* 9 (March 1990): 44-50.

——. "Last Day of the Berlin Mills Railway." *Railfan & Railroad* 17 (May 1998): 28-33.

Moody, Linwood W. *The Maine Two-Footers.* Burbank, CA: Howell-North, 1959.

——. "The Rockport Railroad." *Down East* 14 (July 1968): 44-45, 81-82, 85, 88.

Moody, Linwood W., and W. S. Young. "Six Miles and a Toll Bridge." *Short Line Railroader,* no. 35 (1958).

Morison, Elizabeth Forbes, and Elting E. Morison. *New Hampshire: A Bicentennial History*. Nashville: American Association for State and Local History, 1976.

Morison, Samuel E. *The Story of Mount Desert Island, Maine*. Boston: Little, Brown, 1960.

Morse, Victor. *36 Miles of Trouble: The Story of the West River Railroad*. Brattleboro, VT: Book Cellar, 1959.

Nelligan, Tom. *Bluebirds and Minutemen*. Woodridge, IL: McMillan, 1986.

Nett, Bruce Owen. "Canadian Pacific's Main Line: The Story of CPR's International Maine Division." *Railfan & Railroad* 8 (May 1989): 40-46; (June 1989): 46-53; (July 1989): 34-39.

Niles, Charles, Jr. "Change Trains at Rockingham Junction." *B&M Bulletin* 19, no. 3 (1993): 28-33.

Nimke, R. W. *Green Mountain Railroad*. Walpole, NH: Nimke, 1985.

Peters, Bradley L. *Maine Central Railroad Company: A Story of Success and Independence*. Portland, ME: Maine Central Railroad, 1979.

Peverly, Elaine, and William H. McLin. *The Dummy: A Story of the Pine Tree State's Seaside Railroad*. [S.l.]: Wilson's Printers, 1973.

Philbrook, Dana. "Lake Shore Railroad: The First Forty Years." *B&M Bulletin*, 16, no. 4 (1989): 12-27.

Poor, Henry V. *History of the Railroads and Canals of the United States*. New York: Schultz, 1860.

Potter, Janet Greenstein. *Great American Railroad Stations*. New York: Wiley, 1996.

Rand McNally & Company. *Handy Railroad Atlas of the United States*. Chicago: Rand McNally, 1985 and earlier editions.

Robertson, Edwin B. *Remember the Portland, Maine Trolleys*. Westbrook, ME: Robertson Books, 1975.

Robertson, Edwin B., and Benjamin W. English, Jr. *A Century of Railroading in Crawford Notch*. Westbrook, ME: Robertson Books, 1975.

Robinson, William F. *Abandoned New England*. New York: Little, Brown & Co., 1976.

Shaughnessy, Jim. *Delaware & Hudson: The History of an Important Railroad Whose Antecedent Was a Canal Network to Transport Coal*. San Diego, CA: Howell-North, 1982.

———. "Rails to the Sunrise." *Trains*, April 1966, 44-47.

———. *The Rutland Road*. 2d. ed. San Diego, CA: Howell-North, 1981.

Shaw, Robert B. *A History of Railroad Accidents, Safety Precautions and Operating Practices*. N.p.: Shaw, 1978.

Stevens, G. R. *History of the Canadian National Railways.* New York: Macmillan, 1973.

Thornbury, William D. *Regional Geomorphology of the United States.* New York: Wiley, 1965.

Thurlow, Clinton F. *The WW&F Two-Footer: Hail and Fairwell.* 2d. ed. Weeks Mills, ME: n.p., 1965.

Tobey, Raymond E., "The York Harbor & Beach Railroad: To York Beach in Style." *B&M Bulletin* 9, no. 1 (Fall 1979): 5–15.

Valentine, Donald B., Jr. "A Brief History of the Cheshire Railroad." *New England States Limited* 1 (Summer 1977): 20–29.

Vance, James E., Jr. *The North American Railroad: Its Origin, Evolution and Geography.* Baltimore: Johns Hopkins University Press, 1995.

Waite, Thornton H. "Recycling New Hampshire's Railroad Stations." *B&M Bulletin* 6, no. 4, (Summer 1977).

Walker, Harold S. "The Bangor, Oldtown & Milford Railroad, 1836–1869." *Railway & Locomotive Historical Society Bulletin,* no. 106 (1962): 40–48.

Walker, Mike. *Steam Power Video's Comprehensive Railroad Atlas of North America: North East USA.* Maidstone, England: Steam Powered Publishing, 1993.

Whitney, Roger A. *The Monson Railroad.* Westbrook, ME: Robertson Books, 1989.

Wiggin, Ruby Crosby. *Big Dreams and Little Wheels.* Clinton, ME: n.p., 1971.

Wood, Frederic J. *The Turnpikes of New England.* Abridged with an Introduction by Ronald Dale Karr. Pepperell, MA: Branch Line Press, 1997.

Worthen, S. S. "Steep But Slow." *Trains,* July 1956, 38–42.

Zimmerman, Karl R. *A Decade of the D&H.* Oradell, NJ: Delford Press, 1979.

Zimmermann, Michael W. *The Sunrise Route: A History of the Railroads of Washington County, Maine.* Brewer, ME: Cay-Bel, 1985.

Station Index

Maine

Abbot Village, 59
Adaline, 76
Adams, 61B
Addison, 65
Agamenticus, 15A, 30
Air Base, 76C
Albion, 46
Alder Stream, 54E
Alfred, 13
Allens, 41
Alna Center, 46
Alton, 59
Androscoggin, 40
Annabessacook, 39
Anson, 55
Arey, 61
Arundel, 15
Ashland, 61H, 61I
Ashland Jct., 61, 61H
Askwith, 73
Attean, 73
Attean Landing, 73
Auburn, 39, 41A
Augusta, 44
Austin Jct. , 55, 55A
Ayers Jct., 65, 65A
B&M Transfer, 36
Back Cove, 41
Baileyville, 66
Bakers, 55A
Bald Hill Crossing, 30
Bald Mountain, 55A
Baldwin, 36
Bancroft, 43
Bangor, 39, 42, 43, 63

Bangor Union Sta., 39, 43, 63
Bangs, 55
Bar Mills, 13
Baring, 66
Barnard, 73
Barnjum, 54J
Basin Mills, 43
Bates, 41
Bath, 44A, 45
Bay View House, 33A
Bedell, 31
Bedells, 31
Bedels Crossing, 31
Belfast, 56
Belgrade, 39
Beluga, 55
Bemis, 53
Benson, 73
Benton, 39, 39C
Berlin Mills, 54I
Berwick Jct., 15, 15A
Bethel, 41
Biddeford, 15, 30
Bigelow, 54D
Bingham, 55
Bingham Heights, 55A
Bismarck, 58
Blackstone, 61L
Blair, 73
Blanchard, 59
Blue Point, 15
Bodfish, 73
Boston Ranch, 73
Bowdoinham, 44

Boyd Lake, 59, 61
Brackett Jct., 54G, 54H
Bradbury, 13
Bradford, 61
Bragg Corner, 54F
Branch Switch, 52, 52B
Brannen, 61F
Brassua, 73
Brassua Sta., 73
Brewer, 63, 64
Brewer Jct., 63, 64
Brewer Village, 63
Bridgewater, 61
Bridgton, 38
Bridgton Jct., 36, 38
Brooks, 56
Brocks Crossing, 28, 30
Brownfield, 36
Brownville, 59A, 61
Brownville Jct., 59A, 73
Brunswick, 40A, 44, 44A
Bryant Pond, 41
Bryants Pond, 41
Buckfield, 52
Bucksport, 63
Bucksport Center, 63
Bucksport Jct., 43
Buffalo, 61I
Bugbee, 76
Burnham, 39
Burnham Jct., 39, 56
Buxton, 13
Buxton Centre, 13
Byron, 53
Calais, 66

Concord, NH, at the beginning of the Boston, Concord & Montreal RR, June 1999. (R. D. Karr)

Calais Jct., 63
California Rd., 61G
Camp 12, 73
Camp Benson, 58
Camp Ellis, 33A
Camp Ground, 15, 33A
Campbell, 77
Canibas, 61
Canton, 52
Cape Elizabeth, 30, 44C
Cape Jct., 61, 61A
Cape Jellison, 61A
Caratunk, 55
Caribou, 61, 61G, 77
Carmel, 39
Carrabassett, 54D
Carson, 76, 76B
Cathance, 44
Centraltown, 40
Centre Waterboro, 13
Chamberlains, 43
Chapman, 53
Charlotte, 65
Chelsea, 47
Cherryfield, 65
Chester, 73
Chicks, 30
China, 46
China Lake, 46A
Chipmans, 63
City Point, 56
Clarks, 46A
Clinton, 39
Cobb, 41
Cobbs Brook, 41
Colby, 76B
Coles Corner, 46
Collins, 61
Columbia, 65
Columbia Falls, 65
Congress St., 15
Conway Jct., 28, 30
Cooks, 44A
Cooks Corner, 44A
Coopers Mills, 46
Copsecook Mills, 44B
Corinna, 58
Cornish, 36
Costigan, 43
Craigville, 73
Crossuntic, 43

Crouseville, 76
Crowleys, 40A
Crowleys Jct., 40A, 40B
Cumberland, 39A, 41, 44
Cumberland Center, 44
Cumberland Jct., 39A,
Cumberland Mills, 13, 36
Cumberland Mills Jct., 13
Cummings, 15, 15A
Curtis Corner, 40
Cyrs, 57
Daggett, 77
Dago Jct., 54I, 54K
Dallas, 54F
Damariscotta Mills, 45
Damascus, 39
Danforth, 43
Danville, 41
Danville Jct., 39, 39A, 41
Davidson, 61
Dead River, 40, 54F
Deadwater, 55A
Deering Jct., 13, 44
Dennysville, 65
Derby, 59, 59A, 61
Dexter, 58
Dimmick, 55A
Dixfield, 52
Dolby, 61C
Dolby Rips, 61C
Dover & Foxcroft, 58, 59
Dover-Foxcroft, 58
Dresden, 44
Drew, 43
Dudley, 61H
Dunns, 41
Dunns Corner, 41
Dunstan, 30
Duponts, 57
Dyer Brook, 61
Dyer St., 76
Eagle Lake, 61I
East Baldwin, 36
East Deering, 41
East Dover, 59
East Hebron, 52
East Lebanon, 13
East Livermore, 40
East Lyndon, 77
East Machias, 65
East Millinocket, 61C

East Newport, 39
East Newport [Eastville]),
 39
East Peru, 52
East Poland, 41
East Rd., 61G
East Sumner, 52
East Vassalboro, 46A
East Waldoboro, 13, 45
East Wilton, 40
Eastbrook, 65
Easton, 61E
Eastport, 65A
Eastport Jct., 65, 65A
Eastwood, 13
Eaton, 43
Egerys Mill, 64
Eight Mile Siding, 43
Eighteen Quarry, 60C
Eliot, 30, 65
Ellsworth, 64
Ellsworth Falls, 64
Elmer, 73
Elms, 15
Elmwood, 52
Embden, 55
Empire Rd., 41
Enfield, 43, 43B
Etna, 39
Eustis Jct., 54F, 54I
Exchange St. [MEC Sta.],
 43
Ezarys, 46
Fairbanks, 54A
Fairfield, 39C, 44
Fairmount, 61E
Falmouth, 41, 44
Farmingdale, 44
Farmington, 40, 54A
Ferry Beach Park, 33A
Flag Stop, 43
Forbes, 56
Forest, 43
Forsythe, 55A
Fournier, 61J
Foxcroft, 58
Frankfort, 61
Franklin, 65
Franklin Rd., 64
Freemans, 63
Freeport, 44

Station Index

Frenchville, 61J
Frye, 53
Fryeburg, 36
Fryes, 65
Ft. Fairfield, 61E, 77
Ft. Kent, 61I, 61J, 61K
Ft. Kent Village, 61K
Gardiner, 44, 44B
Gardners, 65
Georges River, 45
Gilbert, 61C
Gilbertville, 52
Gilead, 41
Gilford, 73
Glenburn, 61
Glendon, 45
Golders, 40A
Good Will Farm, 44
Goodrich, 61G
Goodwin, 77
Goodwins, 65
Gorham, 13
Gould Corner, 30
Grand Beach, 15
Grand Isle, 61J
Gray, 39A
Grays Farm, 54H
Great Works, 28, 43
Green Lake, 64
Greenbush, 43
Greene, 39
Greenes Farm, 54I
Greenville, 59, 73
Greenville Jct., 73
Grimes Mill, 61G
Grindstone, 61
Griswold, 61H
Grove Sta., 32
Grovemore, 33A
GT Jct., 13A
Guilford, 59
Guiou, 77
Gull Pond, 54F
Hacketts, 39
Hacketts Switch, 39
Hale, 53
Hallowell, 44
Hampden, 61
Hancock, 64
Hanford, 61L
Hannas, 65

Harding, 44A
Hardings, 44A
Hardy Point, 73
Harfords Point, 73
Harmony, 57
Harrington, 65
Harrison, 38
Hartford, 52
Hartford Center, 52
Hartland, 57
Harvey, 61
Harwards, 44
Harwards Rd., 44
Hawkins, 61H
Head Tide, 46
Hebron, 52
Hebron Pond, 60A
Hermon Center, 39
Hermon Centre, 39
Hermon Pond, 39
Herseys, 43
Highmoor, 40
Highpine, 30
Hillman, 61H
Hillside, 44
Hilltop, 65
Hinckley, 44
Hinks, 63
Hinks Landing, 63
Hiram, 36
Hiram Bridge, 36
Hiram Jct., 36, 38
Hobbs Crossing, 30
Hogtown, 42
Holden, 64
Holeb, 73
Hollis Centre, 13
Hop City, 53
Hopkins, 77
Hotel Rd., 41
Houghton, 53, 53A
Houghtonville, 61G
Houlton, 61, 62
Houstons, 43
Howe Brook, 61H
Howland, 43B
Hoxies, 55
Hudson, 61
Hurd, 77
Iceboro, 44
Indian Pond, 55A

Indian River, 65
Indian Rock, 53
Ingalls, 61
Ingalls Rd., 38
Intervale, 41
Jackman, 73
Jackson Brook, 43
Jacksons Crossing, 41
Jacksonville, 65
Jacobs, 76
Jay, 40
Jay Bridge, 52A
Jemtland, 61
Jewett, 28, 30
Johns Pond, 53
Johnson Brook, 46
Jonesboro, 65
Kamankeag, 53
Katahdin Iron Works, 59A
Keag, 43
Keegan, 61J
Kendall Mills, 39C
Kendalls Mills, 44
Kennebago, 53
Kennebec, 44
Kennebunk, 15, 30, 32
Kennebunk Beach, 32
Kennebunkport, 32
Keough, 73
Kidders, 61
Kineo, 60B
Kineo Sta., 55A
Kingfield, 54B, 54D, 54E
Kingman, 43
Kingsbury, 59
Kinney Shores Sta., 33A
Kirby, 73
Kittery, 30
Kittery Jct., 30, 31
Kittery Point, 31
Knights, 73
Knox, 56
Kyleton, 73
Lagrange, 59, 61
Lake Austin, 55A
Lake House, 64
Lake Moxie, 55A
Lake View, 73
Lakeside, 39
Lambert Lake, 43

Station Index

Langtown, 54I
Lawrences Mills, 44
Ledges, 61K
Leeds Center, 40
Leeds, 39, 40
Leeds Jct., 39, 40, 40A
Lewiston, 39, 40B, 41A
Lewiston Jct., 41, 41A
Lewiston Lower, 40B
Lewiston Upper, 39
Libbys Pit, 40
Ligonia, 15
Lille, 61J
Limestone, 61G
Lincoln, 43
Lincoln Center, 43
Lincoln Mills, 58
Lincolns, 58
Lisbon, 40A
Lisbon Falls, 40A
Little Canada, 61H
Little River, 40A
Littleboro, 40
Littlefield, 41A
Littleton, 61
Livermore Falls, 40, 52A
Lockes Mills, 41
Lombards, 61F
Long A, 61
Long Beach, 31
Long Pond, 73
Long Rd., 61G
Long Sands, 31
Loring AFB, 61G
Lowelltown, 73
Lows Bridge, 59
Lucerne-in-Maine, 64
Ludlow, 61
Lynchs, 65
Machias, 65
Machiasport, 65
Mack Point, 61
Mackamp, 73
Macy Jct., 53
Madawaska, 61J
Madison, 55
Madrid, 54F
Madrid Jct., 54F, 54G
Madrid Village, 54H
Main St., 13
Maines, 77

Mainstream, 57
Maple Grove, 61E
Mapleton, 61F, 61L
Maplewood, 54A
Maranacook, 39
Marbles, 54F
Margison, 76B
Margison Crossroad, 76B
Marion, 65
Marrs, 55A
Mars Hill, 61
Masardis, 61H
Masons, 53
Mattawamkeag, 43, 73
Matthews, 65
Mattocks, 36
Maxcys, 46
Maxys Mills, 46
Maynard, 77
Maysville, 61
McGraw, 77
McKenzies, 64
McNally, 61I
Meadow Brook Siding, 43
Meadowview, 52A
Mechanic Falls, 41, 52
Meddo, 63
Medford, 61B
Mendearth, 53
Merriland, 15
Messalonskee, 39
Middletown, 43
Milford, 42, 43
Mill Creek, 63
Millinocket, 61, 61C
Milltown, 66
Milltown Jct., 66
Milo, 59A, 61
Milo Jct., 59, 59A, 61
Minot, 52
Misery, 55A
Mitchells, 53
Monmouth, 39
Monson, 60, 60A, 60B, 60C
Monson Jct., 59, 60
Montague, 43B
Monticello, 61
Montsweag, 45
Moody, 58
Moodys Mills, 58

Moores, 55A
Moores Camp, 73
Moosehead, 73
Morkill, 73
Morrills, 13
Morrow Rd., 61G
Moscow, 55A
Mosquito, 55A
Mt. Abram, 54C
Mt. Abram Jct., 54B, 54C
Mt. Desert Ferry, 64
Mt. Hope, 43
Murphy Rd., 61G
Muscongus Bay, 45
National Soldiers Home, 47
Navy Yard, 31
Navy Yard Jct., 31, 31A
Navy Yard Sta., 31
Nequasset, 45
New Gloucester, 39A, 41
New Limenfoir, 61
New Limerick, 61
New Meadows, 44A
New Sweden, 61
Newcastle, 45
Newcastle & Damariscotta, 45
Newells Corner, 46
Newhall, 36
Newport, 39
Newport Jct., 39, 58
Nicolin, 64
Nigger Meadow, 46
Nixon, 61I
No. 6, 54G
Nobleboro, 45
Nobles, 44
Norcross, 61
Norlands, 40
Norridgewock, 55
North Anson, 55
North Bangor, 61
North Belgrade, 39
North Berwick, 15, 30
North Bridgton, 38
North Bucksport, 63
North Freeman, 54B
North Jay, 40
North Leeds, 40

Station Index

North Lincoln, 43
North Orrington, 63
North St. Siding, 44
North Vassalboro, 46A
North Whitefield, 46
North Yarmouth, 41
Northern Maine Jct., 39, 61
Norway, 41B
Notre Dame, 61J
Oak Hill, 30, 44
Oakfield, 61
Oakland Farms, 31
Oakland, 39, 55
Oakwood, 44
Ocean Park, 33A
Oceanside, 31
Olamon, 43
Old Orchard Beach, 15, 33A, 33B
Old Town, 42, 43, 59
Oldtown, 43
Olivers Mills, 54B
Onawa, 73
Oquossoc, 53
Orono, 43, 43A
Orrington, 63
Otis Hill, 55
Oxford, 41
Packard, 61B
Packards, 61, 61B
Palermo, 46
Parent, 61J
Park Siding, 76
Parkers, 59,
Parkhurst, 77
Parrot, 59
Parsons, 32
Passadumkeag, 43
Patten, 61D
Patten Jct., 61D
Pauls, 76
Pavilion, 31
Pea Cove, 59
Pea Ridge, 73
Pejepscot, 40A
Pejepscot Mills, 40A
Pembroke, 65A
Perham, 61L
Perham Jct., 54F, 54J
Perham Rd., 76A

Perkins, 30, 61
Perleys Mill, 38
Perry, 65A
Peru, 52
Phair, 61, 61E
Phillips, 54A, 54F
Phillips Lake, 64
Pierces, 63
Pierces Crossing, 63
Pigeon Plains, 46
Pine Point, 15
Pine Point Beach, 15
Pishons, 44
Pishons Ferry, 44
Pittsfield Center, 39
Pittsfield, 39, 57
Pleasant Hill, 15
Pleasant Point, 65A
Pleasantdale, 30
Plummers, 65
Poland, 52
Poland Spring Jct., 39
Poland Springs, 52
Pollard Brook, 43
Portage, 61I
Porters, 53
Porters Siding, 53A
Portland, 36, 44
Portland & Rochester Jct., 13A, 41
Portland [Canal St.], 30
Portland [Commercial St.], 30
Portland GT Sta., 41
Portland India St., 41
Portland Jct., 41
Portland, Preble St. Sta., 13, 13A, 13B, 44C
Portland, Union Sta., 13B, 15
Pownal, 41
Prebles, 46
Presque Isle, 61, 61F, 76, 77
Presque Isle Jct., 76, 76D
Prides Mill, 61H
Princeton, 66
Prospect, 61
PS&P Jct., 33B
Quarry, 59
Quoddy, 65A

Rand Cove, 61B
Randolph, 47
Rangeley, 54F
Rankins Mills, 38
Readfield, 39
Realty, 53
Redington, 54F
Reeds, 54F
Reeds Mill, 53
Riccars, 52
Richmond, 44
Richville, 36
Rigby, 15, 30
Rileys, 52A
River Switch, 43
Riverside, 44
Roberts, 77
Robinson, 61
Rockland, 45
Rockwood, 55A
Rolling Mills, 15
Rowes, 39A
Roxbury, 53
Royal Jct., 39B, 44
Rumford, 52
Rumford Falls, 53
Rumford Jct., 39, 52
Sabattus, 40A
Sabbatusville, 40A
Saccarappa, 13
Saco, 15, 30
Saco [East], 30
Saco River, 13
Salem, 54B
Salmon Falls, 66
Sand Hills, 58
Sanders, 54F
Sands, 76
Sandy Creek, 38
Sandy Point, 61
Sandy River, 54H
Sanford & Springvale, 13
Sangerville, 59
Sawyers, 52A
Scarboro, 15, 30
Scarboro Beach, 15
Scarboro Crossing, 15, 30
Schoodic, 61, 65
Seabury, 31
Searsport, 61
Sebago Lake, 36

Seboois, 73
Seven Mile Brook, 44
Shattucks Siding, 45
Shaw, 61L
Shawmut, 44
Sheepscot, 46
Sheridan, 61I
Sherman, 61
Sherman-Patten, 61
Shipyards, 30A
Shirley, 59
Shirley Mills, 59
Shorey, 61H
Shuy, 40
Sidney, 44
Silvers Mills, 58
Simpsons, 40A
Skillingston, 41
Skinner, 73
Skowhegan, 44
Skunk Brook Camp, 54K
Skyway Industrial Park, 76C
Skyway Jct., 76, 76C
Smiths Mill, 36
Smyrna Mills, 61H
Snow Falls, 41
Snows Falls, 41
Sobins, 63
Soldier Pond, 61I
Solon, 55
Somerset, 73
Somerset Jct., 55A, 73
Somerset Mills, 44
Soule Mill, 54C
Soules Mill, 54C
South Albion, 46
South Berwick, 15, 15A
South Berwick Jct., 15A, 30
South Bethel, 41
South Brewer, 63
South Bridgton, 38
South China, 46A
South Gardiner, 44
South Lagrange, 59, 61, 61B
South Lincoln, 43
South Newcastle, 45
South Orrington, 63
South Paris, 41, 41B

South Portland, 30, 30A, 44C
South Rangeley, 53
South Sebec, 59
South Strong, 54A
South Switch, 61
South Waterboro, 13
South Windham, 36
South Winn, 43
Spaulding, 61L
Sprague, 43
Spragues Falls, 66
Spring Farm, 54D
Springvale, 13
Squa Pan, 61H, 61L
Squaw Brook, 73
St. Croix, 61H
St. Croix Jct., 65, 66
St. David, 61J
St. Francis, 61K
St. John, 61K
St. Luce, 61J
Stacyville, 61
Starbirds, 58
State House Siding, 44
State Rd., 61L
Stebbins, 77
Steep Falls, 36
Stillwater, 42, 43A
Stockholm, 61, 61L
Stockholm Jct. , 61, 61L
Stockton Springs, 61
Stockton, 61
Stovers, 65
Stratton Jct., 54I
Stricklands, 40
Stricklands Ferry, 40
Strong, 54A, 54B
Stronghold, 57
Summit, 53, 54B
Sumner, 52
Surfside, 15
Sweden, 76B
Sweden Siding, 76B
Tarratine, 73
Temple Ave., 15
Ten Degree, 53
The Bridge, 40
The Elms, 15
The Park, 52
The Wye, 52A, 52B

Thomaston, 45
Thompsons, 57
Thorndike, 56
Thurstons Siding, 53A
Togus, 47
Tomah, 43
Topsham, 40A, 44
Troutdale, 55A
Tunk Lake, 65
Tunk Pond, 65
Twin Lake, 38
Tyngston, 40
Union Bluffs, 31
Union Jct., 41
Unionville, 65
Unity, 56
USAF Jct., 76, 76C
Van Buren, 61, 61J
Vanceboro, 43, 44
Veazie, 43
Violette, 61J
Waites, 52A
Waldo, 56
Waldoboro, 45
Wales, 40A
Walker, 61L
Walkers Mills, 41
Wallagrass, 61I
Walnut Hill, 39A, 39B
Wards, 65
Warren, 45
Washburn, 61L, 76, 76A
Washburn Jct., 76D
Washington Jct. , 64, 65
Waterboro, 13
Waterville, 39, 44
Watson, 61
Watts, 65
Waukeag, 64
Wayne Pond, 40
Webbs, 76
Webster, 43
Weeks Mills, 46, 46A
Weeksboro, 61H
Welchs, 53
Wells, 15, 30
Wells Beach, 15
Wells Branch, 30
Wells Depot, 30
Wescott, 13
Wescustogo, 39A

Station Index 389

West Baldwin, 36
West Benton, 39
West Bethel, 41
West Biddeford, 15
West Caribou, 76
West Danville, 41
West Dover, 58
West Falmouth, 44
West Farmington, 40
West Harrington, 65
West Kennebunk, 30
West Minot, 52
West Palmyra, 57
West Paris, 41
West Peru, 52
West Pownal, 41
West Presque Isle, 76
West Scarborough, 30
West Sebago, 38
West Seboois, 61
West Waterville, 39
Westbrook Jct., 13, 44

Westbrook, 13, 44
Westbrook-Cumberland Mills, 36
Westfield, 61
Westmanland, 61L
Westport, 45
Westville, 40
Wheelock, 61K
Whiddens Farm, 66
White Rock, 36
Whitefield, 46
Whitney Brook, 52, 52A
Whitneyville, 65
Wild Goose Club, 57
Wilderness, 43
Williamsburg, 73
Wilton, 40
Windsor, 46
Winn, 43
Winnecook, 56
Winslow, 44, 46A
Winslows Mills, 45

Winterport, 61
Winterport Ferry, 63
Winterville, 61I
Winthrop, 39
Wiscasset, 45, 46
Wiscasset [Boat Landing], 45
Woodard, 73
Woodfords, 13, 44
Woodland, 66A
Woodland Center, 76B
Woodland Jct., 66, 66A
Woodman, 41
Woolwich, 45
Worthley, 52
Wrights, 45
Wytopitlock, 43
Yarmouth Jct., 41, 44
Yarmouth, 41, 44
York Beach, 31
York Harbor, 31

New Hampshire

Alder Brook, 70
Allenstown, 24
Alton, 26
Alton Bay, 26, 27
Ames, 27
Amherst, 11, 22B
Amoskeag, 14A
Anderson, 12
Andover, 51
Antrim, 20
Appalachia, 70B
Apthorp, 70
Ashland, 14C
Ashuelot, 6
Atkinson, 15
Atlantic, 16
Auburn, 23A
Bagley, 21
Baileys, 72
Barnstead, 24
Barrett, 70
Barrington, 12
Bartlett, 36

Base Sta., 70A
Bath, 70
Bayside, 23
Bedford, 22, 22B
Beebe River, 14F
Belknap Point, 27
Bellamy, 25
Belmont, 14E
Belmont Jct., 14C, 14E
Bemis, 36
Bennett Rd., 15
Bennington, 20
Berlin, 41, 70B
Berlin Falls, 41
Berlin Mills, 70B
Bethlehem, 70A, 71A
Bethlehem Jct., 70A, 71, 71A
Blackmount, 14C
Blair, 14F
Blakes, 51A
Blodgett, 24
Blood, 11

Boscawen, 51
Bow, 14A
Bow Jct., 14A, 23
Bow Mills, 14A
Bowman, 70B
Boy Mountain, 70B
Boyce, 14C
Bradford, 21
Breakfast Hill, 16
Bretton Woods, 36,
Bretton Woods-Fabyan, 36, 70A
Bristol, 51A
Brookfield, 29
Brookhurst, 27
Buckley, 27
Burleyville, 28
C&M Jct., 72
Campton, 14F
Campton Village, 14F
Canaan, 51
Candia, 23, 23A
Canobie Lake, 18

Canterbury, 14C
Cardigan, 51
Carrigain, 36
Carroll, 36
Carroll Tank, 36
Cascade, 41
Cavender, 20
Cemetery, 25
Center Barnstead, 24
Center Conway, 36
Centre Barnstead, 24
Centre Ossipee, 28
Chandler, 21
Charlestown, 34, 35
Cherry Mountain, 70B, 70C
Cherry Pond, 70B
Chesham, 19
Cheshire Mills, 8
Chichester, 24
Christian Hill, 6
Claremont, 34
Claremont [Mulberry St.] , 21, 21A
Claremont Center, 21
Claremont Jct., 21, 34
Cochecho, 26
Cocheco, 21
Cocheko, 21
Colby, 22
Cold River, 7
Colebrook, 72
Columbia Bridge, 72
Columbia House, 72
Columbia Valley, 72
Concord, 14A, 14C, 21, 51
Concord Depot, 10
Cones, 72
Contoocook, 21, 21B
Converse, 51
Conway, 28
Conway Center, 36
Coolidge Crossing, 19
Coos Jct., 70, 72
Copperville, 41
Cotton Mill, 28
Cotton Valley, 29
Cottonboro, 29
Crawford Notch, 36
Crawfords, 36

Crescent St., 22
Crocketts Crossing, 15B
Crystal, 41
Cushings, 25
Dalton, 70
Danbury, 51
Danforths Corners, 11
Davis, 26
Deering, 20
Derry, 18
Diamond Crossing, 36
Dimond Corner, 21
Dimonds, 21
Dole Jct., 6, 6A
Doolittle, 6
Dover, 15, 25, 26
Dover Point, 25
Drury, 8
Dublin, 19
Durham, 15
Dye Plant, 25
East Andover, 51
East Candia, 23
East Claremont, 21
East Concord, 14C
East Epping, 23
East Harrisville, 19
East Haverhill, 14C
East Jaffrey, 8
East Kingston, 15
East Lebanon, 51
East Manchester, 23A
East Mathews, 28
East Milford, 11, 22B
East Rochester, 13
East Tilton, 14C
East Wakefield, 28
East Weare, 22
East Westmoreland, 7
Eastside, 14C
Eastview, 19
Eatons, 72
Edgemont, 21
Ellacoya, 27
Elmwood, 19, 20
Elmwood Jct., 19, 20
Emerson, 21B
Enfield, 51
Epping, 12, 23
Epsom, 24
Everett, 22

Exeter, 15
Fabyan, 70A
Fabyans, 36
Fairview, 14F
Farmington, 26
Fernald, 29
Fisherville, 51
Fitzwilliam, 7
Foggs Rd., 14C
Foggs Siding, 41
Folsom St. , 25
Forest Lake, 6
Foundry, 15B, 28
Franklin, 51, 51A
Franklin Falls, 14D
Franklin Falls Dam, 51A
Franklin Jct. , 51, 14D
Freemans Point, 25
Fremont, 12
Ft. Hill, 6A
Gale River, 70
Gale, 51
Gardners Grove, 14E
Garrison, 21
Georges, 72
Gerrish, 51
Gilboa, 7
Gilford, 27
Glen & Jackson, 36
Glen Rd., 70B
Glen Sta., 36
Glencliff, 14C
Glendale, 27
Goffs, 14A
Goffs Falls, 14A
Goffstown, 22
Goffstown Center, 22
Gonic, 26
Gorham Mineral Spring, 70B
Gorham, 41, 70B
Grafton, 51
Grafton Center, 51
Grasmere, 22
Grasmere Jct., 22, 22B
Great Falls, 15B, 28
Greenfield, 11, 19
Greenland, 16, 23
Greenville, 9
Grenier AFB, 18
Greystone, 27

Station Index

Groveton, 41, 70
Groveton Jct., 41, 70
Guild, 21
Hadley, 8
Halcyon, 51
Hallsville, 23A
Hampshire Rd., 18
Hampstead, 12
Hampton, 16
Hampton Falls, 16
Hancock, 19
Hancock Jct., 19, 20
Harrisville, 19
Haverhill, 14C
Haverhill & Newbury, 14C
Hayes, 28
Hayes Crossing, 28
Hazen, 70B
Hazens, 36
Hedding, 23
Henniker, 21B, 22
Henniker Jct., 21B, 22
Highlands, 70B
Hill, 51A
Hillsboro, 20, 21B
Hillsboro Bridge, 21B
Hillsdale, 28
Hilton, 25
Hinsdale, 6
Holderness, 14C
Hollis, 12
Holton, 20
Hooksett, 14A, 14B
Horse Meadow, 14C
Hubbard, 12
Hubbards [East Derry], 12
Hudson, 12
Intervale, 28, 36
Intervale Jct., 36
Jaffrey, 8
Jefferson, 70B, 70C, 72
Jefferson Jct., 70B, 72
Jericho, 41
Joslin, 7
Keene, 6, 7, 19
Keewaydin, 27
Kelly Rd., 18
Kellys, 24
Kellyville, 21

Klondike, 35
Laconia, 14C
Lake Shore Park, 27
Lake Sunapee, 21
Lake Village, 14C
Lake Wentworth, 29
Lakeport, 14C, 27
Lakewood, 28
Lancaster, 70, 72
Lang, 22A
Leadmine Crossing, 41
Lebanon, 51
Lee, 12
Lily Pond, 27
Lincoln, 14F
Lisbon, 70
Little River Jct., 70A
Littlefield, 23
Littles, 10
Littleton, 70
Livermore Falls, 14F
Lochmere, 14C
Londonderry, 18
Loon Cove, 27
Lower Warner, 21
Lyfords Siding, 14F
Madbury, 15
Madison, 28
Maine Central Transfer, 70
Manchester, 14A, 18, 22, 23A
Manchester Airport, 18
Mapleton, 41
Maplewood, 71A
Marlboro, 19
Marlboro Village, 19
Marlborough, 7
Martin, 14A
Martins, 14A
Martins Ferry, 14A
Mascoma, 51
Mason, 9
Mason Centre, 9
Mason Village, 9
Masons, 41, 72
Massabesic, 23A
Mast Yard, 21
Mathews, 28
Meadowbrook, 27
Meadows, 70B

Melvin, 21
Melvin Mills, 21
Meredith, 14C
Meredith Bridge, 14C
Meredith Village, 14C
Merrimack, 14A
Messers, 18
Milan, 41
Milford, 11
Mill Village, 29
Milton, 28
Mineral Springs, 70B
Moores Cossing, 14A
Mountain Rock, 14F
Mountainview, 28
Mountorne, 70
Mt. Madison Springs, 70B
Mt. Major, 27
Mt. Pleasant House, 36
Mt. Sunapee, 21
Mt. Whittier, 28
Nahor, 20
Nashua, 10, 11, 12
Nashua [Concord Depot], 14A
Nashua City Sta., 10, 11
Nashua Jct., 10, 12, 14A
Nashua Main St., 12
Nashua Union Sta., 10, 12, 14A
New Boston, 22A
New Durham, 26
New Hampton, 14C
Newbury, 21
Newfields, 15
Newington, 25
Newmarket, 15
Newmarket Jct., 15, 23
Newport, 21
Newton, 15, 15C
Newton Jct., 15, 15C
Noone, 8
North Boscawen, 51
North Charlestown, 34
North Chichester, 24
North Concord, 14C
North Conway, 28, 36
North Hampton, 16
North Haverhill, 14C
North Lisbon, 70

North Newport, 21
North Stratford, 41, 72
North Stratford Jct., 41, 72
North Wakefield, 28
North Walpole, 34
North Weare, 22
North Woodstock, 14F
Northfield, 14C
Northumberland, 70
Northumberland Falls, 70
Northville, 21
Notchland, 36
Nutts Pond, 18
Oakdale Park, 51A
Oil Mills, 22
Oliverion, 14C
Onway Lake, 23
Ossipee, 28
Ossipee Pit, 28
Ossipee Valley, 28
Parker, 22
Parkers, 22, 22A
Pattee, 51
Pembroke, 23
Penacook, 51
Percy, 41
Peterborough, 8, 20
Pickering, 23, 26
Pierces Bridge, 70A
Pierces Crossing, 8
Pike, 14C
Pinardville, 22
Pine Valley, 11
Piper Hill, 72
Piscataqua, 25
Pittsfield, 24
Place, 26
Plaistow, 15
Pleasant St., 21
Plymouth, 14C, 14F
Ponemah, 11
Portsmouth, 16, 23, 25, 30
Potter Place, 51
Powwow River, 15
Pratt, 9
Pratts, 9
Profile Falls, 51A
Profile House, 71
Putnam, 7

Quebec Jct. , 36, 72
Quincy, 14C
Rand, 8
Randolph, 70B
Raymond, 23
Redstone, 36
Reeds, 14A
Reeds Ferry, 14A
Richardson, 11
Rindge, 8
Rindgemere, 13
Riverdale, 22
Riverhill, 21
Riverton, 72
Robinsons Ferry, 14A
Roby, 21
Robys Corner, 21
Rochester, 12, 13, 26, 28
Rockingham, 15, 23
Rockingham Jct., 15, 23
Rockingham Park, 18A
Rockingham Park Jct., 18, 18A
Rollins Farm, 25
Rollinsford, 15, 15B
Rowes Corner, 23
Rumney, 14C
Russ Crossing, 15
Russell, 11
Salem, 18
Salmon Falls, 15, 28
Sanbornton Bridge, 14C
Sanbornville, 28, 29
Sanbornville Union Sta., 28, 29
Sanders, 27
Sandown, 12
Sargent, 22
Saunders, 27
Sawyer, 25
Sawyer River, 36
Sawyers, 36
Sawyers Crossing, 6
Scotts, 36, 70
Scotts Jct., 36
Seabrook, 16
Severance, 23A
Sewalls, 14C
Sewalls Falls, 14C
Shelburne, 41
Ship Yard, 25

Shirley, 22
Shirley Hill, 22
Short Falls, 24
Silver Lake, 28
Smiths Point, 27
Smithtown, 16
Somersworth, 15B, 28
South Bennington, 19
South Branch Jct., 70B
South Danbury, 51
South Keene, 7, 19
South Lancaster, 70
South Littleton, 70
South Lyndeborough, 11
South Manchester, 14A
South Merrimack, 11
South Milton, 28
South Nashua, 10
South New Market, 15
South Newmarket Jct., 15
South Weare, 22
Spring Haven, 27
Springfield Jct., 35
Stark, 41
Starr King, 72
State Line, 7, 16
Stratford Hollow, 41
Stratford Jct., 41
Stratham, 23
Sugar Hill, 70
Sunapee, 21
Suncook, 14B, 23, 24
Swainboro, 14C
Swanzey, 6, 7
Tarbell, 20
Terrace Hill, 27
Thayers Mills, 70C
Thomas, 8
Thornton, 14F
Thorntons, 14A
Thorntons Ferry, 14A
Tilton, 14C, 14D
Tioga, 14E
Tirell Hill, 22B
Troy, 7
Twin Mountain, 36, 70A
Tyler, 21
Union, 28
Union Bridge, 14C
Upper Bartlett, 36
Wakefield, 28

Station Index

Walpole, 7
Warner, 21
Warren, 14C
Warren Summit, 14C
Washington St., 21
Waterloo, 21
Waumbek Jct., 70B, 72
Webb, 7
Webster Lake, 51
Webster Place, 51
Websters Mills, 24
Weirs, 14C
Weirs Beach, 14C
Wentworth, 14C
West Alton, 27
West Andover, 51
West Canaan, 51
West Claremont, 21A
West Concord, 21
West Deering, 20
West Epping, 23
West Gonic, 12
West Hampstead, 12
West Henniker, 21B
West Hopkinton, 21B
West Lebanon, 51
West Manchester, 22
West Milan, 41
West Ossipee, 28
West Plymouth, 14C
West Rindge, 8
West Rochester, 12
West Rumney, 14C
West Stewartstown, 72
West Swanzey, 6
West Thornton, 14F
West Windham, 12
Westboro, 51
Westmoreland, 7
Westport, 6
Westville, 15
White Mountain House, 36, 70A
White Mountain Transfer, 70
Whitefield, 36, 70B
Whitefield Jct., 70, 70B
Willey, 18
Willey House, 36
Wilson, 18
Wilsons, 18
Wilton, 9, 11
Winchester, 6
Windham, 12, 18
Windham Jct., 12, 18
Wing Rd. , 70, 70A
Winnisquam, 14C
Wolfeboro, 29
Wolfeboro Falls, 29
Wolfeboro Jct., 28, 29
Wolfeboro Lake, 29
Woodlands, 27
Woodmere, 8
Woodstock, 14F
Woodsville, 14C, 70
Zealand, 36, 70A
Zealand Transfer, 70A

Vermont

Abnaki, 2C
Albertson, 48
Alburgh, 2C, 2G, 34A, 75
Alburgh Springs, 34A
Alfrecha, 2B
Anthony, 2E
Arlington, 2B
Barnet, 5
Barnumville, 2B
Barre, 34D, 67A, 67B
Barre Jct., 67, 67B
Barre Transfer, 67
Barton, 5
Barton Landing, 5
Bartonsville, 2A
Beanville, 34
Bee Hive Crossing, 2E
Beecher Falls, 72
Beldens, 2A
Bellows Falls, 2A, 7, 34
Bennington, 2B, 2E
Bethel, 34, 34F, 50
Billings Park, 49A
Blissville, 1B
Bloomfield, 41
Bolton, 34
Boltonville, 67
Boutwells, 50
Bradford, 5
Braintree, 34
Brandon, 2A
Brattleboro, 6A, 17, 34
Bristol, 3
Brockways Mills, 2A
Brooksville, 2A
Burlington, 2A, 2C, 34, 68
Burlington Yard, 2A
Butlers Corners, 68
Cambridge, 68
Cambridge Jct. , 37, 68
Castleton, 1A, 1B
Cavendish, 2A
Center Rutland, 1A, 2A, 48, 48A, 48B
Centervale, 5
Central Park, 34
Charlotte, 2A
Chester, 2A
Clarendon, 2A, 2B
Clarendon Springs, 1C
Cloverdale, 68
Cobb Bridge, 50
Coffeehouse Jct., 67
Colchester, 2C, 34A
Colchester Point, 2C
Cold River, 2B
Concord, 37
Conicut, 5
Coventry, 5
Cuttingsville, 2A
CV Barre Jct., 34D, 34E
Danby, 2B
Danby & Mt. Tabor, 2B
Danville, 37

Station Index

Derby, 5A
Deweys Mills, 49
Dixon, 68
Dow, 37
Dows Crossing, 37
Dummerston, 34
Duxbury, 34
East Alburgh, 34A, 34C, 75
East Barnet, 5
East Barre, 67C
East Berkshire, 69
East Bethel, 34F
East Brighton, 41
East Clarendon, 2A
East Dorset, 2B
East Fairfield, 37
East Fletcher, 37
East Franklin Rd., 69
East Georgia, 34A
East Granville, 34
East Hardwick, 37
East Haven, 37A
East Highgate, 37
East Montpelier, 67
East Putney, 34
East Ryegate, 5
East St. Johnsbury, 37
East Swanton, 34B, 37, 69
East Wallingford, 2A
Edgewater, 67
Elkhurst, 5B, 74
Ellis Quarry [East Bethel], 34F
Ely, 5
Emersons, 50
Enosburg Falls, 69
Essex, 37
Essex Center, 68
Essex Jct. , 34, 34A, 68
Evarts, 34
Fairfield, 37
Fairhaven, 1A
Fairlee, 5
Fairlee & Orford, 5
Fairmont, 67
Ferrisburg, 2A
Fitzdale, 37
Fletcher, 37
Florence, 2A, 48C
Florence Jct., 48A, 48C
Florentine Quarry, 48C
Fonda, 34A
Fonda Jct., 34A, 34B
Fowler, 2A
Ft. Ethan Allen, 34
Gassetts, 2A
Gaysville, 50
Georgia, 34A
Gilman, 37
Grand Isle, 2C
Granite Jct. , 37
Graniteville, 67A
Greens Corner, 69
Greensboro, 37
Greensboro Bend, 37
Groton, 67
Guildhall, 72
Hagers, 4A
Hardwick, 37
Hartford, 34, 49, 49A
Hartland, 34
Healdville, 2A
Highgate, 37
Highgate Center, 37
Highgate Springs, 34B
Hollister Quarry, 48A
Houghs Crossing, 2D
Hubbards, 50
Humphreys, 2A
Hyde Park, 37
Hydeville, 1A
Inwood, 5
Island Pond, 41
Isle La Motte, 2C
Jacksonville, 4
Jamaica, 17
Jeffersonville, 68
Jericho, 68
Joes Pond, 37
Johnson, 37
Jones's, 34
Jonesville, 34
Kendall, 5
Kimball, 5
Knight Point, 2C
Lake Park, 5B
Lake, 41
Lakeside, 67
Lakewood, 34A
Lanesboro, 67
Larrabees Point, 2D
Leicester, 2A
Leicester Jct., 2A, 2D
Lillesville, 50
Lower Rochester, 50
Ludlow, 2A
Lunenburg, 36, 37
Lyndon, 5
Lyndonville, 5
Maidstone, 72
Manchester, 2B
Maquam, 37, 75
Marshfield, 67
McIndoe, 5
McIndoes, 5
McIndoes Falls, 5
McLarans, 5
Middlebury, 2A
Middlesex, 34
Midway, 2A
Miles Pond, 37
Milton, 34A
Missisco, 34A
Missisquoi, 5B
Montpelier, 34D, 67
Montpelier Jct. , 34, 34D
Morrisville, 37
Mount Holly, 2A
Mountain Mills, 4, 4A
New Haven, 2A, 3
New Haven Jct., 2A, 3
Newbury, 5
Newfane, 17
Newport, 5, 5A, 5B
Newport Center, 5B
Norrisville, 5
North Bennington, 2B, 2F
North Clarendon, 2A
North Concord, 37, 37A
North Derby, 5A
North Dorset, 2B
North Duxbury, 34
North Enosburg, 69
North Ferrisburg, 2A
North Georgia, 34A
North Hartland, 34
North Hero, 2C
North Jct., 34A
North Moretown, 34
North Sheldon, 69

Station Index

North Thetford, 5
North Troy, 5B
North Underhill, 68
Northboro, 5
Northfield, 34
Northfield Falls, 34
Norton, 41
Norton Mills, 41
Norwich, 5
Norwich-Hanover, 5
Oakland, 34A
Olcott, 5
Orleans, 5
Orwell, 2D
Paradis, 41
Parker Hill, 1B
Passumpsic, 5
Pawlet, 1B
Pittsford, 2A
Pittsford Quarry, 2A
Plainfield, 67
Pompanoosuc, 5
Poultney, 1B
Proctor, 2A, 48A
Proctorsville, 2A
Putney, 34
Quechee, 49
Queen City Park, 2A
Randolph, 34
Readsboro, 4
Richford, 5B, 69
Richmond, 34
Rickers, 67
Ridleys, 34
Riverside, 2A, 50
Riverside, 68
Riverton, 34
Rochester, 50
Rockingham, 2A
Rocky Point, 67
Roxbury, 34
Roxbury Flat, 34
Royalton, 34
Rupert, 1B
Rutland, 1A, 2A, 2B, 48B

Rye Gate, 5
Salisbury, 2A
Shaftsbury, 2B
Sharon, 34
Shawnville, 37
Shelburne, 2A
Sheldon, 37, 69
Sheldon Jct., 37, 69
Sheldon Springs, 69
Sherman, 4
Shoreham, 2D
South Alburgh, 2C
South Barre, 34E
South Barton, 5
South Franklin, 69
South Hero, 2C
South Londonderry, 17
South Newbury, 5
South Northfield, 34
South Royalton, 34
South Ryegate, 67
South Shaftsbury, 2B
South Vernon, 6
South Wallingford, 2B
St. Albans, 34A, 69
St. Johnsbury, 5, 37
St. Johnsbury Centre, 5
Stafford, 2B
Star Farm Beach, 2C
Stevens, 72
Stevens Mills, 5B
Stockbridge, 50
Summit, 2A, 5, 41
Sunderland, 2B
Sutherland Falls, 2A
Sutton, 5
Swanton, 34A, 37
Swanton Jct., 34A, 34B
Taftsville, 49
Talcville, 50
Thetford, 5
Thompsons Point, 2A
Townshend, 17
Troy Jct., 5B, 74
Tupper, 50

Underhill, 68
Vergennes, 2A
Vernon, 34
Victory, 37A
Walden, 37
Wallingford, 2B
Wardsboro, 17
Waterbury, 34
Websterville, 67A, 67C
Wells River, 5, 14C, 67
Wenlock, 41
West Alburgh, 34A
West Berlin, 34
West Burke, 5
West Concord, 37
West Danville, 37
West Dummerston, 17
West Hartford, 34
West Pawlet, 1B
West River, 34
West Rupert, 1B
West Rutland, 1A, 1C, 48
West Swanton, 34A, 75
West Townshend, 17
Westminster, 34
White River Falls, 5, 34
White River Jct., 5, 34, 49, 51
White River Village, 34
Whiting, 2A, 2D
Whitingham, 4, 4A
Wilder, 5
Williamstown, 34E
Williamsville, 17
Williston, 34
Willoughby, 5
Wilmington, 4, 4A
Windsor, 34
Winhall, 17
Winooski, 34
Wolcott, 37
Woodstock, 34, 49
Woodsville, 5

Main Index

A. L. & W. G. Brown Co., 332
Abbot, ME, 287
Acadia National Park, 316, 367
Addison RR, 42
Agamenticus, ME, 94, 154-155
Albany, NY, 36-38
Albertson, VT, 241
Albion, ME, 233-235, 281
Alburgh, VT, 43, 172, 352
Alder Stream, 267
Allagash, ME, 300
Allan Line, 346
Allenstown, NH, 132
Alton Bay, NH, 137, 139, 141, 143
Alton, NH, 131-132
Ammonoosuc River, 180, 332, 336
Amoskeag Co., 301
Amtrak, 38, 45, 175, 284
Andover & Haverhill RR, 94
Andover & Wilmington RR, 93-94
Andover, MA, 93
Androscoggin & Kennebec RR, 197-198, 202-203, 273
Androscoggin & Kennebec RY, 364
Androscoggin Electric Co., 363
Androscoggin Navigation Co., 256
Androscoggin River, 202, 212, 255-257, 261-262, 333, 363
Androscoggin RR, 200, 202-203
Anson, ME, 273
Antrim, NH, 117
Arbox III Corp., 357
Aroostock Falls, ME, 355
Aroostock Jct., NB, 359
Aroostock River, 359
Aroostook Northern RR, 298, 301

Aroostook River RR, 354-355, 359
Aroostook Valley RR, 299, 354-357, 359
Arundel, ME, 362
Ashland, ME, 298
Ashley, James G., 107
Ashuelot River, 58, 73
Ashuelot RR, 57-59, 61, 113
Athens & Skowhegan RR, 291
Athens, ME, 281, 291
Atlantic & St. Lawrence RR, 197, 207-210, 223, 255, 332
Atlantic & St. Lawrence RY, 331
Atlantic Shore Line RY, 83, 160, 362
Atlantic Shore RY, 362
Atwood, Leonard, 233
Auburn, ME, 197-198, 211-212, 257, 363-364
Auburn, Mechanic Falls & Norway Street RY, 364
Augusta, ME, 198, 223-224, 226, 230, 232, 236-237, 306, 364-365
Austin Jct., ME, 273
Ayer, MA, 67-68
Back Cove, 210-211
Baileyville, ME, 319
Bakers, ME, 275
Bangor & Aroostook Corp., 301
Bangor & Aroostook RR, 287-289, 298-301, 303-304, 347-348, 354-357, 359, 365
Bangor & Bucksport RR, 218
Bangor & Calais RR, 309
Bangor & Katahdin Iron Works Co., 288
Bangor & Katahdin Iron Works RR,

Main Index

298
Bangor & Katahdin Iron Works RY, 288
Bangor & Old Town RY, 214-215
Bangor & Piscataquis Canal & RR, 214
Bangor & Piscataquis RR, 218, 280, 284, 287-288, 291, 298, 300, 365
Bangor Punta Alegre, 301
Bangor Railway & Electric Co., 365
Bangor, ME, 197, 200, 213-215, 217-219, 224, 287, 298, 301, 306, 309, 311, 315, 365
Bangor, Old Town & Milford RR, 215, 217
Bar Harbor, ME, 307, 309, 311
Bar Mills, ME, 81
Baring, ME, 318
Barnjum, ME, 270
Barre & Chelsea RR, 323
Barre Branch RR, 322
Barre Jct., VT, 322-324
Barre RR, 322
Barre, VT, 173, 322, 324
Bartlett & Albany RR, 182
Bartlett, NH, 180, 183-184, 341
Barton Landing, VT, 54
Barton River, 54
Barton, VT, 54
Base Station, NH, 332-333, 366
Bath Iron Works, 223
Bath, ME, 223, 228-229, 364-365
Batten Kill RR, 38
Bay of Fundy, 303, 346
Bay View, ME, 166
Bayonne Lumber Co., 246
Bedford, NH, 125
Beebe, PQ, 55-56
Beecher Falls Manufacturing Co., 341
Beecher Falls, VT, 340-342
Belfast & Moosehead Lake RR, 233, 278-279
Belfast, ME, 278-279
Belgrade, ME, 233
Belknap Point, NH, 143
Bellamy River, 135
Bellows Falls, VT, 44-45, 61, 63, 65, 170-171, 173, 253

Bemis, ME, 180, 260
Bennington & Glastenbury RR, 368
Bennington & Rutland RR, 41-42, 240
Bennington & Woodford Electric RR, 369
Bennington, NH, 74, 114, 117
Bennington, VT, 43, 45, 368
Benton, ME, 198
Berlin Mills RY, 333, 372
Berlin Mills, ME, 269
Berlin Mills, NH, 333
Berlin, NH, 333-334, 341, 372
Berwick, ME, 77, 154-155
Bethel Granite RY, 174
Bethel, ME, 209, 212
Bethel, VT, 246
Bethlehem Jct., NH, 332, 336
Bethlehem, NH, 336-337
Bickford Mountain, 336
Biddeford, ME, 99, 155, 157, 167, 362
Bigelow, ME, 267
Billerica & Bedford RR, 105, 265
Bingham Heights, ME, 274
Bingham, ME, 273-275
Bisbee, George D., 257
Black River, 177, 350
Blackmount, NH, 89
Blanchard & Twitchell Co., 261
Blanchard, ME, 287, 289
Blodgett, NH, 132
Bombardier of Canada, 324
Boscawen, NH, 249, 253
Boston & Albany RR, 65
Boston & Lowell RR, 55, 69-70, 73, 87-88, 93, 97, 111, 113, 121, 141, 187, 249, 251, 332
Boston & Maine RR, 55-56, 58, 62, 65-66, 68, 70-71, 73-74, 77, 81-82, 87-89, 94-96, 98, 101, 103, 110, 113-114, 117, 121, 125, 128-129, 131-132, 134-135, 137, 139, 141, 143, 146-148, 151, 154-157, 159-160, 162-166, 173-175, 177-178, 182-183, 187, 209, 224, 230, 244, 247, 251, 310, 323, 326, 333, 336, 341, 362-363, 366
Boston & Maine Transportation Co.,

68, 73, 251
Boston & Portland RR, 94
Boston Elevated RY, 355
Boston, Barre & Gardner RR, 61, 65, 116
Boston, Concord & Montreal RR, 54-55, 86-88, 119, 131-132, 137, 141-142, 181, 249, 251-252, 322, 331-332, 336, 339, 341
Boston, MA, 44, 55-56, 71, 81, 89, 95-96, 99, 103, 147, 154, 159, 162, 170, 182-183, 198, 207-208, 218, 230, 249, 251, 274, 336
Boston, ME, 310
Boundary, PQ, 345
Bow Jct., NH, 129, 131-132
Bow, NH, 90
Bradford, MA, 94
Bradford, NH, 119-120, 122, 124
Bradlee, Nathaniel J., 147
Brandon & West Rutland RR, 240
Brattleboro & Whitehall RR, 105-106
Brattleboro, VT, 61, 105-106, 171, 173, 175
Brave Boat Harbor, ME, 159
Bretton Woods Conference, 183
Bretton Woods, NH, 183, 333
Brewer, ME, 312
Bridgewater, ME, 301
Bridgton & Harrison RY, 193
Bridgton & Saco River RR, 192, 238, 266
Bridgton Jct., ME, 192
Bridgton, ME, 191-193
Briggs, Wiiliam C., 95
Bristol RR, 47-48
Bristol, NH, 251
Bristol, VT, 47
broad gauge, 197-198, 208-209, 217-218, 287, 304, 306
Brookfield, NH, 150
Brookline & Milford RR , 125
Brown's Lumber Co., 333
Brownville Jct., ME, 288-289, 345, 347-348
Brownville, ME, 288-289, 298, 345-346

Brunswick, ME, 198, 200, 203-204, 223-224, 226, 229-230, 364
Brunswick, VT, 339
Buck, R. P., 306
Buckfield Branch RR, 255-256
Buckfield, ME, 255-256
Bucksport & Bangor RR, 306, 309
Bucksport, ME, 306-307, 309
Buckstown, ME, 306
Budd RDCs, 98, 183, 230, 252, 333
Burleigh, Albert, 298
Burlington & Lamoille RR, 186, 189, 325-326
Burlington International Airport, 326
Burlington, VT, 41, 43, 45-46, 170-172, 186, 326
Burnham, ME, 233, 278
Busiel, Charles A., 141
busses, 73, 251-252, 300-301, 304, 307, 363, 365
Buxton, ME, 83
Byron Logging RR, 261
Byron, ME, 260
Cadillac Mountain, 367
Calais & Baring RR, 303, 318-319
Calais Jct., ME, 307
Calais RY, 318
Calais, ME, 303, 309, 314-316, 318, 320
Cambridge Jct., VT, 326
Cambridge, VT, 186, 326
Camden, ME, 372
Camp Ellis, ME, 166
Canada, 43, 54-55, 86, 171, 173, 176, 180-181, 186, 207-209, 211, 220, 249, 261, 303-304, 314, 339-340, 345, 348, 350, 354, 359
Canada Atlantic RY, 173, 175
Canadian American RR, 289, 348
Canadian Atlantic RY, 220, 320, 347
Canadian National RYs, 174, 176, 210, 218, 300, 346
Canadian Pacific RY, 55, 218-220, 251-252, 281, 288-289, 302, 304, 316, 320, 329, 340-341, 345-347, 350, 355-357, 359
Candia, NH, 128-129

Main Index 399

Cantic, PQ, 173
Canton, ME, 255-258
Cape Elizabeth, ME, 95, 223
Cape Jellison, ME, 299-300
Cape Porpoise, ME, 362
Caribou, ME, 298, 301, 355, 359
Carlows Island, ME, 315
Carrabassett River, 267, 275
Carrabassett, ME, 271
Carroll, NH, 181, 341
Carson, ME, 355
Carver, MA, 212
Cascade, NH, 333
Castine, ME, 309
Castleton, VT, 36-37
Cathance River, 223
Center Barnstead, NH, 132
Center Rutland, VT, 45, 240-241
Central Vermont RR, 42-43, 173-174, 243, 246, 352
Central Vermont RY, 43, 56, 58, 105-106, 174-175, 189, 244, 251, 324-326, 329, 333, 369
Champlain & Connecticut River RR, 41, 171
Champlain & St. Lawrence RR, 249
Champlain Canal, 36
Charleston, ME, 365
Charlestown, NH, 170, 177-178
Charlotte, ME, 314
Chatham & Lebanon Valley RR, 43
Chatham, NY, 43
Chelsea, ME, 237-238
Cherry Mountain, NH, 332
Cherryfield, ME, 314-316
Cheshire Bridge, 177
Cheshire RR, 57-58, 61-62, 65, 73, 113, 119, 170, 249
China Lake, 237
China, ME, 233, 237
Chisolm, Hugh, 257
Claremont & Concord RY, 121
Claremont Center, NH, 121
Claremont Concord RR, 122
Claremont Electric Light Co., 121
Claremont Jct., NH, 121-122
Claremont RY, 122

Claremont RY and Lighting Co., 121
Claremont Street RY, 121
Claremont, NH, 119-120, 122, 124
Clarendon & Pittsford RR, 38, 240-241, 369
Clark's Trading Post, 262
Closson, Henry P., 267
Cobb Bridge, VT, 247
Cobbosseecontee Stream, 224
Cochecho RR, 77, 81, 131, 136-139, 141, 143, 146, 151
Cochecho, NH, 137
Cocheco River, 94, 134-135
Coffeehouse Jct., VT, 322
Coffins Cut, NH, 94
Cold River, NH, 62
Colebrook, NH, 339
Columbia Falls, ME, 315
Columbia, NH, 342
Community Bus Lines, 73
Concord & Claremont RR, 119-120, 122
Concord & Claremont Valley RR, 124
Concord & Manchester Electric Branch, 363
Concord & Montreal RR, 88-89, 124-125, 129, 142, 251, 333, 336, 366
Concord & Portsmouth RR, 87, 128
Concord RR, 70, 86-88, 90, 110, 113, 119, 124, 128-129, 131-132, 333
Concord Street RY, 363
Concord, MA, 71
Concord, NH, 65, 70, 73, 86, 89-90, 116, 119, 128-129, 131, 141, 249, 363
Concord, VT, 186
Connecticut & Passumpsic Rivers RR, 54-56, 249, 322
Connecticut River, 41, 54, 58, 86, 105, 119, 170-171, 175, 177-178, 211, 243, 249, 329, 331, 336, 339
Connecticut River RR, 54, 58, 73, 113, 173
Conrail, 176
Consolidated European & North American RY, 218

Contoocook River, 65, 116, 119, 122
Contoocook River RR, 120-121
Contoocook Valley RR, 65, 116, 119-122, 124
Contoocook, NH, 119, 122
Conway Lumber Co., 147, 182
Conway Scenic RR, 149, 151, 184
Conway, NH, 148, 182
Cookshire, PQ, 340
Coolidge & Shattuck, 229
Coolidge Crossing, NH, 113-114
Coopers Corner, ME, 162
Coopers Mills, ME, 233, 237
Coos Jct., NH, 333-334, 339, 341
Coos Turnpike Corporation, 86
Coos Valley RR, 339
Coplin, ME, 269
Corinna, ME, 283
Corinth, ME, 365
Cotton Valley group, 151
Crawford House Hotel, 181
Crawford Notch, NH, 184
Crawford Pond, 370
Crawford, NH, 183
Crawfords, NH, 180
Crowe Rope Co., 279
Crowell, H. P., 234
Crowleys, ME, 203-204
CSF Acquisitions Corp., 190, 324, 333, 342
Cumberland Jct., ME, 198, 224
Cumberland Mills, ME, 83
Cushman, Samuel B., 264
Dallas, ME, 267, 269
Danforths Corners, NH, 73
Danville Jct., ME, 211
Danville, ME, 198, 208
Danville, VT, 186, 197
Davidson Rubber Co., 139
Dead River, 269
Deadwater, ME, 273
Debec, NB, 303-304
Deer Isle, ME, 157
Deerfield River, 50
Deerfield River Co., 50
Deerfield River RR, 50
Deerfield Valley RR, 50

Deering Jct., ME, 83, 223
Delaware & Hudson Recreational Trail., 38
Delaware & Hudson RR, 37, 42, 105, 175, 240-241
Dennett Island, 160
Dennysville, ME, 315
Derby Line, VT, 55
Derby, ME, 287-289
Derry, NH, 111
Dexter & Newport RR, 284
Dexter & Piscatcquis RR, 284
Dexter, ME, 283
Dingley, Henry M., 363
Dixfield, ME, 258
Dock Lake, 191
Dolby Pond, 213
Dole Jct., NH, 58
Dominion Atlantic RY, 346
Dorset, VT, 370
Dover & Winnipiseogee RR, 81, 137
Dover, ME, 287
Dover, NH, 94, 96-99, 134-135, 137, 139, 141-142, 146, 148, 310, 362
Dover-Foxcroft, ME, 284, 287, 316
Dudswell, PQ, 340
Dumaine, Frederick C., Jr., 301
Durham, NH, 97, 99
Eagle Bridge, NY, 36-37
Eagle Lake, 367
Eagle Lake, ME, 298
East Alburgh, VT, 43, 173, 176, 352
East Augusta, ME, 226
East Barre & Chelsea RR, 322
East Barre RR, 322
East Barre, VT, 322
East Boston, MA, 101, 154
East Branch & Lincoln RR, 89
East Branch RR, 182, 261
East Claremont, NH, 122
East Creek (VT), 37
East Deering, ME, 210-212
East Haven, VT, 188
East Holden, ME, 309
East Kingston, NH, 94, 96, 99
East Lebanon, ME, 83
East Lynn, MA, 97

Main Index 401

East Machias, ME, 309
East Manchester, NH, 129
East Millinocket, ME, 299, 301
East Northfield, MA, 58, 171, 174-175
East Swanton, VT, 189
East Tilton, NH, 90
East Wilton, ME, 202
Eastern Maine RR, 220, 307
Eastern Maine RY, 348
Eastern Propane Co., 139
Eastern RR, 77, 81-82, 95-97, 101, 103, 128, 134, 137, 146-147, 151, 154-155, 159, 167, 182, 207, 309
Eastern Talc Co., 246
Eastman, PQ, 350
Eastport & Calais RR, 309
Eastport Jct., ME, 315
Eastport, ME, 309, 314, 316
Edaville RR, 212, 271, 293
Edmundston, NB, 359
Elliotsville, ME, 281
Ellis, Edmond, 328
Ellsworth High School, 312
Ellsworth, ME, 307, 309-311
Elmhurst, VT, 350
Elmwood, NH, 65, 73-74, 113-114, 117
Embden, ME, 273
Emerson, NH, 117, 121
Emersons, VT, 246
Emons Railroad Group, 211
Enfield, ME, 218, 220
Enfield, NH, 249
Enosburg, VT, 328
Epping, NH, 129
Erie Canal, 36
Essex Center, VT, 326
Essex County RR, 181, 186, 188
Essex Jct., VT, 172, 174, 326
Esterbrooke, W. L. K., 291
Ethan Allen Furniture Co., 341
Euopean & North American RR, 298
European & North American RR, 215, 217-220, 287, 304, 306-307, 316, 346
European & North American RY, 217-218, 319, 345

Eustis RR, 268-270
Eustis, ME, 269
Exeter, NH, 94, 99
Fabyan House, 366
Fabyan, NH, 332-333, 366
Fabyans, NH, 183, 336
Fair Grounds RR, 243
Fairbanks, Horace, 351
Fairfield, ME, 198
Fairmont, ME, 302
Farmington, ME, 202, 233, 264-265, 271
Farmington, NH, 139
Fellheimer & Long, 43
Fernald, NH, 152
Fish River RR, 298
Fitchburg RR, 50, 58, 61, 65, 67-68, 87, 97, 125
Flagstaff Lake, 269
Fletcher Granite Co., 369
Fletcher, VT, 186
floods, 37, 43, 51, 65, 89, 117, 122, 126, 132, 134, 174, 188, 224, 230, 247, 251, 262, 341, 357, 359
Florence Jct., VT, 241
Florence, VT, 38, 241
Florentine Quarry, VT, 241
Fonda Jct., VT, 189
Fonda, VT, 189
Forbes, Clyde S., 190
Fore River, 95-96, 154-155, 223
Fore River Dock and Dredge Co., 157
Foss Manufacturing Co., 103
Four Corners, ME, 162
Four Falls, NB, 359
Foxville, VT, 322
Frankenstein Trestle, 181
Franklin & Bristol RR, 249, 251
Franklin & Megantic RR, 266-267
Franklin & Megantic RY, 267
Franklin & Tilton RR, 251
Franklin Falls Dam, NH, 251
Franklin Falls Flood Control Area, 251
Franklin Falls, NH, 89
Franklin, ME, 314
Franklin, NH, 251
Franklin, Somerset & Kennebec RR,

233
Franklin, VT, 188
Fredericton, NB, 359
French, E. S., 247
Frenchman Bay, 309
Ft. Fairfield, ME, 302, 359
Ft. Kent, ME, 298
Ft. Ticonderoga, NY, 41
Gale River Lumber Co., 336
Gardiner, ME, 224, 237, 266
Gardner, MA, 61, 65
Gateway, NH, 180
Gaysville, VT, 246-247
Georges Valley RR, 229, 370
Georgia-Pacific Corp., 83, 315, 320
Gibson, NB, 359
Gilbert, Bradford Lee, 125
Gilbertville, ME, 204, 257
Gilead, ME, 209
Gilman, VT, 190, 334
Glen Station, NH, 182
Glendale, NH, 143
Goffstown, NH, 125-126
Gonic, NH, 139
Goodall-Sanford mills, 83, 362
Goodwin RR, 90
Gorham, ME, 83
Gorham, NH, 209, 333
Gould, Arthur R., 354-355
Goulds, VT, 177
Grand Falls Flowage, 319
Grand Southern RY, 314
Grand Trunk RY, 43, 54, 81, 172, 174, 192, 198, 209-211, 249, 257, 332-333, 341, 350
Granite Jct., VT, 369
Graniteville, VT, 322
Grant, Ulysses S., 218
Grant's Tomb, 202
Granville, NY, 36
Gray, ME, 363
Grays Farm, ME, 269
Great Bay, 134-135
Great Depression, 16, 37, 48, 238, 244, 274, 363
Great Falls & Conway RR, 77, 146
Great Falls & South Berwick RR, 146

Great Northern RR, 87
Greater Portland Public Development Commission, 157
Green Mountain, 367
Green Mountain RR, 38, 45, 59, 63, 367
Green Mountains, 105
Greenfield RR, 114
Greenfield, MA, 107
Greenfield, NH, 73-74, 113-114
Greenlay, PQ, 350
Greenleaf, Charles H., 336
Greens Corner, VT, 328
Greens Farm, ME, 269
Greensboro, VT, 186
Greenville, ME, 280, 287-289, 291, 345
Greenville, NH, 68
Grenier AFB, NH, 111
Grey, Sarah, 288
Groton Jct., MA, 67
Groveton, NH, 209, 331-334, 341-342
Guildhall, VT, 339
Guilford, 17-18, 38, 56, 66, 71, 74-75, 83, 90, 98-99, 111, 114, 117, 122, 129, 135, 139, 149, 157, 175, 177-178, 183-184, 200, 204, 211, 219, 226, 230, 253, 258, 275, 282, 307, 312, 315-316, 319-320, 329, 333, 342
Guilford, ME, 287, 289
H. E. Salzberg Co., 51
H. K. Webster Co., 328-329
Halifax, NS, 211, 218, 345
Hallock, Donald, 151
Hampton, NH, 103
Hancock Point, ME, 309
Hancock, NH, 73, 113-114
Hanover, NH, 97
Hardings, ME, 226, 230
Hardwick & Woodbury RR, 188, 369
Hardwick, VT, 186, 369
Harmony, ME, 281-282
Harriman, Avril, 51
Harrington, ME, 316
Harrison, ME, 192-193
Harrisville, NH, 113

Main Index

Hartford, ME, 256
Hartford, VT, 243
Hartland, ME, 281-282
Haverhill, MA, 94
Henniker Center, NH, 124
Henniker Jct., NH, 126
Henniker, NH, 119, 124
Henry, J. E., 89, 182
Hereford Branch RY, 339
Hereford RY, 339-340
Highland Lake, 191
Hillsboro, NH, 65, 74, 114, 116-117, 119
Hilton, VT, 243
Hinckley, ME, 225
Hinsdale, NH, 58
Hiram Jct., ME, 192
Hiram, ME, 183, 192
Hobo RR, 90
Holbrook Pond, 309
Holeb, ME, 345-346
Hollister, VT, 241
Holyoke, MA, 50
Hooksett, NH, 89, 131-132
Hoosac Tunnel, 50, 81
Hoosac Tunnel & Wilmington RR, 50
Hopkinton, NH, 120
Hotel Wonolancet, 142
Houghton Logging RR, 261
Houghton, ME, 260-261
Houlton Branch RR, 304
Houlton, ME, 298, 301-304
Howland, ME, 218, 220
Hurricane of 1938, 16, 51, 107, 114, 249
Hyde, Thomas, 223
Indian Pond, 275
Intermodal Surface Transportation Act of 1991, 99
Intercolonial RY, 218, 345
International Paper Co., 204, 258, 315-316
International RY of Maine, 345
Intervale, NH, 148, 182-184
Iron Road RYs, 302
Iron Road, Inc., 56, 347
Island Falls, ME, 298

Island Pond, VT, 209
J. D. Irving Co., 220, 320, 347-348
Jackson Township, NH, 182
Jackson, Paul, 293
Jacksonville, VT, 51
Jaffrey, NH, 65-66
Jamaica, VT, 105
Jefferson Station, NH, 332
Jefferson, NH, 333
Jeffersonville, VT, 326
Jericho, VT, 326
Jewett, ME, 148-149, 157
Johns River RR, 332
Johnson, VT, 190
Jones, Frank, 159
Katahdin Iron Works, ME, 287-288
Keene, NH, 57-59, 61-62, 73, 113-114, 171
Kellas, J. P., 50-51
Kendalls Mills, ME, 224
Kennebago Bus Co., 261
Kennebago, ME, 261
Kennebec & Portland RR, 198, 203, 223-224, 228, 232, 236
Kennebec & Wiscasset RR, 232, 236
Kennebec Central RR, 233-234, 237-238
Kennebec River, 198, 223-226, 229, 233, 237, 266, 275
Kennebec Valley RR, 273
Kennebunk & Kennebunkport RR, 96, 162-164
Kennebunk Beach, ME, 163
Kennebunk, ME, 99, 162, 164, 362
Kennebunkport, ME, 159, 162, 362
Kimball, J. F., 291
Kineo Station, ME, 273-274
Kingfield & Dead River RR, 267
Kingfield, ME, 266-267
Kingsbury, PQ, 350
Kinney Shores, ME, 166
Kittery & York Electric RR, 159
Kittery Navy Yard, ME, 157, 159-160
Kittery Point, ME, 159
Kittery, ME, 154, 156-157, 159, 161, 362
Knox & Lincoln RR, 224-225,

228-230, 370
Knox Lime Co., 370
Knox RR, 229, 370
Lac Frontière, 356
Lac Megantic, 261
Laconia, NH, 142
Lake Anasagunticook, 256
Lake Champlain, 41, 43, 170, 172, 186-187, 352
Lake Hebron, 291
Lake Mascoma, 249
Lake Massabesic, 129
Lake Shore Park, NH, 143
Lake Shore RR, 88, 132, 137, 139, 141, 143, 151
Lake Wentworth, 150
Lake Winnipesaukee, 131, 137, 142, 151
Lakeport, NH, 90, 141-143
Lamoille County RR, 189
Lamoille River, 186
Lamoille Valley Extension RR, 352
Lamoille Valley RR, 183, 186, 189-190, 325-326, 329
Lamprey River, 98
Lancaster, NH, 331-332, 341
Landers, ME, 273
Lang, NH, 126
Langtown, ME, 269-270
Larrabees Point, VT, 44
LaValley Building Supply Co., 122
Lawrence Plywood Co., 271
Lawrence, MA, 110
Lawrence, NB, 303
Lawrenceville, PQ, 350
Lebanon Springs RR, 43
Lebanon, NH, 249, 253
Leeds & Farmington RR, 203
Leeds Jct., ME, 200, 202-204
Lennoxville, PQ, 55
Lewis Pond, VT, 211
Lewis, VT, 211
Lewis, Weston, 266-267, 270
Lewiston & Auburn Electric Light Co., 363
Lewiston & Auburn RR, 209
Lewiston Jct., ME, 209

Lewiston Lower, ME, 204
Lewiston, Augusta & Waterviille Street RY, 364
Lewiston, ME, 197, 200, 202-203, 212, 224, 363-365
Lewy Lake, 319
Lewys Island RR, 318
Libbey, W. Scott, 363
Lily Pond, NH, 143
Lime Ridge, PQ, 340-341
Lime Rock RR, 229, 370
Limestone, ME, 298, 301
Lincoln, L. L., 306-307
Lincoln, NH, 89, 262, 336
Lisbon Falls, ME, 204, 365
Lisgor, Lord, 218
Little Squaw Township, ME, 289
Littlefields, ME, 269
Littleton, NH, 332-334, 336
Livermore Falls, ME, 202, 204, 257
Livermore, NH, 181
Loati, Bruno, 189
Londonderry, NH, 111
Long Lake, 191-193
Long Sands, ME, 159
Longueil, PQ, 208
Lord, George, 96
Loring AFB, ME, 301
Lowell, MA, 69, 86, 291, 310
Lunenburg, VT, 186, 188, 190
Lyndonville, VT, 55
Lyons Granite Co., 106-107
Macdonald, John A., Sir, 345
Machias, ME, 315-316
Mack Point, ME, 300
Madawaska, ME, 301, 359
Madbury, NH, 99
Madison Paper Industries, 275
Madison, ME, 273, 275
Madrid Jct., ME, 268
Madrid RR, 268-269
Madrid, ME, 269-270
Maine Central RR, 83, 95-96, 148, 155, 178, 181-183, 188-189, 193, 198, 200, 203, 209, 217-219, 224-225, 229-230, 233, 237, 256-258, 261-262, 264-265, 267, 270,

Main Index

273-275, 278, 280, 282, 284, 299, 301, 306-307, 309, 311-312, 315, 319, 326, 333, 336, 341, 346, 363-365, 370
Maine Central Transportation Co., 307
Maine Coast RR, 204, 226, 230
Maine Iron Co., 287
Maine Narrow Gauge RR & Museum, 212, 271, 293
Maine Shore Line RR, 309-311, 314
Maine, New Hampshire & Massachusetts RR, 94-95
Mainstream, ME, 281-282
Malone, NY, 50
Manchester & Keene RR, 73, 113, 117
Manchester & Lawrence RR, 87, 110-111
Manchester & North Weare RR, 124
Manchester Center, VT, 369
Manchester International Airport, 111
Manchester, Dorset & Granville RR, 369-370
Manchester, NH, 70, 86, 90, 110, 113, 119, 124, 126, 128-129, 363
Mansfield, George E., 14, 192, 265-266, 291
Mansonville, PQ, 350
Mapleton, ME, 300
Maquam, VT, 187-188, 352
Marbles, John G., 268
Maremont Corp., 157
Marion, ME, 315
Maritime Provinces, 217, 345
Marlboro, NH, 113
Marlow, NH, 73
Marsh, Sylvester, 366-367
Mason Hill, ME, 355
Mason Railroad Trail, 68
Mason Village, NH, 68
Mason, NH, 68
Massachusetts Bay Railroad Enthusiasts, Inc., 51
Massachusetts Bay Transportation Authority, 68
Massawippi Valley RR, 56, 249
Massawippi Valley RY, 54-55
Mast Yard, NH, 119

Mathews, NH, 148
Mattawamkeag, ME, 217-219, 298, 316, 345-346
Mavor Brothers, 261
Maxcy, Josiah, 266-267, 270
McAdam, NB, 303
McIndoes, VT, 54
Mead Paper Corp., 204, 258
Mecham Hill, ME, 270
Mechanic Falls, ME, 208, 255, 257-258
Mechanicville, NY, 37
Medomak River, 229
Medway, ME, 299
Megantic, PQ, 345, 347
Mercer, ME, 233
Meredith, NH, 89-90
Merrimac & Connecticut Rivers RR, 119-120, 124
Merrimack River, 70, 86, 94, 96, 132, 363
Merrimack, NH, 71, 86
Midland RY Co. of Vermont, 350
Milan, NH, 261
Milford, ME, 215, 217
Milford, NH, 73-74, 125
Milford-Bennington RR, 74, 114, 117
Miller platform, 96
Miller, E. S., 183
Millers Falls, MA, 173
Millers River, 65
Millinocket, ME, 299, 301
Milltown, ME, 318-320
Milo Jct., ME, 288
Missisquoi & Clyde Rivers RR , 55, 251
Missisquoi Bay, 352
Missisquoi Pulp & Paper Mill , 329
Missisquoi River, 328-329, 350
Missisquoi RR, 173, 189-190, 327-329
Missisquoi Valley RR, 328
Missisquoi Valley RY, 350
Mitchell, George, 99
mixed trains, 73, 129, 132, 163, 218, 247, 251, 271, 289, 300, 304, 311, 319, 341, 345, 370
Montreal, PQ, 56
Monadnock Paper Co., 117
Monadnock RR, 61, 65, 73, 116, 119

406   *Main Index*

Monroe Bridge, MA, 51
Monson & Athens RR, 291
Monson Jct., ME, 281, 291
Monson RR, 291-293
Monson Slate Co., 291-292
Monson, ME, 289, 291-292
Montague, ME, 218
Monticello, ME, 301
Montpelier & Barre RR, 324
Montpelier & St. Johnsbury RR, 186
Montpelier & Wells River RR, 173, 175, 322-323
Montpelier Jct., VT, 324
Montpelier, VT, 322-324
Montreal, 207
Montreal & Vermont Junction RY, 172
Montreal Board of Trade, 207
Montreal, Portland & Boston RY, 188
Montreal, PQ, 44, 54-55, 143, 163, 172-173, 175, 206-209, 217, 219, 249, 251, 346

Moose Brook, 113
Moosehead Lake, 273, 280, 287
Mooselookmeguntic Lake, 260
Morrill, A. R., 256
Morrill, H. E., 291, 293
Morrison-Knudsen Corp., 189
Morrisville, VT, 186, 189-190
Mousam River, 162, 362
Mt, Desert Ferry, ME, 310
Mt. Abram, ME, 267
Mt. Desert Ferry, 310
Mt. Desert Ferry, ME, 309-310
Mt. Desert Island, 367
Mt. Desert Narrows, 310
Mt. Katahdin, 288
Mt. Kineo House, 274-275
Mt. Kineo, ME, 274
Mt. Pleasant House, 183
Mt. Washington, 336, 366-367
Mt. Washington Hotel, 183
Mt. Washington RY, 332, 366-367
Mt. Washington Summit Rd., 366
Mt. Washington Turnpike, 366
Mt. Whittier, NH, 148
narrow gauge, 105, 159-160, 192, 233, 265-266, 268-271, 291, 304, 307, 332, 336, 359, 371
Nashua & Lowell RR, 68-71, 73, 86, 113, 125
Nashua & Rochester RR, 77, 81, 129
Nashua, NH, 69-71, 73-74, 77, 81, 86, 90, 114
National Association of Railroad Enthusiasts, 51
National Soldiers' Home, 236-238
Navy Yard Jct., ME, 161
Navy Yard Station, ME, 160
Nelson, NH, 113
New Boston RR, 125
New Boston, NH, 125-126
New Brunswick, 206, 302, 318, 320, 348
New Brunswick & Canada RY, 298, 303-304, 319
New Brunswick RY, 218, 304, 345, 359
New Brunswick Southern RY, 320, 348
New England Central RR, 176, 324
New England Power Company, 50-51
New England Public Warehouse, 212
New England Southern RR, 90, 253
New Gloucester, ME, 363
New Hampshire & Vermont RR, 333-334, 342
New Hampshire Central RR, 87, 119, 124, 126, 342
New Hampshire College of Agriculture & Mechanic Arts, 97
New Hampshire Northcoast RR, 99, 139, 149, 151
New Hampshire Stave & Heading Mill, 211
New Haven Jct., VT, 48
New Haven River, 47
New Jersey & Pennsylvania RR, 215
New London Northern RR, 105, 173
New London, CT, 173, 176
New Sharon, ME, 233-234
New Sweden, ME, 355
New York Central RR, 43, 284, 352
New York, New Haven & Hartford RR, 43, 301
New York, NY, 38, 44, 175-176, 202,

Main Index

211, 217, 249, 274, 310-311
Newburyport, MA, 103
Newfane, VT, 105
Newington, NH, 134-135
Newmarket, NH, 94, 98
Newport, ME, 283-284
Newport, NH, 119-120, 122
Newport, VT, 54-56
Newton family, 50
Newton Jct., NH, 96
Newton Jct., NH, 97
Newton, NH, 96
No. 6, ME, 269
Nonesuch River, 98
Norcross-West Marble Co., 369
Norridgewock, ME, 273
North Anson, ME, 273, 275
North Bennington, VT, 41
North Berwick, ME, 95, 97-99, 154, 156-157
North Billerica, MA, 200
North Concord, VT, 188
North Conway Depot Co., 148
North Conway, NH, 147-148, 184
North Derby, VT, 54
North Enosburg, VT, 328
North Haverhill, NH, 252
North Jay, ME, 202
North Pack Monadnock (NH), 65
North Rochester, NH, 139
North Stratford RR, 342
North Stratford, NH, 209, 211, 340-342
North Troy, VT, 55, 350
North Weare, NH, 124
North Yarmouth,ME, 198
Northern Maine Jct., ME, 299, 301
Northern Maine Regional Airport, 357
Northern Maine Seaport RR, 288, 299-300
Northern New England Passenger Rail Authority, 99
Northern RR, 54, 65, 86-87, 116-117, 120-121, 249, 251, 253
Northern RR of New York, 43, 172
Northern Vermont Corp., 189
Northern Vermont RR, 56

Northfield, VT, 170
Norton-Greene, Joseph, 314
Norway Branch RR, 192, 209
Norway, ME, 209, 212
Norwich, VT, 54
Nova Scotia, 206, 346
Oak Terrace, ME, 159
Oakfield, ME, 298
Oakland, ME, 233, 273
Ogdensburg & Lake Champlain RR, 43, 351-352
Ogdensburg, NY, 172
Olamon, ME, 217
Old Colony RR, 215
Old Orchard Beach RR , 96
Old Orchard Beach, ME, 98-99, 165, 167, 362
Old Orchard Junction RR, 167
Old Orchard Transportation Co., 166
Old Town, ME, 213-214, 287-288, 298
Oldhouse Cove, 310
OMYA plant , 241
Onawa, ME, 345
Oquossoc, ME, 261, 268
Orchard Beach RR, 165-166
Ore Mountain, 287
Orford Mountain RY, 350
Orono, ME, 213-214, 217, 220
Ossipee Aggregates, Inc., 149
Ossipee Pit, NH, 149
Ottawa, ON, 173
Otter Creek, 47
Otter Valley RR, 241
Oxford, ME, 208
Oyster River, 97
Pack Monadnock (NH), 65
Packards Brook, 345
Page, John B., 41
Paine, Charles, 170
Palermo, ME, 233
Palmer, MA,, 176
Park Siding, ME, 357
Passamaquoddy tribe, 315
Passumpsic River, 54, 188
Patten & Sherman RR, 298, 300, 302
Patterson, W. D., 233
Pease AFB, NH, 135

Peck, Carson D., 234
Pemigewasset River, 251, 336
Pemigewasset Valley RR, 336
Penacook, NH, 119, 253
Penobscot & Kennebec RR, 197, 228, 287
Penobscot Central RY, 365
Penobscot River, 213, 215, 218, 279, 287, 306
Penobscot, Lincoln & Kennebec RR, 228
Perry, ME, 315
Perth-Andover, NB, 357
Peru, ME, 256
Peterborough & Hillsborough RR, 65, 114, 116
Peterborough & Shirley RR, 67-68
Peterborough RR, 73, 117
Peterborough, NH, 65-68, 73, 114, 116-117
Phair, ME, 302
Philadelphia, PA, 311
Philbrook, Malcom, 234
Phillips & Rangeley RR, 267-269
Phillips, ME, 265-268, 271
Pierce's Bridge, NH, 336
Pinkham Turnpike, 366
Pinsly, Samuel M., 51, 82, 121-122, 189, 324, 362
Piscataqua River, 134, 154, 156-157, 159
Piscataquis Iron Works Co., 288
Piscataquis River, 218, 287, 291
Piscataquog River, 125-126
Pittsfield, ME, 233, 281
Pittsfield, NH, 131-132
Pittsfield, VT, 246
Pittsford & Rutland RR, 240-241
Plaistow, NH, 94, 99
Plattsburgh, NY, 41, 187
Pleasant Point Bar, ME, 315
Pleasantdale, ME, 157
Plymouth, NH, 86, 89, 252, 336
Poland, ME, 258
Poor, John Alfred, 206-207, 215, 217-218
Port Henry, NY, 41

Portland & Kennebec RR, 95, 198, 224, 229, 278
Portland & Ogdensburg RR, 147-148, 180-182, 186-189, 191-192, 332, 341, 351-352, 366
Portland & Oxford Central RR, 256-257
Portland & Rochester RR, 77, 81-82, 223
Portland & Rumford Falls RR, 204, 257-258, 260-261
Portland Jct., ME, 210
Portland RR Co., 361
Portland Terminal RR, 83, 157
Portland Union Railway Station Company, 96
Portland Union Station Co., 210
Portland, Gray & Lewiston RR, 363
Portland, Great Falls & Conway RR, 147, 151
Portland, ME, 77, 81, 83, 94, 96, 99, 101, 103, 143, 154-155, 157, 163-165, 180, 183, 186, 197-198, 200, 203, 206-212, 217, 223-224, 230, 267, 271, 291, 293, 307, 341, 345, 361, 363-364
Portland, Saco & Portsmouth RR, 77, 81, 94-96, 98, 101, 128, 134, 146, 154-157, 159, 167, 207, 209, 223
Portland-Lewiston Interurban RR, 364
Portland-Monson Slate Co., 292
Portsmouth & Concord RR, 128-129, 131
Portsmouth & Dover RR, 134
Portsmouth, Dover & York Beach RY, 362
Portsmouth, Great Falls & Conway RR, 81, 96, 137, 146-147, 150, 157
Portsmouth, New Market & Concord RR, 128
Portsmouth, New Market & Exeter RR, 128
Portsmouth, NH, 101, 103, 128-129, 132, 134-135, 147, 154, 156-160, 362
Poultney, VT, 36
Presque Isle, ME, 298, 300-302,

Main Index

354-357, 359
Princeton, ME, 319
Proctor, ME, 261
Proctor, VT, 240-241
Profile & Franconia Notch RR, 89, 332, 336-337
Profile House, 336-337
Profile Lake, 336
Providence, RI, 157
Punta Alegre Sugar Corp., 301
Putnam, Calvin, 267
Quaker Oats Co., 328
Quarry Station, VT, 369
Quebec Central RY, 55
Quebec Extension RR, 356
Quebec Jct., NH, 341-342
Quechee Gorge, 243-244
Quinn-T Corp., 90
Quoddy, ME, 315
rail busses, 261-262, 271
rail diesel cars, 98, 183, 230, 252, 333
RailTex, 176
Randolph, ME, 237
Rangeley Lake, 261, 268
Rangeley Lakes & Megantic RR, 261
Rangeley Lakes Hotel, 268
Rangeley Lakes, ME, 267
Rangeley RR, 268
Rangeley, ME, 267-268
Raymond, NH, 129
Readsboro, VT, 50-51
Redington Mill, ME, 267
Rensselaer & Saratoga RR, 37
Revere, MA, 101
Richford, VT, 55, 190, 327-328
Richmond, ME, 223
Richmond, PQ, 209
Rigby Yard, ME, 96, 183, 200, 204, 258
Rigby, ME, 155-157
Rileys, ME, 204, 258
Rindge, NH, 65
Rindgemere, NH, 83
Riverside, VT, 326
Rivière-du-Loup, PQ, 359
Robbinston, ME, 314
Rochester, NH, 77, 81-83, 137, 146, 149
Rochester, VT, 246
Rock Island, PQ, 55
Rockingham Park racetrack, 111
Rockingham Planning Commission, 103
Rockingham, NH, 99, 129
Rockland, ME, 228-229, 370
Rockland, Thomaston & Camden Street RY, 370-371
Rockport RR, 371
Rockport, ME, 371
Rockwood, ME, 273
Rocky Branch RR, 182
Rollinsford Jct., NH, 137
Rollinsford, NH, 94, 96, 99, 139, 146, 148, 182
Rome, ME, 233
Rouses Point, NY, 43, 172, 351-352
Royal Jct., ME, 198
Rumford Falls & Buckfield RR, 257
Rumford Falls & Rangeley Lakes RR, 257, 260-262, 268
Rumford Falls, ME, 257
Rumford Jct., ME, 257-258
Rumford, ME, 200, 204, 256-258, 260-262
Rundlett, R. T., 233
Rupert, VT, 36
Rutland & Burlington RR, 41, 171-173
Rutland & Canadian RR, 43
Rutland & Noyan RR, 43
Rutland & Washington RR, 36-37, 240-241
Rutland & Whitehall RR, 37
Rutland Center, VT, 37
Rutland RR, 37, 41-43, 45, 47-48, 61-63, 105, 173-174, 187, 241, 325, 369
Rutland RY, 43-44, 241
Rutland, VT, 36-37, 45, 240-241, 243
S. D. Warren Co., 83, 225
Sabattus, ME, 365
Saco Defense, Inc., 157
Saco River, 81, 166
Saco, ME, 99, 154-155, 157-158, 160, 361
Sadawga Pond, 50

Saint John & Maine RY, 218
Salem, NH, 111
Salem, NY, 37
Salisbury, MA, 103
Salmon Falls Manufacturing Co., 147
Salmon Falls River, 96, 149
Salmon Falls, ME, 318
Salmon Falls, NH, 149
Salzberg, H. E., 51, 189, 271
SamOset Co., 274, 307
Sanbornville, NH, 150, 152
Sandy River, 264, 268
Sandy River & Rangeley Lakes RR, 238, 260, 268-271
Sandy River RR, 193, 204, 233, 257, 264, 266-267
Sanford & Eastern RR, 83, 362
Sanford, ME, 83, 362
SAPPI Co., 83
Sarah Mildred Long Bridge, 156
Saratoga & Washington RR, 36-37
Saratoga Springs, NY, 36
Sargent, S. W., 266
Sargents Purchase, NH, 182
Saunders family, 181
Sawyer, NH, 135
Sawyers River RR, 181
Sawyers River, NH, 181
Scarboro Crossing, ME, 155
Scarborough River, 98
Schoodic Lake, 345
Schoodic Stream RR, 299
Scott Paper Co., 225
Seabrook, NH, 103
Seacoast Scenic RR, 103
Sebasticook & Moosehead RR, 280-282, 291
Sebasticook River, 233
Seboois, ME, 300
Sewall, Arthur, 267
Sewall, S. J., 234
Shaker Mills Co., 249
Shakers, 249
Shawmut, ME, 225
Shediac, NB, 217
Sheepscot River, 229, 232
Sheepscot, ME, 235

Sheldon Jct., VT, 188-190, 329
Sheldon Springs, VT, 328-329
Sherbrooke, PQ, 55, 209, 249, 320, 347
Sherman, ME, 301
Ship Stream, 345
Shipyard RR, 160
Shirley, ME, 289
Silver Lake, 287
Silver Lake Hotel, 288
Simonton Corners, ME, 371
Skowhegan, ME, 224-225, 273
Skyway Industrial Park, 357
Smith, F. O. J., 256
Smith, John, 171
Smithfield, ME, 233
Smithtown, NH, 101
Smithville, ME, 287
Solon, ME, 273
Somerset & Kennebec RR, 223-224, 273
Somerset Jct., ME, 275
Somerset RR, 273-275
Somerset RY, 273
Somersworth, NH, 94, 146, 148-149
Soo Line RR, 251
Souhegan River, 68
South Berwick, ME, 95
South Ashburnham, MA, 61, 63, 65
South Barre, VT, 322
South Berwick Jct., ME, 154
South Berwick, ME, 81, 96, 149, 155, 362
South Bog RR, 261
South Branch RR, 333
South Burlington, VT, 326
South China, ME, 233
South Eastern Counties Jct. RY, 54-55
South Eastern RY, 55, 251, 328
South Franklin, VT, 328
South Hero, VT, 43
South Lagrange, ME, 288-289, 299
South Lawrence, MA, 310
South Londonderry, VT, 105
South Lunenburg, VT, 186
South Lyndeborough, NH, 74
South Milton, NH, 146

Main Index

South Nashua, NH, 70
South Paris, ME, 192, 208
South Portland, ME, 95-96, 155, 157, 183, 200, 223, 258, 361
South Rangeley, ME, 261
South Union, ME, 370
South Vernon, VT, 57-58
South Woodbury, VT, 369
Southern Container Co., 83
Spaulding Turnpike, 135
Spier & Rohns, 210
Sprague Energy Co., 135
Spragues Falls, ME, 319
Springdale, ME, 362
Springfield Electric RY, 177-178
Springfield Terminal RY, 177-178, 320
Springfield, MA, 58, 171, 176
Springfield, VT, 177-178
Springvale, ME, 83, 362
Squa Pan, ME, 299
St. Albans & Richford Plank Rd., 327
St. Albans, VT, 171, 176, 189, 327-329
St. Andrews & Quebec RY, 303
St. Croix & Penobscot RR, 304, 314, 319
St. Croix Paper Co., 319-320
St. Croix River, 303, 318
St. Croix, NB, 217
St. Duchene, NB, 217
St. Francis River, 350
St. Francis, ME, 299-300, 302
St. John & Maine RR, 345
St. John Bridge & Railway Extension Co., 345
St. John River, 300, 357, 359
St. John, NB, 211, 217-219, 345-346
St. Johns, PQ, 172
St. Johnsbury & Lake Champlain RR, 187-189, 325-326, 352, 369
St. Johnsbury & Lamoille County RR, 189
St. Johnsbury, VT, 54, 181, 183, 186, 188-190
St. Lawrence & Atlantic RR, 211, 372
St. Lawrence & Atlantic RY, 207-209
St. Lawrence River, 207-208, 359
St. Regis Paper Co., 211

St. Stephen, NB, 303, 316, 319
Stamp Act Island, 150
Stanstead, PQ, 55
Stanstead, Shefford & Chambly RY, 54
steamboats, 41, 137, 142, 151, 187, 256, 310, 346
Steamtown, 45
Stephen, George, 345
Steven's Brook, 191
Stillwater River, 213
Stillwater, ME, 213-214, 217, 220
Stockbridge, VT, 246-247
Stockholm, ME, 300
Stockton Springs, ME, 299
Stonington, ME, 157
Strasburg RR, 151
Stratton, ME, 269
Strong, ME, 266
Success Pond RR, 372
Sugar River, 122
Sugar River RR, 120-121
Sullivan County RR, 173
Sullivan RR, 119, 170, 173
Sullivan, ME, 307
Sumner, ME, 256
Suncook River, 131
Suncook Valley RR, 89
Suncook Valley Extension RR, 131-132
Suncook Valley Jct., NH, 131
Suncook Valley RR, 89, 129, 131-132, 363
Suncook, NH, 89, 129, 132
Swanton Jct., VT, 172
Swanton, VT, 173, 181, 186-187, 189-190, 326, 351-352
Swazey, Stewall B., 306
Sweden, ME, 355
Swensons Granite quarry, 157
Taft, Richard, 336
Tenth New Hampshire Turnpike, 335, 366
The Elms, ME, 96, 99
The Wye, ME, 257
Thompson Island, ME, 310
Thorndike, ME, 279
Tilton & Belmont RR, 88
Tilton, NH, 90, 142

412 — Main Index

Togus, ME, 232-233, 236-237
Town House, ME, 362
Townsend Center, MA, 68
Township E, ME, 261
trains
  Acadian, 218
  Alouette, 55, 251-252
  Ambassador, 252
  Aroostook Flyer, 301
  Atlantic Limited, 219, 346-347
  Bar Harbor, 229
  Bar Harbor Express, 77, 198, 200, 225, 309-311
  Boston & Mount Desert, 309
  Cannon Ball, 252
  East Wind, 96
  Eastern, 345
  Ethan Allen, 38
  Flying Yankee, 200
  Green Mountain, 44
  Green Mountain Flyer, 46, 62
  Gull, 219
  Maine Coast Special, 143
  Montrealer, 175
  Mount Royal, 44, 62
  Night White Mountains, 183
  North Wind, 183
  Pine Tree, 218
  Pine Tree Limited, 96
  Red Wing, 55, 251
  State of Maine, 96
  State of Maine Express, 77, 310
  Sunday River Silver Bullet Ski Express, 212
  Vermonter, 176
  Western, 345
Trenton, ME, 310
Troutdale, ME, 275
Troy & Boston RR, 41
Troy & Rutland RR, 36-37
Troy Jct., VT, 350
Troy, NH, 61
Troy, NY, 36-37
TTX Corp., 357
Turner Island RR, 157
Turners Island, ME, 154
Twin State Fair, 243

Twin State RR, 183-184, 189
Underhill, VT, 326
Union Mills, ME, 319
Union River, 309
Union, NH, 146
Unity, ME, 279
University of New Hampshire, 97
Upper Coos RR, 333, 339-342
Upper Dam Wharf, ME, 260
Upper Graniteville, VT, 322
Upper Websterville, VT, 322
Valcourt, PQ, 350
Van Buren Internatonal Co., 300
Van Buren, ME, 298-299, 301-302
Van Dyke, George, 339
Vanceboro, ME, 200, 219, 345-346
Vanderbilt, William H., 43, 352
Vassalboro, ME, 234
Veazie RR, 215
Veazie, Samuel, 215
Vermont & Canada RR, 171-172, 249, 328
Vermont & Massachusetts RR, 57-58, 173
Vermont & Province Line RY, 173
Vermont Central RR, 41-42, 54, 105, 170-173, 243, 249, 322, 327-328, 352, 368
Vermont Marble Co., 240, 369
Vermont Northern RR, 189
Vermont RY, 45, 56, 241, 324
Vermont RY, 38
Vermont Valley RR, 58, 171, 173
Vermont White Granite Co., 107
Vermont & Massachusetts RR, 61
VIA Rail Canada, 219, 346-347
Wade, ME, 354
Waldoboro, ME, 229-230
Ware River RR, 61, 65
Warner Sugar Refining Co., 211
Warner, NH, 119-120
Warren, ME, 229, 370
Warren, NH, 86
Washburn Jct., ME, 357, 359
Washburn, ME, 354-357
Washington County RR, 309-310, 312, 314-315, 319, 324

Main Index

Washington County RY, 315
Washington Jct., ME, 311, 315
Washington, DC, 310
Waterboro, ME, 83
Waterford, NY, 36
Waterville & Wiscasset RR, 233
Waterville, ME, 197-198, 200, 223-224, 226, 233, 273, 364
Waukeag, ME, 311
Waumbek House, 333
Waumbek Jct., NH, 333-334, 341-342
Wausau Mosinee facilities, 204
Webb, William Seward, 43
Webster, Daniel, 249
Websterville, VT, 322
Weeks Mills, ME, 233-234
Weld Township, 269
Wellington, MA, 281
Wellington, ME, 280
Wells Beach, ME, 159
Wells River, VT, 54-56, 86, 89, 252, 322-323, 329, 332-333
Wells, ME, 96, 99, 362
West Alburgh, VT, 352
West Alton, NH, 142-143
West Amesbury Branch RR, 96
West Bethel, ME, 209
West Caribou, ME, 357
West Claremont, NH, 121
West Concord, NH, 121
West Dummerston, VT, 106-107
West Enfield, ME, 218
West Falmouth, ME, 363
West Groton, MA, 68
West Hartford, VT, 173
West Hopkinton, NH, 119, 122
West Manchester, NH, 126
West Ossipee, NH, 147-148
West Penobscot Bay, 371
West Presque Isle, ME, 355
West River, 106
West River RR, 105, 107
West Rutland, VT, 240-241
West Stewartstown, NH, 339-340, 342
West Townsend, MA, 68
Westboro, NH, 253
Westbrook, ME, 82

Westbrook-Cumberland Mills, ME, 184
White Creek, NY, 41
White Mountains, 180, 335, 367
White Mountains RR, 87, 181, 331-333, 336, 339, 366, 406
White River, 173, 243, 249
White River Jct., VT, 54, 86, 173-174, 243, 249, 251, 333
White River RR, 246
White River Valley RR, 246
White Star Line, 346
Whitefield & Jefferson RR, 332-333
Whitefield Jct., NH, 333, 341
Whitefield, ME, 235
Whitefield, NH, 183-184, 189, 332-334
Whitehall & Plattsburgh RR, 41
Whitehall, NY, 36-37, 105
Whiting, H. A., 291
Whiting, VT, 44
Whitingham, VT, 50
Whitney Brook, ME, 257
Whitridge, F. W., 315
Wilder, VT, 56
Willey Brook, 181
Williamstown, VT, 173, 322
Wilmington, MA, 93, 95
Wilmington, VT, 50-51
Wilner Wood Products Co., 211
Wilson Stream, 345
Wilton RR, 73
Wilton, NH, 68, 73-74, 113-114
Winchendon RR, 61
Winchendon, MA, 61-62, 65, 73, 119
Windham, NH, 184
Windsor Mills, PQ, 350
Windsor, VT, 170, 173, 175
Wing Road, NH, 332-333, 336, 366
Wing, Herbert S., 271
Winnipesaukee RR, 90, 151
Winnipesaukee Steamboat Co., 142
Winslow, ME, 233-234
Winter, Frank W., 234
Winthrop, ME, 365
Wiscasset & Moosehead Lake RR, 232
Wiscasset & Quebec RR, 232-233, 237, 266
Wiscasset & Waterville RR, 234

Wiscasset, ME, 229, 232-233, 236
Wiscasset, Waterville & Farmington RR, 233, 238, 281
Wiscasset, Waterville & Farmington RY, 234-235
Wolcott, VT, 186
Wolfeboro Lake, NH, 151
Wolfeboro RR, 90, 151
Wolfeboro, NH, 150-152
Wolfeborough RR, 150-151
Wood, Nathaniel, 47
Woodbury, VT, 369
Woodford, VT, 368
Woodfords, ME, 82
Woodland Jct., ME, 319
Woodland, ME, 315, 319
Woodstock RR, 243
Woodstock RY, 243-244
Woodstock, NB, 304, 359
Woodstock, NH, 89
Woodstock, VT, 243-244, 316
Woodsville, NH, 56, 333-334, 342
Woolwich, ME, 229
Worcester & Nashua RR, 77, 81
Worcester, Nashua & Rochester RR, 77
Worthley, ME, 258
Yankee Atomic Power Station, 51
Yarmouth, ME, 197, 223, 228, 364-365
Yarmouth, NS, 346
Yield House Co., 148
York & Cumberland RR, 77, 81, 223
York Beach, ME, 159-161, 362
York Harbor & Beach RR, 159-161
York Harbor, ME, 159
York River, 159
York Utilities Corp., 83, 362
York Village, ME, 159
York, ME, 158
Zealand Transfer, NH, 336
Zealand Valley RR, 182